Klein

Numeric Python

Bernd Klein

Numeric Python

Python Data Analysis with
NumPy, Pandas, and Matplotlib

HANSER

About the author:
Bernd Klein, Singen, bernd@bodenseo.de

Print-ISBN: 978-1-56990-495-4
E-Book-ISBN: 978-1-56990-960-7
ePub-ISBN: 978-1-56990-973-7

Bibliographic information of the German National Library:
The German National Library lists this publication in the German National Bibliography; detailed bibliographic data are available on the Internet at http://dnb.d-nb.de.

© 2026 Carl Hanser Verlag GmbH & Co. KG, Munich
Vilshofener Straße 10 | 81679 Munich | info@hanser.de
www.hanserpublications.com
www.hanser-fachbuch.de
Editor: Brigitte Bauer-Schiewek, Kristin Rothe
Production management: Grazyna Lada
Cover concept: Marc Müller-Bremer, *www.rebranding.de*, Munich
Cover design: Thomas West
Cover picture: © stock.adobe.com/ARTvektor
Typesetting: le-tex publishing services GmbH, Leipzig

Contents

Preface

Data-driven methods have become a central force in contemporary software development. Concepts such as *Big Data* and *Machine Learning* now play a decisive role across research, industry, and applied engineering. As a result, both institutions and individual practitioners face a fundamental question: which programming language is best suited for data-oriented and numerical applications?

In recent years, Python has consistently emerged as one of the most widely used programming languages in this domain. Its rapid development has established it as a core technology for data analysis, scientific computing, and artificial intelligence. While Python was not originally designed for numerical computation, its ecosystem has evolved to fill this gap with remarkable success.

This success is largely attributable to powerful extension libraries such as `NumPy`, `SciPy`, `Matplotlib`, and `Pandas`. Together, these tools have transformed Python into a robust platform that rivals specialized numerical and statistical software packages, both in academic research and in industrial practice.

This book provides a structured and accessible introduction to numerical and data-oriented programming with Python, with a particular focus on `NumPy`, `Matplotlib`, and `Pandas`. It is aimed at readers who already have a basic command of Python and are ready to deepen their skills in scientific and data-driven applications. The book is therefore well suited for students, researchers, engineers, and professionals seeking to extend their Python knowledge into the realm of numerical computing and data analysis.

The present volume is based on the successful German-language book *Numerisches Python* by the same author. The first edition was published on 18 June 2021, and a third, thoroughly revised edition appeared on 14 November 2025. This English-language edition is a translation of the third edition and includes several necessary adaptations for an international readership.

Brigitte Bauer-Schiewek, Editor in January 2026

Acknowledgments

Writing a book requires not only experience and expertise, but above all one essential thing: time. Time beyond the ordinary – time that is often made possible by the support and understanding of one's family. My special thanks therefore go to my wife, Karola, who accompanied me throughout the creation of this book – from the first to the third edition – with great understanding and active support.

A heartfelt thank you also goes to the many participants of my Python courses. Through their questions, feedback, and suggestions, I was able to continuously refine both my didactic approach and the technical concepts presented in this book. I am equally grateful to the many users of my online tutorials at *www.python-kurs.eu* and *www.python-course.eu*, especially those who contacted me with constructive comments and questions.

My sincere thanks also go to Hanser Verlag, which made the publication of this book possible. While this is the first English edition, it is in fact a translation of the third edition of a successful German-language book. I am especially grateful to Ms. Brigitte Bauer-Schiewek (Computer Book Program Planning) for the consistently excellent collaboration, as well as to Kristin Rothe (Editorial Assistant for Computer Books) for her support during the production process.

Finally, I would like to express my sincere gratitude to Python itself, to its creator Guido van Rossum, and to the countless contributors who continue to develop, maintain, and improve this remarkable programming language. The Python community, with its openness, commitment to quality, and emphasis on readability and elegance, has played a decisive role in Python's success and longevity.

I encountered Python for the first time roughly eighteen years ago, and it was an immediate and lasting fascination. Since then, Python has accompanied me throughout my professional career and personal projects alike, shaping the way I think about programming, problem solving, and software design. Its clarity, versatility, and expressive power continue to inspire me, and this book would not exist without the language and the people behind it.

Bernd Klein, Singen   in January 2026

1

Introduction

1.1 The Right Choice

Choosing the right programming language for everyday professional work is of great importance. This choice depends on many factors – and quite often, you don't really have a choice at all. The language is often predetermined by the company, the team, or the specific project. Increasingly, however, developers have the good fortune of being able to work with Python.

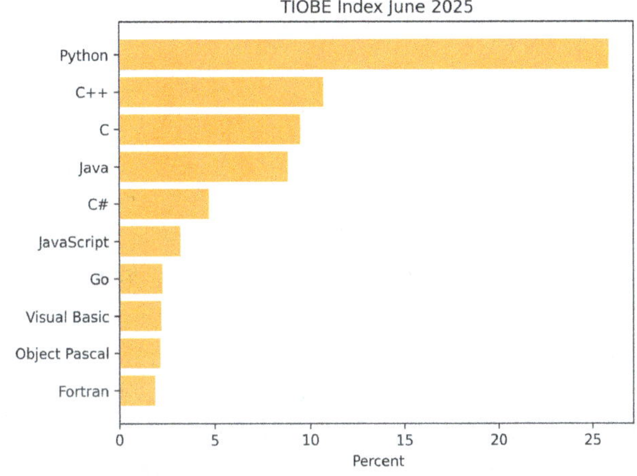

Figure 1.1 Top 10 Programming Languages

If you look at current surveys of the most popular programming languages, Python almost always ranks among the top – mostly at number one. In the TIOBE Index[1], Python now clearly leads all other languages. Back in 2018, when the first edition of this book was published, Python was

---

1 The TIOBE Index, published monthly since 2001 by the Dutch company TIOBE Software BV, ranks programming languages by popularity. The ranking is based on the frequency of search queries containing the language's name in search engines like Google, Bing, or Yahoo!. The index does not measure lines of code or technical quality, but rather the language's visibility on the web.

still in third place in the TIOBE ranking. Even then, it was inducted into the TIOBE Hall of Fame – as the language with the highest popularity growth that year. Since October 2021, Python has held the top spot in the TIOBE Index without challenge.

Of course, it's nice to know that the language you prefer is also popular with many others – and perhaps even widely used in your industry. But one of the most important questions remains: Can your own projects be developed more easily and effectively in Python than in other languages? What we mean by "more easily and effectively" includes aspects like development time, runtime performance, maintainability, and so on.

Programming languages are like shoes: there's no one-size-fits-all. No single pair works equally well for formal events, the office, sports, and hiking. Python, however, is a language that can be used flexibly in most domains – one of the reasons for its great success. But above all, Python owes its rise to the powerful modules NumPy, SciPy, Matplotlib, and Pandas. These make it especially easy to solve numerical problems, thanks to Python's clear and readable syntax. Moreover, NumPy provides data structures that are 10 to 100 times faster than implementations in pure Python or many other languages. Since these modules are largely written in C, they achieve speeds close to native C programs.

1.2 Structure of the Book

This book is about Python and its excellent capabilities for tackling numerical problems – specifically, the modules that have become indispensable for topics like "Big Data" and "Machine Learning". The focus is on using the libraries `NumPy`, `Matplotlib`, and `Pandas`.

The book assumes basic knowledge of Python and is aimed at readers who have already gained some initial experience with the language, for example through an introductory course, online tutorial, or comparable textbook. It is intended for those who are familiar with core Python concepts such as variables, control structures, functions, and modules, and who now wish to extend their skills toward data-oriented and numerical programming.

This book offers a practice-oriented introduction to numerical programming with Python and is divided into several logically structured parts:

Part I: NumPy Begins with the fundamentals of numerical programming and demonstrates how to work efficiently with arrays using `NumPy`. Topics such as array creation, indexing, data types, mathematical operations, broadcasting, and statistical evaluations are systematically covered.

Part II: Matplotlib Introduces the basics of data visualization with `Matplotlib`. The range of presentation options is illustrated, from simple plots to complex diagrams with multiple axes or contour plots.

Part III: Pandas Provides an introduction to working with tabular data. The data structures `Series` and `DataFrame`, handling missing values, grouping, pivot tables, and time and date functions are covered. It also shows how to read and write data from various sources such as `CSV`, `Excel`, or `JSON` files.

Part IV: Applications Presents concrete use cases with `pandas` – including image processing, financial analysis, and analysis of energy production in Germany.

Part V: Solutions Contains the solutions to the exercises in the book for self-assessment.

The book is supplemented by an introductory chapter on the installation and setup of the required libraries.

1.3 This Book and the Tools Behind It

This book was created entirely using LaTeX and `pythontex`. This combines the typographic strengths of LaTeX – such as precise formatting, consistent layout, automatic tables of contents, cross-references, and bibliography management – with the dynamic capabilities of Python. Thanks to `pythontex`, Python code can be embedded directly into the document and executed during compilation. Results such as numerical output, tables, diagrams, or interactive content appear automatically at the correct location in the book.

With syntax highlighting, reproducible code execution, and direct integration into the text, a particularly transparent and consistent didactic workflow is achieved – ideal for a book on data analysis and visualization with Python.

1.4 Download the Examples

All examples used in the book are available for download at

http://www.python-kurs.eu/books/numerical_python

A list of corrections is also available there.

1.5 About the Author

He completed his studies in computer science in 1988 with a diploma from Saarland University. Until 2007, he worked as a software developer in the industry. Since then, he has been active internationally as a lecturer and trainer in software development and programming languages – focusing on the Python programming language since 2009.

He collaborates with universities, research institutions, and companies both in Germany and abroad. Since 2008, he has run the online learning platforms *https://python-kurs.eu* and *https://python-course.eu*, which are used by millions of learners worldwide every year.

Published books:

- Klein, Bernd: *Einführung in Python 3: Für Ein- und Umsteiger.* 4., vollständig überarbeitete Auflage, Carl Hanser Verlag GmbH & Co. KG, Munich, 2021.
  ISBN 978-3-446-46379-0

- Klein, Bernd: *Python–Grundlagen | eLearning.* 1. Auflage, Carl Hanser Verlag GmbH & Co. KG, Munich, 2023.
  ISBN 978-3-446-47992-0

- Klein, Bernd: *Numerisches Python: Arbeiten mit NumPy, Matplotlib und Pandas.* 3., aktualisierte Auflage, Carl Hanser Verlag GmbH & Co. KG, Munich, 2025.
  ISBN 978-3-446-48549-5

- Klein, Bernd; Klein, Philip: *Funktionale Programmierung mit Python.* 1. Auflage, Carl Hanser Verlag GmbH & Co. KG, Munich, 2025.
  ISBN 978-3-446-48191-6

1.6 Suggestions and Feedback

If you notice any inaccuracies or errors in the book, feel free to send an email directly to the author: `bernd.klein@python-kurs.eu`.

This also applies to suggestions, comments, or requests regarding the book.

We will take all feedback into account in future editions.

I wish all readers as much enjoyment reading this book as I had writing it. Have fun exploring, programming, and discovering!

Bernd Klein, January 2026

2

Numerical Programming

2.1 Definition of Numerical Programming

2.2 Overview

The title of this book is "Numerical Python", inspired by the term "numerical programming" – a phrase that, in everyday use, is often vague and sometimes even misleading. One might assume it refers to any kind of programming that deals with numbers – which would apply to almost all programs. Even applications that appear purely text-based, such as search engine algorithms, rely at their core on numerical methods. For example, the original

Figure 2.1 Analog data analysis in the office

PageRank algorithm developed by Google is based on the computation of an extremely large matrix with billions of rows and columns.[1]

---

1   The enormous scale of the matrix used in the PageRank algorithm is illustrated in a lecture at Cornell University: "From the mathematical point of view, once we have M, computing the eigenvectors corresponding to the eigenvalue 1 is, at least in theory, a straightforward task. As in Lecture 1, just solve the system Ax = x! But when the matrix M has size 30 billion (as it does for the real Web graph), even mathematical software such as Matlab or Mathematica are clearly overwhelmed." Source: *https://pi.math.cornell.edu/~mec/Winter2009/RalucaRemus/Lecture3/lecture3.html*

Numerical programming refers to the computer-assisted solution of mathematical problems using numerical methods – for example, solving linear and nonlinear systems of equations, numerical integration, matrix operations, statistical calculations, or optimization problems. These techniques are found in nearly all scientific and technical disciplines. Numerical programming is thus a subfield of scientific programming. The latter includes all types of software development in research and analysis contexts – including visualization, simulation, and data preparation.

The goal of this book is to introduce the key tools needed to implement numerical methods in the fields of data science, statistics, and machine learning with Python. The focus is on practical and efficient libraries such as NumPy, Pandas, and Matplotlib, which form the foundation for data-intensive applications.

2.3 The Relationship Between Python, NumPy, Matplotlib, SciPy, and Pandas

Python is a general-purpose programming language used in a wide variety of fields – such as system administration, web development, computational linguistics, and, as already mentioned, numerical programming, where speed and memory usage are critical. Pure Python – that is, without optimized libraries – is not competitive with specialized tools like MATLAB or R for demanding numerical tasks. The performance of the algorithms used is of utmost importance in numerical applications. For this reason, Python relies on its powerful modules: `NumPy`, `SciPy`, `Matplotlib`, and `Pandas`. As a result, Python is now one of the leading languages in numerical programming – and is often more efficient than MATLAB or R.

- **NumPy** provides the fundamental data structures, particularly multidimensional arrays (ndarrays) and matrices. It includes basic functions for creating, manipulating, and analyzing these structures and serves as the foundation for many other packages.

- **SciPy** builds on NumPy and extends it with a wide range of functionalities from scientific mathematics, such as numerical integration, interpolation, linear algebra, optimization, and Fourier transforms.

- **Matplotlib** enables graphical representation of data, as needed in many scientific contexts. It supports both simple plots and complex visualizations with multiple axes, subplots, or interactive elements.

- **Pandas** is specialized for working with tabular data (DataFrames). It offers powerful tools for time series analysis, grouping, pivot tables, handling missing data, and much more. Pandas also allows for reading and writing a wide range of common formats such as CSV, Excel, or JSON.

2.4 Python – An Alternative to MATLAB

Python is increasingly becoming the preferred programming language for data scientists, analysts, and scientific programmers. While tools like MATLAB and R used to dominate research, engineering, and statistics, the focus has now shifted more and more toward Python. This shift is due to a number of factors – including its high flexibility, a very active community, modular extensibility, and the fact that Python is free and open-source software.

MATLAB was originally developed for numerical computations in engineering and technical fields. It offers a specialized environment with numerous functions for linear algebra, signal processing, system simulation, and optimization. The language is self-contained, proprietary, and based on a paid licensing model. For many academic institutions, students, or startups, the licensing costs – especially for specialized toolboxes – can present a significant barrier.

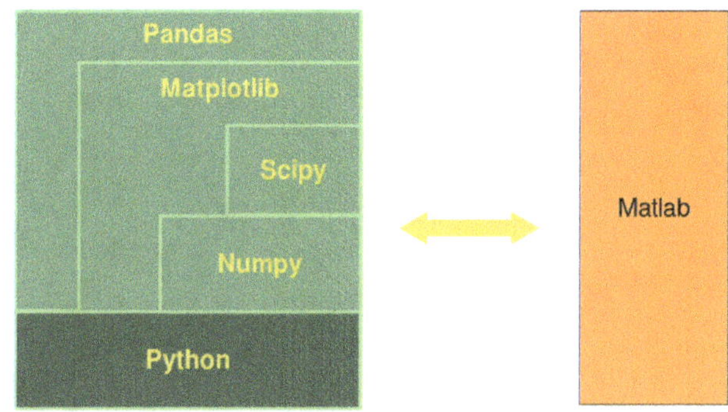

Figure 2.2 Relationship to MATLAB

Python, by contrast, was designed from the beginning as a general-purpose programming language. With libraries such as NumPy, SciPy, Matplotlib, Pandas, SymPy, and scikit-learn, Python is now capable of handling nearly all tasks that were once exclusive to MATLAB – and many more beyond, such as web development, automation, or machine learning.

One major advantage of Python is its seamless integration with modern development environments such as Jupyter Notebooks. This environment allows a combination of code, visualizations, and explanatory text – an ideal format for exploratory data analysis, scientific computing, and teaching.

Another strong point is the openness of its ecosystem: Python supports easy integration with C/C++ libraries, Fortran routines, or external tools. There are also many options for parallel and distributed computing (e.g., using Dask or joblib) as well as GPU-accelerated computing (e.g., CuPy, PyTorch, TensorFlow).

Last but not least, Python benefits from its enormous user base. Its open development culture leads to rapid improvements in tools, extensive documentation, tutorials, conferences, and a wealth of freely available resources.

3

Installation of NumPy, Matplotlib, Pandas, and JupyterLab

3.1 Introduction

This chapter describes how to install the libraries required for the subsequent chapters: NumPy, Matplotlib, Pandas, and JupyterLab.

JupyterLab is the modern, browser-based interface for interactive Python notebooks and is used throughout this book, as it is particularly well suited for experimenting with code, data analysis, and visualizations.

We present two installation methods:

- installation using `pip`, the standard package manager of Python,

- installation using conda, the package manager of Anaconda and Miniconda.

Figure 3.1 Speed Up!

Both methods have their advantages: while `pip` can be used directly with any Python installation, conda simplifies dependency management and provides optimized versions of many packages. Depending on the system and requirements, either method may be preferred.

Important note on Anaconda: Since 2020, Anaconda is no longer completely free for commercial use.[1] Companies and organizations with 200 or more employees require a paid license. For private individuals, students, teachers, as well as smaller companies and non-commercial academic institutions, usage remains free – especially for purely private learning and study purposes.[2] The underlying Python packages included in Anaconda (such as NumPy, Pandas, Matplotlib, and others) are open source and generally available free of charge. The license fees do not apply to the software itself, but to the commercial distribution, maintenance, and integration provided by Anaconda Inc., as well as to associated support services. Users who wish to avoid any potential licensing issues can instead rely on the freely available Miniconda or a custom-configured Python environment using pip.

Miniconda is a lightweight variant of Anaconda that also includes conda as a package manager but does not come with any preinstalled packages. It should be noted that the default channel ("defaults") is operated by Anaconda Inc. Organizations subject to the commercial licensing terms should therefore use alternative package sources such as conda-forge to avoid potential license costs.[3]

3.2 Installation with conda and Miniconda

If the Anaconda or Miniconda distribution is used, the package manager conda is available. This package and environment manager allows for the easy installation and management of numerous scientific Python packages. When using Anaconda, most of the required packages are already installed and do not need to be installed manually as shown below. With Miniconda, the required packages can be installed using:

```
conda install numpy matplotlib pandas jupyterlab
# or alternatively, community-based and license-free:
conda install -c conda-forge numpy matplotlib pandas jupyterlab
```

One advantage of conda is that it automatically resolves dependencies and, in many cases, provides optimized, precompiled versions of packages – especially for numerically demanding applications.

1　See the license information at *https://www.anaconda.com/pricing*
2　Before using Anaconda in a professional or institutional context, the current license terms should always be carefully reviewed.
3　Please note that we cannot guarantee legal correctness here, especially since license terms may change at any time.

3.3 Installation with pip

As an alternative to `conda`, `pip` is the official, standardized tool for package installation and is usually preinstalled with current Python versions. Installing Python packages via `pip` is, from a licensing perspective, the safest and most straightforward method. `pip` accesses the central Python package repository PyPI (Python Package Index), where nearly all widely used packages are published under free open-source licenses (e.g., `MIT`, `BSD`, or `Apache`). These licenses permit both private and commercial use without special permission or license fees.

For the data analysis and visualization examples used in this book, the required packages can be installed as follows:

```
pip install numpy matplotlib pandas jupyterlab
```

If `pip` is not up to date, it can be upgraded using the following command:

```
python -m pip install --upgrade pip
```

Additional packages will be required as the book progresses. We will point these out at the appropriate places. They can then be easily installed later using `pip`.

3.4 Starting JupyterLab

After installation, JupyterLab can be started. The exact command depends on the operating system:

- *Linux/macOS*: Open a terminal and enter the following command:

  ```
  jupyter lab
  ```

- *Windows (Command Prompt or PowerShell)*: Open the Command Prompt (`cmd.exe`) or PowerShell and enter:

  ```
  jupyter lab
  ```

- *Windows (Anaconda users)*: If JupyterLab was installed via Anaconda, it can also be started using the graphical interface:

  1. Open the Anaconda Navigator application.
  2. Select "JupyterLab" from the menu and click "Launch".

After starting, a browser interface opens in which new notebooks can be created and edited. If the browser does not open automatically, the following address can be entered manually:

```
http://localhost:8888/lab
```

If JupyterLab cannot be found after installation, it may be necessary to activate the appropriate environment (when using conda):

```
conda activate my_env
jupyter lab
```

3.5 Why JupyterLab?

Throughout this book, JupyterLab is used frequently because it is ideally suited for interactive programming. It offers:

- step-by-step execution of code,

- direct visualization of plots,

- the combination of code, formulas, and explanations in a single document,

- a modern interface with file explorer, tabs, and integrated terminals.

This greatly facilitates testing code and analyzing data. If JupyterLab is not to be used, all code examples can also be executed in a regular Python environment or in an IDE such as VS Code or PyCharm.

Part I

NumPy

4
NumPy Introduction

4.1 Overview

4.1.1 What is NumPy?

NumPy is a module that provides basic data structures – multidimensional arrays and matrices – as well as important functionalities. These are used by other modules such as Matplotlib, SciPy, and Pandas.

The name NumPy is an acronym for "Numerical Python". From the outset, its design emphasized both memory efficiency and high computational performance. To this end, a significant portion of its core is implemented in C, enabling numerical and mathematical operations to be executed with exceptional speed.[1]

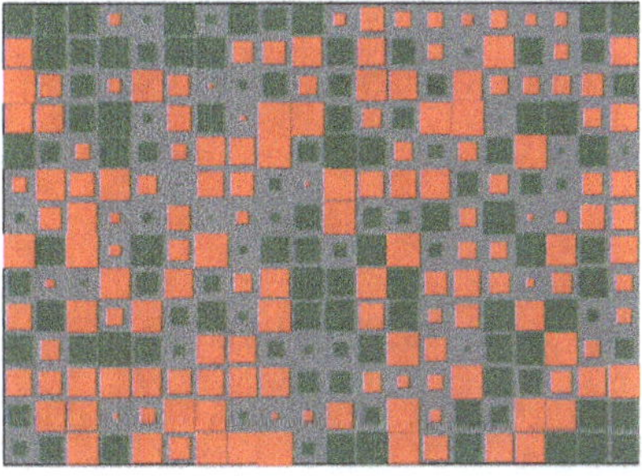

Figure 4.1 Visualization of a matrix as a Hinton diagram

NumPy extends Python with powerful data structures that allow efficient computations with large arrays and matrices – even for extremely large datasets ("Big Data"). In addition, the module provides a variety of high-quality mathematical functions specifically optimized for working with these structures. SciPy ("Scientific Python") is often mentioned alongside NumPy. It extends NumPy with additional functions such as minimization, regression, Fourier transformation, and many other tools.

---

[1] See *https://stackoverflow.com/questions/1825857/how-much-of-numpy-and-scipy-is-in-c*

The diagram in Figure 4.1 was created with Python using NumPy and Matplotlib. It shows a so-called Hinton diagram for visualizing a 14×20 matrix: the size of the squares represents the magnitude of the matrix values, and the color indicates their sign – red for negative and green for positive values.

NumPy is based on two earlier Python modules that dealt with arrays. One of these is Numeric. Like NumPy, Numeric is a Python module for powerful numerical computations, but it is now outdated. Another predecessor of NumPy is Numarray, which was a complete rewrite of Numeric, but this module is also obsolete today. NumPy is the merger of these two, meaning it is built on the code of Numeric and the functionalities of Numarray.

4.1.2 A simple example

To work with NumPy, we first need to import it:

```python
import numpy
# or, much more commonly, to save typing:
import numpy as np
```

In our first simple NumPy example, we define a one-dimensional NumPy array:

```python
C = np.array([20.8, 21.9, 22.5, 22.7, 22.3, 21.0, 21.2, 20.9])
print(C)
```

This is the result of the code:

```
[20.8 21.9 22.5 22.7 22.3 21.  21.2 20.9]
```

Now we want to convert the above temperature values to degrees Fahrenheit. This can be done very easily with a NumPy array. The solution to our problem lies in simple scalar operations:

```python
print(C * 9 / 5 + 32)
```

The code produces the following result:

```
[69.44 71.42 72.5  72.86 72.14 69.8  70.16 69.62]
```

Compared to this approach, the pure Python solution[2], which converts a list to a list of Fahrenheit temperatures using a list comprehension, turns out to be cumbersome:

```python
cvalues = [20.8, 21.9, 22.5, 22.7, 22.3, 21.0, 21.2, 20.9]
fvalues = [x * 9 / 5 + 32 for x in cvalues]
print(fvalues)
```

The result appears as follows:

```
[69.44, 71.42, 72.5, 72.86, 72.14, 69.8, 70.16, 69.62]
```

So far, we have referred to C as an array. However, the internal type designation is ndarray or, more precisely, "C is an instance of the class numpy.ndarray":

```python
print(type(C))
```

The result is:

```
<class 'numpy.ndarray'>
```

In the following, we will usually use "array" and "ndarray" synonymously.

4.2 Comparison of NumPy Data Structures and Lists

4.2.1 Key Differences

The data structures of pure Python, i.e., without NumPy or others, offer significant advantages:

Advantages of Python data structures:
- Integers and floats are implemented as powerful classes. Thus, integer numbers can become almost "infinitely" large or small.[3]
- Lists offer efficient methods for inserting, appending, and deleting elements.
- Dictionaries offer fast lookups.

Advantages of NumPy data structures over Python:
- Array-based computations
- Efficiently implemented multidimensional arrays
- Designed for scientific computing

---

2   That is, Python without using the NumPy module
3   They are ultimately limited by memory size and still infinitely far from "infinite"!

4.2.2 Memory Requirements

The main advantages of NumPy arrays are low memory consumption and optimal
runtime performance. In this chapter of our tutorial, we will take a closer look at the
memory usage of NumPy arrays and compare it with the memory usage of Python lists.

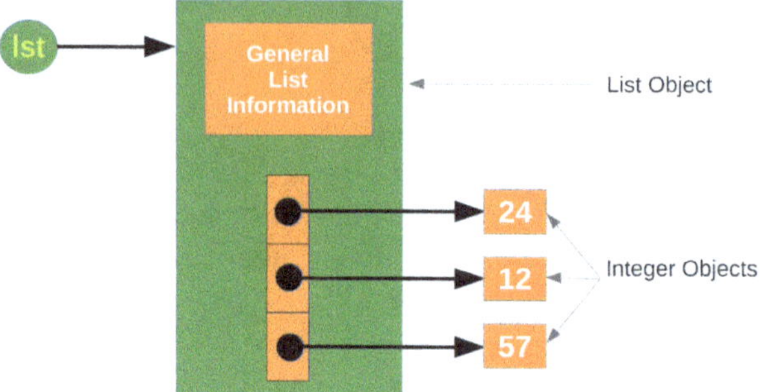

To calculate the memory usage of the list from the previous image, we will use the
`getsizeof` function from the `sys` module:

```python
from sys import getsizeof as size
lst = [24, 12, 57]
size_of_list_object = size(lst)   # only the green box
size_of_elements = len(lst) * size(lst[0])  # 24, 12, 57
total_list_size = size_of_list_object + size_of_elements

print("Size without size of the elements: ", size_of_list_object)
print("Size of all elements: ", size_of_elements)
print("Total size of the list: ", total_list_size)
```

This follows from the code:

```
Size without size of the elements:  88
Size of all elements:  84
Total size of the list:  172
```

The memory requirement of a Python list consists of the size of the general list information, the memory required for the references to the list elements, and the size of all
elements in the list. When we apply `sys.getsizeof` to a list, we only get the memory
usage of the list itself without the size of the list elements. In the example above, we
assumed that all integer elements in our list have the same size. This is, of course, not
generally true, since integers require more memory as their value increases.

We will now check how the memory consumption changes when we add more integer elements to the list. We will also look at the memory usage of an empty list:

```python
lst = [24, 12, 57, 42]
size_of_list_object = size(lst)
size_of_elements = len(lst) * size(lst[0])   # 24, 12, 57, 42
total_list_size = size_of_list_object + size_of_elements
print("Size without size of the elements: ", size_of_list_object)
print("Size of all elements: ", size_of_elements)
print("Total size of the list: ", total_list_size)
empty_lst = []
print("Memory usage of an empty list: ", size(empty_lst))
```

This follows from the code:

```
Size without size of the elements:  88
Size of all elements:  112
Total size of the list:  200
Memory usage of an empty list:  56
```

From the output of the previous code[4] we can conclude that for each integer element we need 8 bytes for the reference. An integer object itself requires 28 bytes in our case. The size of the list "lst" without the memory requirement for the elements themselves can therefore be calculated in our case as follows:

```
56 + 8 * len(lst)
```

To calculate the complete memory usage of an integer list, we must add the memory usage of all integers.

We will now calculate the memory usage of a NumPy array. For this purpose, we first look at the implementation in the following image:

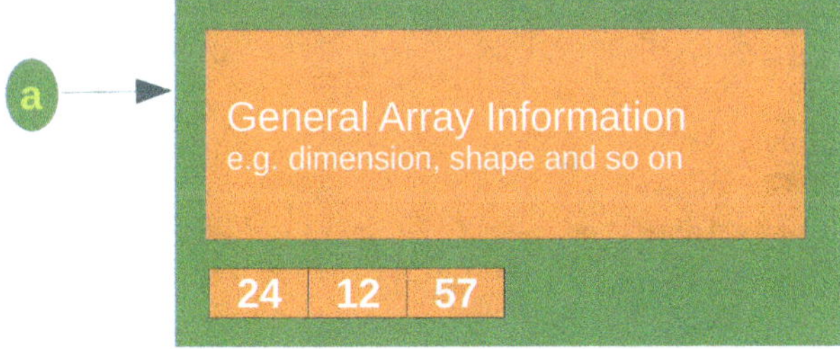

---

4   Depending on the Python version, the values may differ, but this does not change the principle!

We now create the array from the previous image and calculate its memory usage:

```
a = np.array([24, 12, 57])
print(size(a))
```

After execution we get:

```
136
```

The memory requirement for the general array information can be calculated by creating an empty array:

```
e = np.array([])
print(size(e))
```

The script returns:

```
112
```

We can see that the difference between the empty array "e" and the array "a", consisting of 3 integers, is 24 bytes. This means that the memory requirement for an arbitrary integer array with "n" elements is given by:

```
112 + n * 8   bytes
```

In comparison, as we have seen, the memory requirement of an integer list is calculated as:

```
56 + 8 * len(lst) + len(lst) * 28
```

This is a lower bound, since Python integers can become larger than 28 bytes!

When we define a NumPy array, NumPy automatically chooses a fixed integer size, in our case "int64".

We can also specify this size when defining an array. Naturally, this changes the total memory requirement of the array:

```
a8 = np.array([24, 12, 57], np.int8)
a16 = np.array([24, 12, 57], np.int16)
a32 = np.array([24, 12, 57], np.int32)
a64 = np.array([24, 12, 57], np.int64)
print(size(a8), size(a16), size(a32), size(a64))
```

Executing the code yields:

```
115 118 124 136
```

4.2.3 Time Comparison Between Lists and NumPy Arrays

One of the main advantages of NumPy is its time advantage over standard Python. In the following, we define two functions. The first, `pure_python_version`, creates two Python lists using range, while the second creates two NumPy arrays using the NumPy function `arange`. In both functions, we add the elements component-wise:

```python
import numpy as np
import time

size_of_vec = 1000000
def pure_python_version():
    t1 = time.time()
    X = range(size_of_vec)
    Y = range(size_of_vec)
    Z = [X[i] + Y[i] for i in range(len(X))]
    return time.time() - t1

def numpy_version():
    t1 = time.time()
    X = np.arange(size_of_vec)
    Y = np.arange(size_of_vec)
    Z = X + Y
    return time.time() - t1
```

We call these functions and can see the time advantage:

```python
t1 = pure_python_version()
t2 = numpy_version()
print(t1, t2)
print(f'NumPy is {t1 / t2:5.2f} times faster in this case!')
```

Here is the output:

```
0.10400867462158203 0.0036640167236328125
NumPy is 28.39 times faster in this case!
```

Time measurement becomes easier – and above all more accurate – if we use the `timeit` module. In the following script, we will use the Timer class.

The constructor of a Timer object can take two statements: one to be measured and one to act as a setup. Both statements default to 'pass'. Optionally, a timer function can also be passed.

A Timer object has a `timeit` method. The argument of the `timeit` method is the number of loops for which the code should be repeated.

```
timeit(number=1000000)
```

`timeit` returns the time needed for `number` iterations.

```python
import numpy as np
from timeit import Timer

size_of_vec = 1000
def pure_python_version():
    X = range(size_of_vec)
    Y = range(size_of_vec)
    Z = [X[i] + Y[i] for i in range(len(X))]


def numpy_version():
    X = np.arange(size_of_vec)
    Y = np.arange(size_of_vec)
    Z = X + Y


timer_obj1 = Timer("pure_python_version()",
                   "from __main__ import pure_python_version")
timer_obj2 = Timer("numpy_version()",
                   "from __main__ import numpy_version")

print(timer_obj1.timeit(10))
print(timer_obj2.timeit(10))
```

Output:

```
0.0006491319509223104
3.0246912501752377e-05
```

The repeat method is a simplified way to call the `timeit` method several times and get a list of the results:

```python
print(timer_obj1.repeat(repeat=2, number=10))
print(timer_obj2.repeat(repeat=2, number=10))
```

What we obtain is:

```
[0.000644186045974493, 0.0006354820216074586]
[1.6726087778806686e-05, 1.5264027751982212e-05]
```

5

Creation and Structure of Arrays

After learning in the previous chapter how to create NumPy arrays from lists and tuples, we will now systematically examine the internal structure of arrays. In addition, you will get to know further central functions for creating and initializing arrays – including arrays with predefined content such as zeros or ones, as well as those with automatically generated sequences of numbers or random values.

Figure 5.1 Symbolic Array

5.1 Dimensions

5.1.1 Zero-Dimensional Arrays in NumPy

In NumPy arrays of arbitrary dimension can be created – including zero-dimensional arrays. A scalar, that is, a single numerical value without axis or direction, is represented in NumPy as a zero-dimensional array.

In the following example, we create such a zero-dimensional array with the value 42. If we apply the `ndim` method to the array, we obtain its dimension. Moreover, the type of the object can be identified as `numpy.ndarray`.

```python
import numpy as np
x = np.array(42)
print("x: ", x)
print("Type of x: ", type(x))
print("Dimension of x:", np.ndim(x))
```

After execution we get:

```
x:  42
Type of x:  <class 'numpy.ndarray'>
Dimension of x: 0
```

5.1.2 One-Dimensional Array

We have already seen a one-dimensional array – better known as a vector – in our
initial example. What we have not yet mentioned, but is obvious, is the fact that NumPy
arrays are containers that can only contain one type, for example only integers. The
homogeneous data type of an array can be determined with the attribute dtype, as we
can learn in the following example:

```python
F = np.array([1, 1, 2, 3, 5, 8, 13, 21])
V = np.array([3.4, 6.9, 99.8, 12.8])
print(f"{F=}\n{V=}")
print(f"Type of F: {F.dtype}, Type of V: {V.dtype}")
```

We obtain this output:

```
F=array([ 1,  1,  2,  3,  5,  8, 13, 21])
V=array([ 3.4,  6.9, 99.8, 12.8])
Type of F: int64, Type of V: float64
```

5.1.3 Two- and Multi-Dimensional Arrays

Of course, arrays in NumPy are not limited to one dimension. They can have any
number of dimensions. We create them by passing nested lists (or tuples) to NumPy's
array method:

```python
A = np.array([[3.4, 8.7, 9.9],
              [1.1, -7.8, -0.7],
              [4.1, 12.3, 4.8]])
print(f"{A}\n{A.ndim=}")
```

The result of the code is:

```
[[ 3.4  8.7  9.9]
 [ 1.1 -7.8 -0.7]
 [ 4.1 12.3  4.8]]
A.ndim=2
```

5.2 Shape of an Array

The function shape returns the size or the shape of an array in the form of an integer
tuple. These numbers indicate the lengths of the corresponding array dimensions, i.e.,
in the two-dimensional case, the rows and columns. In other words: the shape of an
array is a tuple with the number of elements per axis (dimension). In our example, the
shape is (6, 3). This means we have six rows and three columns.[1]

```
x = np.array([[67, 63, 87],
              [77, 69, 59],
              [85, 87, 99],
              [79, 72, 71],
              [63, 89, 93],
              [68, 92, 78]])
print(np.shape(x))
```

This is the result of the code:

```
(6, 3)
```

There is also an equivalent array property print(x.shape), which produces the same
result.

The shape of an array also tells us something about the order in which the indices are
executed, i.e., first the rows, then the columns, and then possibly another dimension
or further dimensions.

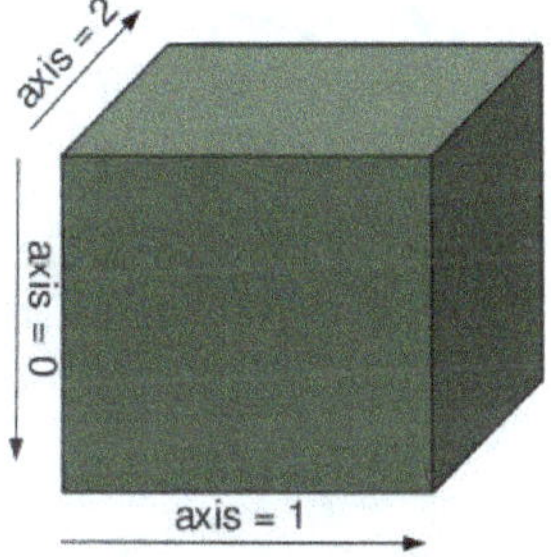

shape can also be used to change the "shape" of an array:

```
x.shape = (3, 6)
print(x)
```

---

[1] In mathematics, in addition to the notion of a matrix's *shape* as used in programming, the terms *size*
or *dimension* are commonly employed. One speaks of an $m \times n$ matrix (read "m-by-n" or "m-cross-n"),
meaning a matrix with m rows and n columns.

The result appears as follows:

```
[[67 63 87 77 69 59]
 [85 87 99 79 72 71]
 [63 89 93 68 92 78]]
```

```
x.shape = (2, 9)
print(x)
```

This is the result of the code:

```
[[67 63 87 77 69 59 85 87 99]
 [79 72 71 63 89 93 68 92 78]]
```

Many will have already guessed that the new shape must correspond to the number of elements of the array, i.e., the total size of the new array must be the same as the old one. An exception is raised if this is not the case, for example if we enter x.shape = (4, 4) in our case.

The shape of a scalar is an empty tuple:

```
x = np.array(11)
print(np.shape(x))
```

Result:

```
()
```

Next we see the shape of a three-dimensional array:

```
B = np.array([[[111, 112], [121, 122]],
              [[211, 212], [221, 222]],
              [[311, 312], [321, 322]]])
print(B.shape)
```

Output:

```
(3, 2, 2)
```

5.3 Indexing and Slicing Operator

Accessing or assigning elements of an array works similarly to Python's sequential data types, i.e., lists and tuples. In addition, we have various options for indexing. This makes indexing in NumPy very powerful and similar to indexing and slicing of lists. Indexing individual elements works as most would probably expect:

```python
F = np.array([1, 1, 2, 3, 5, 8, 13, 21])
print(F[0]) # first element of F
print(F[-1]) # last element of F
```

Output:

```
1
21
```

Indexing multidimensional arrays:

```python
A = np.array([[3.4, 8.7, 9.9],
              [1.1, -7.8, -0.7],
              [4.1, 12.3, 4.8]])
print(A[1][0])


B = np.array([[[111, 112], [121, 122]],
              [[211, 212], [221, 222]],
              [[311, 312], [321, 322]]])
print(B[0][1][0])
```

The result appears as follows:

```
1.1
121
```

We accessed the element in the second row, i.e., the row with index 1, and the first
column (index 0). Alternatively, we can also use just a single pair of brackets, with all
indices separated by commas:

```python
print(A[1, 0])
```

Here is the output:

```
1.1
```

One should be aware that the second method is generally more efficient. In the first
case, as an intermediate step, we create an array A[1] in which we then access the
element with index 0. This corresponds roughly to the following:

```python
tmp = A[1]
print(tmp)
print(tmp[0])
```

After execution we get:

```
[ 1.1 -7.8 -0.7]
1.1
```

The verb *to slice* provides an intuitive metaphor for Python and NumPy slicing: a contiguous subset of a sequence or array is extracted. For one-dimensional arrays, NumPy uses the same slicing syntax as Python lists, while extending it naturally to multidimensional arrays by allowing slices along multiple axes. Slicing uses up to three parameters of the form [start:stop:step]. The following examples illustrate this for a one-dimensional array:

```python
S = np.array([0, 1, 2, 3, 4, 5, 6, 7, 8, 9])
print(S[2:5]) # elements from position 2 (incl.) to 5 (excl.)
print(S[:4])  # elements from start up to position 4 (exclusive)
print(S[6:])  # from position 6 (incl.) to the end
print(S[:])   # from start to end
```

Output:

```
[2 3 4]
[0 1 2 3]
[6 7 8 9]
[0 1 2 3 4 5 6 7 8 9]
```

For multidimensional arrays, ranges are specified for each dimension separated by commas:

```python
A = np.array([
    [11, 12, 13, 14, 15],
    [21, 22, 23, 24, 25],
    [31, 32, 33, 34, 35],
    [41, 42, 43, 44, 45],
    [51, 52, 53, 54, 55]])

print(A[:3, 2:])
```

The code produces the following result:

```
[[13 14 15]
 [23 24 25]
 [33 34 35]]
```

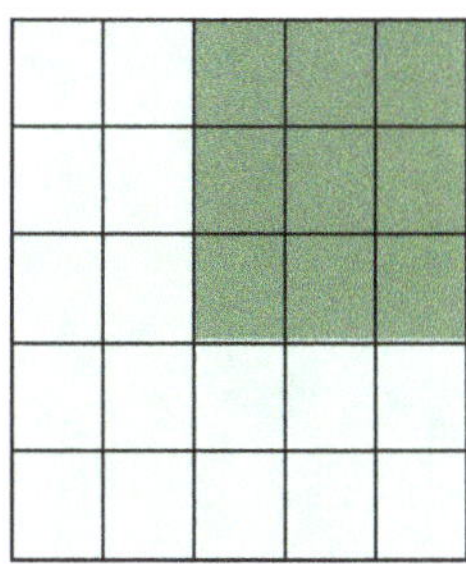

```
print(A[3:, :])
```

We obtain this output:

```
[[41 42 43 44 45]
 [51 52 53 54 55]]
```

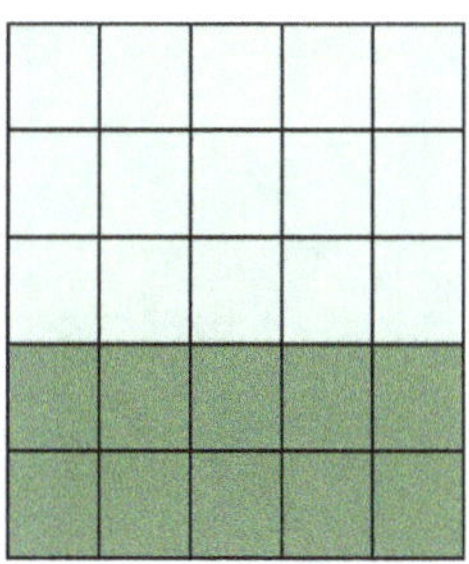

```
print(A[:, 4:])
```

The result follows:

```
[[15]
 [25]
 [35]
 [45]
 [55]]
```

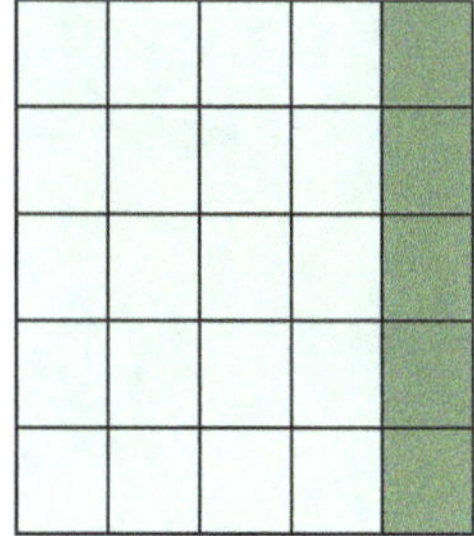

The following two examples also use the third parameter step.

```
X = np.array([[0, 1, 2, 3, 4, 5, 6],
              [7, 8, 9, 10, 11, 12, 13],
              [14, 15, 16, 17, 18, 19, 20],
              [21, 22, 23, 24, 25, 26, 27]])
print(X)
```

The evaluation yields:

```
[[ 0  1  2  3  4  5  6]
 [ 7  8  9 10 11 12 13]
 [14 15 16 17 18 19 20]
 [21 22 23 24 25 26 27]]
```

```
print(X[::2, ::3])
```

Output:

```
[[ 0  3  6]
 [14 17 20]]
```

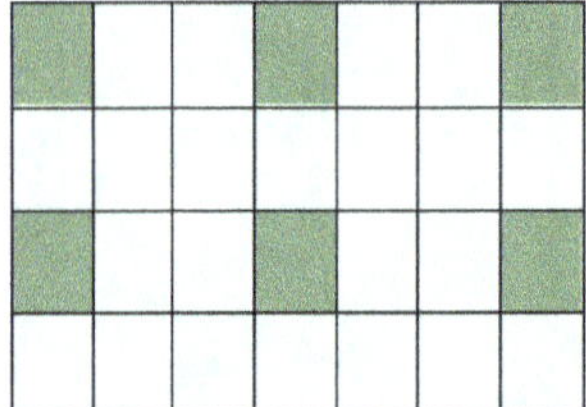

```
print(X[::, ::3])
```

The execution leads to this output:

```
[[ 0  3  6]
 [ 7 10 13]
 [14 17 20]
 [21 24 27]]
```

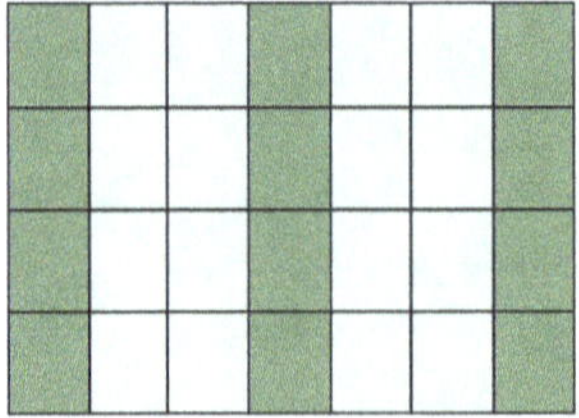

If the number of objects in the selection tuple is smaller than the dimension N, then ":"
is assumed for the remaining, unspecified dimensions:

```
A = np.array(
    [[[45, 12, 4], [45, 13, 5], [46, 12, 6]],
     [[46, 14, 4], [45, 14, 5], [46, 11, 5]],
     [[47, 13, 2], [48, 15, 5], [52, 15, 1]]])

print(A[1:3, 0:2])  # equivalent to print(A[1:3, 0:2, :])
```

Result:

```
[[[46 14  4]
  [45 14  5]]

 [[47 13  2]
  [48 15  5]]]
```

Attention: The slicing operator creates new objects for lists and tuples – in NumPy,
however, it only creates a view of the original array. Changes to this view therefore
directly affect the original array.

```
A = np.array([0, 1, 2, 3, 4, 5, 6, 7, 8, 9])
S = A[2:6]
S[1] = 23
print(A)
```

The result of the code is:

```
[ 0  1  2 23  4  5  6  7  8  9]
```

If we do the same with lists, we see that we get a copy. Strictly speaking, we should say
a shallow copy.

```
lst = [0, 1, 2, 3, 4, 5, 6, 7, 8, 9]
lst2 = lst[2:6]
lst2[1] = 23
print(lst)
```

The processing yields:

```
[0, 1, 2, 3, 4, 5, 6, 7, 8, 9]
```

If you want to check whether two arrays access the same memory area, you can use
the function `np.may_share_memory`:

```
np.may_share_memory(A, B)
```

To determine whether two arrays A and B share memory, the memory bounds of A and
B are calculated. The function returns `True` if they overlap, otherwise `False`.

```python
A = np.array([0, 1, 2, 3, 4, 5, 6, 7, 8, 9])
B = A[2:5]

print(np.may_share_memory(A, B))
```

may_share_memory returns True in the previous code. Even though in most examples it looks like the arrays always share elements when the function returns True, this is not always the case. We show this in the following example. B1 and B2 have no shared data, but their memory locations are interleaved, since both are "just" a view of A:

```python
A = np.array([0, 1, 2, 3, 4, 5, 6, 7, 8, 9])
B1 = A[::2]
B2 = A[1::2]
print(np.may_share_memory(B1, B2))
```

may_share_memory returns True in the previous example, even though the arrays do not actually share memory.

5.4 Three-Dimensional Arrays

Three-dimensional arrays are somewhat harder to imagine in terms of access. Let us consider the following example array:

```python
import numpy as np
X = np.array(
    [[[3, 1, 2],
      [4, 2, 2]],
     [[-1, 0, 1],
      [1, -1, -2]],
     [[3, 2, 2],
      [4, 4, 3]],
     [[2, 2, 1],
      [3, 1, 3]]])

print(X.shape)
```

The output tells us that this array has the shape (4, 2, 3). We now use the slicing functionality to illustrate the slices through the dimensions:

```python
print("Dimension 0 with size ", X.shape[0])
for i in range(X.shape[0]):
    print(f"Output of X[{i:1},:,:]:\n{X[i, :, :]}")
```

```python
print("\nDimension 1 with size ", X.shape[1])
for i in range(X.shape[1]):
    print(f"Output of X[:,{i:1},:]:\n{X[:, i, :]}")

print("\nDimension 2 with size ", X.shape[2])
for i in range(X.shape[2]):
    print(f"Output of X[:,:,{i:1}]:\n{X[:, :, i]}")
```

This follows from the code:

```
Dimension 0 with size  4
Output of X[0,:,:]:
[[3 1 2]
 [4 2 2]]
Output of X[1,:,:]:
[[-1  0  1]
 [ 1 -1 -2]]
Output of X[2,:,:]:
[[3 2 2]
 [4 4 3]]
Output of X[3,:,:]:
[[2 2 1]
 [3 1 3]]

Dimension 1 with size  2
Output of X[:,0,:]:
[[ 3  1  2]
 [-1  0  1]
 [ 3  2  2]
 [ 2  2  1]]
Output of X[:,1,:]:
[[ 4  2  2]
 [ 1 -1 -2]
 [ 4  4  3]
 [ 3  1  3]]

Dimension 2 with size  3
Output of X[:,:,0]:
[[ 3  4]
 [-1  1]
 [ 3  4]
 [ 2  3]]
Output of X[:,:,1]:
[[ 1  2]
 [ 0 -1]
 [ 2  4]
 [ 2  1]]
```

```
Output of X[:,:,2]:
[[ 2  2]
 [ 1 -2]
 [ 2  3]
 [ 1  3]]
```

The following images explain this further:

5.5 Array Creation Functions

Many numerical algorithms require arrays with fixed values or predefined structure at the beginning. NumPy provides functions that allow such arrays to be created easily and efficiently.

NumPy provides two functions to generate intervals with evenly spaced values. `arange` uses a given step size to generate values within specified interval limits, while `linspace` calculates a specified number of values within the given interval limits. The spacing is calculated automatically by `linspace`.

A common scenario is the creation of arrays with evenly spaced values within a given interval. For this, NumPy offers two core functions:

- `arange` uses a fixed step size to generate values within a half-open interval.

- `linspace` generates a defined number of values over an interval with automatically calculated spacing.

5.5.1 arange

The syntax of `arange`:

```
arange([start,] stop[, step], [, dtype=None])
```

`arange` returns evenly spaced values within a given interval. The values are generated within the half-open interval `[start, stop)`. Both integers and floats can be passed as arguments. When this function is used with integer values, it is almost equivalent to the built-in Python function `range`. However, `arange` returns an ndarray, while `range` returns a range object. A range object allows us to iterate over a large range of numbers, generating the numbers only when needed. If the `start` parameter is not provided, it defaults to 0. The end of the interval is determined by the parameter `stop`. Normally, the interval does not include this value, except in cases where `step` is not an integer and floating-point effects influence the length of the output array. The distance between two neighboring values in the output array can be set using the optional parameter `step`. The default value for `step` is 1.

If a value for `step` is specified, the `start` parameter can no longer be optional, i.e., it must also be specified.

The type of the output array can be specified with the parameter `dtype`. If it is not specified, the type is automatically inferred from the provided input values.

```python
import numpy as np

a = np.arange(1, 7)
print(a)
```

```python
x = range(1, 7)
print(x)      # x is an iterator
print(list(x))


x = np.arange(7.3)
print(x)
x = np.arange(0.5, 6.1, 0.8)
print(x)
```

The result is:

```
[1 2 3 4 5 6]
range(1, 7)
[1, 2, 3, 4, 5, 6]
[0. 1. 2. 3. 4. 5. 6. 7.]
[0.5 1.3 2.1 2.9 3.7 4.5 5.3]
```

One must be careful when using a float value for the step parameter, as we can see in
the following example:

```python
x = np.arange(12.04, 12.84, 0.08)
print(x)
```

The code produces the following result:

```
[12.04 12.12 12.2  12.28 12.36 12.44 12.52 12.6  12.68 12.76 12.84]
```

The help text of arange states the following for the stop parameter: "End of interval."
The interval does not include this value, except in some cases where step is not an
integer and floating-point rounding affects the length of the output. This is the case in
our example.

The following use of arange is a bit odd. Why should we use floating-point numbers if
we want integers as a result? Nevertheless, the outcome may be confusing.

```python
x = np.arange(0.6, 10.4, 0.71, int)
print(x)
```

Here is the output:

```
[ 0  1  2  3  4  5  6  7  8  9 10 11 12 13]
```

This result seems to defy all logical explanation. However, it can be explained by the
fact that arange, before starting, truncates the value of the start parameter to the next
lower integer, then calculates the number of steps. In our case, (10.4 - 0.6) / 0.71,
which equals 13.802816901408452. This value is also truncated, i.e., to 13. Only the step

size is rounded, rounded up to 1. Then thirteen "steps" starting at 0 are performed. Moral of the story: if you want integers as a result, you should also use integers as parameters.

5.5.2 linspace

The syntax of `linspace`:

`linspace(start, stop, num=50, endpoint=True, retstep=False)`

`linspace` returns an ndarray consisting of 'num' evenly spaced values from the closed interval `['start', 'stop']` or the half-open interval `['start', 'stop')`. Whether a closed or half-open interval is returned depends on the value of the parameter `endpoint`. `stop` is the last value of the interval if `endpoint` is not set to `False`. The step size differs depending on whether `endpoint` is `True` or `False`:

```
print(np.linspace(1, 10))
print(np.linspace(1, 10, 7))
# now without endpoint:
print(np.linspace(1, 10, 7, endpoint=False))
```

The code produces the following result:

```
[ 1.      1.184  1.367  1.551  1.735  1.918  2.102  2.286  2.469
  2.653  2.837  3.02   3.204  3.388  3.571  3.755  3.939  4.122
  4.306  4.49   4.673  4.857  5.041  5.224  5.408  5.592  5.776
  5.959  6.143  6.327  6.51   6.694  6.878  7.061  7.245  7.429
  7.612  7.796  7.98   8.163  8.347  8.531  8.714  8.898  9.082
  9.265  9.449  9.633  9.816 10.    ]
[ 1.     2.5  4.    5.5  7.    8.5 10.  ]
[1.      2.286 3.571 4.857 6.143 7.429 8.714]
```

So far we have not discussed one interesting parameter. If the parameter `retstep` is set, the function will also return the value of the spacing between two neighboring values of the output array. The function therefore returns a tuple (`'samples'`, `'step'`):

```
import numpy as np

samples, spacing = np.linspace(1, 10,
                              retstep=True)
print(spacing)
samples, spacing = np.linspace(1, 10, 5,
                              endpoint=True,
                              retstep=True)
print(samples, spacing)
samples, spacing = np.linspace(1, 10, 5,
```

```
                                            endpoint=False, retstep=True)
print(samples, spacing)
```

This follows from the code:

```
0.18367346938877551
[ 1.    3.25  5.5    7.75 10.   ] 2.25
[1.   2.8 4.6 6.4 8.2] 1.8
```

Some may wonder why this should be necessary. Can't we simply calculate the spacing as the difference between two neighboring array elements? Let's look at the following example:

```python
import numpy as np
a, spacing = np.linspace(4, 23, endpoint=False, retstep=True)
print(a[:6])

# Spacing between the first 6 array elements:
for i in range(6):
    print(a[i + 1] - a[i])

print(f"{spacing=}")
```

After execution we get:

```
[4.    4.38 4.76 5.14 5.52 5.9 ]
0.3799999999999999
0.3799999999999999
0.3800000000000008
0.379999999999999
0.3800000000000008
0.3799999999999999
spacing=np.float64(0.38)
```

From the output, we can see that the calculated values differ and that none of them match the "true" value, i.e., the value spacing returned by linspace. This is due to rounding issues in floating-point operations.

5.6 Arrays with Zeros and Ones

Arrays can be initialized with zeros and ones in two ways. The method ones(t) takes as parameter a tuple t with the shape of the array and generates an array filled with ones accordingly. By default, it is filled with float ones. If integer ones are required, you can set the optional parameter dtype to int:

```python
import numpy as np

E = np.ones((2, 3))
print(E)


F = np.ones((3, 4), dtype=int)
print(F)
```

This output is obtained:

```
[[1. 1. 1.]
 [1. 1. 1.]]
[[1 1 1 1]
 [1 1 1 1]
 [1 1 1 1]]
```

What we said about the method ones applies analogously to the method zeros, as we can see in the following example:

```python
Z = np.zeros((2, 4))
print(Z)


Z = np.zeros((2, 4), dtype=int)
print(Z)
```

Here is the output:

```
[[0. 0. 0. 0.]
 [0. 0. 0. 0.]]
[[0 0 0 0]
 [0 0 0 0]]
```

There is also another interesting way to create an array of ones or zeros if it should have the same shape as another existing array a. For this purpose, NumPy provides the methods ones_like and zeros_like:

```python
x = np.array([2, 5, 18, 14, 4])
E = np.ones_like(x)
print(E)


Z = np.zeros_like(x)
print(Z)
```

Here is the output:

```
[1 1 1 1 1]
[0 0 0 0 0]
```

5.7 Identity Matrix

In linear algebra, the identity matrix is defined as a square matrix whose main diagonal elements are ones and all other elements are zeros. NumPy provides two ways to create such arrays:

- identity
- eye

5.7.1 The identity Function

We can generate identity arrays using the function identity:

identity(n, dtype=None)

Parameter	Meaning
n	An integer value that defines the number of rows and columns of the output, i.e., 'n' x 'n'
dtype	An optional argument that defines the data type of the result. The default is 'float'

The output of identity is an n x n array in which the elements on the main diagonal are set to 1 and all other elements are set to 0.

```python
import numpy as np


print(np.identity(4))
```

Here is the result of the code:

```
[[1. 0. 0. 0.]
 [0. 1. 0. 0.]
 [0. 0. 1. 0.]
 [0. 0. 0. 1.]]
```

```python
print(np.identity(4, dtype=int))
```

Result:

```
[[1 0 0 0]
 [0 1 0 0]
 [0 0 1 0]
 [0 0 0 1]]
```

5.7.2 The eye Function

The function eye provides another way to create identity arrays, but also general diagonal arrays, filled with ones. The output of eye is a two-dimensional array in which the elements on the main diagonal are set to 1 and all other elements are set to 0.

```
eye(N, M=None, k=0, dtype=float)
```

Parameter	Meaning
N	An integer that specifies the number of rows of the output array.
M	An integer that specifies the number of columns of the output array. If this parameter is not set or is None, it defaults to 'N'.
k	Specifies the position of the diagonal. The default is 0. 0 denotes the main diagonal. A positive value refers to an upper diagonal and a negative value to a lower diagonal.
dtype	An optional argument that defines the data type of the result. The default is 'float'.

eye returns an ndarray with shape (N, M). All elements of this array are 0 except those on the k-th diagonal, which are set to 1.

```python
import numpy as np


print(np.eye(5, 8, k=1, dtype=int))
```

Here is the result of the code:

```
[[0 1 0 0 0 0 0 0]
 [0 0 1 0 0 0 0 0]
 [0 0 0 1 0 0 0 0]
 [0 0 0 0 1 0 0 0]
 [0 0 0 0 0 1 0 0]]
```

The behavior of the parameter k of eye is illustrated in the following diagram:

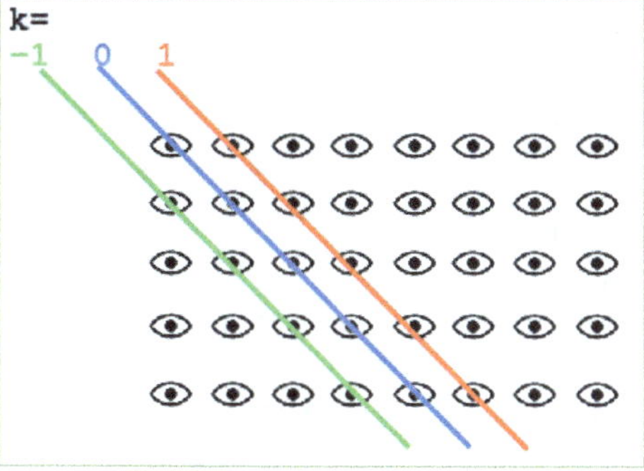

5.8 Data Types

So far, we have only briefly mentioned, or touched on indirectly, that the integers or floats used in NumPy arrays differ fundamentally from the Python data types `int` and `float`.

Data Type	Comment
int8	from -128 to 127, 1 Byte
int16	from -32768 to 32767, 2 Bytes
int32	from -2147483648 to 2147483647, 4 Bytes
int64	from -9223372036854775808 to 9223372036854775807, 8 Bytes
uint8	from 0 to 255, unsigned int, 1 Byte
uint16	from 0 to 65535, unsigned int, 2 Bytes
uint32	from 0 to 4294967295, unsigned int, 4 Bytes
uint64	from 0 to 18446744073709551615, unsigned int, 8 Bytes
float16	Half precision floating-point number: sign bit, 5 bits exponent, 10 bits mantissa
float32	Single precision floating-point number: sign bit, 8 bits exponent, 23 bits mantissa
float64	Double precision floating-point number: sign bit, 11 bits exponent, 52 bits mantissa
complex64	Complex number represented by two 32-bit floats.
complex128	Complex number represented by two 64-bit floats.

Further information on the float types can be displayed using the function `finfo`:

```python
import numpy as np
print(np.finfo(np.float16))
print(np.finfo(np.float32))
print(np.finfo(np.float64))
```

The output shows:

```
Machine parameters for float16
---------------------------------------------------------------
precision =   3   resolution = 1.00040e-03
machep =    -10   eps =          9.76562e-04
negep =     -11   epsneg =       4.88281e-04
minexp =    -14   tiny =         6.10352e-05
maxexp =     16   max =          6.55040e+04
nexp =        5   min =          -max
smallest_normal = 6.10352e-05   smallest_subnormal = 5.96046e-08
---------------------------------------------------------------
```

```
Machine parameters for float32
---------------------------------------------------------------
precision =   6   resolution = 1.0000000e-06
machep =    -23   eps =           1.1920929e-07
negep =     -24   epsneg =        5.9604645e-08
minexp =   -126   tiny =          1.1754944e-38
maxexp =    128   max =           3.4028235e+38
nexp =        8   min =              -max
smallest_normal = 1.1754944e-38   smallest_subnormal = 1.4012985e-45
---------------------------------------------------------------


Machine parameters for float64
---------------------------------------------------------------
precision =  15   resolution = 1.0000000000000001e-15
machep =    -52   eps =           2.2204460492503131e-16
negep =     -53   epsneg =        1.1102230246251565e-16
minexp =  -1022   tiny =          2.2250738585072014e-308
maxexp =   1024   max =           1.7976931348623157e+308
nexp =       11   min =              -max
smallest_normal = 2.2250738585072014e-308   smallest_subnormal =
↪   4.9406564584124654e-324
---------------------------------------------------------------
```

Here, eps is the difference between 1.0 and the next representable float greater than
1.0. epsneg is the difference between 1.0 and the next representable float smaller than
1.0. max denotes the largest representable number. min corresponds to the smallest
representable number. maxexp stands for the smallest positive power of the base (2)
that causes an overflow. tiny is the smallest positive floating-point number with full
precision.

Every numerical array in NumPy consists of values of one of these types. In fact, you
should specify the type when creating arrays. We show this in the following examples:

```python
import numpy as np


a1 = np.array([2, 4, -5], dtype=np.int8)
a2 = np.array([4.564, 8.987, 0.32], dtype=np.float32)
a3 = np.zeros((3, 4), dtype=np.uint8)
a4 = np.identity(3, dtype=np.uint16)
print(f"{a1=}\n{a2=}\n{a3=}\n{a4=}")
```

Result:

```
a1=array([ 2,  4, -5], dtype=int8)
a2=array([4.564, 8.987, 0.32 ], dtype=float32)
a3=array([[0, 0, 0, 0],
       [0, 0, 0, 0],
       [0, 0, 0, 0]], dtype=uint8)
```

```
a4=array([[1, 0, 0],
          [0, 1, 0],
          [0, 0, 1]], dtype=uint16)
```

If no type is assigned to `dtype`, a default value is used, which usually corresponds to the largest possible data type. In many cases, this is a waste of memory.

5.9 Copying Arrays

5.9.1 numpy.copy(A) and A.copy()

To copy a NumPy array A, there are generally two options:
- `numpy.copy(A)`
- `A.copy()`

Both functions are very similar and each returns a new array containing a copy of the data of A. They differ, however, in the default value of the optional argument `order`. In `numpy.copy(obj)` the default value is `order='K'`, while in `obj.copy()` it is `order='C'`.

Parameter	Meaning
`obj`	Array-like input data
`order`	Possible values are {`'C'`, `'F'`, `'A'`, `'K'`}. This parameter controls the memory layout of the copy. `'C'` means C-order or C-contiguous, `'F'` means Fortran-contiguous, `'A'` behaves like `'F'` if the object `obj` is in Fortran-order, otherwise like `'C'`. `'K'` means that the layout of `obj` should be preserved as closely as possible.

5.9.2 Contiguous Arrays

To understand the parameter `order`, we need to briefly discuss the concept of "contiguous." The memory structure of an array is called contiguous if the array is stored either in C-contiguous order (`C_CONTIGUOUS`) or Fortran-contiguous order (`F_CONTIGUOUS`). Let's consider the following array:

$$
\begin{array}{cccc}
a_{11} & a_{12} & a_{13} & a_{14} \\
a_{21} & a_{22} & a_{23} & a_{24} \\
a_{31} & a_{32} & a_{33} & a_{34}
\end{array}
$$

If this array is stored row by row – as shown in the following image – it is called
C-contiguous.

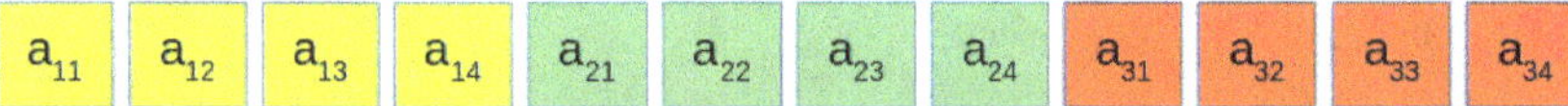

If an array is stored column by column, it is called Fortran-contiguous:

We now demonstrate how the storage type can be determined using the parameter
order:

```python
import numpy as np


F = np.array([[11, 12, 13, 14],
              [21, 22, 23, 24],
              [31, 32, 33, 34]], order='F')


C = F.copy()
C2 = np.copy(F)


print("F array: \n", F)
print("C array: \n", C)


print("Is F 'C contiguous?': ", F.flags['C_CONTIGUOUS'])
print("Is C 'C contiguous?': ", C.flags['C_CONTIGUOUS'])
print("Is C2 'C contiguous?': ", C2.flags['C_CONTIGUOUS'])
```

The script returns:

```
F array:
 [[11 12 13 14]
 [21 22 23 24]
 [31 32 33 34]]
C array:
 [[11 12 13 14]
 [21 22 23 24]
 [31 32 33 34]]
Is F 'C contiguous?':  False
Is C 'C contiguous?':  True
Is C2 'C contiguous?':  False
```

When an array is transposed, the data is not rearranged in memory; instead, only the
strides attribute is adjusted, i.e., the storage is interpreted differently.

```python
T = C.transpose()
print(f"{C.flags['C_CONTIGUOUS']=}, {T.flags['C_CONTIGUOUS']=}")
print(f"C strides: {C.strides}, T strides: {T.strides}")
```

The corresponding output can be seen here:

```
C.flags['C_CONTIGUOUS']=True, T.flags['C_CONTIGUOUS']=False
C strides: (32, 8), T strides: (8, 32)


T = F.transpose()
print(F.flags['C_CONTIGUOUS'])
print(T.flags['C_CONTIGUOUS'])
print(T.strides, F.strides)
```

We obtain this output:

```
False
True
(24, 8) (8, 24)
```

We see that `F.strides` returns the tuple `(8, 24)`. This means you have to skip 24 bytes
– which corresponds to three numbers of 8 bytes each – to get from one array element
to the neighboring element in the same row. In other words: due to Fortran-contiguous
storage, between the values of `F[1, 1]` and `F[1, 2]` lie the values of `F[2, 1]` and
`F[3, 1]`. The first component of `F.strides` indicates that you need to skip 8 bytes to
get to the next element of the following row. So between the values of `F[1, 1]` and
`F[2, 1]`, there are no further values.

The following code illustrates how the different possible values of `order` affect the
memory layout of an array:

```
order_values = ['C', 'F', 'A', 'K']
for order in order_values:
    R1 = F.copy(order=order)
    R2 = C.copy(order=order)
    print(f"R1: order='{order}': ",
          R1.flags['C_CONTIGUOUS'],
          R1.flags['F_CONTIGUOUS'])
    print(f"R2: order='{order}': ",
          R2.flags['C_CONTIGUOUS'],
          R2.flags['F_CONTIGUOUS'])
```

Here is the output:

```
R1: order='C':  True False
R2: order='C':  True False
R1: order='F':  False True
R2: order='F':  False True
R1: order='A':  False True
R2: order='A':  True False
R1: order='K':  False True
R2: order='K':  True False
```

5.10 Exercises

Exercise 1

(Solution: 33.1, Solution 1)

Create an arbitrary one-dimensional array with the name "v".

Exercise 2

(Solution: 33.1, Solution 2)

Now create an array consisting of the odd indices of the previously created array "v".

Exercise 3

(Solution: 33.1, Solution 3)

Create an array from "v" in reverse order.

Exercise 4

(Solution: 33.1, Solution 4)

What does the output of the following code look like?

```python
a = np.array([1, 2, 3, 4, 5])
b = a[1:4]
b[0] = 200
print(a[1])
```

Exercise 5

(Solution: 33.1, Solution 5)

Create a two-dimensional array with the name "m".

Exercise 6

(Solution: 33.1, Solution 6)

Create an array from m with each row reversed.

Exercise 7

(Solution: 33.1, Solution 7)

Another array in which the rows are reversed.

Exercise 8

(Solution: 33.1, Solution 8)

Create an array from "m" in which both rows and columns are in reverse order.

Exercise 9

(Solution: 33.1, Solution 9)

Remove the first and the last row and column.

6

Data Type Object: dtype

6.1 dtype

In the previous chapters, we dealt with ndarrays. In the two-dimensional case, one can view them as a rectangular arrangement of data of the same type. In the NumPy arrays that we have used in our examples so far, we have only used simple data types such as integers and floating-point numbers (floats). Two-dimensional NumPy arrays correspond to mathematical matrices. We have seen that we can also calculate with them as with matrices. Matrices are a key concept of linear algebra, and they are used in almost all areas of mathematics.

Figure 6.1 Countries and population density

However, if we look at the way data is represented in spreadsheet programs like Excel, it becomes clear that the previous concept is not flexible enough. To be able to model such data in NumPy as well, we are provided with the data type object dtype. This is an instance of the numpy.dtype class.

dtype objects are created from a combination of basic data types such as integers or floats. With the help of dtype we are able to create "structured arrays," also known as "record arrays." Structured arrays give us the possibility of having different data types in different columns. Structured arrays therefore – as already mentioned – are similar to Excel or CSV documents. Using dtype, data like that shown in the following table can be modeled.

Country	Population density	Area	Population
Netherlands	477	37 378	17 942 942
Belgium	383	30 667	11 832 049
United Kingdom	97	505 983	48 610 458
Germany	236	357 569	83 445 000
Liechtenstein	1715	316	563 443
Italy	195	302 079	58 989 749
Switzerland	138	42 925	5 961 249
Luxembourg	255	2 595	672 050
France	107	638 475	68 401 977
Austria	109	83 878	9 158 750
Greece	79	131 694	10 397 193
Ireland	74	69 947	5 343 805
Sweden	16	338 411	5 603 851
Finland	16	338 424	5 424 687
Norway	24	385 207	5 424 687

Before we start with complex data like the above, we want to introduce dtype with a very simple example. We define a Pixel data type that corresponds to a numpy.uint8 data type.

The elements of the list lst are converted into pixel types in order to create the two-dimensional array A. We can see that float values are also automatically converted into pixel data types, i.e., numpy.uint8. The conversion does not occur by rounding, but by truncating the decimal places.

```
import numpy as np

Pixel = np.dtype(np.uint8)
print(Pixel)

lst = [[115, 230.9, 229.2, 234],
       [117, 229, 232.1, 235],
       [116, 140, 141, 142]]

A = np.array(lst, dtype=Pixel)

print(A)
```

The processing yields:

```
uint8
[[115 230 229 234]
 [117 229 232 235]
 [116 140 141 142]]
```

In the previous example, we merely introduced a new name for a basic data type. This can, for example, improve the readability and understandability of a program. This has nothing to do with "structured arrays," which we mentioned at the beginning of this chapter.

6.2 Structured Arrays

ndarrays are homogeneous data objects, i.e., all elements of an array have the same data type. The data type dtype, on the other hand, allows us to declare types column by column.

Now we take the first step towards implementing the table of European countries with the information about area, population, and population density.

We create a structured array with a column density. We define the data type as np.dtype([('density', np.int32)]). We assign this data type to the variable Density. We used a capital letter for the variable so that one can see the difference from density in the type definition itself. We then use the data type Density in the definition of the NumPy array, in which we use the first three values:

```python
import numpy as np

Density = np.dtype([('density', np.int32)])

x = np.array([(393,), (337,), (256,)],
             dtype=Density)

print(x)

print("\nThe internal representation:")
print(repr(x))
```

The resulting output is:

```
[(393,) (337,) (256,)]

The internal representation:
array([(393,), (337,), (256,)], dtype=[('density', '<i4')])
```

We can access the `density` column by entering `density` as a key. It is similar to a
dictionary access in Python:

```python
print(x['density'])
```

The execution leads to this output:

```
[393 337 256]
```

One might wonder that we used `np.int32` in our definition, but that the internal representation shows <i4.

In a `dtype` definition, we can use the type directly, for example `np.int32`, or we can
use a string, such as `i4`.

In our example, we could also have defined our `dtype` as follows:

```python
Density = np.dtype([('density', 'i4')])
x = np.array([(393,), (337,), (256,)],
             dtype=Density)


print(x)
```

This follows from the code:

```
[(393,) (337,) (256,)]
```

The `i` stands for integer, and the 4 means "4 bytes." But what does the less-than sign
before the 4 mean? We could just as well have written '<i4'. We can prefix a type with '<'
or '>'. '<' means that little-endian is used for memory organization, and '>' accordingly
means that big-endian is used. Without a prefix, the natural byte order of the system
is used. We demonstrate this in the following example by defining a double-precision
floating-point number in different byte orders:

```python
# little-endian byte order
dt = np.dtype('<d')
print(dt.name, dt.byteorder, dt.itemsize)

# big-endian byte order
dt = np.dtype('>d')
print(dt.name, dt.byteorder, dt.itemsize)

# native byte order
dt = np.dtype('d')
print(dt.name, dt.byteorder, dt.itemsize)
```

Here is the result of the code:

```
float64 = 8
float64 > 8
float64 = 8
```

The equals sign '=' stands for the native byte order, defined by the operating system. In our case this means little-endian, because we are on a Linux machine.

A possible pitfall with the density array: We defined the array with a list of 1-tuples. One might assume that a list with single-element lists would also work – but that is not the case. Only tuples are allowed to define the records – in our case these consist only of the population density ('density') – and the list is the 'container' for the records. The tuples define the atomic elements of the structure and the lists the dimensions.

Now we will add the country names, the areas, and the populations to our type:

```python
dt = np.dtype([('country', 'S20'),
               ('density', 'i4'),
               ('area', 'i4'),
               ('population', 'i4')])
population_table = np.array([
    ('Netherlands', 477, 37378, 17942942),
    ('Belgium', 383, 30667, 11832049),
    ('United Kingdom', 97, 505983, 48610458),
    ('Germany', 236, 357569, 83445000),
    ('Liechtenstein', 1715, 316, 563443),
    ('Italy', 195, 302079, 58989749),
    ('Switzerland', 138, 42925, 5961249),
    ('Luxembourg', 255, 2595, 672050),
    ('France', 107, 638475, 68401977),
    ('Austria', 109, 83878, 9158750),
    ('Greece', 79, 131694, 10397193),
    ('Ireland', 74, 69947, 5343805),
    ('Sweden', 16, 338411, 5603851),
    ('Finland', 16, 338424, 5424687),
    ('Norway', 24, 385207, 5424687)],
    dtype=dt)


print(population_table[:4])
```

The evaluation yields:

```
[(b'Netherlands', 477,  37378, 17942942)
 (b'Belgium', 383,  30667, 11832049)
 (b'United Kingdom',  97, 505983, 48610458)
 (b'Germany', 236, 357569, 83445000)]
```

We can access each element individually:

```python
print(population_table['density'])
print(population_table['country'])
print(population_table['area'][2:5])
```

This is the result of the code:

```
[ 477  383   97  236 1715  195  138  255  107  109   79   74
    16   16   24]
[b'Netherlands' b'Belgium' b'United Kingdom' b'Germany'
 b'Liechtenstein' b'Italy' b'Switzerland' b'Luxembourg'
 b'France' b'Austria' b'Greece' b'Ireland' b'Sweden' b'Finland'
 b'Norway']
[505983 357569    316]
```

The country names are instances of the NumPy class `numpy.bytes_`. They can be
converted back into Unicode strings with the function `str`. Further below we will also
see how one can work directly with Unicode strings in `dtype` arrays.

```python
s = population_table['country'][0]
print(s, type(s))
s = str(s)
print(s, type(s))
```

The result follows:

```
b'Netherlands' <class 'numpy.bytes_'>
b'Netherlands' <class 'str'>
```

6.3 Input and Output of Structured Arrays

In most applications it is necessary to save the data from a program into a file. We
will now save our previously created array into a file using the command `savetxt`. A
detailed introduction to this topic can be found in Chapter 11 (Reading and Writing
Data Files).

```python
np.savetxt("population_table.csv",
           population_table,
           fmt="%s;%d;%d;%d",
           delimiter=";")
```

Very likely one will later want to read back the data from the file just saved. We can accomplish this with the command `genfromtxt`.

```python
dt = np.dtype([('country', 'U20'),
               ('density', 'i4'),
               ('area', 'i4'),
               ('population', 'i4')])

x = np.genfromtxt("population_table.csv",
                  dtype=dt,
                  delimiter=";")

print(x[:3])   # output of the first three rows
```

The evaluation yields:

```
[("b'Netherlands'", 477,  37378, 17942942)
 ("b'Belgium'", 383,  30667, 11832049)
 ("b'United Kingdom'",  97, 505983, 48610458)]
```

Instead of `genfromtxt`, one can also use `loadtxt`:

```python
dt = np.dtype([('country', 'U25'),
               ('density', 'i4'),
               ('area', 'i4'),
               ('population', 'i4')])

x = np.loadtxt("population_table.csv",
               dtype=dt,
               delimiter=";")

print(x[:3])    # output of the first three rows
```

We obtain this output:

```
[("b'Netherlands'", 477,  37378, 17942942)
 ("b'Belgium'", 383,  30667, 11832049)
 ("b'United Kingdom'",  97, 505983, 48610458)]
```

6.4 Unicode Strings in Arrays

We had already pointed out that the strings in our previous example array had a small b as a prefix. This happened because in our dtype definition we wrote ('country', 'S20') and thereby defined our country names as binary strings.

To obtain Unicode strings, we must change to ('country', np.unicode_, 20). We modify the definition for population_table as follows:

```python
dt = np.dtype([('country', 'U25'),
               ('density', 'i4'),
               ('area', 'i4'),
               ('population', 'i4')])
population_table = np.array([
    ('Netherlands', 477, 37378, 17942942),
    ('Belgium', 383, 30667, 11832049),
    ('United Kingdom', 97, 505983, 48610458),
    ('Germany', 236, 357569, 83445000),
    ('Liechtenstein', 1715, 316, 563443),
    ('Italy', 195, 302079, 58989749),
    ('Switzerland', 138, 42925, 5961249),
    ('Luxembourg', 255, 2595, 672050),
    ('France', 107, 638475, 68401977),
    ('Austria', 109, 83878, 9158750),
    ('Greece', 79, 131694, 10397193),
    ('Ireland', 74, 69947, 5343805),
    ('Sweden', 16, 338411, 5603851),
    ('Finland', 16, 338424, 5424687),
    ('Norway', 24, 385207, 5424687)],
    dtype=dt)


print(population_table[:4])
```

Output:

```
[('Netherlands', 477,  37378, 17942942)
 ('Belgium', 383,  30667, 11832049)
 ('United Kingdom',  97, 505983, 48610458)
 ('Germany', 236, 357569, 83445000)]
```

6.5 Renaming Column Names

Now we want to rename the column names into German designations. You can access
the column names with the `names` property of `dtype`:

```python
print(population_table.dtype.names)
```

The result appears as follows:

```python
('country', 'density', 'area', 'population')
```

Renaming is very straightforward. You simply assign this property a new tuple with
the new names:

```python
population_table.dtype.names = ('Land',
                               'Bevölkerungsdichte',
                               'Fläche',
                               'Bevölkerung')


print(population_table['Land'])
```

The processing yields:

```python
['Netherlands' 'Belgium' 'United Kingdom' 'Germany'
 'Liechtenstein' 'Italy' 'Switzerland' 'Luxembourg' 'France'
 'Austria' 'Greece' 'Ireland' 'Sweden' 'Finland' 'Norway']
```

6.6 Replacing Column Values

Now we also want to translate the country names from English into German. To do
this, we create a list `lands`. We can convert this into an array with `np.array` and then
completely replace the existing column `population_table['Land']`:

```python
lands = ['Niederlande', 'Belgien', 'Vereinigtes Königreich',
         'Deutschland', 'Liechtenstein', 'Italien', 'Schweiz',
         'Luxemburg', 'Frankreich', 'Österreich', 'Griechenland',
         'Irland', 'Schweden', 'Finnland', 'Norwegen']

population_table['Land'] = np.array(lands, dtype='<U25')

print(population_table)
```

Result:

```
[('Niederlande',  477,  37378, 17942942)
 ('Belgien',  383,  30667, 11832049)
 ('Vereinigtes Königreich',   97, 505983, 48610458)
 ('Deutschland',  236, 357569, 83445000)
 ('Liechtenstein', 1715,   316,   563443)
 ('Italien',  195, 302079, 58989749)
 ('Schweiz',  138,  42925,  5961249)
 ('Luxemburg',  255,   2595,   672050)
 ('Frankreich',  107, 638475, 68401977)
 ('Österreich',  109,  83878,  9158750)
 ('Griechenland',   79, 131694, 10397193)
 ('Irland',   74,  69947,  5343805)
 ('Schweden',   16, 338411,  5603851)
 ('Finnland',   16, 338424,  5424687)
 ('Norwegen',   24, 385207,  5424687)]
```

6.7 More Complex Example

In the previous examples we created our arrays directly. Normally, however, we must obtain the data for our structured arrays from databases or files. We will now use a list that was created using the `pickle` module. When we read the pickled file `cities_and_times.pkl`, we obtain a list of tuples, each containing a city name, followed by a day, and a two-tuple with a time.

The first task is therefore to "unpickle" this file:

```python
import pickle
with open("cities_and_times.pkl", "rb") as fh:
    cities_and_times = pickle.load(fh)
    for i in range(5):
        print(cities_and_times[i])
```

Script output:

```
('Amsterdam', 'Sun', (8, 52))
('Anchorage', 'Sat', (23, 52))
('Ankara', 'Sun', (10, 52))
('Athens', 'Sun', (9, 52))
('Atlanta', 'Sun', (2, 52))
```

Now we convert our data into a structured array:

```python
time_type = np.dtype([('city', 'U30'),
                      ('day', 'U3'),
                      ('time', [('h', int), ('min', int)])])

times = np.array(cities_and_times, dtype=time_type)
print(times[:4])
```

The corresponding output can be seen here:

```
[('Amsterdam', 'Sun', ( 8, 52)) ('Anchorage', 'Sat', (23, 52))
 ('Ankara', 'Sun', (10, 52)) ('Athens', 'Sun', ( 9, 52))]
```

```python
lst = []
for row in times:
    t = row[2]
    t = f"{t[0]:02d}:{t[1]:02d}"
    lst.append((row[0], row[1], t))

time_type = np.dtype([('city', 'U30'),
                      ('day', 'U3'),
                      ('time', 'U5')])
times2 = np.array(lst, dtype=time_type)

print(times2[:10])
```

Here is the output:

```
[('Amsterdam', 'Sun', '08:52') ('Anchorage', 'Sat', '23:52')
 ('Ankara', 'Sun', '10:52') ('Athens', 'Sun', '09:52')
 ('Atlanta', 'Sun', '02:52') ('Auckland', 'Sun', '20:52')
 ('Barcelona', 'Sun', '08:52') ('Beirut', 'Sun', '09:52')
 ('Berlin', 'Sun', '08:52') ('Boston', 'Sun', '02:52')]
```

Now we save the data into a CSV file. To ensure correct processing of non-ASCII characters, we must set the encoding to utf-8:

```python
with open('cities_and_times.csv', 'w', encoding='utf-8') as fh:
    np.savetxt(fh, times2, fmt='%s')
```

6.8 Exercises

Before we continue, we want to deepen what we have learned with practice exercises.

Exercise 1

(Solution: 33.2, Solution 1)

Define a structured array with two columns. The first column should contain the ID of a product, which can be represented as int32. The second column should contain the price of this product.

How can you output the column with the product IDs?

How can you output the first row?

How can you access the third item, i.e., the item in the 3rd row?

Exercise 2

(Solution: 33.2, Solution 2)

Create an array of the same length as the one just created. The contents of this array are integers that correspond to the number of units sold for the respective product IDs. Compute the sales revenues per item and the total sum.

Exercise 3

(Solution: 33.2, Solution 3)

Define a structured array for time entries with hours, minutes, and seconds. The indices should be "h," "min," and "sec."

Exercise 4

(Solution: 33.2, Solution 4)

Add a temperature value to each of the time entries from the previous exercise.

Exercise 5

(Solution: 33.2, Solution 5)

Create a CSV file in which each row contains a time and a temperature value, e.g.
```
14:56:19 23.8 16:08:04 32.8
```

7 Combining and Reshaping Arrays

Anyone who works with `arrays` sooner or later encounters situations in which the shape – i.e., the `shape` – of an array or its dimensions need to be changed. The functionalities required for this are introduced in this chapter.

We will show how to combine arrays (concatenate) and how existing arrays can be extended by additional dimensions. We also demonstrate how multiple arrays can be "stacked" horizontally or vertically (`stack`). Finally, we will see how new arrays can be created by repeating existing arrays (`tile`).

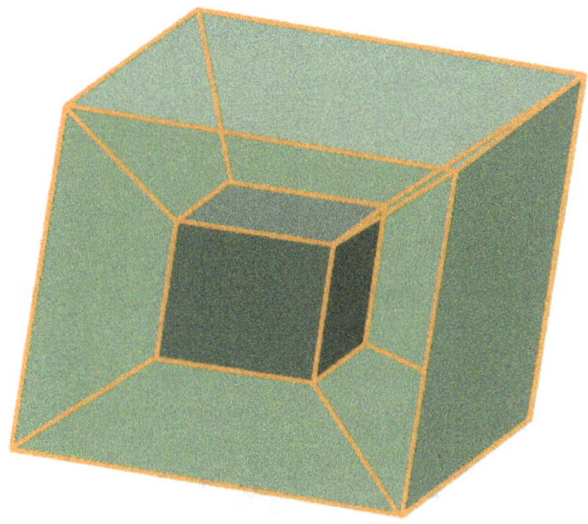

Figure 7.1 Tesseract

In Figure 7.1, an illustration of four-dimensional space is shown. Depicted is a **tesseract**, also known as a four-dimensional *hypercube*. A tesseract can be understood as an extension of the concept of a three-dimensional cube into four-dimensional space – just as a cube relates to a square, a tesseract relates to a cube.

7.1 Reduction and Reshaping of Arrays

There are several methods to reduce a multidimensional array:

- `flatten`
- `ravel`
- `reshape`

7.1.1 flatten

flatten is an ndarray method with an optional parameter order, which can take the values C, F, and A. The default value of order is C. C means that flattening is done in C-style row-major order, i.e., the rightmost index "changes fastest." In other words: in row-major order, the row index changes the slowest, while the column index changes the fastest, so that a[0, 1] follows a[0, 0]. F stands for "Fortran column-major order." A stands for preserving the "C/Fortran order."

```python
import numpy as np

A = np.array([[[ 0,  1,  2,  3],
               [ 4,  5,  6,  7],
               [ 8,  9, 10, 11]],

              [[12, 13, 14, 15],
               [16, 17, 18, 19],
               [20, 21, 22, 23]]])

Flattened_X = A.flatten()
print(Flattened_X)

print(A.flatten(order="C"))
print(A.flatten(order="F"))
print(A.flatten(order="A"))
```

The result follows:

```
[ 0  1  2  3  4  5  6  7  8  9 10 11 12 13 14 15 16 17 18 19 20
 21 22 23]
[ 0  1  2  3  4  5  6  7  8  9 10 11 12 13 14 15 16 17 18 19 20
 21 22 23]
[ 0 12  4 16  8 20  1 13  5 17  9 21  2 14  6 18 10 22  3 15  7
 19 11 23]
[ 0  1  2  3  4  5  6  7  8  9 10 11 12 13 14 15 16 17 18 19 20
 21 22 23]
```

7.1.2 ravel

The order of elements returned by ravel() is by default in "C-style."

```
ravel(X, order='C')
```

ravel creates a linearized, i.e., one-dimensional, array. A copy is only created if necessary. The optional parameter order can take the values C, F, A, or K.

C: C-style order, where the last axis index changes fastest, back to the first axis index, which changes the slowest. C is the default.

F: Fortran-style index order, where the first index changes fastest and the last index slowest.

A: Fortran-style index order if the array 'a' is stored in Fortran order in memory; otherwise C-style order is used.

K: Elements are read as they are stored in memory, except for reversals in case of negative strides.

```python
print(A.ravel())
print(A.ravel(order="A"))
print(A.ravel(order="F"))
print(A.ravel(order="K"))
```

Executing the code yields:

```
[ 0  1  2  3  4  5  6  7  8  9 10 11 12 13 14 15 16 17 18 19 20
 21 22 23]
[ 0  1  2  3  4  5  6  7  8  9 10 11 12 13 14 15 16 17 18 19 20
 21 22 23]
[ 0 12  4 16  8 20  1 13  5 17  9 21  2 14  6 18 10 22  3 15  7
 19 11 23]
[ 0  1  2  3  4  5  6  7  8  9 10 11 12 13 14 15 16 17 18 19 20
 21 22 23]
```

7.1.3 Differences between `ravel` and `flatten`

- `ravel` generally does not return a copy, but a view adapted to the dimension of the original array.
- `flatten` always returns a copy.
- `ravel` is faster than `flatten`, because it does not need to create a copy.

We show this in examples:

```python
import numpy as np

A = np.array([[1, 2, 3],
              [4, 5, 6]])

B = A.flatten()
B[4] = 42

print("B: \n", B)
print("A: \n", A)
```

```python
print(np.may_share_memory(A, B))

print("\n... and now the same with ravel:")
B = A.ravel()
B[4] = 42

print("B: \n", B)
print("A: \n", A)
print(np.may_share_memory(A, B))
```

What we obtain is:

```
B:
 [ 1  2  3  4 42  6]
A:
 [[1 2 3]
 [4 5 6]]
False


... and now the same with ravel:
B:
 [ 1  2  3  4 42  6]
A:
 [[ 1  2  3]
 [ 4 42  6]]
True
```

7.1.4 reshape

The reshape method converts an array into a new shape without changing the data it contains. This means that the data in memory does not have to be copied, as long as this is possible. The method call is of the form:

```python
reshape(a, newshape, order='C')
```

Here, a refers to the array (or an array-like structure) to be reshaped. The parameter newshape specifies the new shape, either as an integer value (for one-dimensional arrays) or as a tuple of dimensions, e.g., (3, 4, 2). It is important that the product of the dimensions in newshape matches the number of elements in the original array. The optional parameter order controls the traversal order of the array during reshaping, as with flatten and ravel.

With reshape we can also linearize an array:

```python
A = np.array([[1, 2, 3],
              [4, 5, 6]])
```

```
B = A.reshape((6,))
print(B)
```

Output:

```
[1 2 3 4 5 6]
```

Thus, reshape can take over the tasks of ravel and flatten. But reshape can do more. We can use it to transform an array A into any desired shape x, as long as the product of A's shape components equals the product of the shape components of x, i.e.,

`np.prod(A.shape) == np.prod(x)`

```
X = np.arange(24)
Y1 = X.reshape((3, 4, 2))
print(Y1)
new_shape = (2, 3, 4)
Y2 = Y1.reshape(new_shape)
print(Y2)
```

The resulting output is:

```
[[[ 0  1]
  [ 2  3]
  [ 4  5]
  [ 6  7]]

 [[ 8  9]
  [10 11]
  [12 13]
  [14 15]]

 [[16 17]
  [18 19]
  [20 21]
  [22 23]]]
[[[ 0  1  2  3]
  [ 4  5  6  7]
  [ 8  9 10 11]]

 [[12 13 14 15]
  [16 17 18 19]
  [20 21 22 23]]]
```

The comparison

```
print(np.prod(Y1.shape) == np.prod(new_shape))
```

yields True

7.2 Adding Dimensions

Additional dimensions can be added to an array in two main ways: by using `reshape` or by inserting axes using slicing with `np.newaxis`.

The `reshape` method allows you to change the overall shape of an array – including increasing its dimensionality – as long as the total number of elements remains the same.

Alternatively, `np.newaxis` can be used to explicitly insert new axes of length one at specific positions. This technique is especially readable when you only want to add additional dimensions without changing the order of the elements.

In the following example we show the use of `np.newaxis`:

```python
x = np.array([2, 5, 18, 14, 4])
y = x[:, np.newaxis]
print(y)
```

We obtain: [[2] [5] [18] [14] [4]]

The same result can also be achieved with `reshape`:

```python
x = np.array([2, 5, 18, 14, 4])
y = x.reshape((x.shape[0], 1))
print(y)
```

We obtain: [[2] [5] [18] [14] [4]]

7.3 Concatenation and Stacking of Arrays

In the following subsections we will look at various NumPy functions for combining and stacking arrays. Depending on the desired behavior – for example, whether stacking is done along an existing or a new axis – different functions are used:

- `concatenate`: Joins arrays along an existing axis.
- `stack`: Joins arrays along a new axis.
- `vstack`: Vertical stacking (row-wise, along the first axis).
- `hstack`: Horizontal stacking (column-wise, along the second axis).
- `column_stack`: Stacks 1D arrays as columns into a 2D array.
- `dstack`: Stacks along the third axis (depth).
- `dsplit`: Splits an array along the third axis.

7.3.1 concatenate

The function concatenate

```
concatenate((a1, a2, ...), axis=0,
            out=None, dtype=None,
            casting="same_kind")
```

joins a sequence of arrays a1, a2, ... along an existing axis. The default axis is 0.

In the following example we concatenate three one-dimensional arrays into one. The elements of the second array are appended horizontally to the first array. Then the elements of the third array are also appended horizontally:

```python
import numpy as np
x = np.array([11, 22])
y = np.array([18, 7, 6])
z = np.array([1, 3, 5])
c = np.concatenate((x, y, z))
print(c)
```

The evaluation yields:

```
[11 22 18  7  6  1  3  5]
```

When we merge multidimensional arrays, we must pay attention to the axes. The arrays must have the same shape except in the dimension along which we want to concatenate them. The default is axis = 0:

```python
import numpy as np
x = np.arange(8)
x = x.reshape((2, 4))
y = np.arange(100, 112)
y = y.reshape((3, 4))
z = np.concatenate((x, y))
print(f'x:\n{x}\n\ny:\n{y}\n\nz:\n{z}')
```

The script returns:

```
x:
[[0 1 2 3]
 [4 5 6 7]]

y:
[[100 101 102 103]
 [104 105 106 107]
 [108 109 110 111]]
```

```
z:
[[  0   1   2   3]
 [  4   5   6   7]
 [100 101 102 103]
 [104 105 106 107]
 [108 109 110 111]]
```

If we want to concatenate along `axis = 1`, then `x.shape[0] == y.shape[0]` must hold. The value at index 1 can then be different. In the following example we construct x and y accordingly:

```python
import numpy as np
x = np.arange(8).reshape((4, 2))
y = np.arange(100, 112).reshape((4, 3))
z = np.concatenate((x, y), axis=1)
print(f'{x=}\n{y=}\n{z=}')
```

Here is the result of the code:

```
x=array([[0, 1],
       [2, 3],
       [4, 5],
       [6, 7]])
y=array([[100, 101, 102],
       [103, 104, 105],
       [106, 107, 108],
       [109, 110, 111]])
z=array([[  0,   1, 100, 101, 102],
       [  2,   3, 103, 104, 105],
       [  4,   5, 106, 107, 108],
       [  6,   7, 109, 110, 111]])
```

In the following, we demonstrate the functionality of `concatenate` in three-dimensional space. We concatenate two arrays along the first axis. We create two 3-dimensional arrays x and y whose shapes differ only at index 1:

```python
import numpy as np
x = np.arange(24).reshape((2, 3, 4))
y = np.arange(100, 116).reshape((2, 2, 4))
z = np.concatenate((x, y), axis=1)
print(f'{x=}\n\n{y=}\n\n{z=}')
```

The following result is generated:

```
x=array([[[  0,   1,   2,   3],
        [  4,   5,   6,   7],
        [  8,   9,  10,  11]],
```

```
       [[12, 13, 14, 15],
        [16, 17, 18, 19],
        [20, 21, 22, 23]]])

 y=array([[[100, 101, 102, 103],
        [104, 105, 106, 107]],

       [[108, 109, 110, 111],
        [112, 113, 114, 115]]])

 z=array([[[  0,   1,   2,   3],
        [  4,   5,   6,   7],
        [  8,   9,  10,  11],
        [100, 101, 102, 103],
        [104, 105, 106, 107]],

       [[ 12,  13,  14,  15],
        [ 16,  17,  18,  19],
        [ 20,  21,  22,  23],
        [108, 109, 110, 111],
        [112, 113, 114, 115]]])
```

7.3.2 stack

The stack function stack(arrays, axis=0, out=None) joins arrays along a new axis. This is the essential difference from the concatenate function.

We demonstrate how it works in the following example. First we create four arrays of shape (2, 3) using a list comprehension:

```
[np.random.randn(2, 3) for _ in range(4)]
```

Since our arrays to be joined arrays are two-dimensional, we can insert the new axis in three positions: before, in the middle, and at the end. We see this in the shape values: (4, 2, 3), (2, 4, 3), and (2, 3, 4).

```python
import numpy as np
arrays = [np.random.randn(2, 3) for _ in range(4)]
for axis in range(3):
    res = np.stack(arrays, axis=axis)
    print(f'{axis=}\n{res.shape=}\nres:\n{res}\n')
```

The execution leads to this output:

```
axis=0
res.shape=(4, 2, 3)
```

```
res:
[[[ 0.095  0.686 -1.384]
  [-1.907 -0.391  0.148]]

 [[ 0.672 -0.246  0.436]
  [-0.536  0.729  0.435]]

 [[-0.348 -0.958 -0.227]
  [-1.827  0.467  1.025]]

 [[-0.727  0.484  0.269]
  [ 1.502 -0.817  1.073]]]

axis=1
res.shape=(2, 4, 3)
res:
[[[ 0.095  0.686 -1.384]
  [ 0.672 -0.246  0.436]
  [-0.348 -0.958 -0.227]
  [-0.727  0.484  0.269]]

 [[-1.907 -0.391  0.148]
  [-0.536  0.729  0.435]
  [-1.827  0.467  1.025]
  [ 1.502 -0.817  1.073]]]

axis=2
res.shape=(2, 3, 4)
res:
[[[ 0.095  0.672 -0.348 -0.727]
  [ 0.686 -0.246 -0.958  0.484]
  [-1.384  0.436 -0.227  0.269]]

 [[-1.907 -0.536 -1.827  1.502]
  [-0.391  0.729  0.467 -0.817]
  [ 0.148  0.435  1.025  1.073]]]
```

An interesting application of this function will appear in Chapter 31 (Image Processing
Techniques). There we use the function to create a three-dimensional pseudo-color
image from a two-dimensional grayscale image:

```python
import numpy as np
grey_image = np.array([[0,    1,    2, 11],
                       [4,    5,    6,  7],
                       [1,  157,  149,  8],
```

```
                    [3, 145, 148, 12],
                    [8,   9,  10, 13]])
```

```
# (grey_image,)*3 is equivalent to (grey_image, grey_image, grey_image)
colour_image = np.stack((grey_image,) * 3, axis=2)
print(colour_image.shape)
print(colour_image)
```

Output:

```
(5, 4, 3)
[[[  0   0    0]
  [  1   1    1]
  [  2   2    2]
  [ 11  11   11]]

 [[  4   4    4]
  [  5   5    5]
  [  6   6    6]
  [  7   7    7]]

 [[  1   1    1]
  [157 157  157]
  [149 149  149]
  [  8   8    8]]

 [[  3   3    3]
  [145 145  145]
  [148 148  148]
  [ 12  12   12]]

 [[  8   8    8]
  [  9   9    9]
  [ 10  10   10]
  [ 13  13   13]]]]
```

The color values of a pixel are, of course, all the same and correspond to the original
grayscale value at that position:

```
row, column = 2, 1
print(f'{colour_image[row, column]}\n{grey_image[row, column]}')
```

The evaluation yields:

```
[157 157 157]
157
```

7.3.3 dstack

dstack(tup) Stacks arrays depth-wise, i.e., along the third axis.

This function is most meaningful for arrays with up to three dimensions. For example, for pixel data with height (first axis), width (second axis), and RGB channels (third axis).

The parameter tup contains the sequence of arrays to be stacked. The shapes of these arrays must be the same except for the third axis if they are three-dimensional. The arrays must match in shape along all axes except the third. For one- and two-dimensional arrays, the shapes must be identical.

```python
a = np.array((1, 2, 3))
print(a.shape)
b = np.array((11, 12, 13))
res1 = np.dstack((a, b))
print(f'{res1.shape=}')
# equivalent with
res2 = np.stack((a, b), axis=1)
print(f'{res2.shape=}')
# add a dimension at axis 0:
res2 = np.expand_dims(res2, axis=0)
print(f'with new dimension: {res2.shape=}')
print(f'res1:\n{res1}\n\nres2:\n{res2}')
```

The result is:

```
(3,)
res1.shape=(1, 3, 2)
res2.shape=(3, 2)
with new dimension: res2.shape=(1, 3, 2)
res1:
[[[ 1 11]
  [ 2 12]
  [ 3 13]]]

res2:
[[[ 1 11]
  [ 2 12]
  [ 3 13]]]
```

We see that two one-dimensional arrays with dstack are combined into a three-dimensional array of shape (1, 3, 2). We also see that we can reach the same result using stack:

```python
res2 = np.stack((a, b), axis=1)
```

```python
# add a dimension at axis 0:
res2 = np.expand_dims(res2, axis=0)
```

Now let's look at an example with two two-dimensional arrays.

```python
a = np.array([[1],
              [2],
              [3]])
b = np.array([[11],
              [12],
              [13]])
print(f'np.dstack((a, b)):\n{np.dstack((a, b))}')
# equivalent with
print(f'np.stack((a, b), axis=2):\n{np.stack((a, b), axis=2)}')
```

The processing yields:

```
np.dstack((a, b)):
[[[ 1 11]]

  [[ 2 12]]

  [[ 3 13]]]
np.stack((a, b), axis=2):
[[[ 1 11]]

  [[ 2 12]]

  [[ 3 13]]]
```

We see that in this case we can more easily – i.e., without adding a new dimension – simulate the functionality with stack.

Further Example:

In the following example of dstack, we show how three-dimensional arrays can be stacked. The result is, in this case, also a three-dimensional array. Using np.arange, we create five arrays of shape (4, 3, 2). These five arrays are stored in a list list_of_arrays:

```python
list_of_arrays = []
for i in range(5):
    a = np.arange(i*100, i*100 + 24).reshape(4, 3, 2)
    list_of_arrays.append(a)

# output of the 1st array in list_of_arrays:
print(f"1st array:\n{list_of_arrays[0]}")
```

The following result is generated:

```
1st array:
[[[ 0  1]
  [ 2  3]
  [ 4  5]]

 [[ 6  7]
  [ 8  9]
  [10 11]]

 [[12 13]
  [14 15]
  [16 17]]

 [[18 19]
  [20 21]
  [22 23]]]
```

We can imagine this array in three-dimensional space as follows:

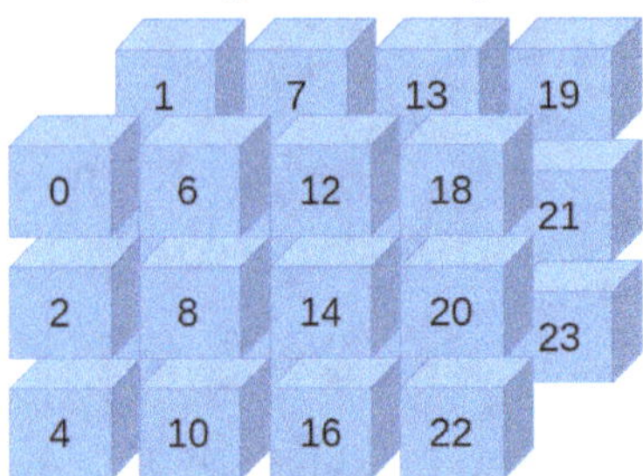

The 2nd array looks like this:

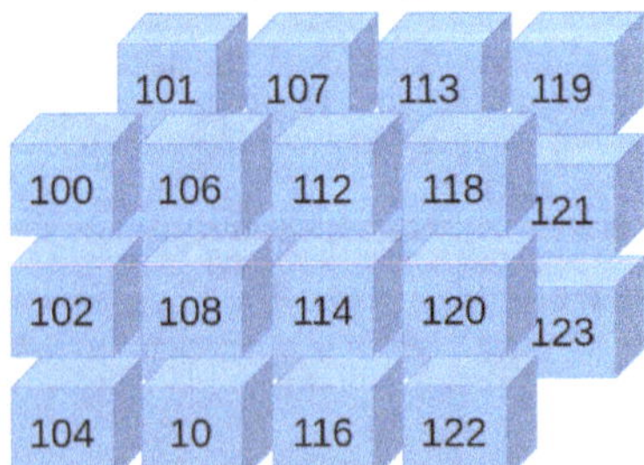

Now we want to stack the 5 arrays of our list `list_of_arrays` using `dstack` along the third axis:

```python
stacked = np.dstack(list_of_arrays)
print(f"Shape: {stacked.shape}")
```

The script returns:

```
Shape: (4, 3, 10)
```

The newly created array can be imagined as in the following graphic. The five original arrays from which the new stacked array is composed have been colored in different shades of blue. The first array of the original list corresponds to the lightest shade of blue.

The 1st array of our list `list_of_arrays[0]` corresponds to `stacked[:, :, :2]`.

The following holds:

```python
for i in range(5):
    print(f"{i+1}th array of the list: ", end="")
    print(np.array_equal(stacked[:, :, 2*i:2*i+2],
                         list_of_arrays[i]))
```

Check for equality:

```
1th array of the list: True
2th array of the list: True
3th array of the list: True
4th array of the list: True
5th array of the list: True
```

7.3.4 vstack

vstack stacks arrays vertically, i.e., row-wise. `row_stack` is an alias of `vstack`. It is also equivalent to `concatenate` when concatenating along the first axis. Let's look at an example with one-dimensional arrays:

```python
import numpy as np
a = np.array([1, 2, 3])
b = np.array([4, 5, 6])
print(np.vstack((a, b)))
```

The output we get is:

```
[[1 2 3]
 [4 5 6]]
```

This is equivalent to a `np.stack` call:

```python
print(np.stack((a, b)))
```

The evaluation yields:

```
[[1 2 3]
 [4 5 6]]
```

Next is an example with two-dimensional arrays:

```python
import numpy as np
a2 = np.array([[1, 2], [3, 4], [5, 6]])
b2 = np.array([[11, 12], [13, 14], [15, 16]])
print(np.vstack((a2, b2)))
```

We obtain this output:

```
[[ 1  2]
 [ 3  4]
 [ 5  6]
 [11 12]
 [13 14]
 [15 16]]
```

7.3.5 hstack

`hstack` stacks arrays horizontally, i.e., column-wise. It is equivalent to `concatenate` when concatenating along the second axis, except in the one-dimensional case, where concatenation happens along the first axis.[1]

```python
import numpy as np
a = np.array([1, 2, 3])
b = np.array([4, 5, 6])
print(np.hstack((a, b)))
```

---

[1] If `row_stack` and `column_stack` appear in code, note that these functions have been **deprecated** since NumPy 1.24 and should no longer be used. Instead, `vstack` should be used as a replacement for `row_stack` and `hstack` as a replacement for `column_stack` to ensure future compatibility.

Output:

```
[1 2 3 4 5 6]
```

This is equivalent to a `np.concatenate` call:

```python
print(np.concatenate((a, b)))
```

Output:

```
[1 2 3 4 5 6]
```

Now let's look at the two-dimensional case:

```python
a2 = np.array([[1, 2], [3, 4], [5, 6]])
b2 = np.array([[11, 12], [13, 14], [15, 16]])
print(np.hstack((a2, b2)))
```

This output is obtained:

```
[[ 1  2 11 12]
 [ 3  4 13 14]
 [ 5  6 15 16]]
```

This is equivalent to a `np.concatenate` call:

```python
print(np.concatenate((a2, b2), axis=1))
```

Output:

```
[[ 1  2 11 12]
 [ 3  4 13 14]
 [ 5  6 15 16]]
```

It is also equivalent to a call to `column_stack`:

```python
print(np.column_stack((a2, b2)))
```

What we obtain is:

```
[[ 1  2 11 12]
 [ 3  4 13 14]
 [ 5  6 15 16]]
```

Finally, let's look at an example that leads us into the next chapter:

```python
A = np.array([[1, 2],
              [3, 4]])
```

```python
X = np.hstack((A, A, A))
result = np.vstack((X, X, X))

print(result)
```

This follows from the code:

```
[[1 2 1 2 1 2]
 [3 4 3 4 3 4]
 [1 2 1 2 1 2]
 [3 4 3 4 3 4]
 [1 2 1 2 1 2]
 [3 4 3 4 3 4]]
```

Looking at the previous example, we see that we have created a new array by repeating
the array A horizontally and vertically. If one thinks of A as a tile, we have created the
following pattern:

```
array([[1, 2, 1, 2, 1, 2],
       [3, 4, 3, 4, 3, 4],
       [1, 2, 1, 2, 1, 2],
       [3, 4, 3, 4, 3, 4],
       [1, 2, 1, 2, 1, 2],
       [3, 4, 3, 4, 3, 4]])
```

Tile is also the name of a function that we will discuss in the following subsection.
In essence, `tile` allows us to achieve the same result that we previously constructed
more laboriously using `column_stack` and `row_stack`.

7.4 dsplit

The function `dsplit` splits a three-dimensional array along the third axis (i.e., along
depth). `dsplit` only works with arrays that have at least three dimensions. For 2D
arrays or 1D arrays, the functions `hsplit` and `vsplit` are available instead.

`np.dsplit(array, indices_or_sections)`

The parameters are:

- `array`: An array of shape (`m`, `n`, `p`) – i.e., a three-dimensional array.

- `indices_or_sections`: Either an integer specifying into how many equal parts
  the array should be split along the third axis, or a list of indices at which to cut.

`dsplit` is thus the counterpart of the function `dstack`, which joins arrays along the
third axis.

```python
import numpy as np

A = np.arange(24).reshape((2, 3, 4))
print("A:\n", A)

# Split A along the third axis into 2 parts
B = np.dsplit(A, 2)
for i, b in enumerate(B):
    print(f"Part {i+1}:\n", b)
```

We obtain this output:

```
A:
 [[[ 0  1  2  3]
  [ 4  5  6  7]
  [ 8  9 10 11]]

 [[12 13 14 15]
  [16 17 18 19]
  [20 21 22 23]]]
Part 1:
 [[[ 0  1]
  [ 4  5]
  [ 8  9]]

 [[12 13]
  [16 17]
  [20 21]]]
Part 2:
 [[[ 2  3]
  [ 6  7]
  [10 11]]

 [[14 15]
  [18 19]
  [22 23]]]
```

7.5 Repeating Arrays with tile

Similar to how tiles are regularly placed next to each other in a bathroom, with the function `np.tile()` the contents of an array can be repeated in a regular structure. In this way a new matrix can be created consisting of multiple copies of an existing array – either along specific axes or across multiple dimensions. This is useful when you want to transfer a small pattern to a larger area.

Example: We want to transform the one-dimensional array `array([ 3.4 ])` into the array `array([ 3.4, 3.4, 3.4, 3.4, 3.4 ])`.

Another example: We want to use a two-dimensional array like `np.array([ [1, 2], [3, 4] ])` as a building block to create an array of shape (6, 8):

The construction idea is shown in the following diagram:

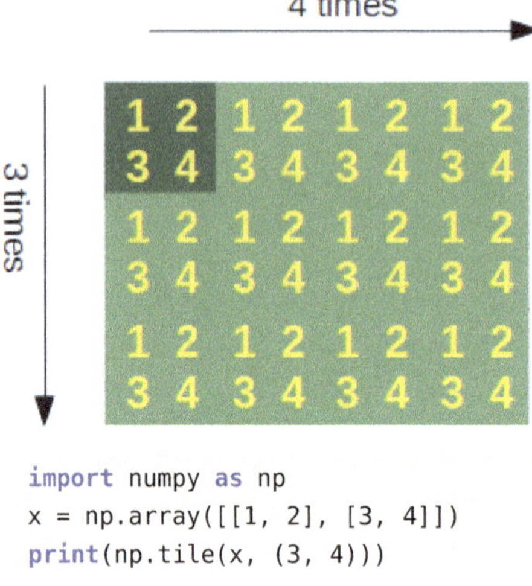


```python
import numpy as np
x = np.array([[1, 2], [3, 4]])
print(np.tile(x, (3, 4)))
```

The code produces the following result:

```
[[1 2 1 2 1 2 1 2]
 [3 4 3 4 3 4 3 4]
 [1 2 1 2 1 2 1 2]
 [3 4 3 4 3 4 3 4]
 [1 2 1 2 1 2 1 2]
 [3 4 3 4 3 4 3 4]]
```

```python
import numpy as np

x = np.array([3.4])

y = np.tile(x, (5,))

print(y)
```

The following result is generated:

```
[3.4 3.4 3.4 3.4 3.4]
```

In the previous `tile` example we could just as well have written `y = np.tile(x, 5)`.

If we write reps as a tuple or list, or consider reps = 5 as a substitute for reps = (5,), then the following is true:

If reps has length n, then the dimension of the resulting array will be at most n and A.ndim.

If A.ndim < n, then A is promoted to n dimensions by prepending new axes. For example, an array of shape (5,) is promoted to (1, 5) for 2D replication or to shape (1, 1, 5) for 3D replication. If this is not the desired behavior, then A should be adjusted to the desired shape before calling the tile function.

If A.ndim > n, then reps is adjusted to A.ndim by prepending 1's. For example, an array A of shape (2, 3, 4, 5) with reps = (2, 2) is treated as (1, 1, 2, 2).

Further examples:

```python
import numpy as np
x = np.array([[1, 2], [3, 4]])
print(np.tile(x, 2))
```

Executing the code yields:

```
[[1 2 1 2]
 [3 4 3 4]]
```

```python
import numpy as np
x = np.array([[1, 2], [3, 4]])
print(np.tile(x, (2, 1)))
```

The result appears as follows:

```
[[1 2]
 [3 4]
 [1 2]
 [3 4]]
```

```python
import numpy as np
x = np.array([[1, 2], [3, 4]])
print(np.tile(x, (2, 2)))
```

This follows from the code:

```
[[1 2 1 2]
 [3 4 3 4]
 [1 2 1 2]
 [3 4 3 4]]
```

7.6 Exercises

Exercise 1

(Solution: 33.3, Solution 1)

In subsection dstack we introduced an example with a list of five 3-dimensional arrays. There the arrays were stacked along the third axis using dstack.

Now use an appropriate NumPy function to **stack** the five arrays along the axis axis=0 into a single array, so that the first dimension expands accordingly.

Exercise 2

(Solution: 33.3, Solution 2)

We are given a one-dimensional NumPy array symbolically representing three colors:

```python
import numpy as np

colours = np.array([1, 2, 3])  # Red, Green, Blue
```

This array should now be used to create a simple color mosaic.

1. Use np.tile to create a new row in which the color pattern [1, 2, 3] repeats a total of four times.

2. Create a two-dimensional array (color mosaic) consisting of five identical rows, each with the pattern above.

3. Create a mosaic in which each row is cyclically shifted by one element to the left compared to the previous row (Hint: np.roll shifts the elements of an array cyclically by a specified number of positions, e.g., np.roll(array, -1) for a left shift by 1 position).

8

Numerical Operations on NumPy Arrays

So far, we have mainly dealt with the creation of NumPy data structures. But what would arrays be without operators? We want to add them, multiply them, or combine them with scalars – just as easily as with numbers or strings. With two arrays, the question also arises: how do we form the matrix product? Of course, only under the condition that the shapes of the two arrays are compatible.

Figure 8.1 Operators fractal representation

In NumPy, mathematical operators can be applied directly to arrays. The matrix product of two arrays is also possible, provided their shapes are compatible. Operations with scalars are carried out component-wise.

8.1 Operations with Scalars

Let's start with a simple everyday example: a table of foods and their energy content in calories – i.e., their quantitative nutritional value.

Table 8.1 Caloric content of selected foods per 100 g

Food	kcal per 100 g
Watermelon	30
Apple	52
Banana	88
Carrot	36
Potato	86
Avocado	160
Beef fillet	115

In the following example, we have placed the calorie values from the table above into an array called `calorie_table`. Strictly speaking, the unit calorie (cal) is an outdated measure of energy. Therefore, we want to convert the values into joules – more precisely, kilojoules. One calorie corresponds to about 4.1868 joules.

```python
import numpy as np
calorie_table = np.array([30, 52, 88, 36, 86, 160, 115])
joule_table = calorie_table * 4.1868
print(joule_table)
```

The result of the code is:

```
[125.604 217.714 368.438 150.725 360.065 669.888 481.482]
```

We see that all values of the array `calorie_table` have been multiplied by the factor `4.1868`. Since the calorie values are approximate, it makes no sense to keep the decimal places, as they would suggest a misleading precision. So instead of the calculation above, we could also proceed as follows:

```python
joule_table = np.round((calorie_table * 4.1868), 0)
print(joule_table)
```

The processing yields:

```
[126. 218. 368. 151. 360. 670. 481.]
```

It also makes sense to define this array as an integer array:

```python
joule_table = joule_table.astype(np.int16)
print(joule_table)
```

The result appears as follows:

```
[126 218 368 151 360 670 481]
```

We have just successfully multiplied an array (or mathematically speaking, a vector) component-wise with a scalar. Addition, subtraction, and division can be performed just as easily:

```python
consumption_in_grams = np.array([240, 95, 135, 120, 200, 160, 290])


consumption_in_kg = consumption_in_grams / 1000
print(consumption_in_kg)

# Diet: eat 10% less
reduced_consumption_in_kg = np.round(consumption_in_kg * 0.9, 2)
print(reduced_consumption_in_kg)
```

The result follows:

```
[0.24  0.095 0.135 0.12  0.2   0.16  0.29 ]
[0.22 0.09 0.12 0.11 0.18 0.14 0.26]
```

8.2 Operations between and on Arrays

In addition to combining with scalars, arrays can also be combined with each other. In this case, the elements of both arrays are linked component-wise, e.g., through addition or multiplication. NumPy also offers functions for aggregating array values, such as calculating the sum or the mean of all elements.

```python
import numpy as np
calorie_table = np.array([30, 52, 88, 36, 86, 160, 115])
consumption_in_grams = np.array([240, 95, 135, 120, 200, 160, 290])
calories_consumed = calorie_table * consumption_in_grams / 100
print(calories_consumed)
```

The result of the code is:

```
[ 72.   49.4 118.8  43.2 172.  256.  333.5]
```

If we want to calculate how many calories our health-conscious person has consumed in total, we can use the function sum. The average calorie intake can be determined with mean:

```python
print(f"Sum: {calories_consumed.sum()}")
print(f"Mean: {calories_consumed.mean()}")
```

We obtain this output:

```
Sum: 1044.9
Mean: 149.27142857142857
```

In the next example, we use two two-dimensional arrays to demonstrate component-wise addition and multiplication:

```python
import numpy as np

A = np.array([[11, 12, 13], [21, 22, 23], [31, 32, 33]])
B = np.array([[5, 4, 2], [1, 0, 2], [3, 8, 2]])

print("Addition of two arrays: ")
print(A + B)

print("\nMultiplication of two arrays: ")
print(A * B)
```

After execution we get:

```
Addition of two arrays:
[[16 16 15]
 [22 22 25]
 [34 40 35]]

Multiplication of two arrays:
[[ 55  48  26]
 [ 21   0  46]
 [ 93 256  66]]
```

A * B in the previous example should by no means be confused with matrix multiplication. As already mentioned, in our example the arrays are only multiplied component-wise!

8.3 Matrix Multiplication and Dot Product

8.3.1 Definition of the dot Function

The syntax of the dot function is as follows:

```
dot(a, b, out=None)
```

The function dot returns the dot product of its arguments.

- If both a and b are scalars or both are one-dimensional arrays, a scalar is returned.

- Otherwise, an array is returned.

For one-dimensional arrays, it corresponds to the inner (scalar) product, also called inner product, of vectors, but without complex conjugation.

For two-dimensional arrays, the dot product corresponds to matrix multiplication.

For N dimensions, the sum product is formed over the last axis of a and the second-to-last axis of b.

For example, if a and b are three-dimensional, then `np.dot(a, b)` is four-dimensional and `dot(a, b)[i,j,k,m] = sum(a[i,j,:] * b[k,:,m])`.

We will illustrate this case with examples in the following.

The function raises a `ValueError` if the shape of the last dimension of a is not the same size as the shape of the second-to-last dimension of b, i.e. it must hold that `a.shape[-1] == b.shape[-2]`.

8.3.2 Examples of the dot Function

We begin with the cases where both arguments are scalars or one-dimensional arrays:

```python
print(np.dot(3, 4))


x = np.array([3])
y = np.array([4])
print(np.dot(x, y))


x = np.array([3, -2])
y = np.array([-4, 1])
print(np.dot(x, y))
```

Result:

```
12
12
-14
```

In the two-dimensional case, the dot function performs matrix multiplication. Let us consider the following example:

```python
import numpy as np


A = np.array([[11, 12, 13, 14],
              [21, 22, 23, 24],
              [31, 32, 33, 34]])
B = np.array([[5, 4, 2],
              [1, 0, 2],
              [3, 8, 2],
              [24, 12, 57]])
print(np.dot(A, B))
```

This is the result of the code:

```
[[ 442   316   870]
 [ 772   556  1500]
 [1102   796  2130]]
```

Since Python 3.5, there is an infix operator for matrix multiplication, denoted by @. In NumPy, the expression $A@B$ is equivalent to np. matmul(A, B).

For two-dimensional arrays, the operations

np. matmul(A, B)   and   np. dot(A, B)

coincide. However, for higher-dimensional arrays, these operations generally differ.

```
print(A @ B)
```

The evaluation yields:

```
[[ 442   316   870]
 [ 772   556  1500]
 [1102   796  2130]]
```

For matrix multiplication of two matrices A and B in the two-dimensional case, it must hold that A.shape[-1] == B.shape[-2]:

```
print(A.shape[-1] == B.shape[-2])
```

The result follows:

```
True
```

From the previous example, we learn that the number of columns of the first two-dimensional array must equal the number of rows of the second two-dimensional array.

8.3.3 The dot Product in the Three-Dimensional Case

Things get quite tricky when we use three-dimensional arrays as arguments of dot. In the first example, we use two symmetric three-dimensional arrays:

```
import numpy as np

X = np.array([[[3,1,2],[4,2,2],[2,4,1]],
              [[3,2,2],[4,4,3],[4,1,1]],
              [[2,2,1],[3,1,3],[3,2,3]]])
```

```
Y = np.array([[[2,3,1],[2,2,4],[3,4,4]],
              [[1,4,1],[4,1,2],[4,1,2]],
              [[1,2,3],[4,1,1],[3,1,4]]])

R = X @ Y
print(f"{X.shape=}, {Y.shape=}, {R.shape=}\n{R=}")
```

Output:

```
X.shape=(3, 3, 3), Y.shape=(3, 3, 3), R.shape=(3, 3, 3)
R=array([[[14, 19, 15],
          [18, 24, 20],
          [15, 18, 22]],

         [[19, 16, 11],
          [32, 23, 18],
          [12, 18,  8]],

         [[13,  7, 12],
          [16, 10, 22],
          [20, 11, 23]]])
```

Note that the operator @ follows the semantics of `np.matmul`. Let X and Y be arrays with

$$X.\texttt{shape} = (3, 3, 3) \quad \text{and} \quad Y.\texttt{shape} = (3, 3, 3).$$

The leading dimension is interpreted as a batch dimension, and the result has shape

$$(3, 3, 3),$$

that is,

$$R[i] = X[i]@Y[i].$$

In contrast, `np.dot(X, Y)` contracts the last axis of X with the second-to-last axis of Y and therefore returns an array of shape

$$(3, 3, 3, 3).$$

Now let us consider the product of two non-symmetric three-dimensional arrays:

```
import numpy as np
X = np.array([[[11, 12, 13], [14, 15, 16], [17, 18, 19]],
              [[21, 22, 23], [24, 25, 26], [27, 28, 29]],
              [[31, 32, 33], [34, 34, 35], [36, 37, 39]]])
```

```python
Y = np.array([[[0, 0, 0],
               [0, 1, 0],
               [0, 0, 1]]])

R = np.dot(X, Y)
print(f"{X.shape=}, {Y.shape=}, {R.shape=}\n{R=}")
```

Here is the result of the code:

```
X.shape=(3, 3, 3), Y.shape=(1, 3, 3), R.shape=(3, 3, 1, 3)
R=array([[[[ 0, 12, 13]],

          [[ 0, 15, 16]],

          [[ 0, 18, 19]]],


         [[[ 0, 22, 23]],

          [[ 0, 25, 26]],

          [[ 0, 28, 29]]],


         [[[ 0, 32, 33]],

          [[ 0, 34, 35]],

          [[ 0, 37, 39]]]])
```

The squeeze function allows us to shrink dimensions by removing single-dimensional entries from the shape of an array. We show this with a simple example:

```python
x = np.array([3, 5, 7]).reshape(1, 3, 1)
print(f"x.squeeze() =\n{x.squeeze()}")
print(f"x.squeeze(axis=0) =\n{x.squeeze(axis=0)}")
print(f"x.squeeze(axis=2) =\n{x.squeeze(axis=2)}")
```

Output:

```
x.squeeze() =
[3 5 7]
x.squeeze(axis=0) =
[[3]
 [5]
 [7]]
```

```
x.squeeze(axis=2) =
[[3 5 7]]
```

Now we apply squeeze to the array R to shrink its shape from (3, 3, 1, 3) to (3, 3, 3):

```
print(R.shape)
R = np.squeeze(R, axis=2)
print(R.shape, R)
```

After execution we get:

```
(3, 3, 1, 3)
(3, 3, 3) [[[ 0 12 13]
  [ 0 15 16]
  [ 0 18 19]]

 [[ 0 22 23]
  [ 0 25 26]
  [ 0 28 29]]

 [[ 0 32 33]
  [ 0 34 35]
  [ 0 37 39]]]
```

To show how the dot product works in the three-dimensional case, we will now use two non-symmetric three-dimensional arrays:

```
import numpy as np
X = np.array(
    [[[3, 1, 2],
      [4, 2, 2]],

     [[-1, 0, 1],
      [1, -1, -2]],

     [[3, 2, 2],
      [4, 4, 3]],

     [[2, 2, 1],
      [3, 1, 3]]])

Y = np.array(
    [[[2, 3, 1, 2, 1],
      [2, 2, 2, 0, 0],
      [3, 4, 0, 1, -1]],
```

```
        [[1, 4, 3, 2, 2],
         [4, 1, 1, 4, -3],
         [4, 1, 0, 3, 0]]])

 R = np.dot(X, Y)
 print(f"{X.shape = }, {Y.shape = }, {R.shape = },\n{R[:2]=}")
```

Executing the code yields:

```
 X.shape = (4, 2, 3), Y.shape = (2, 3, 5), R.shape = (4, 2, 2, 5),
 R[:2]=array([[[[ 14,  19,   5,   8,   1],
         [ 15,  15,  10,  16,   3]],

        [[ 18,  24,   8,  10,   2],
         [ 20,  20,  14,  22,   2]]],


       [[[  1,   1,  -1,  -1,  -2],
         [  3,  -3,  -3,   1,  -2]],

        [[ -6,  -7,  -1,   0,   3],
         [-11,   1,   2,  -8,   5]]]]])
```

Let us now look at the following sum products:

```
 i = 0
 for j in range(X.shape[1]):
     for k in range(Y.shape[0]):
         for m in range(Y.shape[2]):
             fmt = "    sum(X[{}, {}, :] * Y[{}, :, {}] :   {}"
             arguments = (i, j, k, m, sum(X[i, j, :] * Y[k, :, m]))
             print(fmt.format(*arguments))
```

We obtain this output:

```
        sum(X[0, 0, :] * Y[0, :, 0] :   14
        sum(X[0, 0, :] * Y[0, :, 1] :   19
        sum(X[0, 0, :] * Y[0, :, 2] :   5
        sum(X[0, 0, :] * Y[0, :, 3] :   8
        sum(X[0, 0, :] * Y[0, :, 4] :   1
        sum(X[0, 0, :] * Y[1, :, 0] :   15
        sum(X[0, 0, :] * Y[1, :, 1] :   15
        sum(X[0, 0, :] * Y[1, :, 2] :   10
        sum(X[0, 0, :] * Y[1, :, 3] :   16
        sum(X[0, 0, :] * Y[1, :, 4] :   3
        sum(X[0, 1, :] * Y[0, :, 0] :   18
        sum(X[0, 1, :] * Y[0, :, 1] :   24
```

```
sum(X[0, 1, :] * Y[0, :, 2] :   8
sum(X[0, 1, :] * Y[0, :, 3] :   10
sum(X[0, 1, :] * Y[0, :, 4] :   2
sum(X[0, 1, :] * Y[1, :, 0] :   20
sum(X[0, 1, :] * Y[1, :, 1] :   20
sum(X[0, 1, :] * Y[1, :, 2] :   14
sum(X[0, 1, :] * Y[1, :, 3] :   22
sum(X[0, 1, :] * Y[1, :, 4] :   2
```

Hopefully, you noticed that the values we produced correspond to the elements of R[0]:

```
print(R[0])
```

The result of the code is:

```
[[[14 19  5  8   1]
  [15 15 10 16   3]]

 [[18 24  8 10   2]
  [20 20 14 22   2]]]
```

This means that we could also have generated the array R using sum products. To "prove" this, in the following example we will create an array R2 using sum products and then check whether R2 is equal to R.

```python
def sum_prod(X, Y):
    """ sum product for 3-dimensional arrays """
    res_shape = X.shape[:-1] + Y.shape[:-2] + (Y.shape[-1],)
    R = np.zeros(res_shape, dtype=X.dtype)
    for i in range(X.shape[0]):
        for j in range(X.shape[1]):
            for k in range(Y.shape[0]):
                for m in range(Y.shape[2]):
                    R[i, j, k, m] = sum(X[i, j, :] * Y[k, :, m])
    return R

print(np.array_equal(np.dot(X, Y), sum_prod(X, Y)))
```

Executing the code yields:

```
True
```

So what we stated at the beginning holds true:

```
dot(X, Y)[i,j,k,m] = sum(X[i,j,:]  * Y[k,:,m])
```

8.4 Comparison Operators

We are already familiar with comparison operators in Python, which we have applied to integers, floats, or strings. They return `True` or `False`.

When we compare two arrays, we do not get a "simple" Boolean value back. The comparisons are carried out elementwise. This means that we get a Boolean array as the return value:

```python
import numpy as np


A = np.array([[11, 12, 13], [21, 22, 23], [31, 32, 33]])
B = np.array([[11, 102, 13], [201, 22, 203], [31, 32, 303]])


print(A == B)
```

Here is the result of the code:

```
[[ True False  True]
 [False  True False]
 [ True  True False]]
```

We can also check arrays for complete equality. For this we use the function `array_equal`, which returns `True` if two arrays have the same shape and all elements are equal. Otherwise, `False` is returned.

```python
print(np.array_equal(A, B))
print(np.array_equal(A, A))
```

The output shows:

```
False
True
```

8.5 Logical Operators

We can also compare arrays component-wise with a logical "or" or a logical "and." For this there are the functions `logical_or` and `logical_and`.

```python
a = np.array([[True, True], [False, False]])
b = np.array([[True, False], [True, False]])


print(np.logical_or(a, b))
print(np.logical_and(a, b))
```

Output:

```
[[ True  True]
 [ True False]]
[[ True False]
 [False False]]
```

8.6 Broadcasting

Up to now, we have assumed that arrays must have the same shape in order to apply numerical operators to them.

Under the name "broadcasting," NumPy provides a powerful mechanism that allows us to apply arithmetic operators to arrays with different shapes. To perform the operation, the "smaller" array is either transformed into a "matching form" or applied multiple times to the "larger" array.

In other words: under certain conditions, the smaller array is "broadcast" until it has the same shape as the larger one.

Broadcasting allows us to avoid loops in our Python programs. Looping then happens implicitly inside NumPy's implementation, i.e. in C. This also prevents unnecessary copies of our data.

In principle, there are three different forms of broadcasting:
- in the horizontal direction
- in the vertical direction
- in both horizontal and vertical directions

Broadcasting in NumPy for two arrays follows these rules:

Rule 1 If the two arrays differ in their number of dimensions, the shape of the array with fewer dimensions is padded with ones on the left.

Rule 2 If the shapes of two arrays do not match at a certain position, the shape entry that is equal to 1 is adjusted (repeated) to match the other array's size.

Rule 3 If in any dimension the sizes differ and neither of them is 1, an error is raised.

We will see more clearly in the following what applying these rules means.

A particularly simple case of broadcasting we have already encountered: scalar multiplication.

```python
import numpy as np

v = np.array([3, 5, 1])
x = 4
print(v * x)
```

Result:

```
[12 20  4]
```

Instead of a scalar for x, we could also have used the vector `np.array([4, 4, 4])`
and would have obtained the same result:

```python
import numpy as np

v = np.array([3, 5, 1])
x = np.array([4, 4, 4])
print(v * x)
```

This follows from the code:

```
[12 20  4]
```

Normally, however, this is not what we mean when we talk about broadcasting.

8.6.1 Row-wise Broadcasting

Let us consider the two arrays A and B and their shapes:

```python
import numpy as np

A = np.array([[11, 12, 13],
              [21, 22, 23],
              [31, 32, 33]])
B = np.array([1, 2, 3])

print(A.shape)
print(B.shape)
```

What we obtain is:

```
(3, 3)
(3,)
```

```python
print("Multiplication with broadcasting: ")
print(A * B)
print("... and now addition with broadcasting: ")
print(A + B)
```

The output we get is:

```
Multiplication with broadcasting:
[[11 24 39]
 [21 44 69]
 [31 64 99]]
... and now addition with broadcasting:
[[12 14 16]
 [22 24 26]
 [32 34 36]]
```

The following diagram illustrates how broadcasting works:

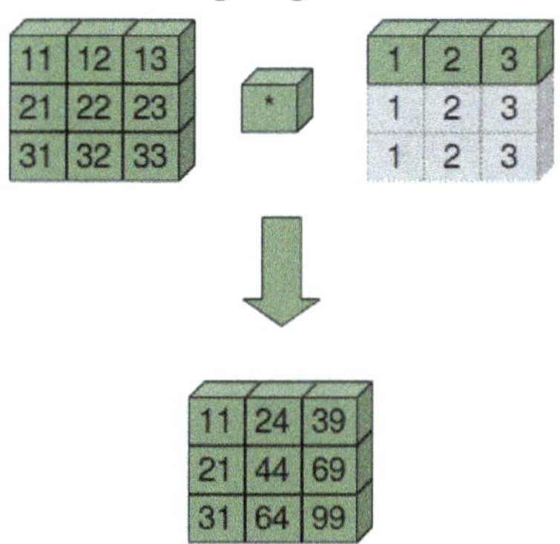

Array B is treated as if it were structured as follows:

```python
B = np.array([1, 2, 3])
print("Shape of B at the start: ", B.shape)
# Application of rule 1:
B = B[np.newaxis, :]
print("Shape after applying the first rule: ", B.shape)
# Application of rule 2:
B = np.tile(B, (3, 1))
print("Shape after applying the second rule: ", B.shape)
print()
print(B)
```

The corresponding output can be seen here:

```
Shape of B at the start:  (3,)
Shape after applying the first rule:  (1, 3)
Shape after applying the second rule:  (3, 3)

[[1 2 3]
 [1 2 3]
 [1 2 3]]
```

"Row-wise" therefore means that we treat a one-dimensional array as the row to be broadcast.

Broadcasting also works for higher dimensions, as long as the first two rules can be successfully applied. We demonstrate this in the following example:

```python
Y = np.array(
    [[[2, 3, 1, 2, 1],
      [2, 2, 2, 0, 0],
      [3, 4, 0, 1, -1]],

     [[1, 4, 3, 2, 2],
      [4, 1, 1, 4, -3],
      [4, 1, 0, 3, 0]]])

print(Y.shape)
X = np.array([1, 2, 3, 4, 5])
print(X + Y)
```

Executing the code yields:

```
(2, 3, 5)
[[[3 5 4 6 6]
  [3 4 5 4 5]
  [4 6 3 5 4]]

 [[2 6 6 6 7]
  [5 3 4 8 2]
  [5 3 3 7 5]]]
```

Again in this case, we want to see what one would have to do to simulate broadcasting step by step according to the rules:

```python
print(Y.shape)
X = X[np.newaxis, np.newaxis, :]
print("Shape after applying the first rule: ", X.shape)
X = np.tile(X, (2, 3, 1))
print("Shape after applying the second rule: ", X.shape)
print()
print(X + Y)
```

This is the result of the code:

```
(2, 3, 5)
Shape after applying the first rule:  (1, 1, 5)
Shape after applying the second rule:  (2, 3, 5)
```

```
[[[3 5 4 6 6]
  [3 4 5 4 5]
  [4 6 3 5 4]]

 [[2 6 6 6 7]
  [5 3 4 8 2]
  [5 3 3 7 5]]]
```

Now let us show a simple application of row-wise broadcasting. Given a matrix A, we compute the mean values of its columns. We obtain a vector with three elements, then perform a subtraction in which broadcasting is applied.

```python
import numpy as np
A = np.array([[1, 2, 3],
              [4, 5, 6],
              [7, 8, 9],
              [10, 11, 12]])

# Compute column means:
mean = A.mean(axis=0)


res = A - mean
print(res)
```

Output:

```
[[-4.5 -4.5 -4.5]
 [-1.5 -1.5 -1.5]
 [ 1.5  1.5  1.5]
 [ 4.5  4.5  4.5]]
```

The following diagram illustrates the previous example:

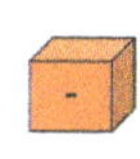
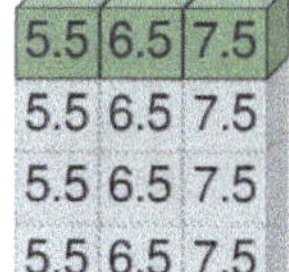

8.6.2 Column-wise Broadcasting

In this case we again have a one-dimensional array, but we now treat it as a column vector of the broadcast array.

For this example we need to know how to convert a row vector into a column vector. There are two options. Using reshape:

```python
B = np.array([1, 2, 3])
print(B.reshape((B.shape[0], 1)))
```

We obtain this output:

```
[[1]
 [2]
 [3]]
```

Alternatively, we can use newaxis:

```python
B = np.array([1, 2, 3])
print(B[:, np.newaxis])
```

We obtain this output:

```
[[1]
 [2]
 [3]]
```

Now we can perform multiplication with broadcasting:

```python
import numpy as np

A = np.array([[11, 12, 13],
              [21, 22, 23],
              [31, 32, 33]])

X = A * B[:, np.newaxis]
print(X)
```

Result:

```
[[11 12 13]
 [42 44 46]
 [93 96 99]]
```

Array B is treated as if it were structured as follows:

```python
B = np.array([1, 2, 3])
B = B.reshape((B.shape[0], 1))
print("Shape after applying the first rule: ", B.shape)
B = np.tile(B, (1, 3))
print("Shape after applying the second rule: ", B.shape)
print()

print(B)
```

The output we get is:

```
Shape after applying the first rule:   (3, 1)
Shape after applying the second rule:   (3, 3)


[[1 1 1]
 [2 2 2]
 [3 3 3]]
```

Now let us show a simple application of column-wise broadcasting. Given a matrix A, we compute the mean values of its rows. We obtain a vector with three elements. Before we can perform subtraction, we must add a new dimension to the mean vector so that column-wise broadcasting can work.

```python
import numpy as np
A = np.array([[1, 2, 3],
              [4, 5, 6],
              [7, 8, 9],
              [10, 11, 12]])

# Compute row means
mean = A.mean(axis=1)
res = A - mean[:, np.newaxis]
print(res)
```

We obtain this output:

```
[[-1.  0.  1.]
 [-1.  0.  1.]
 [-1.  0.  1.]
 [-1.  0.  1.]]
```

The following diagram illustrates the previous example:

8.6.3 Broadcasting with Two One-Dimensional Arrays

Now let us consider the case where we want to combine two one-dimensional arrays. We want to treat the first as a column vector and the second as a row vector.

In principle, we now combine the procedures from the two previous cases – column-wise and row-wise broadcasting:

```
A = np.array([10, 20, 30])
B = np.array([1, 2, 3])

# reshape A into a column vector:
A = A.reshape(A.shape[0], 1)
print(A)
# now we can perform broadcasting:
print(A * B)
```

The script returns:

```
[[10]
 [20]
 [30]]
[[10 20 30]
 [20 40 60]
 [30 60 90]]
```

8.7 Distance Matrix

In mathematics, computer science, and especially in graph theory, a distance matrix refers to a two-dimensional array that contains the "distances" between the elements of a set pairwise. The size of this two-dimensional array is $n \times n$ if the set consists of n elements.

A practical example of a distance matrix is a matrix with the distances between stations along a railway line, in our example some train stations on the route from Saarbrücken to Salzburg:

```python
stations = ["Saarbrücken", "Homburg (Saar)", "Kaiserslautern",
            "Neustadt (Weinstr)", "Ludwigshafen (Rhein)",
            "Mannheim", "Stuttgart", "Ulm", "Günzburg",
            "Augsburg", "München", "Rosenheim",
            "Prien am Chiemsee", "Traunstein", "Salzburg"]


minutesFromStart = [0, 21, 46, 70, 88, 94, 141, 199, 213, 245,
                    280, 320, 336, 356, 398]


route = np.array(minutesFromStart)
dists = np.abs(route - route[:, np.newaxis])


print(route)
print(dists)
```

The script returns:

```
[  0  21  46  70  88  94 141 199 213 245 280 320 336 356 398]
[[  0  21  46  70  88  94 141 199 213 245 280 320 336 356 398]
 [ 21   0  25  49  67  73 120 178 192 224 259 299 315 335 377]
 [ 46  25   0  24  42  48  95 153 167 199 234 274 290 310 352]
 [ 70  49  24   0  18  24  71 129 143 175 210 250 266 286 328]
 [ 88  67  42  18   0   6  53 111 125 157 192 232 248 268 310]
 [ 94  73  48  24   6   0  47 105 119 151 186 226 242 262 304]
 [141 120  95  71  53  47   0  58  72 104 139 179 195 215 257]
 [199 178 153 129 111 105  58   0  14  46  81 121 137 157 199]
 [213 192 167 143 125 119  72  14   0  32  67 107 123 143 185]
 [245 224 199 175 157 151 104  46  32   0  35  75  91 111 153]
 [280 259 234 210 192 186 139  81  67  35   0  40  56  76 118]
 [320 299 274 250 232 226 179 121 107  75  40   0  16  36  78]
 [336 315 290 266 248 242 195 137 123  91  56  16   0  20  62]
 [356 335 310 286 268 262 215 157 143 111  76  36  20   0  42]
 [398 377 352 328 310 304 257 199 185 153 118  78  62  42   0]]
```

Suppose Tobias, who lives near Kaiserslautern, wants to visit his girlfriend in Traunstein. From the previously calculated matrix, he can easily look up the upcoming travel time:

```python
t = dists[stations.index("Kaiserslautern"),
          stations.index("Traunstein")]
print(f"{t} min or {t//60}:{t%60}h")
```

Here is the output:

```
310 min or 5:10h
```

8.8 ufuncs

In NumPy, "ufunc" stands for "universal function". A ufunc is a general functionality in NumPy that can operate on arrays of any shape and size, performing operations elementwise.

For example, a ufunc can be used to square all elements of an array or add all elements of two arrays together.

The purpose of NumPy ufuncs is to perform fast and efficient operations on arrays, enabled by optimized C implementations. Ufuncs are functions that can be applied to elements of NumPy arrays to carry out mathematical operations quickly, without having to write a loop over all array elements.

This means that by using ufuncs, complex operations on arrays can be executed very quickly and simply – which is especially important in data analysis.

NumPy contains a wide variety of ufuncs, including mathematical functions such as sine and cosine, as well as arithmetic operations such as addition and multiplication.

The key aspect of ufuncs is the *vectorization* of sequential datatypes like lists, tuples, or ranges. It means that operations are executed elementwise in optimized compiled code without explicit Python loops. Vectorization is significantly faster than iterating over the individual elements of sequential structures or arrays.

In addition, ufuncs also provide broadcasting functionality and additional methods such as `reduce` and `accumulate`, which are extremely useful for mathematical computations.

Another advantage of ufuncs is that they can work with a wide variety of datatypes and formats.

In principle, most NumPy functionalities are implemented as ufuncs. Thus, in addition to the infix operators we already know (+, -, *, etc.), there are also functional forms like `add`, `subtract`, `multiply`, `divide`, `remainder`, `power`, and others.

But there are also functions for which no infix variant exists, since they expect only one argument (unary operators): `arccos`, `arccosh`, `arcsin`, `arcsinh`, `arctan`, `arctanh`, `cos`, `cosh`, `tan`, `tanh`, `log10`, `sin`, `sinh`, `sqrt`, `absolute`, `fabs`, `floor`, `ceil`, `fmod`, `exp`, `log`, `conjugate`, `maximum`, `minimum`.

For the infix comparison operators <, <=, ==, >, >=, !=, and so on, there are corresponding functional variants as well: `greater`, `greater_equal`, `equal`, `less`, `less_equal`, `not_equal`, `logical_or`, `logical_xor`, `logical_not`, `logical_and`, `bitwise_or`, `bitwise_xor`, `bitwise_not`, `bitwise_and`, `rshift`, `lshift`.

8.8.1 Application of ufuncs

The functional and infix variants are equivalent:

```python
import numpy as np
from numpy import add


x = np.array([3, 5, -1, 0])
y = np.array([1, -2, 0, 3])


print(x + y)
# equivalent form
print(add(x, y))
print("Type of the 'add' function:", type(add))
```

The result appears as follows:

```
[ 4  3 -1  3]
[ 4  3 -1  3]
Type of the 'add' function: <class 'numpy.ufunc'>
```

Ufuncs can be applied to arbitrary Python sequences, as long as they consist of numeric datatypes and are compatible in length and shape. This has the advantage that we can combine different but compatible numeric datatypes without explicit type conversion:

```python
import numpy as np


a = np.array([1, -1.2, 4])
list1 = [2, 5, 6.7]
list2 = [4, 6, 7.8]
t = (1.3, 4.5, 0)


# Additive combination of np.array and list:
print(a, list1)
```

```python
# or the other way around:
print(list1, a)

# Additive combination of arrays and numeric tuples:
print(np.add(a, t))

# Addition of two numeric lists:
print(np.add(list1, list2))

# Addition of arbitrary sequential datatypes:
print(np.add(t, list2))
print(np.add(t, range(3, 6)))

# other functions:
print(np.sin(a))
print(np.cos(list1))
print(np.tan(range(1001, 1010)))
```

Here is the output:

```
[ 1.  -1.2  4. ] [2, 5, 6.7]
[2, 5, 6.7] [ 1.  -1.2  4. ]
[2.3 3.3 4. ]
[ 6.  11.  14.5]
[ 5.3 10.5  7.8]
[4.3 8.5 5. ]
[ 0.841 -0.932 -0.757]
[-0.416  0.284  0.914]
[-2.347 -0.17   1.098 -3.742 -0.32   0.826 -8.324 -0.485  0.611]
```

The return value is always a `numpy.ndarray`. Ufuncs can also be applied to instances of the built-in `int` and `float` classes. In these cases, the return values are of type `numpy.int64` or `numpy.float64`:

```python
res = np.sin(2)
print(res, type(res))


res = np.ceil(2.3)
print(res, type(res))
```

Output:

```
0.9092974268256817 <class 'numpy.float64'>
3.0 <class 'numpy.float64'>
```

8.8.2 Output Parameters in ufuncs

Another special feature of ufuncs is that they can also take an output parameter for the result object. This is especially important for writing efficient code.

Suppose we want to multiply an array x by a scalar, and in the subsequent program flow we only need the newly computed array and no longer the old one. There are four ways to do this. All are logically correct, but two are inefficient and should be avoided, especially with large data structures. We demonstrate this in the following example:

```python
import numpy as np

print('Method 1:')
x = np.array([25.6, 29.3, 30.9])
print(f'before: {id(x)=}')
x = x * 1.8
print(f'after: {id(x)=}')

print('\nMethod 2:')
x = np.array([25.6, 29.3, 30.9])
print(f'before: {id(x)=}')
x *= 1.8
print(f'after: {id(x)=}')

print('\nMethod 3:')
x = np.array([25.6, 29.3, 30.9])
print(f'before: {id(x)=}')
x = np.multiply(x, 1.8)
print(f'after: {id(x)=}')

print('\nMethod 4:')
x = np.array([25.6, 29.3, 30.9])
print(f'before: {id(x)=}')
np.multiply(x, 1.8, x)
print(f'after: {id(x)=}')
```

The evaluation yields:

```
Method 1:
before: id(x)=125292150720144
after: id(x)=125291232402320

Method 2:
before: id(x)=125292150720144
after: id(x)=125292150720144
```

```
Method 3:
before: id(x)=125291231938384
after: id(x)=125291232402320


Method 4:
before: id(x)=125291231938384
after: id(x)=125291231938384
```

From the id function outputs above we can see that in Methods 1 and 3 a new array is created, and the old array is discarded (since no variable references it anymore). This is inefficient.

In Method 2, however, the operator *= updates the array in place – the id remains the same, meaning no new array is created.

Method 4 shows another special feature: we specify a third parameter, which designates the variable (or memory space) into which the result should be written. If provided, it must have the appropriate shape. If not provided (or None), a new array is allocated. Thus, Method 4 is just as efficient as Method 2.

We can also explicitly use the keyword parameter out:

```
np.multiply(x, 1.8, out=x)
```

The main benefit of using += or ufuncs with the out parameter becomes clear with very large arrays. Suppose we have only 1 GB of free memory, and we have an array x that already takes up 1.2 GB. If we execute x = x * 1.8, NumPy must allocate another 1.2 GB for the new array – which we cannot afford. With x *= 1.8, no extra space is required, so the program runs without issues.

In the previous example, the out parameter did not offer much additional advantage, since we could just use +=. But it becomes essential in cases where no shorthand operator exists.

For example, suppose we have three arrays, a, b, and c, all with the same shape. If we compute a = b + c, NumPy allocates a new array for the result. To avoid this, we can use the out parameter:

```python
import numpy as np


rows, cols = 30, 40   # Bigger advantage for larger dimensions
a = np.random.randint(1, 20, (rows, cols))
b = np.random.randint(1, 20, (rows, cols))
c = np.random.randint(1, 20, (rows, cols))


print(f'Before execution: {id(a)=}')
np.add(b, c, out=a)      # instead of a = b + c
print(f'After execution: {id(a)=}')
```

Output:

The result appears as follows:

```
Before execution: id(a)=125291232400400
After execution: id(a)=125291232400400
```

Both forms technically work, but the explicit form `np.add(b, c, out=a)` is clearer and more readable. The shorter `np.add(b, c, a)` works only because a is passed in the third positional argument, which happens to map to `out`. This is discouraged because it is:

✗ less readable,

✎ easy to misinterpret (especially with multiple optional arguments), and

✎ error-prone if the ufunc signature changes or is misunderstood.

8.8.3 accumulate

The `accumulate` method can be applied to ufunc functions. It applies the operator cumulatively to all elements of the array. When applied to `np.add`, the result is equivalent to `np.cumsum`, as shown in the following example:

```python
import numpy as np

x = np.arange(1, 6)
print(x)
print(np.add.accumulate(x))
print(np.cumsum(x))
```

After execution we get:

```
[1 2 3 4 5]
[ 1  3  6 10 15]
[ 1  3  6 10 15]
```

For multidimensional arrays, the optional parameter `axis` can be used. The following example illustrates this clearly:

```python
import numpy as np

x = np.arange(24).reshape((6, 4))
print(x)
print("Accumulation over rows, i.e. axis = 0:")
print(np.add.accumulate(x))
print("Accumulation over rows, i.e. axis = 0:")
print(np.add.accumulate(x, axis=0))
```

```python
print("Accumulation over columns, i.e. axis = 1:")
print(np.add.accumulate(x, axis=1))
print("Accumulation over rows and columns:")
print(np.add.accumulate(np.add.accumulate(x, axis=0), axis=1))
```

Output:

```
[[ 0  1  2  3]
 [ 4  5  6  7]
 [ 8  9 10 11]
 [12 13 14 15]
 [16 17 18 19]
 [20 21 22 23]]
Accumulation over rows, i.e. axis = 0:
[[ 0  1  2  3]
 [ 4  6  8 10]
 [12 15 18 21]
 [24 28 32 36]
 [40 45 50 55]
 [60 66 72 78]]
Accumulation over rows, i.e. axis = 0:
[[ 0  1  2  3]
 [ 4  6  8 10]
 [12 15 18 21]
 [24 28 32 36]
 [40 45 50 55]
 [60 66 72 78]]
Accumulation over columns, i.e. axis = 1:
[[ 0  1  3  6]
 [ 4  9 15 22]
 [ 8 17 27 38]
 [12 25 39 54]
 [16 33 51 70]
 [20 41 63 86]]
Accumulation over rows and columns:
[[  0   1   3   6]
 [  4  10  18  28]
 [ 12  27  45  66]
 [ 24  52  84 120]
 [ 40  85 135 190]
 [ 60 126 198 276]]
```

8.8.4 reduce

The behavior of `reduce` in the one-dimensional case can be described as follows:

Suppose `op` is a function such as `numpy.add` or `numpy.multiply`. When we apply `op.reduce` to an object `x` (which may be a numerical Python sequence or a one-dimensional array), it returns a single value.

The computation proceeds as follows: If `x` is empty, the result is `0.0`. If `x` has only one element, that element is returned. If `x` has more than one element, op is applied first to the first two elements, then to that result and the next element, and so on, until no elements remain. The final result is returned:

```python
import numpy as np


x = np.arange(1, 5)


print(np.add.reduce(x))        # equivalent to sum
print(np.multiply.reduce(x))   # equivalent to factorial
```

Executing the code yields:

```
10
24
```

In the multidimensional case, reduce reduces along one axis. A reduction over all dimensions is obtained by setting `axis=None`:

```python
import numpy as np


x = np.arange(12).reshape((3, 4))
print(x)
print("Reduce over rows, i.e. axis = 0:")
print(np.add.reduce(x))
print("Reduce over columns, i.e. axis = 1:")
print(np.add.reduce(x, axis=1))
print("Reduce over rows and columns:")
print(np.add.reduce(np.add.reduce(x)))
print("The simpler way with axis=None:")
print(np.add.reduce(x, axis=None))
```

The output we get is:

```
[[ 0  1  2  3]
 [ 4  5  6  7]
 [ 8  9 10 11]]
```

```
Reduce over rows, i.e. axis = 0:
[12 15 18 21]
Reduce over columns, i.e. axis = 1:
[ 6 22 38]
Reduce over rows and columns:
66
The simpler way with axis=None:
66
```

8.8.5 outer

`op.outer(A, B)` applies the operation op to all pairs `(a, b)` with a in A and b in B.

In mathematics, this special product of two vectors is known as the "dyadic product" or "tensor product." The result is a matrix.

The following diagram illustrates the working principle of `outer`:

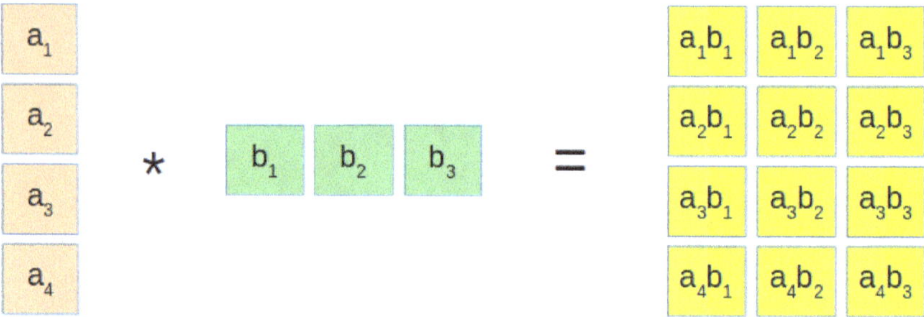

And here is the same example with real values:

```python
import numpy as np

x = np.multiply.outer([1, 2, 3, 4], [11, 22, 33])
print(x)
```

The output we get is:

```
[[ 11  22  33]
 [ 22  44  66]
 [ 33  66  99]
 [ 44  88 132]]
```

8.8.6 at

at(a, indices, b=None) performs an unbuffered in-place operation on the elements of a specified by indices. For addition, for example, this is equivalent to a[indices] += b, except that repeated indices are accumulated rather than overwritten.

```python
import numpy as np

a = np.array([3, 5, 12, 5])
b = np.array([3, 11])
np.add.at(a, [0, 2], b)
print(a)

# equivalent with direct indexing
a = np.array([3, 5, 12, 5])
a[[0, 2]] += b
print(a)

# now with repeated indices:
a = np.array([3, 5, 12, 5])
np.add.at(a, [0, 0], b)
print(a)

a[[0, 0]] += b
print(a)
```

Result:

```
[ 6  5 23  5]
[ 6  5 23  5]
[17  5 12  5]
[28  5 12  5]
```

8.9 Exercises

Exercise 1

(Solution: 33.4, Solution 1)

Given an array B = np.array([1, 2, 3]).

Automatically generate an array of the form:

```
[[[1 1 1]]
 [[2 2 2]]
 [[3 3 3]]]
```

This array has the shape (3, 1, 3).

Exercise 2

(Solution: 33.4, Solution 2)

Create an integer array A with shape (3, 4). Create a one-dimensional array Z with the row minima and a one-dimensional array S with the column minima. What is the absolute minimum of the array?

Exercise 3

(Solution: 33.4, Solution 3)

Suppose we have a NumPy array representing the number of steps walked by a person each day of the week:

```python
import numpy as np


steps = np.array([3000, 4500, 4000, 5000, 3500, 6000, 5500])
```

Task: Compute the cumulative number of steps after each day.

Exercise 4

(Solution: 33.4, Solution 4)

Suppose you run a small business and want to calculate the total costs for different order quantities of several products.

You are given:

- An array prices containing the unit prices (in dollars) of 4 different products: [10.0, 15.0, 25.0, 50.0].

- An array quantities representing how many units a customer might order: [1, 2, 3, 4, 5].

```python
import numpy as np

# Unit prices for 4 different products
prices = np.array([10.0, 15.0, 25.0, 50.0])  # in dollars

# Order quantities from 5 different customers
quantities = np.array([1, 2, 3, 4, 5])
```

9
Statistics and Probability

9.1 Introduction

"Every American should have above average income, and my administration is going to see they get it." (Bill Clinton)[1]

Statistics and probability theory surround us almost everywhere in daily life. We constantly have to deal with them, often when choosing between alternatives. Can we go hiking tomorrow or will it rain? The weather forecast tells us that the probability of precipitation is 30 %. What now – can we risk it? Another scenario: you play the lottery every

Figure 9.1 Dice

week and dream of a distant island. What are the chances of winning the jackpot so you can live in paradise without having to work? Not very high. But imagine you actually won the jackpot. What is the probability that on your **dream island**, far from home, you might run into your neighbor? Maybe they also won the lottery. How likely is such a coincidence? Uncertainty surrounds us, and only a few people truly understand the foundations of statistics and probability theory.

The Python programming language and the NumPy and SciPy modules do not help us to understand everyday problems like those above. However, Python and NumPy do provide powerful functionality for performing calculations in statistics and probability theory. In this chapter we will look at the `random` module as well as the separate but similarly named NumPy submodule `numpy.random`.

---

1   Although this quotation is extremely widespread, we were unfortunately unable to find a citable source!

9.2 Functions Based on the random Module

These two modules are not part of NumPy, but they are widely used. In later subsections we will focus specifically on the corresponding functionality provided by NumPy. The `secrets` module was only introduced in Python 3.6. It generates cryptographically strong pseudo-random numbers, suitable for passwords, tokens, and similar use cases. It was designed for exactly this purpose. Internally, it contains a CSPRNG (Cryptographically Strong Pseudo Random Number Generator). By contrast, Python's built-in random module was not developed with cryptographic applications in mind. Instead, its focus is on modeling and simulation. The documentation of the random module even contains an explicit warning:

Warning: Please note that the pseudo-random number generator in the random module should **not** be used for security-critical purposes. Use `secrets` in Python 3.6+ or `os.urandom()` in earlier versions.[2]

That said, you can use the `SystemRandom` class from the random module, which relies on the secure `os.urandom` system function.

`random.SystemRandom` and `secrets.SystemRandom` are functionally identical, as both use `os.urandom()`. The `secrets` module, however, is specifically intended for cryptographic applications, whereas `random.SystemRandom` is just a class inside the random module that also relies on `os.urandom()`.

With the function `random.random` we can generate a pseudo-random number in the half-open interval [0, 1). Since this module uses the Mersenne Twister algorithm, the numbers are not cryptographically secure. If cryptographic security is needed, you can use `SystemRandom().random()`, which is based on true OS entropy.

```python
import random
random_number = random.random()
print(random_number)
```

This is the result of the code:

```
0.6394267984578837
```

Now let's generate a cryptographically strong random number:

```python
from secrets import SystemRandom
# from random import SystemRandom   # equivalent
crypto = SystemRandom()
print(crypto.random())
```

The corresponding output can be seen here:

```
0.5700634608381924
```

---

2   Original: "Note that the pseudo-random generators in the random module should NOT be used for security purposes. Use `secrets` on Python 3.6+ and `os.urandom()` on Python 3.5 and earlier."

9.2.1 True Random Numbers

True random numbers can be obtained from physical phenomena – for example, radioactive decay or electronic noise. Simpler but less practical are analog methods like tossing a coin or rolling dice. These are usually too slow or technically cumbersome.

As we have seen, neither Python's random module nor NumPy's numpy.random submodule produces "true" random numbers. For most applications, however, pseudo-random numbers are good enough. What about the SystemRandom class from the secrets module? Can this class generate cryptographically strong random numbers – that is, numbers that are unpredictable and non-deterministic?[3] The answer lies in the fact that SystemRandom uses the os.urandom function. According to the built-in help, os.urandom "returns a bytestring of 'n' bytes suitable for cryptographic use."[4] However, the very next section of the help text adds a qualification: "This function returns random bytes from an OS-specific randomness source. The returned data should be unpredictable enough for cryptographic applications, though its exact quality depends on the OS implementation."[5]

The website RANDOM.ORG[6] claims to generate "true" random numbers by harnessing atmospheric noise. The numerical values produced in this way are often better suited for many applications than pseudo-random numbers from a computer program. However, obtaining these random numbers over the internet is generally unsuitable unless you have a trusted, authenticated channel and a threat model that accepts reliance on a third party.

9.2.2 Generating a List of Random Numbers

In many cases we need more than just a single random number. We demonstrate two approaches to achieving this: first, with a custom function random_list, to show how this could be implemented without NumPy. Afterwards we present the NumPy version in Section 9.3 (The random Submodule of NumPy), which is the preferred practical solution.

The parameter secure lets us control whether the numbers should be generated using SystemRandom for security:

```
import random
```

---

3   That is, numbers that cannot be precomputed by another program and that do not exhibit predictable patterns.

4   Return a bytestring of size random bytes suitable for cryptographic use.

5   This function returns random bytes from an OS-specific randomness source. The returned data should be unpredictable enough for cryptographic applications, though its exact quality depends on the OS implementation.

6   *http://www.random.org*

```python
def random_list(n, secure=True):
    random_floats = []
    if secure:
        crypto = random.SystemRandom()
        random_float = crypto.random
    else:
        random_float = random.random
    for _ in range(n):
        random_floats.append(random_float())
    return random_floats

print(random_list(3, secure=False))
```

The script returns:

```
[0.025010755222666936, 0.27502931836911926, 0.22321073814882275]
```

As we can see below, the price of security is a significant increase in computation time:

The evaluation yields:

```
random_list(100, secure=True)
114.6 \textmu s $\pm$ 16.3 \textmu s per loop (mean $\pm$ std. dev. of 7
↪  runs, 1000 loops each)
```

Output:

```
random_list(100, secure=False)
5.2 \textmu s $\pm$ 416.9 ns per loop (mean $\pm$ std. dev. of 7 runs,
↪  10000 loops each)
```

The simplest approach in terms of programming effort, and the fastest in terms of runtime, is to generate random numbers using the random submodule of numpy:

```python
import numpy as np

print(np.random.random(10))
```

Executing the code yields:

```
[0.375 0.951 0.732 0.599 0.156 0.156 0.058 0.866 0.601 0.708]
```

The result is:

```
np.random.random(100)
2.6 \textmu s $\pm$ 758.3 ns per loop (mean $\pm$ std. dev. of 7 runs,
↪  10000 loops each)
```

However, these are not cryptographically secure random numbers!

9.2.3 Random Integers

Everyone is familiar with generating random numbers without a computer. When you roll a die, you obtain a random number between 1 and 6. In probability theory, we call "rolling a die" an experiment, and its set of possible outcomes is {1, 2, 3, 4, 5, 6}. This set is also referred to as the "sample space."

We can generate integer values relatively easily using what we have already learned. Our function produces numbers in the half-open interval between `start` and `stop`, i.e., `[start, stop)`:

```python
import random
random.seed(42)


def randint(start, stop, secure=True):
    if secure:
        crypto = random.SystemRandom()
        rnd = crypto.random
    else:
        rnd = random.random
    result = int(rnd() * (stop - start)) + start
    return result


print([randint(3, 7) for i in range(20)])
```

The result appears as follows:

```
[3, 6, 4, 4, 4, 4, 5, 5, 4, 4, 3, 6, 3, 3, 4, 3, 5, 4, 3, 4]
```

9.2.4 Samples or Selections

`choice` is another extremely useful function of the `random` module. It can be used to select a random element from a non-empty sequence.

Sequences can be, for example, lists, strings, or tuples, but also iterators. This means that we can select a random character from a string, or a random element from a list or a tuple:

```python
from random import seed, choice
seed(42)


professions = ["scientist", "philosopher", "engineer", "priest"]
print(choice("abcdefghij"))
print(choice(professions))
print(choice(("apples", "bananas", "cherries")))
print(choice(range(10)))
```

The output shows:

```
b
scientist
cherries
4
```

The function `choice` randomly returns one object from a non-empty sequence, with each element having an equal chance of being selected. For instance, when calling `choice(profession)`, the chance of returning `scientist` is 1/4.

This, of course, does not reflect reality. To better model real-world scenarios, we need weighted selection – similar to the case of a loaded die.

We now define a function `weighted_choice`, which, like `random.choice`, returns a random element from a sequence, but where the elements of the sequence are assigned weights.

9.2.5 Random Intervals

Before designing weighted choice, we define a helper function `find_interval(x, partition)`, which we will need for our `weighted_choice` function. `find_interval` expects two arguments:

- a numerical value x
- a list or tuple of numerical values $p_0, p_1, p_2, \ldots p_n$

The function returns i if $p_i < x < p_{i+1}$. It returns -1 if x is smaller than p_0 or greater than or equal to p_n.

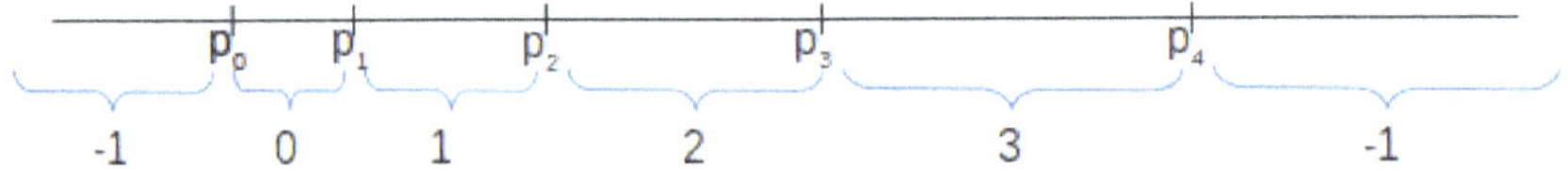


```python
def find_interval(x, partition):
    """ find_interval -> i
        partition is a sequence of numeric values
        x is an int or float number
        The return value "i" is the index
        for which partition[i] < x < partition[i+1],
        if such an index exists. Otherwise -1
    """

    for i in range(0, len(partition)):
        if x < partition[i]:
            return i-1
    return -1
```

```python
I = [0, 3, 5, 7.8, 9, 12, 13.8, 16]
for x in [-1.3, 0, 0.1, 3.2, 5, 6.2, 7.9, 13.9, 15, 16, 16.5]:
    print(find_interval(x, I), end=", ")
```

The result of the code is:

```
-1, 0, 0, 1, 2, 2, 3, 6, 6, -1, -1,
```

9.2.6 Seed or Initial Value

A "seed" is an initial value used to initialize a random number generator. It ensures that a pseudo-random sequence remains reproducible: with the same seed, the same sequence of numbers is generated. In cryptography, however, a seed must not be predictable – it must itself be chosen randomly, for example from user inputs such as mouse movements.

When we call `random.random()`, we expect a random value between 0 and 1. `random.random()` computes a new random value based on the previous random value. But what happens if we use this function for the very first time in our program? Exactly: there is no previous random value yet. When a random generator is called for the first time, the first "random" value must be created somehow.

If we set the initial value, i.e., the seed, of a pseudo-random number generator, we provide the first random value. From this, a sequence of further random values is then generated deterministically. If we restart a random sequence with the same initial value, we obtain exactly the same sequence of values again. Thus, if the initial value is known, the values derived from it can also be calculated.

Therefore, whenever security is involved, we need a way to use a true random value as the initial value. In many programming languages, random initial values are generated from the system state, which is usually the system time.

This is also true for Python. According to `help(random.seed)`, if the function is called with `None` or with no argument, the seed value is generated from the current system time or another system-specific randomness source.

Calling `seed` without parameters will therefore use either the current time or a system-specific randomness source as the seed. If you provide a value, it will be used to compute the initial seed.

The seed function yields a deterministic sequence of random numbers. The sequence can be repeated as often as needed, for example to debug certain situations.

```python
import random

random.seed(42)

for _ in range(10):
    print(random.randint(1, 10), end=", ")

print("\nThe same random numbers again:")
random.seed(42)
for _ in range(10):
    print(random.randint(1, 10), end=", ")
```

The result is:

```
2, 1, 5, 4, 4, 3, 2, 9, 2, 10,
The same random numbers again:
2, 1, 5, 4, 4, 3, 2, 9, 2, 10,
```

9.2.7 Weighted Random Selection

We can now define the `weighted_choice` function. Suppose we have three weights, namely 1/5, 1/2, and 3/10. We compute the cumulative sum of the weights with `np.cumsum(weights)`.

```python
import numpy as np

weights = [0.2, 0.5, 0.3]
cum_weights = [0] + list(np.cumsum(weights))
print(cum_weights)
```

After execution we get:

```
[0, np.float64(0.2), np.float64(0.7), np.float64(1.0)]
```

If we generate a random number x between 0 and 1 using `random.random()`, then the probability that x lies in the interval `[0, cum_weights[0])` is 1/5. The probability that x lies in the interval `[cum_weights[0], cum_weights[1])` is 1/2. Finally, the probability that x lies in the interval `[cum_weights[1], cum_weights[2])` is 3/10.

The basic idea on which `weighted_choice` is based can now be understood:

```python
from collections import Counter


def weighted_choice(sequence, weights):
    """
    weighted_choice selects a random element from
    'sequence' while taking into account the
    list or tuple of weights.
    """
    x = np.random.random()
    cum_weights = [0] + list(np.cumsum(weights))
    index = find_interval(x, cum_weights)
    return sequence[index]
```

Example: We can now use the function `weighted_choice` for the following task: Let us imagine a loaded die, such that the probabilities for rolling a 6 or a 1 are P(6)=3/12 and P(1)=1/12. The probabilities for all other possible outcomes are equal, i.e., P(2) = P(3) = P(4) = P(5) = p. We can compute p as 1 - P(1) - P(6) = 4 x p, which gives p = 1/6. How can we simulate this die with our `weighted_choice` function?

We call `weighted_choice` with the faces of the die and the list of corresponding weights. Each call corresponds to one roll of the loaded die. After 10,000 rolls we see that the estimated probabilities correspond to the weighting.

```python
faces_of_dice = [1, 2, 3, 4, 5, 6]
weights = [1/12, 1/6, 1/6, 1/6, 1/6, 3/12]

outcomes = []
n = 10000
for _ in range(n):
    outcomes.append(weighted_choice(faces_of_dice, weights))

c = Counter(outcomes)
for key in c:
    c[key] = c[key] / n

print(sorted(c.values()))
```

After execution we get:

```python
[0.0862, 0.1643, 0.1684, 0.1697, 0.17, 0.2414]
```

The values of the partition list define the intervals in which we expect the value x. If x is smaller than p_0 or greater than or equal to p_n, we return −1.

We could define our first partition as an interval from $-\infty$ to p_0 and return 0. The last partition would then be an interval from p_n to ∞. To distinguish between both cases, we extend the function find_interval with the parameter "endpoints." "True" corresponds to our initial approach. "False" corresponds to the alternative just described. In other words, if "endpoints" is False, the following applies:

- i is returned if x is smaller than p_i.

- len(partition) is returned if x is greater than or equal to $p_{len(partition)-1}$.

We demonstrate this in the following diagram:

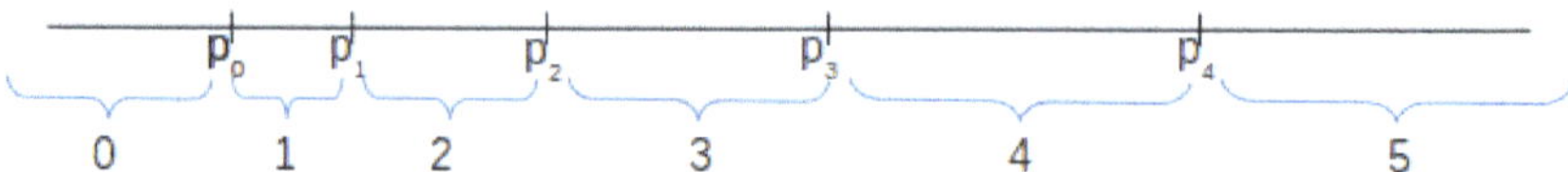

The new function looks as follows:

```python
def find_interval(x, partition, endpoints=True):
    """
    Returns the interval index for x.
    If endpoints=True: return i with partition[i-1] < x < partition[i];
        else -1.
    If endpoints=False: return i with x < partition[i]; if not found: len(
        partition).
    """

    for i in range(0, len(partition)):
        if x < partition[i]:
            return i - 1 if endpoints else i
    return -1 if endpoints else len(partition)

I = [0, 3, 5, 7.8, 9, 12, 13.8, 16]
print("Endpoints included:")
for x in [-1.3, 0, 0.1, 3.2, 5, 6.2, 7.9, 13.9, 15, 16, 16.5]:
    print(find_interval(x, I), end=", ")
print("\nEndpoints not included:")
for x in [-1.3, 0, 0.1, 3.2, 5, 6.2, 7.9, 13.9, 15, 16, 16.5]:
    print(find_interval(x, I, endpoints=False), end=", ")
```

Here is the result of the code:

```
Endpoints included:
-1, 0, 0, 1, 2, 2, 3, 6, 6, -1, -1,
Endpoints not included:
0, 1, 1, 2, 3, 3, 4, 7, 7, 8, 8,
```

9.2.8 Sampling with Python

A sample can be regarded as a representative subset of a larger group, which we call the "population."

The standard module random provides the function sample, which produces samples from a population. The population is a sequence, for example a list, set, or string.

The function sample(population, k) randomly selects k elements from the given population and returns them as a list. If the population does not contain duplicates, the result list will not contain any either.

If we want to draw a sample from a range of integer values, we can – or rather should – use range as the argument for the population. In the following example, we draw six numbers from the range between 1 and 49 (inclusive). This corresponds to a lottery draw in Germany:

```python
import random
random.seed(42)


print(random.sample(range(1, 50), 6))
```

Output:

```
[41, 8, 2, 18, 16, 15]
```

```python
def weighted_sample(population, weights, k):
    """

    weighted_sample draws a random sample of length k
    from the sequence 'population' according to the list of weights.
    """

    sample = set()
    population = list(population)
    weights = list(weights)
    while len(sample) < k:
        choice = weighted_choice(population, weights)
        sample.add(choice)
        index = population.index(choice)
        weights.pop(index)
        population.remove(choice)
        weights = [x / sum(weights) for x in weights]
    return list(sample)
```

An alternative Implementation

```python
def weighted_sample_alternative(population, weights, k):
    """
```

```
    weighted_sample draws a random sample of
    size k from the sequence 'population'
    according to the list of weights.
    """
    sample = set()
    population = list(population)
    weights = list(weights)
    while len(sample) < k:
        choice = weighted_choice(population, weights)
        if choice not in sample:
            sample.add(choice)
    return list(sample)
```

Example:

Suppose we have eight sugar cubes in the colors red, green, blue, yellow, black, white, pink, and orange. Our friend Peter has the following "weighted" preferences for the colors: 1/24, 1/6, 1/6, 1/12, 1/12, 1/24, 1/8, 7/24. Peter may choose 3 sugar cubes:

```
balls = ["red", "green", "blue", "yellow", "black",
         "white", "pink", "orange"]
weights = [1/24, 1/6, 1/6, 1/12, 1/12, 1/24, 1/8, 7/24]
for i in range(5):
    print(weighted_sample(balls, weights, 3))
```

This follows from the code:

```
['white', 'blue', 'orange']
['blue', 'green', 'pink']
['black', 'green', 'orange']
['red', 'orange', 'pink']
['blue', 'green', 'orange']
```

Next, we compare the two variants for calculating weighted samples:

```
n = 10000
orange_counter = 0
orange_counter_alternative = 0
for i in range(n):
    if "orange" in weighted_sample(balls, weights, 3):
        orange_counter += 1
    if "orange" in weighted_sample_alternative(balls, weights, 3):
        orange_counter_alternative += 1

print(orange_counter / n)
print(orange_counter_alternative / n)
```

The script returns:

```
0.7158
0.7055
```

We will see in the chapter on `numpy.random` that it is directly possible in NumPy to generate weighted samples.

9.2.9 Cartesian Choice

The function `cartesian_choice`, which we will define below, is named after the Cartesian product from set theory.[7]

9.2.10 Cartesian Product

The Cartesian product, also called set product, is a construction principle for building a new set from given sets.

For two sets A and B, the Cartesian product A x B is the set of all ordered pairs (a, b) for which a ∈ A and b ∈ B:

A x B = { (a, b) | a ∈ A and b ∈ B }

In general, the Cartesian product of several sets consists of the set of all tuples of elements of the sets, where the order of the sets, and thus of the corresponding elements, is fixed. The result of the Cartesian product is also called product set, cross set, or connection set.

If we have n sets $A_1, A_2, \ldots A_n$, we can form the Cartesian product as follows:

$$A_1 \times A_2 \times \cdots \times A_n = \{(a_1, a_2, \ldots, a_n) \mid a_1 \in A_1,\ a_2 \in A_2, \ldots,\ a_n \in A_n\}$$

The Cartesian product of n sets is sometimes also called the n-fold Cartesian product.

9.2.11 Cartesian Choice: cartesian_choice

We now write a function `cartesian_choice`, which expects an arbitrary number of iterable arguments and returns a list containing a random selection from each iterator in the corresponding order.

From a mathematical point of view, the result of the function `cartesian_choice` can be regarded as an element of the Cartesian product of the passed iterable arguments.

---

[7]   The Cartesian product is named after the French mathematician René Descartes.

```python
import random

def cartesian_choice(*iterables):
    """Creates a list whose i-th element is a random selection
    from the i-th input argument.

    The result corresponds to a random element from the
    Cartesian product of the given iterable objects."""
    return [random.choice(population) for population in iterables]


res = cartesian_choice(["The", "A"],
                       ["red", "green", "blue", "yellow", "grey"],
                       ["car", "house", "fish", "light"],
                       ["smells", "dreams", "blinks"])

print(res)
```

Script output:

```
['The', 'red', 'fish', 'smells']
```

We now define a weighted version of the previously defined function:

```python
import random

def weighted_cartesian_choice(*iterables):
    """
    Returns a list with weighted random selections,
    each from the passed (population, weight) tuples.

    The order of the input is preserved in the output.
    """
    return [weighted_choice(population, weight) for population, weight in
            iterables]


determiners = (["The", "A", "Each", "Every", "No"],
               [0.3, 0.3, 0.1, 0.1, 0.2])
colours = (["red", "green", "blue", "yellow", "grey"],
           [0.1, 0.3, 0.3, 0.2, 0.2])
nouns = (["door", "elephant", "fish", "light",
          "programming language", "Python"],
         [0.2, 0.2, 0.1, 0.1, 0.3, 0.1])
nouns2 = (["of happiness", "of chocolate", "of wisdom",
           "of challenges", "of air"],
          [0.5, 0.2, 0.1, 0.1, 0.1])
```

```python
verb_phrases = (["smells", "dreams", "thinks",
                 "is made", "consists"],
                [0.1, 0.3, 0.3, 0.2, 0.1])


print("It may or may not be true:")
for i in range(7):
    res = weighted_cartesian_choice(determiners,
                                    colours,
                                    nouns,
                                    verb_phrases,
                                    nouns2)
    print(" ".join(res) + ".")
```

The code produces the following result:

```
It may or may not be true:
The green elephant consists of happiness.
The green programming language dreams of chocolate.
A blue elephant thinks of happiness.
The green elephant thinks of happiness.
The green elephant is made of chocolate.
No green fish dreams of chocolate.
Each yellow Python thinks of air.
```

In the following version, we check whether all "probabilities" are correct:

```python
sentences = []
for i in range(10000):
    res = weighted_cartesian_choice(determiners,
                                    colours,
                                    nouns,
                                    verb_phrases,
                                    nouns2)
    sentences.append(" ".join(res) + ".")

words = ["smells", "dreams", "thinks", "is made of"]
c = Counter()
for sentence in sentences:
    for word in words:
        if word in sentence:
            c[word] += 1

wsum = sum(c.values())
for key in c:
    print(key, c[key] / wsum)
```

We obtain this output:

```
is made of 0.0948
smells 0.4025
dreams 0.3028
thinks 0.1999
```

9.2.12 Gaussian Normal Distribution

With `random.gauss` and `random.normalvariate` we have two different implementations of functions that both return normally distributed random numbers.

We now want to generate 1000 random numbers between 130 and 230 that follow a Gaussian distribution with a mean `mu = 180` and a standard deviation of `sigma = 30`.

Looking at the help information, we see that the essential difference is that `gauss` is somewhat faster but not thread-safe, while `random.normalvariate` is thread-safe.

```
import random


help(random.normalvariate)
help(random.gauss)
```

The following result is generated:

```
Help on method normalvariate in module random:

normalvariate(mu=0.0, sigma=1.0) method of random.Random instance
    Normal distribution.

    mu is the mean, and sigma is the standard deviation.

Help on method gauss in module random:

gauss(mu=0.0, sigma=1.0) method of random.Random instance
    Gaussian distribution.

    mu is the mean, and sigma is the standard deviation.  This is
    slightly faster than the normalvariate() function.

    Not thread-safe without a lock around calls.
```

We now use the `gauss` function to calculate 1000 random numbers with a mean of 180 and a standard deviation of 30:

```
from random import gauss


n = 1000
```

```python
values = []
frequencies = {}

while len(values) < n:
    value = int(gauss(180, 30))
    if 130 < value < 230:
        frequencies[value] = frequencies.get(value, 0) + 1
        values.append(value)
print(values[:7])
```

The result appears as follows:

```python
[175, 174, 176, 201, 176, 135, 189]
```

The following program plots the random values we just generated. We have not covered the module `matplotlib` yet. However, this is not strictly necessary to understand the following code:

```python
import matplotlib.pyplot as plt

freq = sorted(frequencies.items())


plt.plot(*list(zip(*freq)))
plt.savefig('../MatplotlibImages/frequencies.pdf')
```

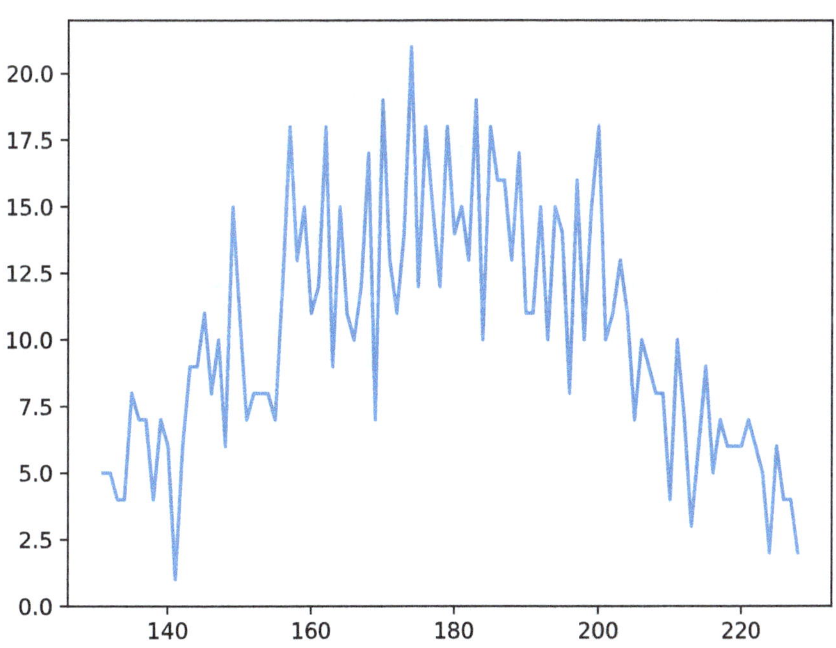

We can, of course, also carry this out with the `normalvariate` function:

```python
from random import normalvariate

n = 1000

values = []
frequencies = {}

while len(values) < n:
    value = int(normalvariate(180, 30))
    if 130 < value < 230:
        frequencies[value] = frequencies.get(value, 0) + 1
        values.append(value)

freq = sorted(frequencies.items())


plt.plot(*list(zip(*freq)))
plt.savefig('../MatplotlibImages/frequencies2.pdf')
```

9.2.13 Exercise with Binary Transmitter

It may be a good idea to implement the following function as an exercise. The function should be called with a parameter p, which contains a probability value between 0 and 1. The function should return a 1 with probability p, i.e. in p percent of cases ones are returned, and zeros in (1-p) percent of cases:

```python
import random


def random_ones_and_zeros(p):
    """ p: probability 0 <= p <= 1
        returns a 1 with the probability p
    """
    x = random.random()
    if x < p:
        return 1
    else:
        return 0
```

We now test our little function:

```python
n = 1000000
s = sum(random_ones_and_zeros(0.8) for i in range(n)) / n
print(s)
```

Script output:

```
0.800622
```

Another good idea is to implement the task with a generator.

```python
import random


def random_ones_and_zeros(p):
    while True:
        x = random.random()
        yield 1 if x < p else 0


def firstn(generator, n):
    for i in range(n):
        yield next(generator)
```

```
n = 1000000

firstn_values = firstn(random_ones_and_zeros(0.8), n)
s = sum(x for x in firstn_values) / n
print(s)
```

We obtain this output:

```
0.800479
```

Our zeros-and-ones generator can be thought of as a transmitter that emits zeros and ones with probability p, respectively (1-p).

We now write another generator that receives this bitstream. The task of this new generator is to read the bitstream and generate another bitstream of zeros and ones with probability 0.5, without knowing the probability p. It should work for any arbitrary value of p.[8]

```
def ebitter(bitstream):
    while True:
        bit1 = next(bitstream)
        bit2 = next(bitstream)
        if bit1 + bit2 == 1:
            bit3 = next(bitstream)
            if bit2 + bit3 == 1:
                yield 1
            else:
                yield 0


def ebitter2(bitstream):
    bit1 = next(bitstream)
    bit2 = next(bitstream)
    bit3 = next(bitstream)
    while True:
        if bit1 + bit2 == 1:
            if bit2 + bit3 == 1:
                yield 1
            else:
                yield 0
        bit1, bit2, bit3 = bit2, bit3, next(bitstream)
```

---

8   I would like to thank Dr. Hanno Baehr, who drew my attention to the problem of "randomness extraction."
    Hanno developed the theoretical framework. During a night session after a Python seminar in January
    2014 at the bar "Zeit & Raum" (Eng. "Time & Space") in Nuremberg, I implemented a Python program to
    empirically support his theoretical solution.

```
n = 1000000
s = sum(x for x in firstn(ebitter(random_ones_and_zeros(0.8)), n)) / n
print(s)
```

What we obtain is:

```
0.499454
```

```
n = 1000000
s = sum(x for x in firstn(ebitter2(random_ones_and_zeros(0.8)), n)) / n
print(s)
```

This output is obtained:

```
0.500214
```

Foundations of the theory:

Our first generator produces a bitstream B_0, B_1, B_2, ...

We now examine an arbitrary pair of consecutive bits B_i, B_{i+1}, ...

Such a pair can have the values 01, 10, 00, or 11. The probability p(01) = (1-p) × p and the probability p(10) = p × (1-p) gives a combined probability that the consecutive bits are either 01 or 10 of 2 × (1-p) × p.

Let us now consider another bit B_{i+2}. What is the probability of the two conditions

$B_i + B_{i+1} = 1$

and

$B_{i+1} + B_{i+2} = 1$?

The possible outputs fit the conditions, and the associated probabilities are listed in the following table:

Probability	B_i	B_{i+1}	B_{i+2}
$p^2 \times (1-p)$	0	1	0
$p \times (1-p)^2$	1	0	1

We denote the result sum(B_i, B_{i+1})=1 as X_1 and accordingly sum(B_{i+1}, B_{i+2})=1 as X_2.

The joint probability $P(X_1, X_2) = p^2 \times (1-p) + p \times (1-p)^2$ can be simplified to p × (1-p).

The conditional probability of X_2 given X_1:

$P(X_2 \mid X_1) = P(X_1, X_2) / P(X_2)$

$P(X_2 \mid X_1) = p \times (1-p) / 2 \times p \times (1-p) = 1/2$

9.3 The random Submodule of NumPy

In the previous subsections we used the standard module "random". We now turn
to "numpy.random", which is specifically optimized for numerical computations with
NumPy arrays. It therefore provides functions for generating random numbers that
are designed for NumPy arrays. "numpy.random" is in most cases faster and more
powerful than the standard module "random".

9.3.1 Randomly generating integers and floats

The `randint` method from `numpy.random` can be used to generate both individual
random integers as well as whole arrays of them.

The formal definition:

`numpy.random.randint(low, high=None, size=None)`

This function returns random integers between "low" (inclusive) and "high" (exclusive). In other words: `randint` returns random integers from the discrete uniform
distribution in the "half-open" interval [low, high). If `high` is None or not provided,
the results are in the range [0, low). In other words, `low` then denotes the upper bound.
The parameter `size` defines the shape of the result. If `size` is None or not provided,
the function generates a single integer. Otherwise, the result is an array. `size` should
be a tuple. If an integer n is passed as `size`, this corresponds to the tuple (n,).

The following examples illustrate the behavior of the parameters:

```python
import numpy as np

print("An integer between 1 (incl.) and 7 (excl.):",
      np.random.randint(1, 7))
print("\nA one-dimensional array with one element:\n",
      np.random.randint(1, 7, size=1))
print("\nA one-dimensional array with ten elements:\n",
      np.random.randint(1, 7, size=10))
print("\nAs above, but alternative size definition:\n",
      np.random.randint(1, 7, size=(10,)))
print("\nTwo-dimensional array:\n",
      np.random.randint(1, 7, size=(5, 4)))
```

The output we get is:

```
An integer between 1 (incl.) and 7 (excl.): 2

A one-dimensional array with one element:
 [1]

A one-dimensional array with ten elements:
 [6 4 3 3 4 3 2 6 3]
```

```
As above, but alternative size definition:
 [3 3 1 1 5 2 5 4 2 2]

Two-dimensional array:
 [[5 1 6 5]
 [5 2 2 3]
 [3 2 1 2]
 [1 3 5 2]
 [6 5 3 1]]
```

We can simulate rolling a die with the code `np.random.randint(1, 7, size=1)` from the NumPy module. We assume that our die is fair, i.e. the probability for each side is 1/6. We simulate multiple dice rolls (`number_of_rolls`) with the following program:

```python
import numpy as np
from collections import Counter

number_of_rolls = 100000
outcome = np.random.randint(1, 7, size=number_of_rolls)

c = Counter(outcome)
for die_face in c:
    print(f"Dice face: {die_face}, \
        relative frequency: {c[die_face]/number_of_rolls:7.5f}")
```

After execution we get:

```
Dice face: 1,          relative frequency: 0.16527
Dice face: 2,          relative frequency: 0.16564
Dice face: 3,          relative frequency: 0.16680
Dice face: 5,          relative frequency: 0.16969
Dice face: 6,          relative frequency: 0.16526
Dice face: 4,          relative frequency: 0.16734
```

We can also determine the number of rolls per face with the NumPy function bincount:

```python
import numpy as np

number_of_rolls = 100000
outcome = np.random.randint(1, 7, size=number_of_rolls)
frequencies = np.bincount(outcome)[1:]
print(f'Frequencies per dice face:\n{frequencies}')
```

The output shows:

```
Frequencies per dice face:
[16608 16690 16621 16644 16768 16669]
```

Analogous to `randint`, we can use `rand` to generate random float numbers between 0 (inclusive) and 1 (exclusive):

```python
import numpy as np

# A random number between 0 (inclusive) and 1 (exclusive):
x = np.random.rand()
print(f'{x=}')

# One-dimensional array with 4 random numbers from [0, 1):
a = np.random.rand(4)
print(f'{a=}')

# 2-dim. array with 3 rows and 4 columns
b = np.random.rand(3, 4)
print(f'{b=}')
```

After execution we get:

```
x=0.7808730730389412
a=array([0.245, 0.599, 0.684, 0.598])
b=array([[0.122, 0.405, 0.877, 0.047],
        [0.616, 0.244, 0.147, 0.363],
        [0.325, 0.715, 0.425, 0.107]])
```

9.3.2 numpy.random.choice

The function `numpy.random.choice()` works similarly to `random.choice()` from the "random" module, but is specialized for NumPy arrays. The function allows selecting random elements from a NumPy array or a list of elements.

The function has several parameters, including the array or list of elements from which a random element should be chosen, as well as the sample size, i.e. how many elements should be selected. We demonstrate its behavior with the following examples:

Generate a uniform random sample of size 3 from `np.arange(5)`:

```python
x = np.random.choice(5, 3)
print(x)

# equivalent to:
y = np.random.randint(0, 5, 3)
print(y)
```

The execution leads to this output:

```
[0 2 0]
[0 3 0]
```

In the previous example the probability was uniform, i.e. each number had the same chance of being drawn. One can also provide the keyword parameter p with a sequence of probability values and thus define an individual distribution. In the following example we simulate a loaded die. With the for loop we simulate 10 rolls:

```python
import numpy as np

for i in range(10):
    x = np.random.choice(range(1, 7),
                         1,
                         p=[0.1, 0.1, 0.1, 0.1, 0.1, 0.5])
    print(x, end=',')
```

This output is obtained:

```
[6],[6],[6],[6],[5],[6],[1],[1],[3],[6],
```

Now we generate a random sample without replacement, which we achieve by setting the keyword parameter replace to False:

```python
for i in range(4):
    x = np.random.choice(range(5), 4, replace=False)
    print(x)
```

The script returns:

```
[0 4 2 3]
[2 1 4 3]
[3 1 0 4]
[1 2 0 4]
```

For comparison, once again with True, which is the default value:

```python
for i in range(4):
    x = np.random.choice(range(5), 4, replace=True)
    print(x)
```

Executing the code yields:

```
[4 2 1 2]
[0 3 0 4]
[3 4 4 0]
[4 0 2 1]
```

Each of the above examples can be repeated with any array-like object instead of integers. In the following example we have a group of people spending, say, a long weekend in a ski hut. Now the task is to use Python to select two volunteers who will do the evening dishes:

Guido, who loves Python as much as he hates washing dishes, manipulates the algorithm by using the parameter p. Since he knows that Eddie likes to wash dishes, he increases Eddie's probability to 0.4. One must ensure here that the probabilities sum to 1!

```python
people = ['Silke', 'Swen', 'Eddie', 'Guido', 'Sarah', 'Maria']
volunteers = np.random.choice(people,
                              2,
                              replace=False,
                              p=(0.15, 0.15, 0.4, 0, 0.15, 0.15))
print("The chosen ones are: ", volunteers)
```

Result:

```
The chosen ones are:  ['Sarah' 'Silke']
```

9.3.3 numpy.random.random_sample

The module numpy.random contains the function random_sample, which returns random float values in the half-open interval [0.0, 1.0). The results are uniformly distributed over the given interval. The function expects only one parameter size, which defines the shape of the output. If we specify size, for example, as (3, 4), we obtain an array with the shape (3, 4), filled with random values:

```python
import numpy as np

x = np.random.random_sample((3, 4))
print(x)
```

This is the result of the code:

```
[[0.375 0.951 0.732 0.599]
 [0.156 0.156 0.058 0.866]
 [0.601 0.708 0.021 0.97 ]]
```

If random_sample is called with an integer value, we obtain a one-dimensional array. An integer value has the same effect as a simple tuple as argument:

```python
x = np.random.random_sample(7)
print(x)

y = np.random.random_sample((7,))
print(y)
```

This output is obtained:

```
[0.375 0.951 0.732 0.599 0.156 0.156 0.058]
[0.866 0.601 0.708 0.021 0.97  0.832 0.212]
```

It is also possible to generate arrays from an arbitrary interval [a, b), where a must be smaller than b. This can be done as follows:

```
(b - a) * random_sample() + a
```

Example:

```
a = -3.4
b = 2

A = (b - a) * np.random.random_sample((3, 4)) + a

print(A)
```

The result of the code is:

```
[[-1.377  1.734  0.553 -0.167]
 [-2.557 -2.558 -3.086  1.277]
 [-0.154  0.424 -3.289  1.838]]
```

9.4 Synthetic Sales Figures

In this subsection we present an example of how numpy.random can be used to generate synthetic data. For this purpose, we create a file with sales figures of a fictitious chain of stores in various European cities.

We begin with an array sales containing sales figures for the year 2001:

```
import numpy as np

sales = np.array([1245.89, 2220.00, 1635.77, 1936.25, 1002.03,
                  2099.13, 723.99, 990.37, 541.44, 1765.00,
                  1802.84, 1999.00])
```

The goal is to create a comma-separated list as we know it from Excel. The file should contain fictitious sales figures for our non-existent stores for the years 2001 through 2021. We add random values to the sales figures for each year. For this we construct an array of growth rates. The growth rates can vary between a minimum percentage value (min_percent) and a maximum percentage value (max_percent):

```
import numpy as np
```

```python
min_percent = 0.98  # corresponds to 98 %
max_percent = 1.06  # corresponds to 106 %

sample = np.random.random_sample(12)
print(sample)
growthrates = (max_percent - min_percent) * sample + min_percent
print(growthrates)
```

The script returns:

```
[0.832 0.212 0.182 0.183 0.304 0.525 0.432 0.291 0.612 0.139
 0.292 0.366]
[1.047 0.997 0.995 0.995 1.004 1.022 1.015 1.003 1.029 0.991
 1.003 1.009]
```

For the new sales figures after one year we multiply the sales array by the growthrates array:

```python
print(sales * growthrates)
```

This output is obtained:

```
[1303.943 2213.311 1626.849 1925.934 1006.378 2145.27   734.528
  993.637  557.114 1749.397 1808.918 2017.609]
```

To obtain sustainable sales development, we change the growth rates every 4 years. Here is our complete program, which stores the data in the file sales_figures.csv:

```python
import numpy as np

cities = ["Frankfurt", "Munich", "Berlin", "Zurich", "Hamburg",
          "London", "Paris", "Luxembourg", "Vienna", "Amsterdam",
          "Rotterdam", "The Hague"]

with open("sales_figures.csv", "w", encoding="utf-8") as fh:
    fh.write("Year," + ",".join(cities) + "\n")
    sales = np.array([
        1245.89, 2220.00, 1635.77, 1936.25, 1002.03, 2099.13,
        723.99, 990.37, 541.44, 1765.00, 1802.84, 1999.00])

    # Creates an array of 1.0 values with the same shape as sales
    # means no growth until overwritten
    growthrates = np.ones_like(sales)

    for year in range(2001, 2022):
        fh.write(str(year) + "," + ",".join(map(str, sales)) + "\n")
```

```python
    # Update growth rates every 4th year
    if year % 4 == 0:
        min_percent = 0.98
        max_percent = 1.06
        sample = np.random.random_sample(len(sales))
        growthrates = (max_percent - min_percent) * sample +
            min_percent

    sales = np.around(sales * growthrates, 2)
```

The result can be found in the file `sales_figures.csv`.

We will use this data again in a later chapter (Reading and Writing in NumPy).

9.5 Exercises

Exercise 1

(Solution: 33.5, Solution 1)

We begin with a small dice task. Prove empirically – by writing a simulation program – that the probability for the combined event "Whatever number was rolled" and "A number greater than 2 was rolled" is 1/3.

Exercise 2

(Solution: 33.5, Solution 2)

The file "universities_uk.txt"[9] contains a list of universities in the United Kingdom by enrollment between 2013–2014. (Source: Wikipedia):

```
Rank  Institution  Undergraduates  Postgraduates  Total students
1   Open University in England  112,535  10,955  123,490
2   University of Manchester  26,485  11,440  37,925
3   University of Nottingham  24,885  8,385  33,270
4   Sheffield Hallam University  25,985  7,115  33,100
5   University of Birmingham  19,185  13,150  32,335
6   Manchester Metropolitan University  26,635  5,525  32,160
7   University of Leeds  23,265  7,710  30,975
8   Cardiff University  21,495  8,685  30,180
9   University of South Wales  23,890  5,310  29,195
10  University College London  15,415  13,015  28,430
...
```

Write a function that returns a tuple '(universities, enrollments, total_students)' with:

- `universities`: list of university names

---

9   Available for download at: *http://www.python-kurs.eu/buecher/numerical_python*

- enrollments: corresponding list with enrollment numbers per university
- total_students: sum of students across all universities

Now simulate the enrollment of 100,000 fictitious students with probabilities corresponding to the "real" enrollments.

Exercise 3

(Solution: 33.5, Solution 3)

Figure 9.2 Pythonia

In this task we want to go on a time travel. We return to ancient Pythonia (Πηθωνια). It was the time when King Pysseus ruled as a benevolent dictator. The time when Pysseus sent his envoys out into the world to proclaim that it was time for his princes Anacondos (Ανακονδος), Cobrion (Κομπριον), Boatos (Μποατος) and Addokles (Ανδοκλης) to marry. To find suitable candidates, Pysseus organized a programming competition – between those fair and brave Amazons known throughout the realm as the Pythanians of Pythonia. Eleven Amazons succeeded in this programming competition, probably also because they used the then still young programming language Python:

1. The ethereal Airla (Αιρλα)
2. Barbara (Βαρβαρα), the one from the foreign land
3. Eos (Ηως), divine to behold in the dawn
4. The sweet Glykeria (Γλυκερια)
5. The graceful Hanna (Αννα)
6. Helen (Ελενη), the light in the darkness
7. The good angel Agathangelos (Αγαθαγγελος)
8. The violet-tinged cloud Iokaste (Ιοκαστη)
9. Medousa (Μεδουσα), the guardian
10. The self-determined Sofronia (Σωφρονια)
11. Andromeda (Ανδρομεδα), the one who thinks like a man or a warrior

The lot was to decide which four would become princesses. At first all had the same chance of being chosen. For reasons no longer known today, however, Pysseus knew that the probabilities changed with each passing day: With each new day the probability of each of the first seven Amazons being chosen decreased by 1/13, while for each of the last four Amazons it increased by 1/12. Because the last four Amazons perfectly matched the king's taste, Pysseus postponed the lottery for a few more days.

How long did the king have to wait until he could be 90 % sure that his princes Anacondas, Cobrion, Boatos and Addokles would marry the Amazons Iokaste, Medousa, Sofronia and Andromeda?

10
Boolean Masking and Indexing

In this chapter we deal with Boolean masking and so-called Boolean masks. We show how values in NumPy arrays can be modified with them. Masking is helpful for extracting, modifying, counting, or binarizing data with certain properties – for example, setting all values above a threshold to a fixed value, and all values below to another. Masks are not only easy to use but also usually highly efficient.

In the first example, we compare all elements of array A with a number. The result is an array of the same shape, in which True appears wherever the original contained a 4, otherwise False.

Figure 10.1 Masked Matrix

```python
import numpy as np
A = np.array([4, 7, 3, 4, 2, 8])
print(A == 4)
```

We obtain the following result: [True False False True False False]

Analogously, one can also process the individual components with the comparison operators "<", "<=", ">", and ">=". The working principle is the same as in the previous case:

```python
print(A < 5)
```

The evaluation yields:

```
[ True False  True  True  True False]
```

This can also be applied to higher-dimensional arrays:

```python
B = np.array([[42, 56, 89, 65],
              [99, 88, 42, 12],
              [55, 42, 17, 18]])


print(B >= 42)
```

Script output:

```
[[ True  True  True  True]
 [ True  True  True False]
 [ True  True False False]]
```

In this way, arrays can also be binarized. If we regard the following array A as a grayscale image, we can binarize it using the threshold 15:

```python
import numpy as np


A = np.array([[12, 13, 14, 12, 16, 14, 11, 10,  9],
              [11, 14, 12, 15, 15, 16, 10, 12, 11],
              [10, 12, 12, 15, 14, 16, 10, 12, 12],
              [ 9, 11, 16, 15, 14, 16, 15, 12, 10],
              [12, 11, 16, 14, 10, 12, 16, 12, 13],
              [10, 15, 16, 14, 14, 14, 16, 15, 12],
              [13, 17, 14, 10, 14, 11, 14, 15, 10],
              [10, 16, 12, 14, 11, 12, 14, 18, 11],
              [10, 19, 12, 14, 11, 12, 14, 18, 10],
              [14, 22, 17, 19, 16, 17, 18, 17, 13],
              [10, 16, 12, 14, 11, 12, 14, 18, 11],
              [10, 16, 12, 14, 11, 12, 14, 18, 11],
              [10, 19, 12, 14, 11, 12, 14, 18, 10],
              [14, 22, 12, 14, 11, 12, 14, 17, 13],
              [10, 16, 12, 14, 11, 12, 14, 18, 11]])

B = A < 15
print(B.astype(np.int8))
```

The output shows:

```
[[1 1 1 1 0 1 1 1 1]
 [1 1 1 0 0 0 1 1 1]
 [1 1 1 0 1 0 1 1 1]
 [1 1 0 0 1 0 0 1 1]
 [1 1 0 1 1 1 0 1 1]
 [1 0 0 1 1 1 0 0 1]
 [1 0 1 1 1 1 1 0 1]
```

```
[1 0 1 1 1 1 1 0 1]
[1 0 1 1 1 1 1 0 1]
[1 0 0 0 0 0 0 0 1]
[1 0 1 1 1 1 1 0 1]
[1 0 1 1 1 1 1 0 1]
[1 0 1 1 1 1 1 0 1]
[1 0 1 1 1 1 1 0 1]
[1 0 1 1 1 1 1 0 1]]
```

All values of the original array A have been replaced by 0 or 1. If you look at the image with slightly blurred vision, you can recognize a large A.

10.1 Fancy Indexing

The principle of "fancy indexing" is quite simple: instead of a single index, you use an array of indices. In this way, you can address several elements at once.

```python
A = np.array([34, 8, 99, 12, 1, 102, 44])
# cumbersome:
B = np.array([A[1], A[3], A[5]])
print(B)
# elegant with fancy indexing:
B2 = A[[1, 3, 5]]
print(B2)
```

The evaluation yields:

```
[  8  12 102]
[  8  12 102]
```

Now we use the Boolean mask of one array to select the corresponding elements of another array, concretely, we index array C with a mask that we create by masking array A. We obtain a copy, not a view. Array R contains all the elements from C for which in array A the test A <= 5 returns True.

```python
A = np.array([4, 7, 2, 8, 6, 9, 5])
C = np.array([123, 188, 190, 99, 77, 88, 100])
print(A <= 5)
R = C[A <= 5]
print(R)
```

Output:

```
[ True False  True False False False  True]
[123 190 100]
```

10.2 Indexing with an Integer Array

Indexing can also be done, for example, with an integer array or an integer list. We do
the latter in the next example:

```python
C = np.array([123, 188, 190, 99, 77, 88, 100])
lst = [0, 2, 3, 1, 4, 1]
print(C[lst])
```

Here is the result of the code:

```
[123 190  99 188  77 188]
```

As we can see, indices may occur multiple times and in any order!

10.3 nonzero and where

The method `nonzero` returns the indices of those elements in an array that are not zero
(non-zero). The indices are returned as a tuple of one-dimensional arrays, one for each
dimension. The corresponding non-zero values of an array A can then be obtained via
Boolean indexing:

`A[numpy.nonzero(A)]`

```python
import numpy as np

A = np.array([[0, 2, 3, 0, 1],
              [1, 0, 0, 7, 0],
              [5, 0, 0, 1, 0]])

print(A.nonzero())
print(A[A.nonzero()])
```

The output we get is:

```
(array([0, 0, 0, 1, 1, 2, 2]), array([1, 2, 4, 0, 3, 0, 3]))
[2 3 1 1 7 5 1]
```

If you want the elements as pairs of rows and columns, you can use `transpose`:

`transpose(nonzero(A))`

This produces a two-dimensional array. Each row corresponds to the indices of a non-
zero element in the form `[row, column]`.

```python
print(np.transpose(A.nonzero()))
```

Here is the result of the code:

```
[[0 1]
 [0 2]
 [0 4]
 [1 0]
 [1 3]
 [2 0]
 [2 3]]
```

The function nonzero can also be used to obtain the indices from an array where the condition is True. In the following script we create the Boolean array B >= 42:

```
B = np.array([[42, 56, 89, 65],
              [99, 88, 42, 12],
              [55, 42, 17, 18]])


print(B >= 42)
```

Executing the code yields:

```
[[ True  True  True  True]
 [ True  True  True False]
 [ True  True False False]]
```

np.nonzero(B >= 42) produces the indices from B for which the condition holds.

```
B = np.array([[42, 56, 89, 65],
              [99, 88, 42, 12],
              [55, 42, 17, 18]])


print(np.nonzero(B >= 42))
```

The result appears as follows:

```
(array([0, 0, 0, 0, 1, 1, 1, 2, 2]), array([0, 1, 2, 3, 0, 1, 2, 0, 1]))
```

10.4 Example Applications with np.where

The function np.where is first introduced with simple array examples, but it is equally suitable for practical applications – for example, for the targeted overlay of images with watermarks. An illustrative example of this follows in Section 31.9 (Chapter 31). At this point we omit it, since the fundamentals of matplotlib and central aspects of image processing must be covered first.

An interesting intermediate application is the *clipping* of temperature values with
np.where: A temperature sensor provides measurements in degrees Celsius; due to
outliers or measurement errors implausible values may occur – for example below
35 °C or above 42 °C. These should automatically be restricted ("clipped") to a realistic
range. Although clipping can be implemented using np.where, NumPy provides the
specialized function np.clip, which is faster and clearer.

```python
import numpy as np
import matplotlib.pyplot as plt

temps = np.array([36.5, 34.0, 37.8, 45.2, 33.9, 39.0, 42.5])
clipped = np.clip(temps, 35, 42)
print(clipped)
```

The script returns:

```
[36.5 35.  37.8 42.  35.  39.  42. ]
```

For illustration, the following diagram is used:

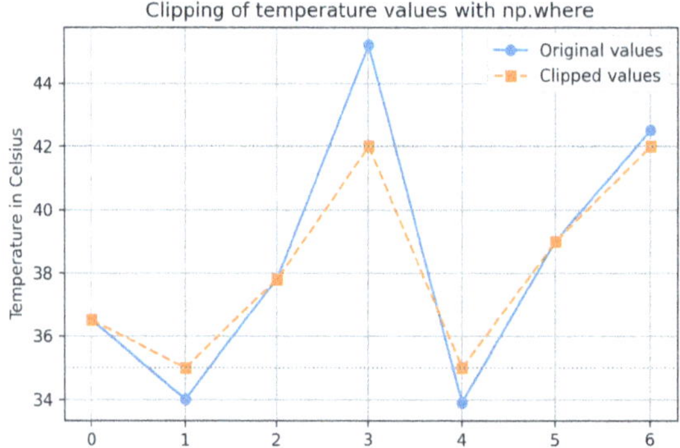

Figure 10.2 Clipped temperature profile: values outside the range [35, 42] were replaced.

Example: Categorization of Point Scores into Grades

The function np.where is also suitable for classification or recoding of data – for example, for converting point scores into school grades. In this example, numerical point
values from an exam are translated into verbal grade levels:

```python
import numpy as np

punkte = np.array([91, 78, 65, 42, 88, 59, 73, 96])
```

```
noten = np.where(punkte >= 90, "Very good",
        np.where(punkte >= 75, "Good",
        np.where(punkte >= 60, "Satisfactory", "Fail")))
```

```
print(noten)
```

The result is:

```
['Very good' 'Good' 'Satisfactory' 'Fail' 'Good' 'Fail' 'Satisfactory'
 'Very good']
```

The following diagram shows the point scores, color-coded by grade:

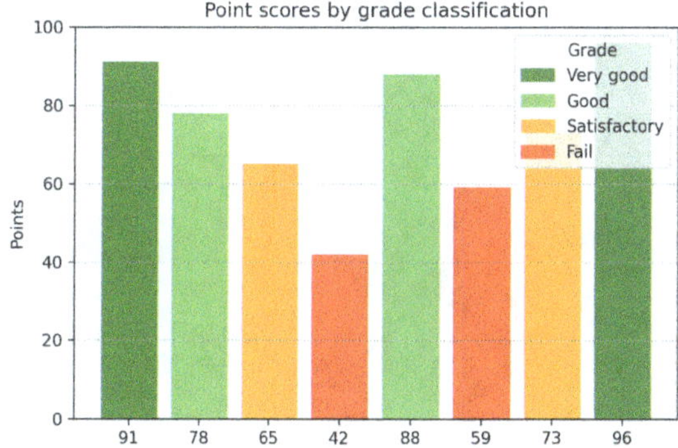

Figure 10.3 Point scores from an exam, color-coded by grade levels.

10.5 Exercises

1. Exercise

(Solution: 33.6, Solution 1)

Extract from the array `np.array([3, 4, 6, 10, 24, 89, 45, 43, 46, 99, 100])`, using Boolean indexing, the values that:

- are not divisible by 3
- are divisible by 5
- are divisible by both 3 and 5
- are divisible by 3, and set these to 42

2. Exercise

(Solution: 33.6, Solution 2)

Compute the prime numbers between 0 and 100 using a Boolean array.

3. Exercise

(Solution: 33.6, Solution 3)

A sensor provides temperature values in degrees Celsius – including outliers. All values outside the range [−50 °C, 60 °C] should be replaced by `np.nan`.

- Create an arbitrary array with example values.
- Use `np.where` to replace all values < −50 or > 60 with `np.nan`.
- Print the result.

Tip: use a logical OR connection with `|`.

11
Reading and Writing Data Files

The powerful data structures and extensive functionality of NumPy for data analysis and scientific computing would be of limited use if there were no way to read data from files and write it back to files.

Of course, file processing can also be handled entirely with Python's built-in tools, but this is often impractical and inefficient for NumPy applications. A detailed

Figure 11.1 The Art of Reading and Writing

treatment of Python's basic file input/output lies outside the scope of this chapter and is not especially relevant for the specialized data structures we are focusing on here.

Instead, NumPy provides optimized methods tailored to its array-based architecture, allowing entire arrays to be read or written with a single command. Supported formats include CSV, text files, and binary data. In Chapter 6 (Data Type Object: dtype) we introduced central functions such as `genfromtxt`, `loadtxt`, and `savetxt`. In this chapter, we examine these functions in more detail, along with additional tools for file handling in NumPy.

As illustrated by monks reading and writing in a medieval library (Figure 11.1), the capture and interpretation of data has long been central to intellectual work. Although the tools have changed fundamentally, the need for structured storage and access to information remains.

11.1 Saving text files with savetxt

The first two functions we want to look at are `savetxt` and `loadtxt`.

We define an array x and save it to a text file with `savetxt`.

```python
import numpy as np


x = np.array([[1, 2],
              [3, 4],
              [5, 6]], np.int32)


np.savetxt("test.txt", x)
```

Viewed from the terminal, `test.txt` contains:

```
$ more test.txt

1.000000000000000000e+00  2.000000000000000000e+00
3.000000000000000000e+00  4.000000000000000000e+00
5.000000000000000000e+00  6.000000000000000000e+00
```

Although the array contains integers, `np.savetxt()` writes floating-point values by
default. The output format can be controlled via `fmt`. Below, the array is saved to
`test2.txt` with three decimal places and to `test3.txt` as zero-padded four-digit integers. The field separator can be set with `delimiter`. Although multi-character
delimiters are supported, they are discouraged because many tools – including
`np.loadtxt()` – expect single-character separators. Using a single uncommon charac-
ter (e.g. | or \t) is preferable.

```python
np.savetxt("test2.txt", x, fmt="%2.3f", delimiter=",")
np.savetxt("test3.txt", x, fmt="%04d", delimiter="|")
```

The newly created files look as follows:

```
$ more test2.txt

1.000,2.000
3.000,4.000
5.000,6.000

$ more test3.txt

0001|0002
0003|0004
0005|0006
```

The complete syntax of `savetxt` looks like this:

```
savetxt(fname,
        X,
        fmt='%.18e',
        delimiter=' ',
        newline='\n',
        header='',
        footer='',
        comments='# ')
```

Parameter	Meaning
X	Array-like data to be saved into a text file.
fmt	String or sequence of strings, optional. A single format string (%10.5f), a sequence of string formats, or a multi-format string, e.g. 'Iteration %d – %10.5f', in which case the "delimiter" is ignored. For complex "X" the following options are allowed for "fmt": a) A single format specification, "fmt='%.4e'", produces a number formatting like "' (%s+%sj)' % (fmt, fmt)". b) A full specification string, covering all real and imaginary parts, e.g. "' %.4e %+.4j %.4e %+.4j %.4e %+.4j'" for 3 columns. c) A list of specifications, one per column – in this case the real and imaginary parts must have separate specifiers, i.e. "['%.3e + %.3ej', '(%.15e%+.15ej)']" for 2 columns.
delimiter	A string used to separate columns.
newline	A string that terminates a line instead of the standard line ending.
header	A string written at the beginning of the file.
footer	A string written at the end of the file.
comments	A string prepended to "header" and "footer" to mark them as comments. The default is the hash symbol "#".

11.2 Loading text files with loadtxt

11.2.1 loadtxt without parameters

Now we will read in the file "test.txt" that we created in the previous subsection:

```
y = np.loadtxt("test.txt")
print(y)
```

The result follows:

```
[[1. 2.]
 [3. 4.]
 [5. 6.]]
```

11.2.2 Custom delimiters

The delimiter of the file can be specified again via the parameter `delimiter`:

```python
y = np.loadtxt("test2.txt", delimiter=",")
print(y)
```

Reading the file with a vertical bar as separator also yields no surprises:

```python
y = np.loadtxt("test3.txt", delimiter="|")
print(y)
```

The output we get is:

```
[[1. 2.]
 [3. 4.]
 [5. 6.]]
```

11.2.3 Selective column reading

Often, only specific columns of a file are needed. For this, you pass a tuple of column indices to the `usecols` parameter; indexing starts at 0. To illustrate `usecols`, we first create and save an array with ten columns:

```python
Z = np.random.randint(-10, 10, size=(4, 10))
print(Z)
np.savetxt("test5.txt", Z, fmt="%1d", delimiter=" ")
```

This follows from the code:

```
[[ -6  -8   1  -3  -8 -10  -8  -6   4   3]
 [ -8 -10  -6   3  -4  -2   4   4  -1   2]
 [  8  -4   6   9  -7  -6  -4   2   4   0]
 [ -7   2  -4   8  -9  -1   2  -5   1   1]]

y = np.loadtxt("test5.txt",
               delimiter=" ",
               usecols=(0, 1, 6))
print(y)
```

The corresponding output can be seen here:

```
[[ -6.  -8.  -8.]
 [ -8. -10.   4.]
 [  8.  -4.  -4.]
 [ -7.   2.   2.]]
```

11.2.4 Data conversion during import

Quite often the data in a file needs to be converted. For example, a file may contain values in Fahrenheit, but we want them in Celsius. If you simply read in the data as we did earlier, you would need a post-processing step to convert to Celsius. A more efficient way is to specify directly during loading which functions should be applied to which columns. This is done with the keyword parameter `converters`, which expects a dictionary: the keys are integer column indices, the values are functions to be applied to that column. We demonstrate this with the file `temperatures.txt`:

```
Chicago New York Boston Dallas
74.3 69.7 76.1 77.5
80.2 73.8 82.4 84.2
86.3 79.4 89.2 90.2
```

The first line contains column descriptions. We must skip this line while reading. For this, we set the parameter `skiprows` to 1.

```python
def fahrenheit2celsius(t):
    return (float(t) - 32) * 5 / 9


converters_dict = {0: fahrenheit2celsius,
                   1: fahrenheit2celsius,
                   2: fahrenheit2celsius,
                   3: fahrenheit2celsius}
# Alternatively:
# converters_dict = dict(zip(range(4), [fahrenheit2celsius]*4)
y = np.loadtxt("temperatures.txt",
               delimiter=" ",
               skiprows=1,
               converters=converters_dict)

print(y)
```

The result appears as follows:

```
[[23.5   20.944 24.5   25.278]
 [26.778 23.222 28.    29.   ]
 [30.167 26.333 31.778 32.333]]
```

In the next example, we want to read in the file "times_and_temperatures.txt". Each line contains a time stamp in the format hh::mm::ss and a random temperature between 10.0 and 25.0 °C. We need to convert the time string into a float. The time is given in hours, minutes, and seconds. We define a function that converts hh::mm::ss into minutes:

```python
def time2float_minutes(time):
    if isinstance(time, bytes):
        time = time.decode()
    t = time.split(":")
    minutes = float(t[0])*60 + float(t[1]) + float(t[2])*0.05/3
    return minutes

for t in ["06:00:10", "06:27:45"]:
    print(time2float_minutes(t))
```

The evaluation yields:

```
360.1666666666667
387.75
```

You may have noticed that we checked whether the time value is a binary type. The reason is that our function time2float_minutes will be used inside loadtxt in the next example. The keyword parameter converters holds a dictionary that assigns a function to each column index. This function converts the string data of that column into floats. The string data is passed as byte strings, which is why we need to decode the parameter to a Unicode string in our function:

```python
y = np.loadtxt("times_and_temperatures.txt",
               converters={0: time2float_minutes})
print(y)
pass
```

Here is the output:

```
[[ 360.     20.1]
 [ 361.5   16.1]
 [ 363.    16.9]
 ...
 [1375.5   22.5]
 [1377.    11.1]
 [1378.5   15.2]]
```

11.3 tofile

tofile is a function that allows writing the contents of an array to a file, either in binary format or in text format.

```
A.tofile(fid, sep=' ', format='%s')
```

The data from ndarray A is now written in "C" order, regardless of A's original memory layout. The file written with this method can be loaded again with fromfile().

Parameter	Meaning
fid	Open file object or filename as string.
sep	The string "sep" specifies the separator between elements. An empty string produces a binary file (equivalent to file.write(a.tostring())).
format	Format string for text output. Each entry in the array is formatted by first converting it to the next Python type and then applying "format".

Note: Information about byte order and precision is lost. Therefore, it is not a good idea to use this function for archiving data or transporting it between machines with different byte orders. Some of these issues can be worked around, but outputting the data as a text file comes at the cost of speed and file size.

```python
dt = np.dtype([('time', [('min', int), ('sec', int)]),
               ('temp', float)])


x = np.zeros((1,), dtype=dt)
x['time']['min'] = 10
x['temp'] = 98.25
print(x)


with open("test6.txt", "bw") as fh:
    x.tofile(fh)
```

This output is obtained:

```
[((10, 0), 98.25)]
```

11.4 fromfile

fromfile reads data that has been written with tofile. It is possible to read binary data if the data type is known. It is also possible to parse simply formatted text files. The data from the file is returned as an array.

The general syntax looks as follows:

```
numpy.fromfile(file, dtype=float, count=-1, sep='')
```

Parameter	Meaning
file	'file' can either be an open file object or a string with a filename to be read.
dtype	defines the data type of the array to be constructed from the data file. For binary files, it determines the size and byte order of the file elements.
count	defines the number of elements to be read. -1 means that all are read.
sep	The string "sep" specifies the separator to be used if the file is a text file. If the string is empty (''), the file is treated as a binary file. A space (' ') in a separator stands for 0 or more spaces. A separator consisting only of spaces must consist of at least one space.

```python
with open("test4.txt", "rb") as fh:
    print(np.fromfile(fh, dtype=dt))
```

Script output:

```
[((  4294967296,  12884901890), 1.061e-313)
 (( 30064771078,  38654705672), 2.334e-313)
 (( 55834574860,  64424509454), 3.607e-313)
 (( 81604378642,  90194313236), 4.881e-313)
 ((107374182424, 115964117018), 6.154e-313)
 ((133143986206, 141733920800), 7.427e-313)
 ((158913789988, 167503724582), 8.700e-313)
 ((184683593770, 193273528364), 9.973e-313)]
```

```python
import numpy as np
import os

data = np.arange(50, dtype=np.int32)
data.tofile("test4.txt")

fh = open("test4.txt", "rb")
# 4 * 32 = 128
fh.seek(128, os.SEEK_SET)

x = np.fromfile(fh, dtype=np.int32)

print(x)
```

Result:

```
[32 33 34 35 36 37 38 39 40 41 42 43 44 45 46 47 48 49]
```

Caution: Problems can occur if `tofile` and `fromfile` are used for storage, because binary files are not platform independent. `tofile` does not store information about byte order or data types. Data can be stored in a platform-independent way using the .npy format, if you use `save` and `load` instead.

11.5 Recommended methods

The recommended way to efficiently store and load NumPy arrays within Python applications is to use `save` and `load`. These functions store data in a binary format that preserves the structure and metadata of the array. In the following example, we use a temporary file.[1] .

```python
from tempfile import TemporaryFile
import numpy as np

outfile = TemporaryFile()

x1 = np.arange(10)
print(f'{x1=}')
np.save(outfile, x1)

# jump back to the beginning of the file:
outfile.seek(0)
x2 = np.load(outfile)
print(f'{x2=}')
```

Executing the code yields:

```
x1=array([0, 1, 2, 3, 4, 5, 6, 7, 8, 9])
x2=array([0, 1, 2, 3, 4, 5, 6, 7, 8, 9])
```

11.6 Another option: `genfromtxt`

Another way to read tabular data from a file and create NumPy arrays is the function `genfromtxt`. As the name suggests, the input file should be a text-based file. This function can also read compressed archives – specifically formats like `.gz` (gzip) and `.bz2` (bzip2). The archive type is automatically recognized based on the file extension.

`genfromtxt` is more flexible than `loadtxt`, but also a bit slower. A key advantage is its ability to handle missing values gracefully. Internally, `genfromtxt` works in two phases: first, the lines are read as strings, then the conversion to the target data structure takes place. `loadtxt`, on the other hand, performs this conversion in a single step, making it faster but less fault-tolerant. Use `loadtxt` when data is clean; use `genfromtxt` when missing values or irregular formats are expected.

---

1   The `tempfile` module in Python provides functions to create temporary files and directories. One such function is `TemporaryFile`, which creates temporary files. These files are either created in memory (RAM) or on disk, depending on the options specified at creation. The file exists only for the duration of the program run and is automatically deleted when no longer needed or when the program ends.

Example: Reading a file with missing values

Suppose we have a file data.txt with the following content:

```
1.0, 2.0, 3.0
4.0, ,    6.0
7.0, 8.0, 9.0
```

The second line contains a missing value. If we try to read this file with loadtxt, an error is raised:

```python
import numpy as np

# This results in a ValueError because of the missing value
data = np.loadtxt("data/data.txt", delimiter=",")
```

With genfromtxt, however, the missing value can be handled automatically:

```python
import numpy as np

data = np.genfromtxt("data/data.txt", delimiter=",")
print(data)
```

The execution leads to this output:

```
[[ 1.  2.  3.]
 [ 4. nan  6.]
 [ 7.  8.  9.]]
```

Missing entries are filled with np.nan, which makes it much easier to work with incomplete datasets.

Part II

Matplotlib

12 Introduction

matplotlib is a library for creating charts and plots. As Python has become more widespread, the popularity of matplotlib has steadily grown. The library is particularly attractive as an open-source alternative to MATLAB – especially in combination with NumPy and SciPy. While MATLAB is commercial and proprietary, matplotlib is free, open, and open-source. In addition, matplotlib supports object-oriented structures and can be integrated into GUI frameworks such as wxPython, Qt, or GTK+. matplotlib is excellent for producing figures for scientific work. Graphics can be exported in many formats such as PDF, PNG, or SVG.

matplotlib is quick to learn, and you can achieve appealing results with little prior knowledge. The official website puts it this way: "Matplotlib tries to make easy things easy and hard things possible. You can generate plots, histograms, power spectra, bar charts, error charts, scatter plots, etc., with just a few lines of code."[1]

Figure 12.1 Plots as art.

---

1 "Matplotlib tries to make easy things easy and hard things possible. You can generate plots, histograms, power spectra, bar charts, error charts, scatter plots, etc., with just a few lines of code."

12.1 A first example

We begin with a simple plot – so simple that it can hardly get any simpler. A plot in `matplotlib` is a two- or three-dimensional graphical representation that visualizes relationships using points, lines, bars, or other elements. The horizontal axis (x) represents the independent values, and the vertical axis (y) represents the dependent ones.

For our first steps we use the `pyplot` submodule. `pyplot` offers a MATLAB-like, procedural interface that is particularly suitable for simple and interactive applications. Under the hood, it is fully based on `matplotlib`'s object-oriented architecture, which you can also access directly if needed.

By convention, `matplotlib.pyplot` is imported under the short name `plt`. In our first example we use the `plot` function, to which we pass a list of values. `plot` interprets these values as y-values; the corresponding x-values are automatically determined by their position in the array (starting at 0).

Note: In most examples in this book, we do not use the statement `plt.show()`. This is because we work with `pythontex` or in Jupyter notebooks – in these environments, plot output is displayed automatically, and calling `plt.show()` can even be counter-productive in the case of `pythontex`.

When using Matplotlib in traditional Python scripts (so-called standalone applications), you must explicitly call `plt.show()` at the end of a script so that the plot window is displayed.

```python
import matplotlib.pyplot as plt
plt.plot([-1, -4.5, 16, 23, 15, 59, 45, 21])
```

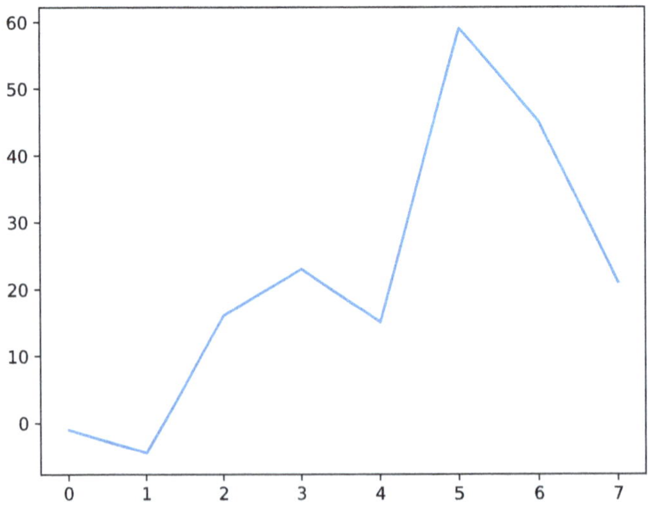

We see a continuous plot even though we only provided discrete values for the ordinate, also commonly called the y-axis. For the abscissa, i.e. the x-axis, the indices were used. By passing a format string when calling the function, we can produce a plot with discrete values – in our case with blue filled circles. The format string defines how the discrete points are displayed:

```python
import matplotlib.pyplot as plt
plt.plot([-1, -4.5, 16, 23, 15, 59, 45, 21], "ob")
```

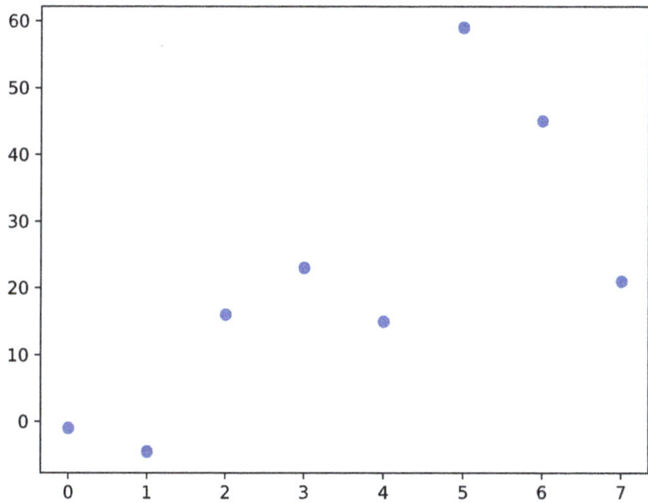

12.2 Format parameters of plot

In our previous example we used ob as the format parameter. It consists of two characters. The first defines the line style or the representation of discrete values, the markers. With the second character you choose the color for the plot. The order of the two characters could also be reversed, i.e. we could have written bo. If no format parameter is given, as in our first example, b- is used as the default value, i.e. a continuous blue line. The following color abbreviations are available:

Table 12.1 Color abbreviations in `matplotlib`

Character	Color	Character	Color	Character	Color
'b'	blue	'c'	cyan	'k'	black
'g'	green	'm'	magenta	'w'	white
'r'	red	'y'	yellow		

The following characters are accepted in a format string to control line style or markers:

Table 12.2 Characters and their graphical meaning in `matplotlib`

Character	Description	Character	Description
'-'	solid line	'3'	tri-left marker
'-'	dashed line	'4'	tri-right marker
'-.'	dash-dot line	's'	square marker
':'	dotted line	'p'	pentagon marker
'.'	point marker	'*'	star marker
','	pixel marker	'h'	hexagon marker 1
'o'	circle marker	'H'	hexagon marker 2
'v'	triangle down	'+'	plus marker
'^'	triangle up	'x'	x marker
'<'	triangle left	'D'	diamond marker
'>'	triangle right	'd'	thin diamond marker
'1'	tri-down marker	'|'	vertical line
'2'	tri-up marker	'_'	horizontal line

As some may have already guessed, you can also pass explicit x-values to the `plot` function. In the following example we pass a list of the multiples of 3 between 0 and 21 as x-values:

```python
import matplotlib.pyplot as plt
days = list(range(0, 22, 3)) # x-values
# y-values:
celsius_values = [25.6, 24.1, 26.7, 28.3, 27.5, 30.5, 32.8, 33.1]
plt.plot(days, celsius_values, 'bo-')
```

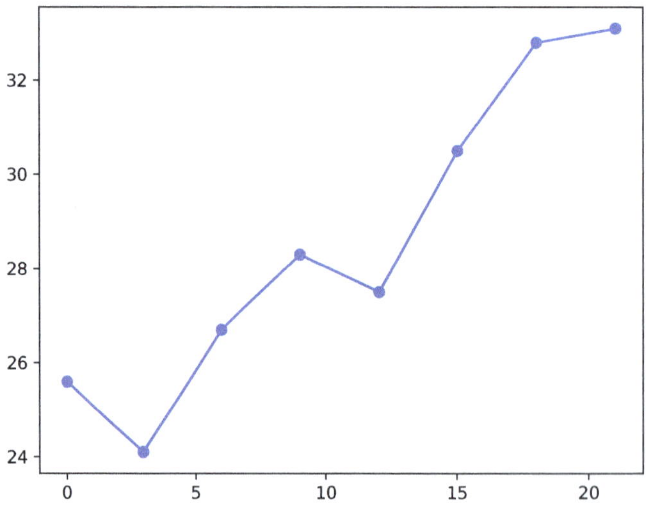

Lines and points can be given different colors, and the marker here is a diamond:

```python
plt.plot(days, celsius_values, 'g-')
plt.plot(days, celsius_values, 'rD')
```

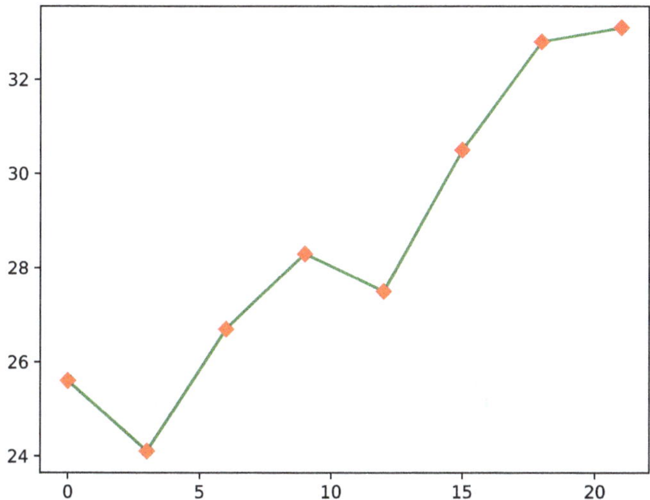

12.3 Multiple data series with axis labels

In a single plot you can display several data series at once. The `plot` function allows you to pass any number of x-value, y-value, and format string combinations.

In the following example we show minimum and maximum daily temperatures over eight days. In addition we label the axes with `xlabel` and `ylabel` to provide context.

```python
import matplotlib.pyplot as plt

days = list(range(1, 9))
celsius_min = [19.6, 24.1, 26.7, 28.3, 27.5, 30.5, 32.8, 33.1]
celsius_max = [24.8, 28.9, 31.3, 33.0, 34.9, 35.6, 38.4, 39.2]

plt.xlabel('Day')
plt.ylabel('Temperature in degC')
plt.title('Daily minimum and maximum temperatures')

plt.plot(days, celsius_min,
         days, celsius_min, "oy",
         days, celsius_max,
         days, celsius_max, "or")
```

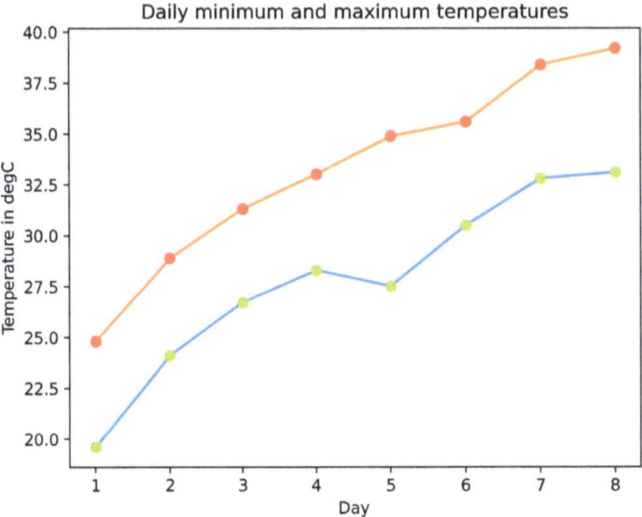

The previous code draws each dataset twice and is not good practice. It should be done like this:

```
ax.plot(days, celsius_min, 'y-o')
ax.plot(days, celsius_max, 'r-o')
```

13
Object-Oriented Plotting

In the previous chapter we showed how to quickly create a plot with only a few lines of code. For this we used the submodule `matplotlib.pyplot` under the alias `plt`. It provides functions reminiscent of MATLAB and allows the creation of simple plots.

For simple examples – as in the last chapter – this is convenient and effective. But as complexity grows, we soon reach limitations. When it comes to structuring multiple plots cleanly or configuring them in detail, an object-oriented approach becomes much more helpful.

This chapter therefore introduces the object-oriented usage of Matplotlib. At its core are the `Figure` and `Axes` objects, which

Figure 13.1 Stone piles

together form a hierarchical structure – comparable to carefully stacked stones in a pile. This structure gives our plots more control, flexibility, and clarity.

Step by step we will learn how to work with these objects, and in doing so create more sophisticated plots – systematically, transparently, and modularly.

Matplotlib is built in an object-oriented way. A graphic is not simply an image, but a *hierarchical structure* of objects that interact like building blocks. The central elements of this structure are the Figure and Axes objects.[1]

- The Figure object forms the outer frame of an entire graphic. It provides the canvas on which one or more plots appear. Methods such as savefig, which is used to save a graphic, belong to the Figure.

- The Axes object represents the actual plotting area – what one would commonly call the "plot": with axes, grid, curves, labels, and titles.

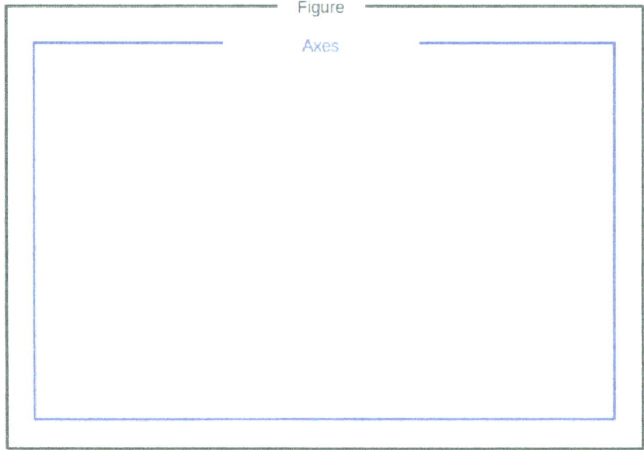

Figure 13.2 Structure of a Matplotlib graphic with one Figure and one Axes

A Figure can contain *one or more* Axes – either side by side (e.g., in columns), stacked vertically (in rows), or in more complex arrangements. The relationship is always the same: the Figure is the container, the Axes are the drawing areas.

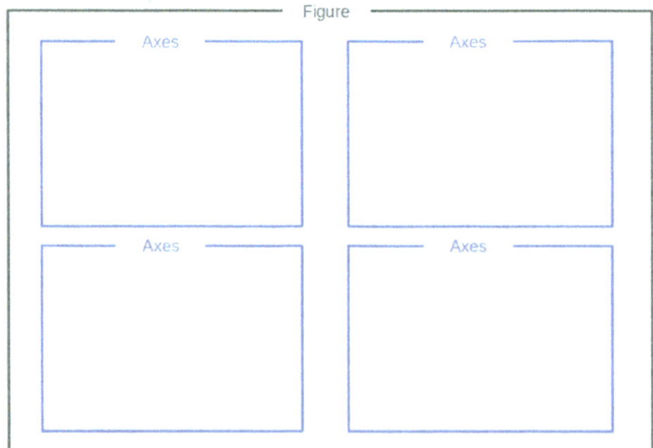

Figure 13.3 Structure of a Matplotlib graphic with one Figure and four Axes

---

1   The term Axes often causes confusion: it is the plural of Axis, but here it does *not* mean multiple axes. Instead, it refers to a complete plot object – including the axes themselves and many other elements. A more intuitive name might have been "Plot."

The following graphic illustrates further concepts such as `Spine`,[2] `Tick`, and `Axis`.

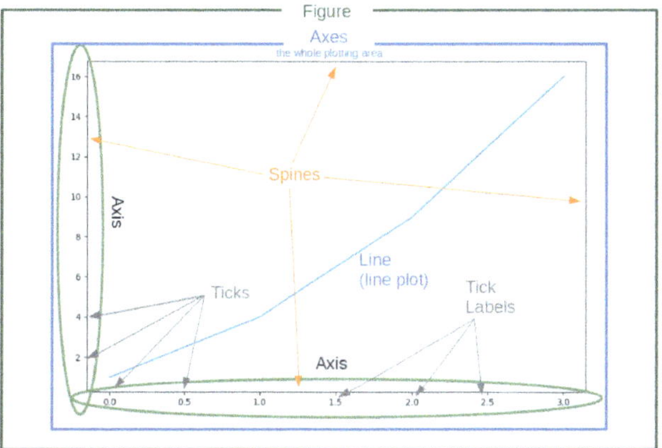

Figure 13.4 Explanation of terms in Matplotlib: Spine, Tick, Ticklabel, and Axis are visually marked.

13.1 Creating a Figure and Axes

To work with Matplotlib's object-oriented structure, we first need to create a `Figure` and a corresponding `Axes`. The easiest way to do this is with the `subplots` method from the `pyplot` module.

```python
import matplotlib.pyplot as plt
fig, ax = plt.subplots()
print(type(fig))
print(type(ax))
```

Output of the object types:

```
<class 'matplotlib.figure.Figure'>
<class 'matplotlib.axes._axes.Axes'>
```

This shows us that `fig` is an object of the class `Figure` and `ax` is an object of the class `Axes` – the central building blocks for object-oriented work with Matplotlib.

The `subplots` method creates a Figure and one or more Axes. In our previous example we called the function without parameters and received one Figure and one Axes in return. Later we will see how to create multiple Axes with this call.

---

[2] In Matplotlib Spine refers to the border lines of a plot – i.e., the lines along the axis edges.

Let's now extend our previous example into a complete plot. We can see that we now apply the `plot` method directly to the Axes (`ax`) and no longer to `plt`. This avoids ambiguities in more complex applications:

```python
import matplotlib.pyplot as plt
X = [2, 4, 6, 8, 10]
Y = [1, 4, 9, 19, 39]
fig, ax = plt.subplots()
ax.plot(X, Y)
```

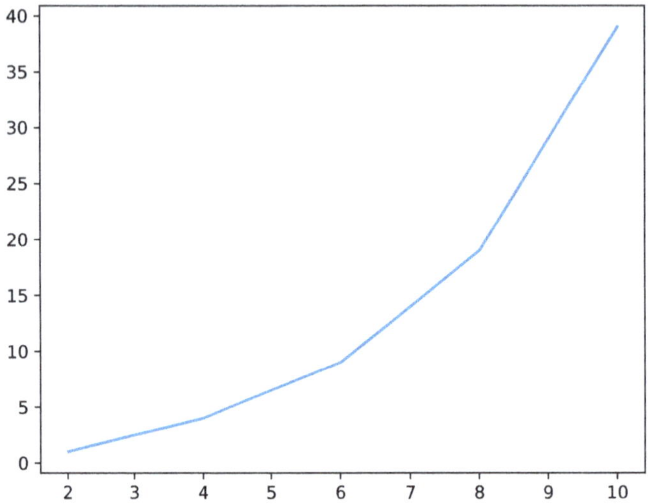

13.2 Axis Labels and Title

Matplotlib provides two equivalent ways to set labels and a title for an Axes:

1. **Set multiple properties at once with set()**
   The `set` method allows you to define several attributes in one step. This is especially convenient for compact examples:

   ```python
   ax.set(xlabel='Days',
          ylabel='Temperature in Celsius',
          title='Temperature Graph')
   ```

   This variant is short and clear, especially when several properties need to be set at the same time. It is well-suited for smaller scripts or interactive work in a notebook.

2. **Set individual properties with specific methods**

   Alternatively, you can set the properties with the explicit methods `set_xlabel`, `set_ylabel`, and `set_title`:

   ```python
   ax.set_xlabel('Days')
   ax.set_ylabel('Temperature in Celsius')
   ax.set_title('Temperature Graph')
   ```

   This variant is a bit more verbose and therefore particularly easy to read. It makes the object structure clearer and is well-suited for didactic purposes, e.g., in textbooks or for beginners.

Both methods lead to the same result – which one you choose depends on personal style, the application context, and the desired readability of the code. In the following code example, we opt for the more explicit variant with individual functions:

```python
import matplotlib.pyplot as plt

days = list(range(1, 9))
celsius_values = [25.6, 24.1, 26.7, 28.3, 27.5, 30.5, 32.8, 33.1]

fig, ax = plt.subplots()
ax.plot(days, celsius_values)
ax.set_xlabel('Days')
ax.set_ylabel('Temperature in Celsius')
ax.set_title('Temperature Graph')
```

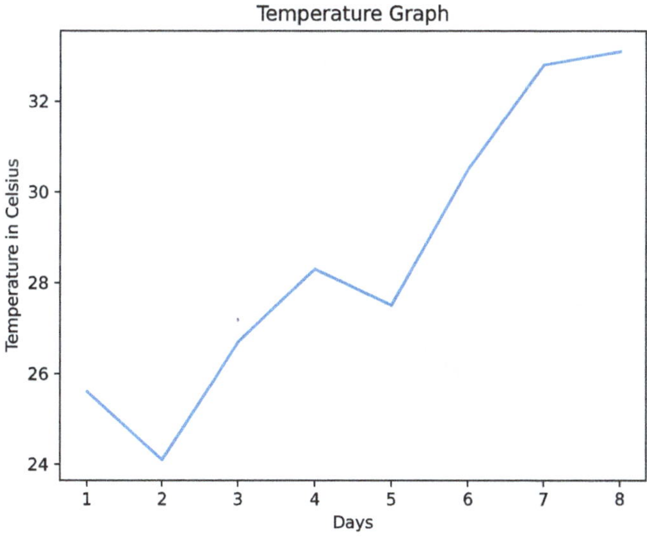

13.3 The Plot Method

We have already been using the `plot` method all along without looking at it in detail. Now is a good time to take a closer look: What exactly can this method do – and how flexible is it?

The `plot` method is used to display data graphically in an Axes object. Any number of groups of x, y, and format specifications (`fmt`) can be passed. The format specifications control, for example, whether points or lines are used and in which color – such as 'oy' for yellow circles or 'or' for red circles.

We now extend our previous temperature example and show both minimum and maximum temperatures. This demonstrates how multiple value pairs and format specifications can be combined in a single call to the `plot` method:

```python
import matplotlib.pyplot as plt

days = list(range(1, 9))
celsius_min = [19.6, 24.1, 26.7, 28.3, 27.5, 30.5, 32.8, 33.1]
celsius_max = [24.8, 28.9, 31.3, 33.0, 34.9, 35.6, 38.4, 39.2]

fig, ax = plt.subplots()

ax.set_xlabel('Days')
ax.set_ylabel('Temperature in Celsius')
ax.set_title('Temperature Graph')

ax.plot(days, celsius_min,
        days, celsius_min, "oy",
        days, celsius_max,
        days, celsius_max, "or")
```

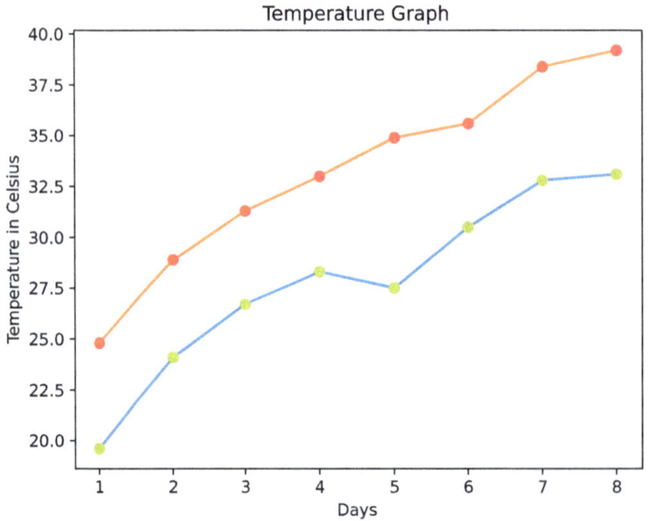

This draws each dataset twice and is not good practice. The optimal way is to write it like this:

```python
ax.plot(days, celsius_min, 'y-o')
ax.plot(days, celsius_max, 'r-o')
```

13.4 Axis Ranges

We can query and change the axis ranges with the `axis` method. If called without arguments, it returns the current limits:

```python
import matplotlib.pyplot as plt

days = list(range(1, 9))
celsius_values = [25.6, 24.1, 26.7, 28.3, 27.5, 30.5, 32.8, 33.1]

fig, ax = plt.subplots()
ax.plot(days, celsius_values)
ax.set(xlabel='Days',
       ylabel='Temperature in Celsius',
       title='Temperature Graph')

print("The current axis limits are:")
xmin, xmax, ymin, ymax = ax.axis()
# alternatively you can define them like this:
#xmin, xmax = ax.get_xlim()
#ymin, ymax = ax.get_ylim()

print(f"x: {xmin:.2f}, {xmax:.2f}, y: {ymin:.2f}, {ymax:.2f}")

print("Changing to the following values:")
ax.axis([0, 10, 14, 45])
xmin, xmax, ymin, ymax = ax.axis()
print(f"x: {xmin:.2f}, {xmax:.2f}, y: {ymin:.2f}, {ymax:.2f}")
```

Output:

```
The current axis limits are:
x: 0.65, 8.35, y: 23.65, 33.55
Changing to the following values:
x: 0.00, 10.00, y: 14.00, 45.00
```

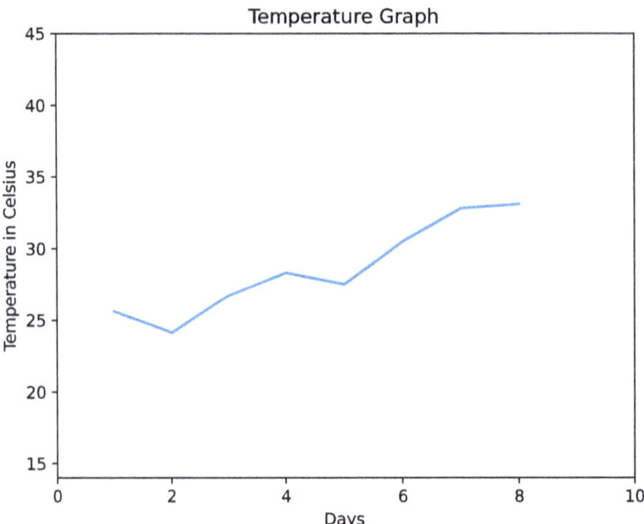

In the following example we introduce some interesting keyword parameters of
the `plot` method. With the parameters `color`, `marker`, `linestyle`, `linewidth`, and
`markersize`, you can control color, marker symbol, line type, line width, and marker
size explicitly.

```python
import matplotlib.pyplot as plt

days = list(range(1,9))
celsius_min = [19.6, 24.1, 26.7, 28.3, 27.5, 30.5, 32.8, 33.1]
celsius_max = [24.8, 28.9, 31.3, 33.0, 34.9, 35.6, 38.4, 39.2]

fig, ax = plt.subplots()

ax.set(xlabel='Days',
       ylabel='Temperature in Celsius',
       title='Temperature Graph')

ax.plot(days, celsius_min,
        color="magenta",
        marker="o",
        linestyle="dashed",
        linewidth=3,
        markersize=18)

ax.plot(days, celsius_max,
        color="green",
        marker="x",
        linestyle="solid",
        linewidth=7,
        markersize=24)
```

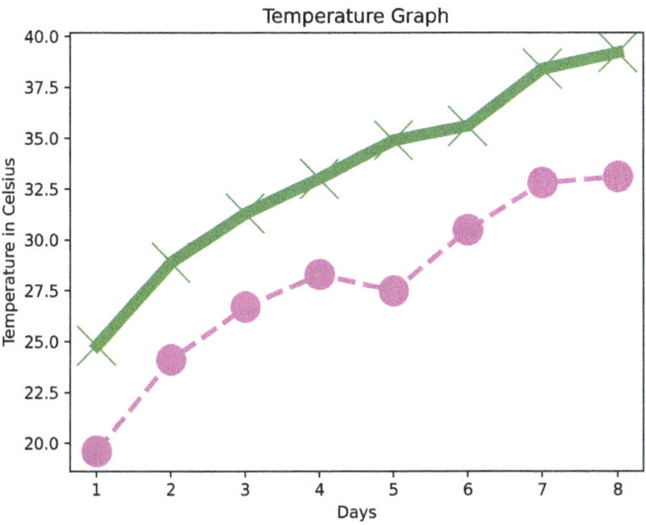

13.5 Plotting Multiple Functions

The following shows how to display multiple functions in a single Axes. In principle we
already saw this in the example with minimum and maximum temperatures. In this
example we also use NumPy's `linspace` function to generate evenly spaced x-values:

```python
import numpy as np
import matplotlib.pyplot as plt


num_x_values = 50
start, end = -2 * np.pi, 2 * np.pi
X = np.linspace(start, end,
                num=num_x_values,
                endpoint=True)
F1 = 3 * np.sin(X)
F2 = np.sin(2*X)
F3 = 0.3 * np.sin(X)


fig, ax = plt.subplots()
startx, endx = start - 0.1, end + 0.1
starty, endy = -3.1, 3.1
ax.axis([startx, endx, starty, endy])
ax.plot(X, F1, X, F2, X, F3)
ax.plot(X, F1, 'ro', X, F2, 'bx', X, F3, 'g4')
```

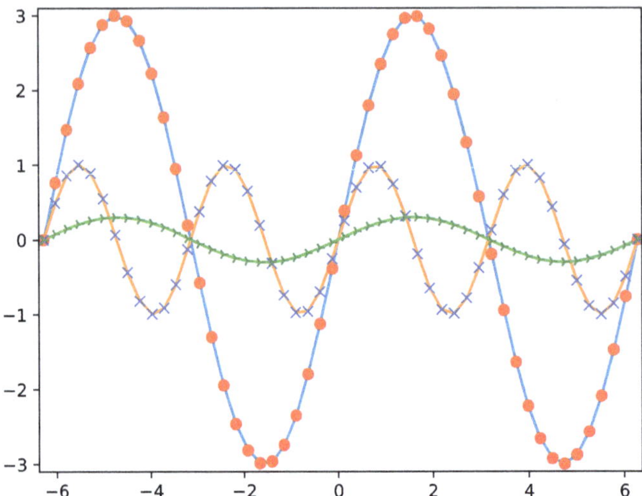

Even though Figures with multiple Axes will not be covered until the next chapter, it
makes sense to show an example now, since many readers will wonder how to display
the three functions separately in subplots.

```python
import numpy as np
import matplotlib.pyplot as plt


X = np.linspace(-2 * np.pi, 2 * np.pi, 50, endpoint=True)
Funcs = 3 * np.sin(X), np.sin(2*X), 0.3 * np.sin(X)
fmts = 'ro', 'bx', 'g4'


rows, cols = 1, 3
fig, ax = plt.subplots(rows, cols, sharey='row')
startx, endx = -2 * np.pi - 0.1, 2*np.pi + 0.1
starty, endy = -3.1, 3.1
for i in range(len(ax)):
    ax[i].axis([startx, endx, starty, endy])
    ax[i].plot(X, Funcs[i])
    ax[i].plot(X, Funcs[i], fmts[i])
```

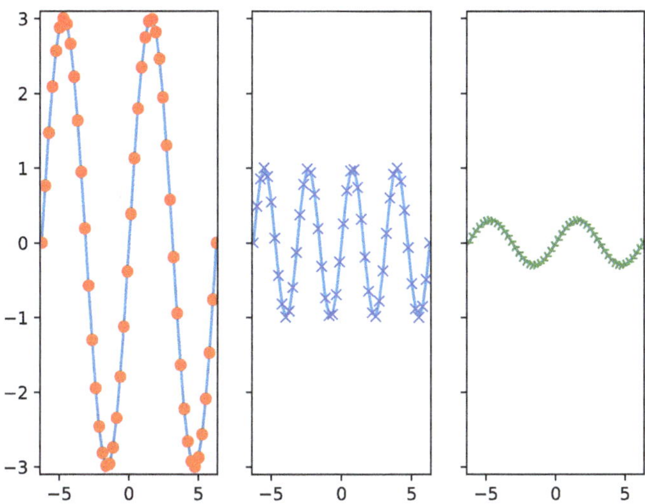

13.6 Scatter Plots

With the Axes method `scatter`, you can create scatter plots – also known as point diagrams. The method requires at least two arguments x and y, i.e. the x- and y-coordinates of a point. With the keyword parameter s we can specify the size of the marker. The following example displays a single point at position (4, 7):

```python
import matplotlib.pyplot as plt
fig, ax = plt.subplots()
ax.scatter(4, 7, s=42)
```

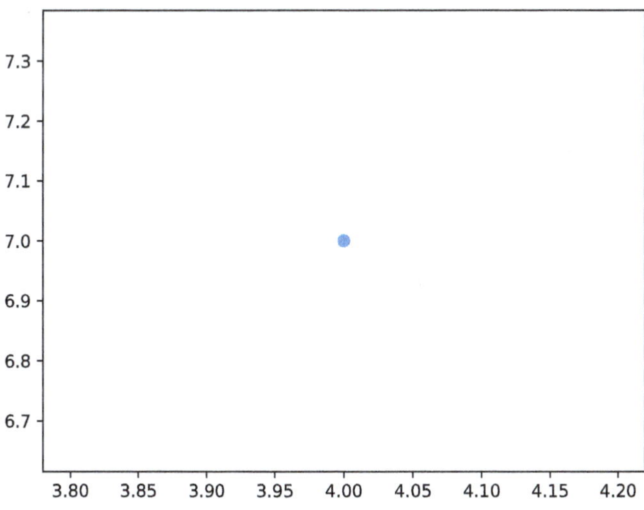

Next we generate 40 random points and plot them with `scatter`:

```python
import matplotlib.pyplot as plt
import numpy as np
X = np.random.randint(0, 100, (40,))
Y = np.random.randint(0, 100, (40,))
fig, ax = plt.subplots()
ax.scatter(X, Y, s=42)
```

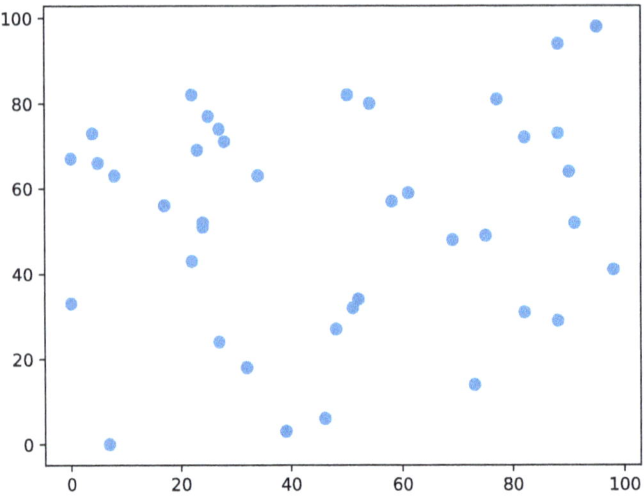

With scatter plots, you can even "draw":

```python
import matplotlib.pyplot as plt
import numpy as np

fig, ax = plt.subplots()

# Face (circle of points)
theta = [i * 0.2 for i in range(32)]
x_face = [4 + 3 * np.cos(t) for t in theta]
y_face = [4 + 3 * np.sin(t) for t in theta]

# Eyes
x_eyes = [3, 5]
y_eyes = [5, 5]

# Nose
x_nose = [4]
y_nose = [4]
```

```python
# Mouth (half-circle curve)
theta_mouth = [i * 0.3 for i in range(11)]
x_mouth = [4 + 2 * np.cos(t) for t in theta_mouth]
y_pos = 3.5
y_mouth = [y_pos - 0.5 * np.sin(t) for t in theta_mouth]

# Combine all points
X = x_face + x_eyes + x_nose + x_mouth
Y = y_face + y_eyes + y_nose + y_mouth

ax.scatter(X, Y, s=100)
ax.set_aspect('equal')
ax.set_xticks([])
ax.set_yticks([])
```

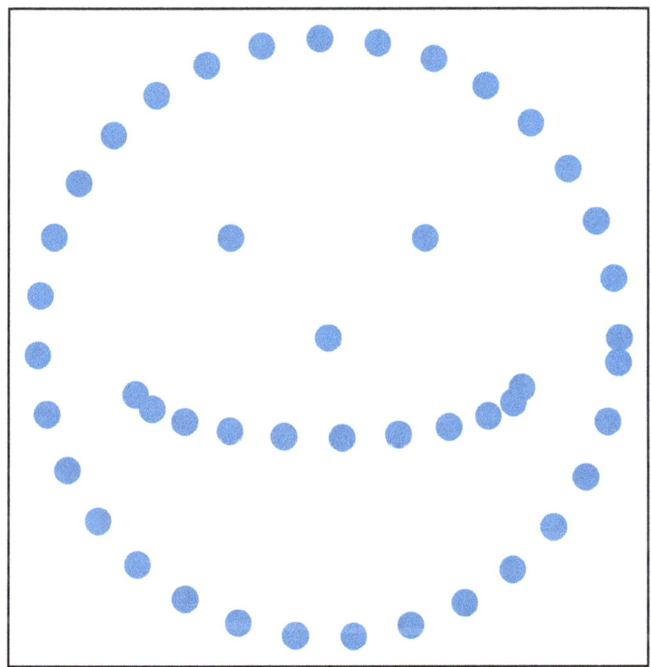

The following example adds some color and variety:

```python
import numpy as np
import matplotlib.pyplot as plt
# Set seed value for reproducibility:
np.random.seed(19680801)
n = 50
x, y = np.random.rand(n), np.random.rand(n)
```

```
colors = np.random.rand(n)
area = (30 * np.random.rand(n))**2
fig, ax = plt.subplots()
ax.scatter(x, y, s=area, c=colors, alpha=0.5)
```

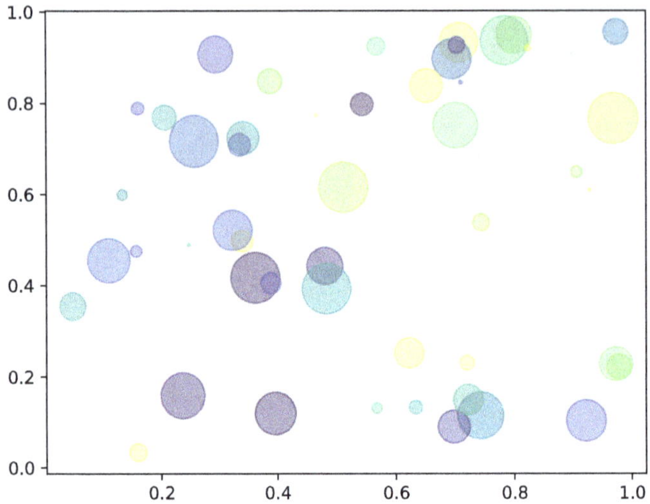

13.7 Filling Areas

As the last example of a method on the Axes object, we introduce the `fill_between`
method. It allows you to shade or color the area between curves or between curves
and the axes. In the following example, we fill the area between the x-axis and the
graph of the function `sin(2*X)`:

```
import numpy as np
import matplotlib.pyplot as plt
n = 256
X = np.linspace(-np.pi,np.pi,n,endpoint=True)
Y = np.sin(2*X)

fig, ax = plt.subplots()
ax.plot(X, Y, color='blue', alpha=1.0)
ax.fill_between(X, 0, Y, color='blue', alpha=.2)
```

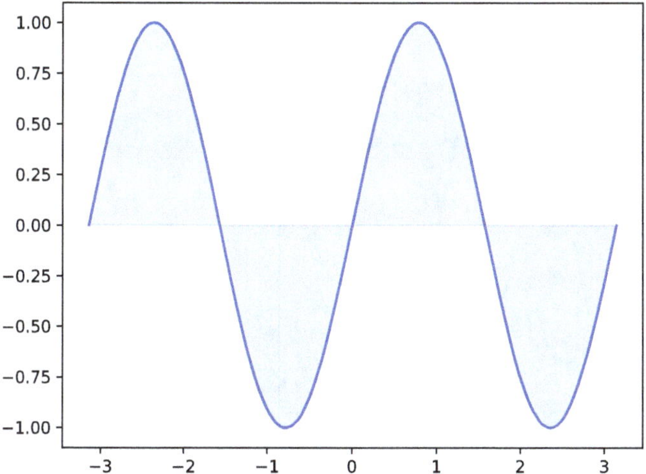

The general syntax of `fill_between`:

```
fill_between(x, y1, y2=0, where=None, interpolate=False, **kwargs)
```

The parameters of `fill_between`:

Parameter	Meaning
x	An array with N elements of x-values
y1	An array with N elements (or a scalar) of y-data
y2	An array with N elements (or a scalar) of y-data
where	If set to None, everything is filled by default. Otherwise, a NumPy boolean array with N elements is expected. Only the regions where where==True are filled.
interpolate	If True, the intersection between two lines is interpolated to find the exact crossing point. Otherwise, start and end values only appear as explicit values at the region boundaries.
kwargs	Keyword arguments passed on to PolyCollection.

We now fill the area above the function:

```python
import numpy as np
import matplotlib.pyplot as plt

n = 256
X = np.linspace(-np.pi,np.pi,n,endpoint=True)
Y = np.sin(2*X)
fig, ax = plt.subplots()
ax.plot(X, Y, color='blue', alpha=1.00)
ax.fill_between(X, Y, 1, color='blue', alpha=.1)
```

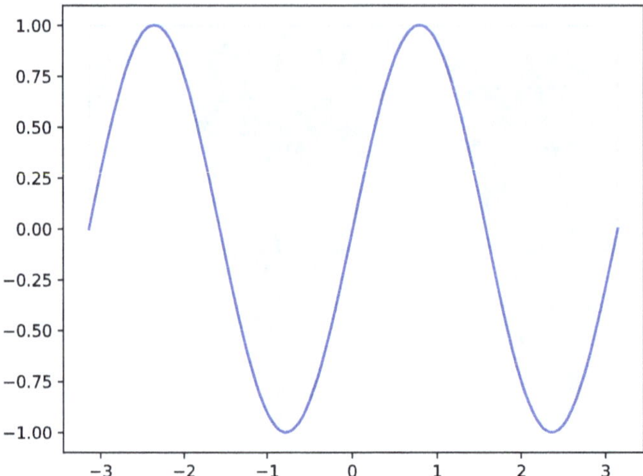

In the next example, we fill the area between the two functions F1 and F2:

```python
import numpy as np
import matplotlib.pyplot as plt

X = np.linspace(0, 2 * np.pi, 50, endpoint=True)
F1 = 3 * np.sin(X)
F2 = np.sin(2*X)

fig, ax = plt.subplots()
ax.plot(X, F1, color="blue", linewidth=2.5, linestyle="-")
ax.plot(X, F2, color="red", linewidth=1.5, linestyle="-")
ax.fill_between(X, F1, F2, color='blue', alpha=.1)
```

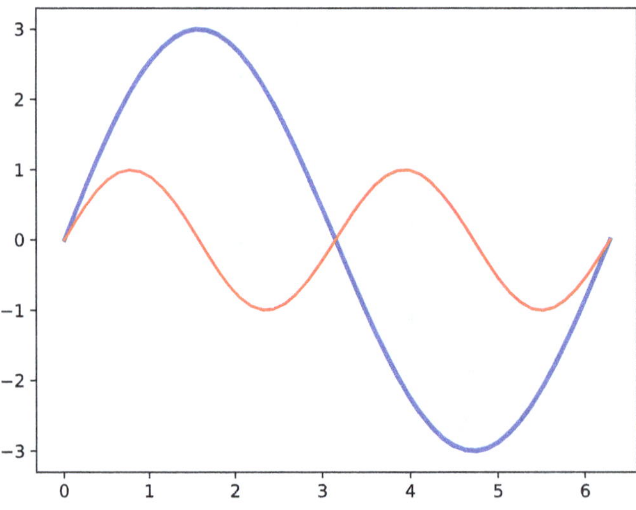

13.8 Exercises

Exercise 1

(Solution: 33.7, Solution 1)

Create a line chart with `matplotlib` that shows your jogging times (in minutes) for one week. For Monday to Sunday, for example, the values are: 30, 42, 35, 50, 45, 60, 45

- Use the object-oriented Matplotlib interface with `subplots()`.
- Label the axes and give the diagram a title.
- Display the data with markers and a line.

Exercise 2

(Solution: 33.7, Solution 2)

In two cities, the daily maximum temperatures were measured over eight consecutive days:

- City A: 21, 23, 24, 25, 26, 27, 29, 30
- City B: 18, 20, 22, 23, 25, 28, 31, 33

Create a diagram with `matplotlib` that shows both temperature series:

Hint: To distinguish the cities, you can use the `label` parameter in `plot(...)` and then call `ax.legend()`.

Exercise 3

(Solution: 33.7, Solution 3)

In an experiment, 15 lemons and 14 oranges are examined with respect to their sweetness (x-axis) and acidity (y-axis). Create a scatter plot to visualize the differences:

- Generate 15 points for lemons with low sweetness and high acidity.
- Generate 14 points for oranges with higher sweetness and lower acidity.
- Display the fruits as colored points in the same diagram – e.g., yellow for lemons, orange for oranges.
- Label the axes with "Sweetness" and "Acidity" and give the plot a suitable title.

Hint: Use `ax.scatter(...)` and optionally specify color (`c=...`) and transparency (`alpha=...`).

14
Multiple Plots and Dual Axes

In numerous examples so far, we have seen how to create diagrams and graphs. Now we turn to the question of how to place multiple plots in one figure.

In the simplest case, this means having one curve and overlaying another on top of it. The more interesting case, however, is when two plots are desired in one window. In one window means that there are two subplots, i.e. they are not drawn over each other. The idea is to have more than one graph in a window, with each graph appearing in its own subplot.

Figure 14.1 Multiple plots à la Gridspec

We present two different ways to achieve this:

- subplot
- gridspec

We believe that `gridspec` is the best option, as it is easier to use when the layout becomes more complex.

14.1 Subplots with subplot

We already encountered the subplot function in Section 13.1 (Creating a Figure and Axes). We saw that if subplot is called without parameters, it returns a Figure and an Axes. Now we are interested in having more than one Axes returned. In this case, a Figure and a two-dimensional array of Axes are returned. The following table introduces some parameters to control this:

Parameter	Meaning
nrows	Number of rows in the returned Axes array (default: 1).
ncols	Number of columns accordingly.
sharex	Controls x-axis sharing. Possible values are True, False, none, all, row, and col (default: False). True or all share the x-axis across all subplots; False or none keep axes independent; row shares per row; col shares per column.
sharey	Analogous to sharex.

In the first example, we create two Axes objects arranged in one row.

```python
import matplotlib.pyplot as plt
fig, (ax1, ax2) = plt.subplots(1, 2, sharey='row', figsize=(6, 4))

ax1.text(0.5, 0.5, "left",  color="green", fontsize=18, ha='center')
ax2.text(0.5, 0.5, "right", color="green", fontsize=18, ha='center')
```

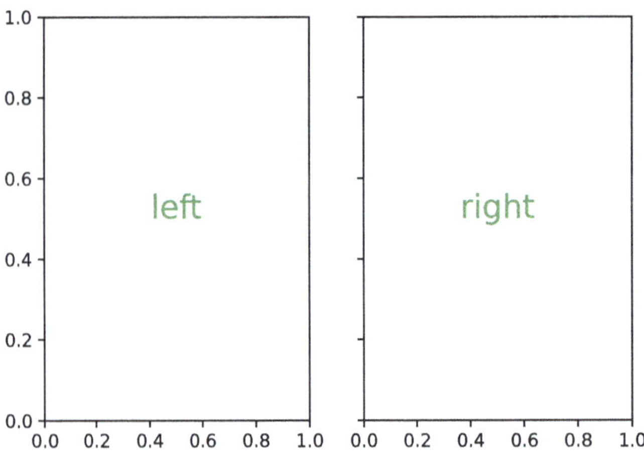

If we omit the sharey parameter, i.e.

```python
fig, (ax1, ax2) = plt.subplots(1, 2)
```

we obtain the following plot:

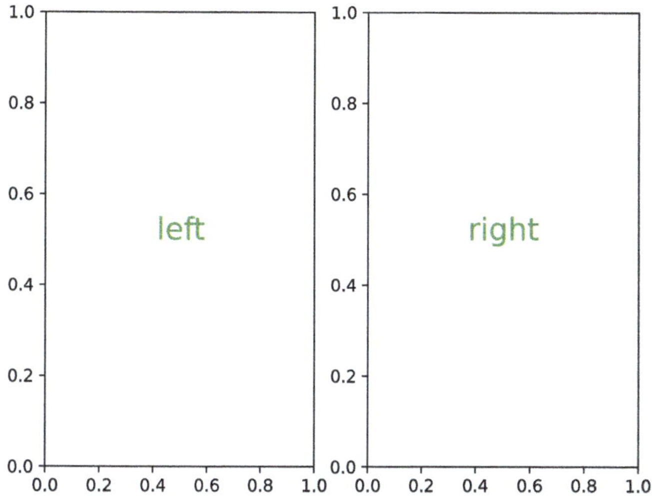

Now let us look at the same with actual function graphs:

```python
import numpy as np
import matplotlib.pyplot as plt


x = np.linspace(0, 2*np.pi, 400)
y = np.sin(x**2) + np.cos(x)
derivative = 2 * x * np.cos(x**2) - np.sin(x)

fig, (ax1, ax2) = plt.subplots(1, 2, sharey='row')
ax1.plot(x, y)
ax1.set_title('Sharing Y axis')
ax2.plot(x, derivative)
```

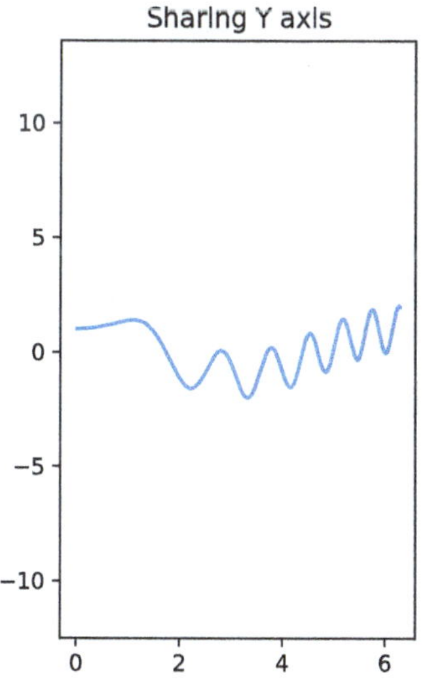

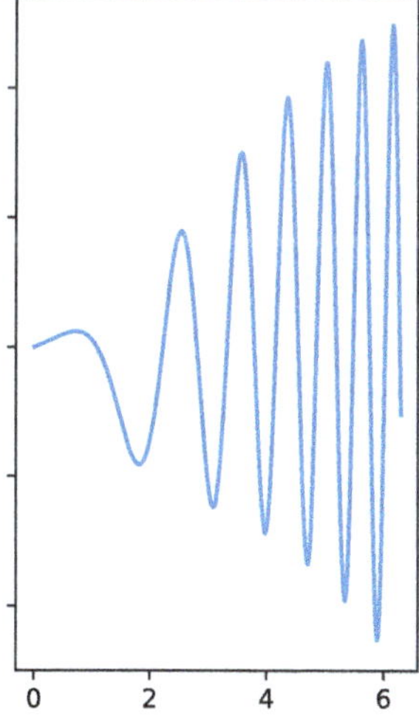

If we omit `sharex` or set it to `False`, i.e.

```
fig, (ax1, ax2) = plt.subplots(1, 2)
```

we see that now the y-scales of both functions differ:

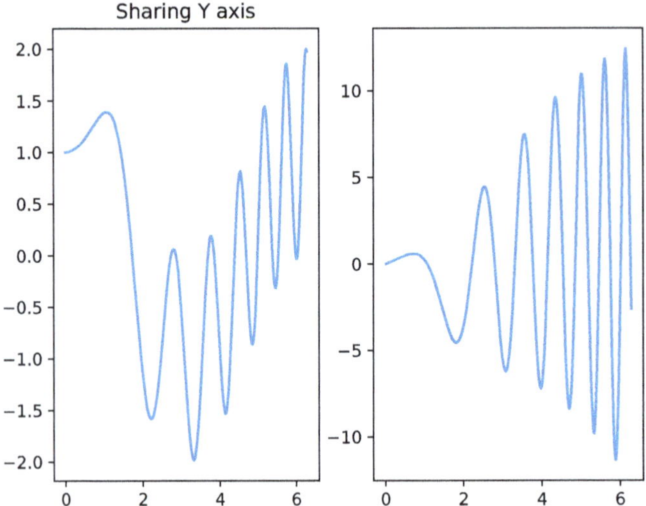

In the following example, we demonstrate how to create a subplot for polar plotting. To do this, the key `polar` is set to `True` in the `subplot_kw` dictionary:

```
import numpy as np
import matplotlib.pyplot as plt

fig, ax = plt.subplots(1, subplot_kw=dict(polar=True))

x = np.linspace(0, 2*np.pi, 400)
ax.plot(x, np.sin(x) * np.cos(x), "--g")
```

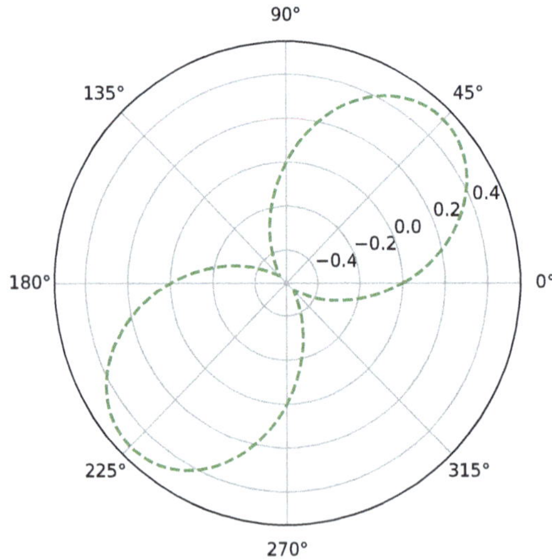

The first two parameters of subplots determine the number of rows and columns. We demonstrate this in the following example. To illustrate the structure, we use the text method of the Axes objects.

```python
import matplotlib.pyplot as plt

rows, cols = 2, 3
fig, ax = plt.subplots(rows, cols,
                       sharex='col',
                       sharey='row')

for row in range(rows):
    for col in range(cols):
        ax[row, col].text(0.5, 0.5,
                          str((row, col)),
                          color="green",
                          fontsize=18,
                          ha='center')
```

Next, we create a similar structure with two rows and two columns, containing polar coordinate plots:

```python
import matplotlib.pyplot as plt
import numpy as np
x = np.linspace(0, 2*np.pi, 400)
y = np.sin(x**2) + np.cos(x)
derivative = 2 * x * np.cos(x**2) - np.sin(x)

rows, cols = 2, 2
fig, axes = plt.subplots(rows, cols, subplot_kw=dict(polar=True))
axes[0, 0].plot(x, y)
```

```
axes[0, 1].plot(x, np.sin(x**2) + np.cos(x**3))
axes[1, 0].plot(x, np.cos(x) * np.sin(x**2))
axes[1, 1].plot(x, derivative, "g--")
```

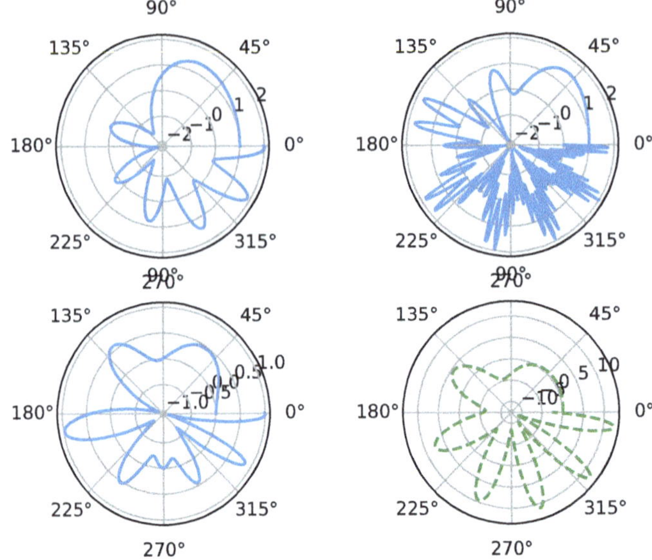

With the function `subplots_adjust`, you can adjust the layout parameters of the sub-plots. For example, the parameter `hspace` controls the spacing between rows.

The parameters of `subplots_adjust`:

Parameter	Meaning
left	A floating-point number that sets the position of the left edge of the subplots as a fraction of the figure width.
right	A floating-point number that sets the position of the right edge of the subplots as a fraction of the figure width.
bottom	A floating-point number that sets the position of the bottom edge of the subplots as a fraction of the figure height.
top	A floating-point number that sets the position of the top edge of the subplots as a fraction of the figure height.
wspace	A floating-point number that sets the width of the space between subplots as a fraction of the average Axes width.
hspace	A floating-point number that sets the height of the space between subplots as a fraction of the average Axes height.

```
import matplotlib.pyplot as plt
import numpy as np
x = np.linspace(0, 2*np.pi, 400)
y = np.sin(x**2) + np.cos(x)
derivative = 2 * x * np.cos(x**2) - np.sin(x)
```

```python
rows, cols = 2, 2
fig, axes = plt.subplots(rows, cols, subplot_kw=dict(polar=True))
fig.suptitle('Various Plots')
axes[0, 0].set(title=r"$\sin(x) + \cos(x)$")
axes[0, 0].plot(x, y)
axes[0, 1].set(title="derivative")
axes[0, 1].plot(x, np.sin(x**2) + np.cos(x**3))
axes[1, 0].set(title=r"$\cos(x) + \sin(x^2)$")
axes[1, 0].plot(x, np.cos(x) * np.sin(x**2))
axes[1, 1].set(title="derivative")
axes[1, 1].plot(x, derivative, "g--")

plt.subplots_adjust(left=0,
                    right=1,
                    bottom=0,
                    top=0.8,
                    wspace=0.0,
                    hspace=0.8)
```

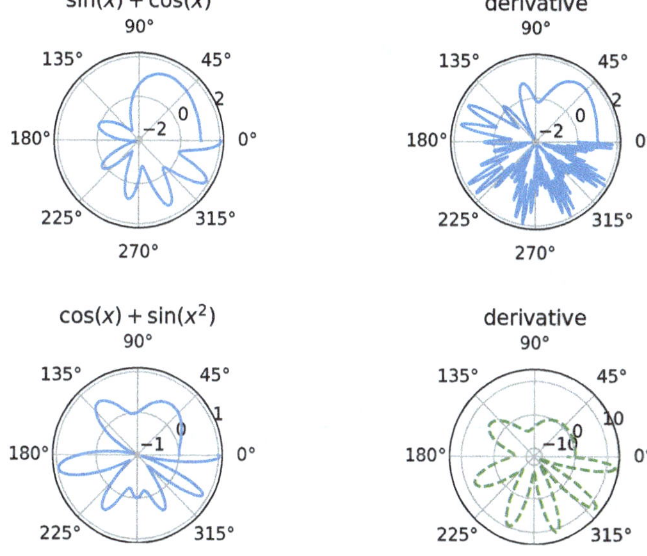

In the next example, we will see how to color plots:

```python
import numpy as np
import matplotlib.pyplot as plt


def f(x):
    return np.sin(x) - x * np.cos(x)
```

```python
def fp(x):
    """ The derivative of f """
    return x * np.sin(x)


X = np.arange(-5, 5.0, 0.05)

fig, ax = plt.subplots(2,
                       sharex='col',
                       sharey='row',
                       facecolor='xkcd:seafoam green')
ax[0].plot(X, f(X), 'bo', X, f(X), 'k')
ax[0].set(title='The function f')
ax[0].set_facecolor('y')
ax[0].xaxis.label.set_color("yellow")
ax[0].yaxis.label.set_color("green")
ax[1].plot(X, fp(X), 'go', X, fp(X), 'k')
ax[1].set(xlabel='X Values', ylabel='Y Values',
          title='Derivative Function of f')
ax[1].set_facecolor('tab:orange')
```

Additional colors from the T10 color palette[1]: 'tab:blue', 'tab:orange', 'tab:green', 'tab:red', 'tab:purple', 'tab:brown', 'tab:pink', 'tab:gray', 'tab:olive', 'tab:cyan'.

Some other arbitrarily chosen colors from xkcd[2]: 'cloudy blue', 'dark pastel green', 'dust', 'electric lime', 'light eggplant', 'macaroni and cheese', 'pig pink'.

---

1   Default color cycle

2   These are the 954 most common RGB screen colors, as defined by several hundred thousand participants in the xkcd color survey. An overview of the colors can be found on the xkcd website: *https://xkcd.com/ color/rgb*.

14.2 Flexible Layouts with GridSpec

In Section 14.1 Subplots with `subplot`, we showed how to create a figure with multiple axes (subplots) using the `subplots` function. In this section, we will learn about the `gridspec` submodule from `matplotlib`. It allows us to explicitly control the placement of subplots within a figure.

Concretely, a `GridSpec` object defines a grid in which the individual subplots are placed. This gives us much more control over the arrangement – including margins and spacing between plots.

Another advantage: with `gridspec` we can create axes that span multiple grid cells – e.g., wide or tall subplots that flexibly integrate into the overall layout.

With the following code we create a figure with four axes in a 2×2 grid – just like in the previous chapter using `subplots`:

```
import matplotlib.pyplot as plt
import matplotlib.gridspec as gridspec

fig, axes = plt.subplots(ncols=2,
                         nrows=2,
                         constrained_layout=True)
```

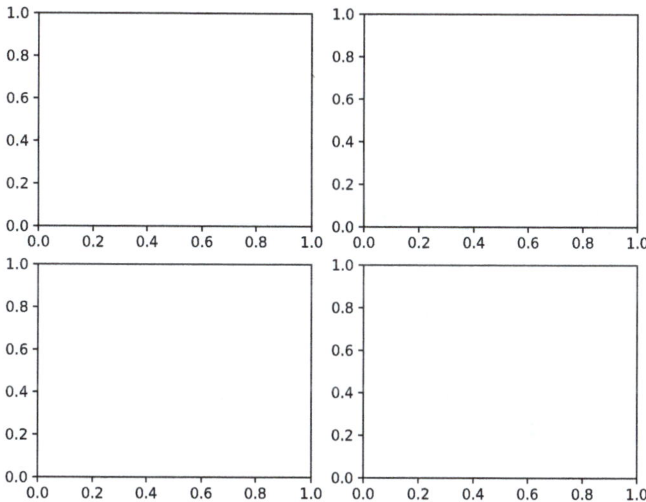

Figure 14.2 Subplots with `plt.subplots()`

We now want to replicate this simple example using the gridspec module. To do this, we first create a Figure object and pass it to a GridSpec object via the figure argument. We then explicitly create the four axes with fig.add_subplot(...). Accessing individual grid cells works just like NumPy arrays – using square brackets and indices.

```python
import matplotlib.pyplot as plt
import matplotlib.gridspec as gridspec


fig = plt.figure(constrained_layout=True)
spec = gridspec.GridSpec(ncols=2, nrows=2, figure=fig)
ax1 = fig.add_subplot(spec[0, 0])
ax2 = fig.add_subplot(spec[0, 1])
ax3 = fig.add_subplot(spec[1, 0])
ax4 = fig.add_subplot(spec[1, 1])
```

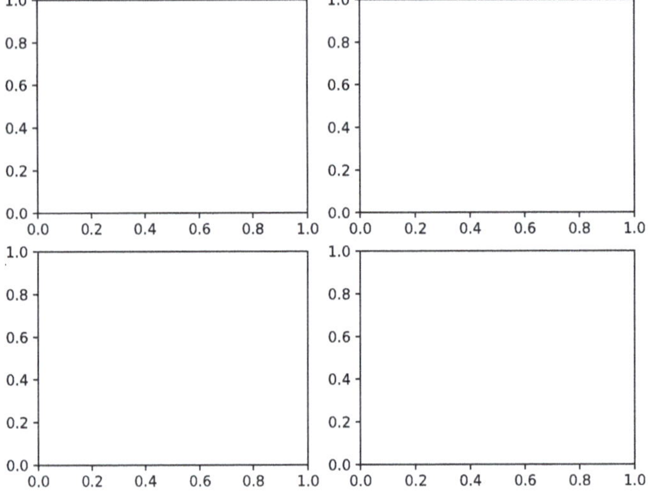

Figure 14.3 Subplots with GridSpec

The above example shows that in simple cases – like an evenly divided 2×2 grid – using GridSpec does not provide an immediate advantage over subplots. On the contrary, the code even becomes a bit more cumbersome.

The real strength of `GridSpec` shows up when subplots are not all the same size but should span multiple rows or columns. An example:

```python
import matplotlib.pyplot as plt
import matplotlib.gridspec as gridspec

fig = plt.figure(constrained_layout=True)
gs = fig.add_gridspec(3, 3)
ax1 = fig.add_subplot(gs[0, :])
ax1.set_title('gs[0, :]')
ax2 = fig.add_subplot(gs[1, :-1])
ax2.set_title('gs[1, :-1]')
ax3 = fig.add_subplot(gs[1:, -1])
ax3.set_title('gs[1:, -1]')
ax4 = fig.add_subplot(gs[-1, 0])
ax4.set_title('gs[-1, 0]')
ax5 = fig.add_subplot(gs[-1, -2])
ax5.set_title('gs[-1, -2]')
```

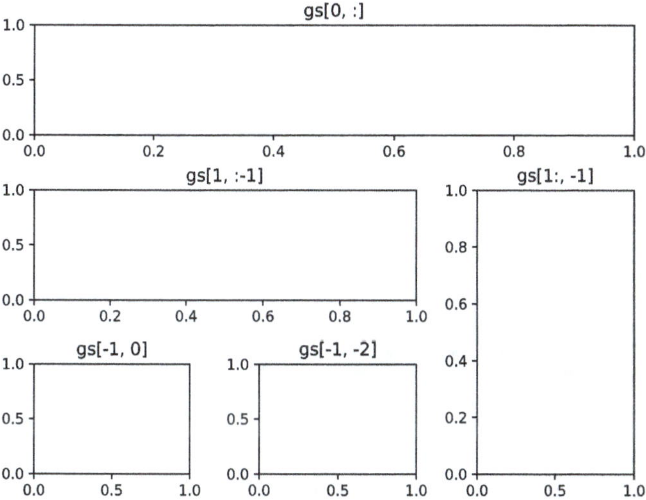

Figure 14.4 Flexible subplot arrangement with `GridSpec`: subplots spanning multiple grid cells

`matplotlib.gridspec` is also essential for creating subplots of different widths using multiple methods.

The method shown here is similar to the one above: it initializes a uniform grid specification and then uses NumPy indexing and slices to assign multiple "cells" to a given subplot.

```python
fig = plt.figure(constrained_layout=True)
spec = fig.add_gridspec(ncols=2, nrows=2)
optional_params = dict(xy=(0.5, 0.5),
                       xycoords='axes fraction',
                       va='center',
                       ha='center')

ax = fig.add_subplot(spec[0, 0])
ax.annotate('GridSpec[0, 0]', **optional_params)
fig.add_subplot(spec[0, 1]).annotate('GridSpec[0, 1:]',
                                     **optional_params)
fig.add_subplot(spec[1, 0]).annotate('GridSpec[1:, 0]',
                                     **optional_params)
fig.add_subplot(spec[1, 1]).annotate('GridSpec[1:, 1:]',
                                     **optional_params)
```

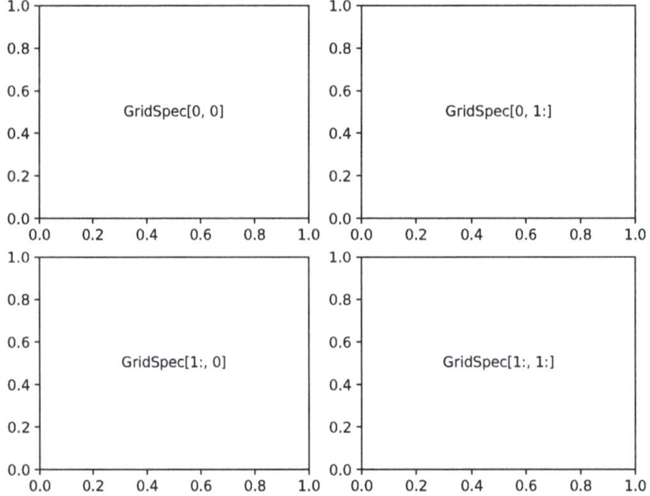

Figure 14.5 Subplots of different sizes by combining grid cells

We can also use the parameters `width_ratios` and `height_ratios`. These keyword parameters are lists of numbers. Note that absolute values are irrelevant – only relative proportions matter. This means that `width_ratios=[2, 4, 8]` is equivalent to `width_ratios=[1, 2, 4]` when the relative widths are the same.

```python
fig5 = plt.figure(constrained_layout=True)
widths = [2, 3, 1.5]
heights = [1, 3, 2]
spec5 = fig5.add_gridspec(ncols=3,
                          nrows=3,
                          width_ratios=widths,
                          height_ratios=heights)
for row in range(3):
    for col in range(3):
        ax = fig5.add_subplot(spec5[row, col])
        label = f'Width: {widths[col]}\nHeight: {heights[row]}'
        ax.annotate(label,
                    (0.1, 0.5),
                    xycoords='axes fraction',
                    va='center')
```

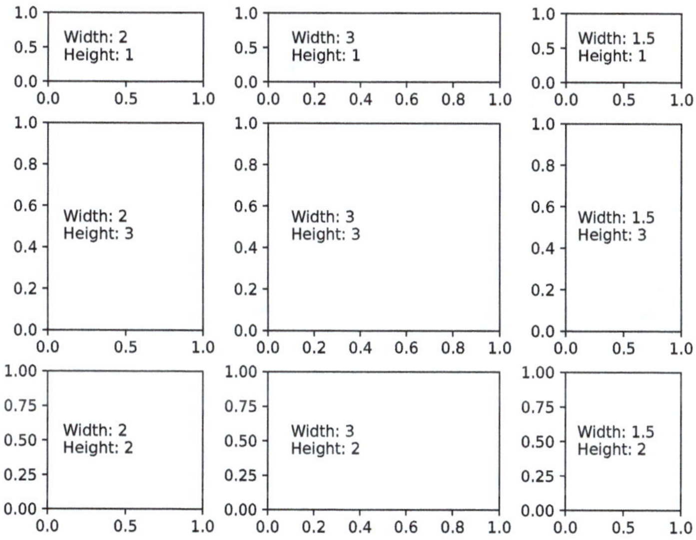

We now show how to use `matplotlib` to visualize the **Power Spectral Density. (PSD)** The PSD is a commonly used tool in **signal processing** to analyze how the power of a signal is distributed across different frequencies.

NumPy and `matplotlib` provide convenient functions for computing and visualizing the PSD. The following example demonstrates how this can be done:

```python
import matplotlib.pyplot as plt
import numpy as np

dt = 0.01
t = np.arange(0, 10, dt)
nse = np.random.randn(len(t))
r = np.exp(-t / 0.05)

cnse = np.convolve(nse, r, mode='full') * dt
cnse = cnse[:len(t)]
s = 0.1 * np.sin(2 * np.pi * t) + cnse

fig, axs = plt.subplots(2, 1, figsize=(10, 6))
axs[0].plot(t, s)
axs[0].set_title("Signal")

# Power Spectral Density
axs[1].psd(s, NFFT=512, Fs=1/dt)
axs[1].set_title("Power Spectral Density")

plt.tight_layout()
```

This kind of flexible grid alignment is very versatile. It is particularly useful for creating multi-axis histograms like the one shown here:

```python
# Generate normally distributed data
mean = [0, 0]
cov = [[1, 1], [1, 2]]
x, y = np.random.multivariate_normal(mean, cov, 3000).T

fig = plt.figure(figsize=(6, 6))
grid = plt.GridSpec(4, 4, hspace=0.2, wspace=0.2)
main_ax = fig.add_subplot(grid[:-1, 1:])
y_hist = fig.add_subplot(grid[:-1, 0],
                         xticklabels=[],
                         sharey=main_ax)
x_hist = fig.add_subplot(grid[-1, 1:],
                         yticklabels=[],
                         sharex=main_ax)

# Scatterplot on the main axis - orange markers
main_ax.plot(x, y,
             'o', color='orange', markersize=3, alpha=0.2)
```

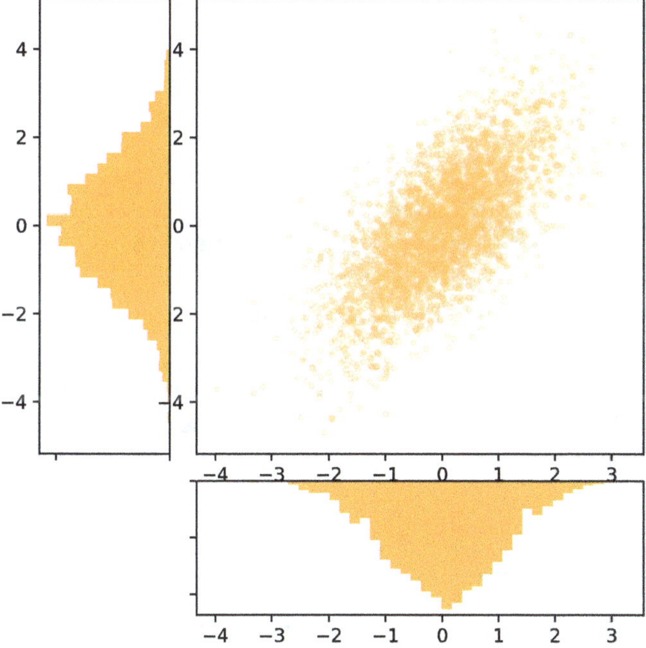

Figure 14.6 Visualization of scatter and marginal histograms with GridSpec

```python
# Histograms on the left and bottom axes
x_hist.hist(x,
            40,
            histtype='stepfilled',
            orientation='vertical',
            color='orange')
x_hist.invert_yaxis()

y_hist.hist(y,
            40,
            histtype='stepfilled',
            orientation='horizontal',
            color='orange')
y_hist.invert_xaxis()
```

14.3 Dual Axes

In many applications a single y-axis is sufficient to display a dataset. But sometimes one wants to show two different quantities with different scales on the same x-axis – for example: temperature and electricity consumption, speed and RPM, or revenue and advertising expenses.

For such situations, Matplotlib provides the option of dual axes – more precisely: a second y-axis on the right-hand side of the figure. This allows two data series to be compared without converting them into the same unit of measurement.

Matplotlib provides the methods `twinx()` (for two y-axes) and `twiny()` (for two x-axes).

In the following example, we demonstrate the use of dual axes with a practical scenario. The goal is to relate the electricity consumption of a group of houses to the outside temperature. This way we can examine whether there is a relationship between electricity consumption and temperature.

To generate the temperature values, we use a sine function that models a typical daily cycle – with a minimum in the early morning and a maximum in the afternoon:

$$\texttt{temperature} = 10 + 10 \cdot \sin\left(\tfrac{\pi}{12} \cdot (\texttt{hours} - 6)\right)$$

The temperature oscillates sinusoidally between 0 °C and 20 °C with a mean of 10 °C. The shift by 6 hours ensures that the maximum occurs at 2 p.m.

The electricity consumption is then modeled as a combination of two effects:

$$\texttt{consumption} = 30 - 0.8 \cdot \texttt{temperature} + 5 \cdot \exp\left(-\left(\tfrac{\texttt{hours}-18}{3}\right)^2\right)$$

The first term models the typical relationship: at lower temperatures, electricity consumption rises (e.g. due to heating). The second term describes an evening peak around 6 p.m. – caused, for example, by cooking, lighting, and electronics. The bell-shaped function is based on a Gaussian distribution and generates a realistic, locally limited increase.

```python
import matplotlib.pyplot as plt
import numpy as np


hours = np.arange(0, 24)
temperature = 10 + 10 * np.sin((hours - 6) * np.pi / 12)
consumption = 30 - 0.8 * temperature + 5 * np.exp(-((hours - 18)/3)**2)


fig, ax1 = plt.subplots()
# Left axis: Temperature
ax1.plot(hours, temperature, 'tab:red', label='Temperature (degC)')
ax1.set_xlabel('Hour of the day')
ax1.set_ylabel('Temperature (degC)', color='tab:red')
ax1.tick_params(axis='y', labelcolor='tab:red')


# Right axis: Electricity consumption
ax2 = ax1.twinx()
ax2.plot(hours,
         consumption,
         'tab:blue',
         label='Electricity consumption (kWh)')
ax2.set_ylabel('Electricity consumption (kWh)', color='tab:blue')
ax2.tick_params(axis='y', labelcolor='tab:blue')


fig.suptitle('Relationship between Temperature and Electricity Consumption
     ')
fig.tight_layout()
```

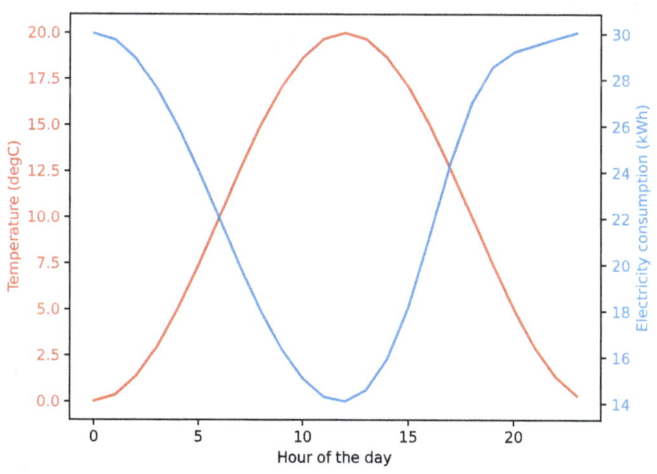

Figure 14.7 Dual axes: electricity consumption and outside temperature

14.4 Exercises

1. Exercise

(Solution: 33.8, Solution 1)

Create a diagram with multiple subplots using `plt.subplot()`. The diagram should look roughly like this:

2. Exercise

(Solution: 33.8, Solution 2)

As in the previous exercise, but now for the following figure:

3. Exercise

(Solution: 33.8, Solution 3)

Create a diagram for the figure from the previous exercise with six labeled areas using `matplotlib.gridspec`. The resulting diagram should look like this:

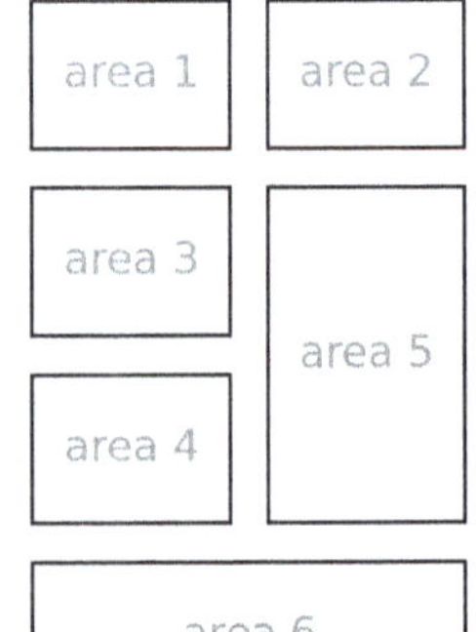

15

Axes and Tick Marks

15.1 Axes and Spines

In Matplotlib, we encounter the term *spine*, a concept that is not commonly used in MATLAB or many other plotting libraries.

In Matplotlib, a *spine* refers to one of the lines that form the rectangular frame surrounding the plot area. There are four spines in total: top, bottom, left, and right.

In Matplotlib's default configuration, the x-axis is drawn along the bottom spine and the y-axis along the left spine. In simple cases, these spines may therefore appear to coincide with the axes. From a technical standpoint, however, spines are only the frame lines of the plot. The axes themselves consist of additional elements, including tick marks, tick labels, and axis labels.

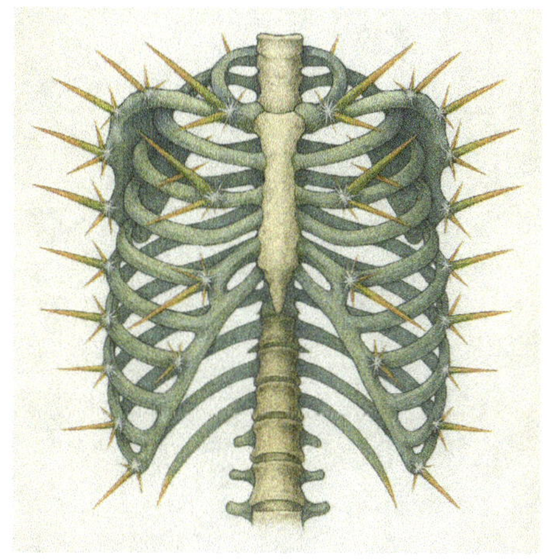

Figure 15.1 Rib cage and cactus spines

The following image illustrates a plot in which all four spines are explicitly labeled.

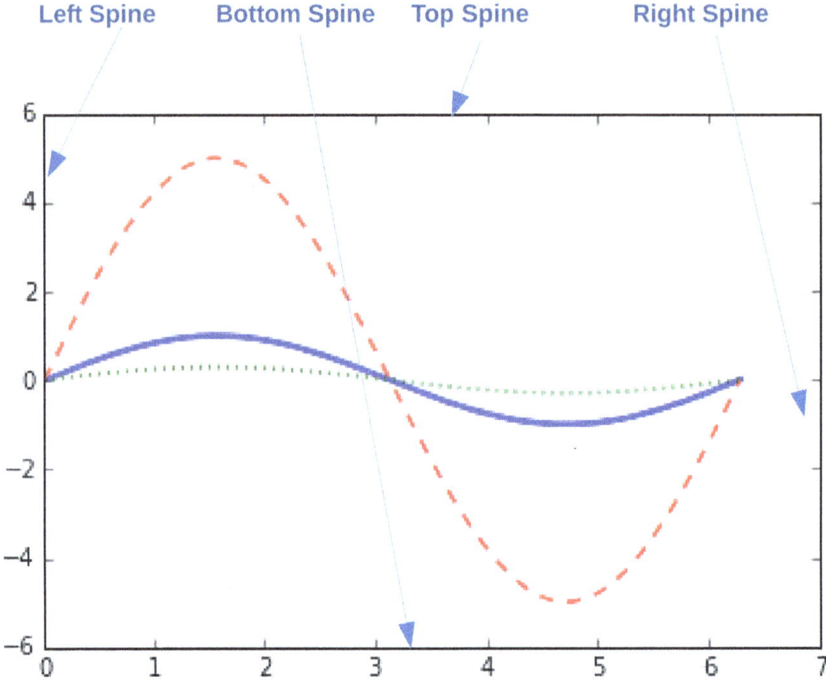

Figure 15.2 Illustration of spines

In the following program, we show how the spines can be shifted. In doing so, we create the appearance of a classical coordinate system by hiding the top and right spines and shifting the bottom (x-axis) and left (y-axis) spines:

```python
import numpy as np
import matplotlib.pyplot as plt


X = np.linspace(-2*np.pi, 2*np.pi, 70, endpoint=True)
F1 = np.sin(2 * X)
F2 = (2 * X**5 + 4 * X**4 - 4.8 * X**3 + 1.2 * X**2 + X + 2) * np.exp(-X
    **2)


fig, ax = plt.subplots()
# Make the top and right axes invisible:
ax.spines['top'].set_color('none')
ax.spines['right'].set_color('none')
# Move the bottom axis to the y=0 position:
ax.xaxis.set_ticks_position('bottom')
ax.spines['bottom'].set_position(('data', 0))
# Move the left axis to the x=0 position:
ax.yaxis.set_ticks_position('left')
ax.spines['left'].set_position(('data', 0))
ax.plot(X, F1, X, F2)
```

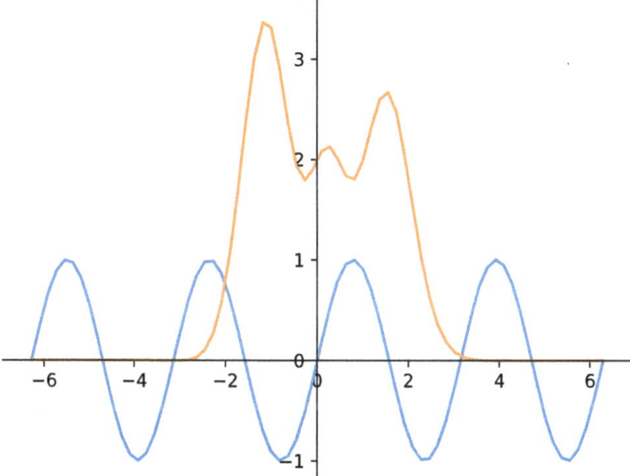

Up to now – in all previous examples – Matplotlib has automatically determined the spacing of the points on the axis. In our previous example, we saw that the X-axis was labeled with `-8, -6, -4, -2, 0, 2, 4, 6, 8`, while the Y-axis was labeled with `-2.0, -1.5, -1.0, -0.5, 0, 0.5, 1.0, 1.5, 2.0`.

The method `xticks` is used to query or change the positions and labels of the ticks on the X-axis. The same applies to the `yticks` method.

In addition, the methods get_xticklabels and get_yticklabels are used to read out the current tick labels, while set_xticklabels and set_yticklabels can be used to set custom labels.

```python
import matplotlib.pyplot as plt
fig, ax = plt.subplots()

xticks = ax.get_xticks()
xticklabels = ax.get_xticklabels()
print(f"{xticks=}\n{xticklabels=}")
print(f"{type(xticklabels[0])=}")

yticks = ax.get_yticks()
yticklabels = ax.get_yticklabels()
print(f"{yticks=}\n{yticklabels=}")
```

We obtain this output:

```
xticks=array([0. , 0.2, 0.4, 0.6, 0.8, 1. ])
xticklabels=[Text(0.0, 0, '0.0'), Text(0.2, 0, '0.2'), Text(0.4, 0, '0.4')
↪ , Text(0.6000000000000001, 0, '0.6'), Text(0.8, 0, '0.8'), Text(1.0,
↪ 0, '1.0')]
type(xticklabels[0])=<class 'matplotlib.text.Text'>
yticks=array([0. , 0.2, 0.4, 0.6, 0.8, 1. ])
yticklabels=[Text(0, 0.0, '0.0'), Text(0, 0.2, '0.2'), Text(0, 0.4, '0.4')
↪ , Text(0, 0.6000000000000001, '0.6'), Text(0, 0.8, '0.8'), Text(0,
↪ 1.0, '1.0')]
```

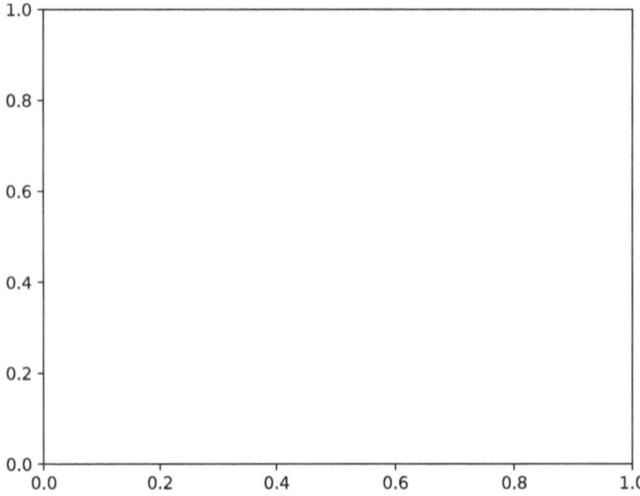

One can see that the labels are a list of Text xticklabel objects or Text yticklabel objects. The ticklabel objects are "empty" because the axis is labeled only with numerical values and not with text.

As already mentioned, `xticks` can also be used to change the position of the ticks on the
X-axis. In addition, in the following example we set the labels to city names (strings):

```python
import matplotlib.pyplot as plt
fig, ax = plt.subplots()

ax.set_xticks([5, 13, 23, 33, 42, 58])
xticks = ax.get_xticks()
ax.set_xticklabels(['Berlin', 'Frankfurt',
                    'Hamburg', 'Munich',
                    'Zurich', 'Geneva'])
xticklabels = ax.get_xticklabels()

print(f"{xticks=}\n{xticklabels=}")
```

The output we get is:

```
xticks=array([ 5, 13, 23, 33, 42, 58])
xticklabels=[Text(5, 0, 'Berlin'), Text(13, 0, 'Frankfurt'), Text(23, 0, '
↪    Hamburg'), Text(33, 0, 'Munich'), Text(42, 0, 'Zurich'), Text(58, 0, '
↪    Geneva')]
```

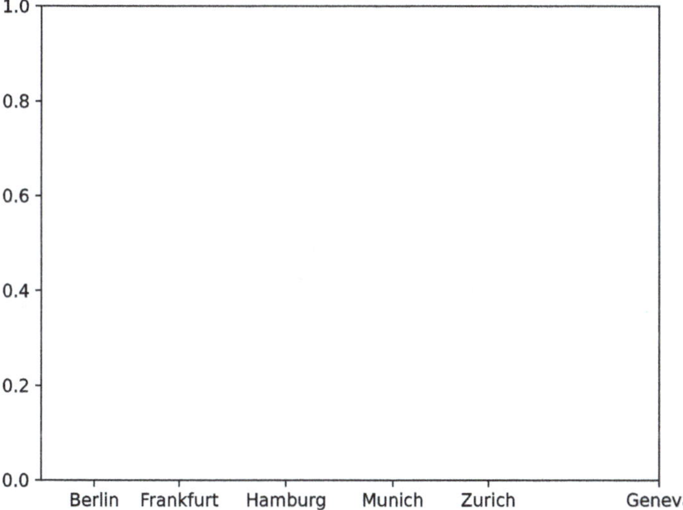

Let us return once more to the initial example of the trigonometric functions. Most users will prefer labeling the X-axis in fractions or multiples of pi:

```python
import numpy as np
import matplotlib.pyplot as plt


X = np.linspace(-2*np.pi, 2*np.pi, 70, endpoint=True)
F1 = np.sin(X**2)
F2 = X * np.sin(X)


fig, ax = plt.subplots()
# make the top-right spine invisible:
ax.spines['top'].set_color('none')
ax.spines['right'].set_color('none')
# move the bottom spine to the y=0 position:
ax.xaxis.set_ticks_position('bottom')
ax.spines['bottom'].set_position(('data', 0))
# move the left spine to x=0:
ax.yaxis.set_ticks_position('left')
ax.spines['left'].set_position(('data', 0))


ax.set_xticks([-6.28, -3.14, 0, 3.14, 6.28])
ax.set_yticks([-3, -1, 0, +1, 3])
ax.plot(X, F1)
ax.plot(X, F2)
```

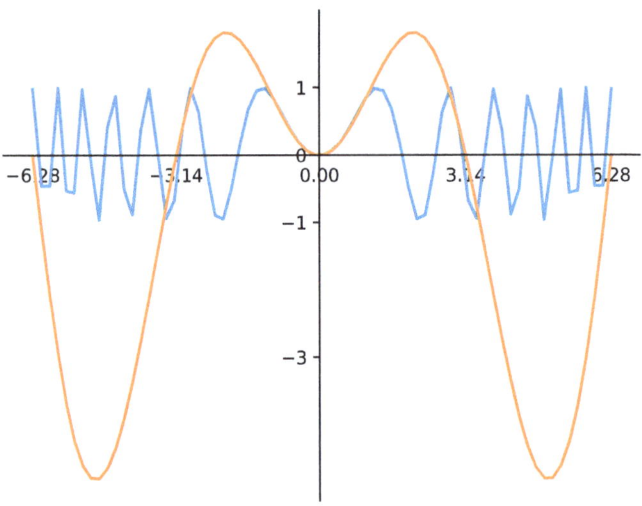

15.2 Changing Axis Labels

We now want to rename the labels of the X-axis and replace them with our own markers. To set the positions, we use the `set_major_locator` method of `ax.xaxis`. We use the `set_major_formatter` method of `ax.xaxis` to set the labels. To this method, we pass a list of strings that must have the same length as the list of positions (`positions`). To display the Greek pi as well as fractions, we use LaTeX notation. These must be written as raw strings (prefixed with 'r') in order to disable Python's escape mechanism, since backslashes are frequently used in LaTeX.

```python
import numpy as np
import matplotlib.pyplot as plt
import matplotlib.ticker as ticker


X = np.linspace(-2*np.pi, 2*np.pi, 100)
F1, F2 = np.sin(X), 3 * np.sin(X)


fig, ax = plt.subplots()
positions = [np.pi / 2 * x for x in range(-4, 5)]
labels = [r'$-2\pi$', r'$-\frac{3\pi}{2}$', r'$-\pi$',
          r'$-\frac{\pi}{2}$', 0, r'$\frac{\pi}{2}$',
          r'$+\pi$', r'$\frac{3\pi}{2}$', r'$+2\pi$']
ax.xaxis.set_major_locator(ticker.FixedLocator(positions))
ax.xaxis.set_major_formatter(ticker.FixedFormatter(labels))
ax.plot(X, F1, X, F2)
```

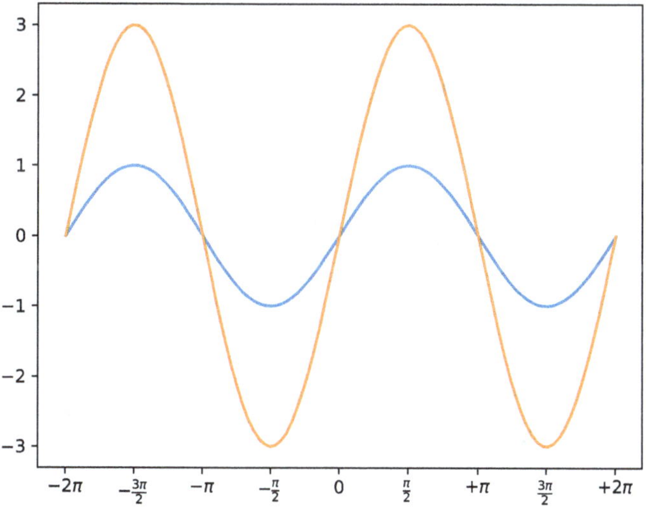

15.3 Adjustment of Tick Labels

In the following, we now increase the readability of the tick labels. To do this, we enlarge the font and draw it on a semi-transparent background.

```python
import numpy as np
import matplotlib.pyplot as plt
import matplotlib.ticker as ticker


X = np.linspace(-2*np.pi, 2*np.pi, 170, endpoint=True)
F1 = np.sin(X**3 / 2)
fig, ax = plt.subplots()
positions = [np.pi / 2 * x for x in range(-4, 5)]
labels = [r'$-2\pi$', r'$-\frac{3\pi}{2}$', r'$-\pi$',
          r'$-\frac{\pi}{2}$', 0, r'$\frac{\pi}{2}$',
          r'$+\pi$', r'$\frac{3\pi}{2}$', r'$+2\pi$']
ax.xaxis.set_major_locator(ticker.FixedLocator(positions))
ax.xaxis.set_major_formatter(ticker.FixedFormatter(labels))
descr_dict = dict(facecolor='white', edgecolor=None, alpha=0.7)
for xtick in ax.get_xticklabels():
    xtick.set_fontsize(18)
    xtick.set_bbox(descr_dict)
for ytick in ax.get_yticklabels():
    ytick.set_fontsize(14)
    ytick.set_bbox(descr_dict)
ax.plot(X, F1, label=r"$\sin(x^3/2)$")
```

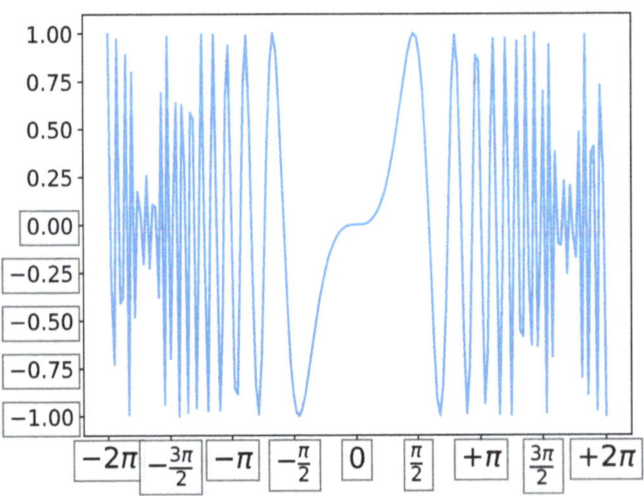

16
Legends and Annotations

16.1 Adding a Legend

When looking at the line plots from the previous examples, you always have to read the code to know which function is shown. This information should be contained directly in the diagram – that's what legends are for. The term comes from the Latin *legenda* ("that which must be read").

Originally used on maps, legends there explain symbols and colors. In diagrams, they provide information about the functions or values behind lines and curves.

The following shows how to add a legend to a plot. A legend consists of one or more entries, each linking a plotted line to a label.

Figure 16.1 Apollo and Diana slay the Python, Marcantonio Bassetti, 1618–1729

Adding one is simple: on the Axes object, call the `legend` method and pass it a list of label strings. For example:

```
import matplotlib.pyplot as plt

fig, ax = plt.subplots()
# Change height and width of the figure:
fig.set_figheight(2)
```

```
fig.set_figwidth(8.5)
ax.plot([1, 2, 3, 4])
ax.legend(['A straight line'])
```

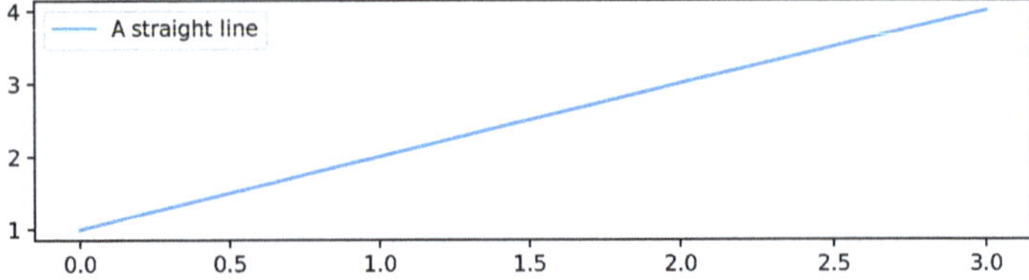

Figure 16.2 Simple legend for a line

Some might wonder why the string was in a list. The `legend` method expects an iterable of strings (e.g. list, tuple, or array) as its first parameter. This corresponds to the keyword parameter `labels`. The number of strings should match the number of plots in the Axes object.

```
ax.plot([1, 2, 3, 4])
ax.plot([4, 3, 2, 1])
ax.plot([2, 2, 2, 2])
ax.legend(labels=['A straight line', 'A 2nd line', 'Another one'])
```

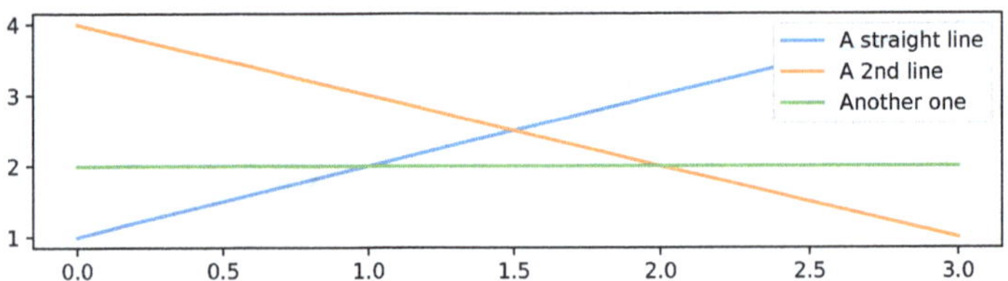

If the `labels` object contains fewer strings than there are plots, some plots won't appear in the legend. The strings are assigned to the plots in the order they were created. Here's the same example again, but with a shorter `legend` call:

```
ax.legend(['A straight line', 'A 2nd line'])
```

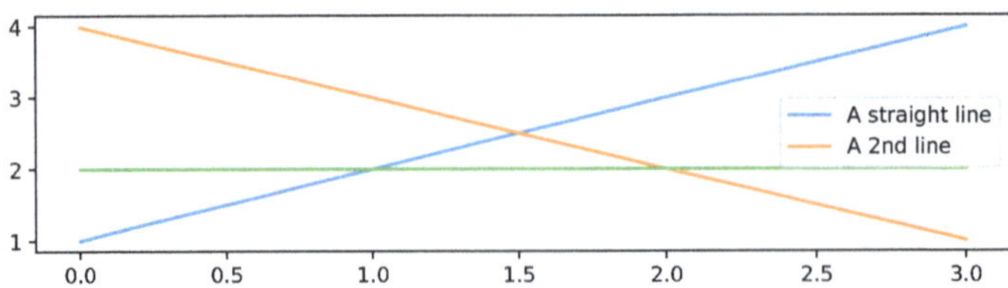

Alternatively, you can specify labels for the functions directly when plotting, using the `label` keyword parameter of the `plot` method. Then you can call `legend` without arguments:

```python
import numpy as np
import matplotlib.pyplot as plt
x = np.linspace(0, 25, 1000)
y1 = np.sin(x)
y2 = np.cos(x)

fig, ax = plt.subplots()
fig.set_figheight(4)
ax.plot(x, y1, '-', label='sine')
ax.plot(x, y2, '-', label='cosine')
ax.legend()
ax.set_ylim(-1.1, 1.3)
```

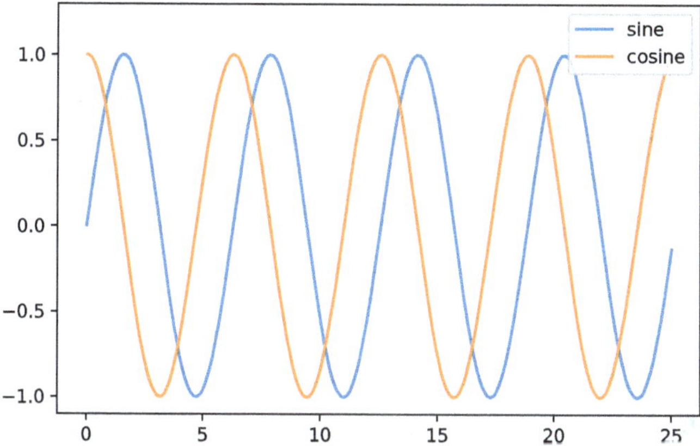

So far we let Matplotlib decide where to place the legend. By default, `legend` tries to find a position that avoids covering up data. But with the keyword parameter `loc`, we can control the placement explicitly:

- Corners: `upper left`, `upper right`, `lower left`, `lower right`
- Centered on a side: `upper center`, `lower center`, `center left`, `center right`
- In the exact center of the axes plot: `center`
- The option `best` places the legend where it overlaps the data the least. With large datasets, this may be slower; a fixed placement can speed things up.
- The position can also be a 2-tuple giving the axes coordinates of the lower-left corner of the legend.

In the following example, we place the legend explicitly in the upper left corner:

```python
ax.legend(loc='upper left')
```

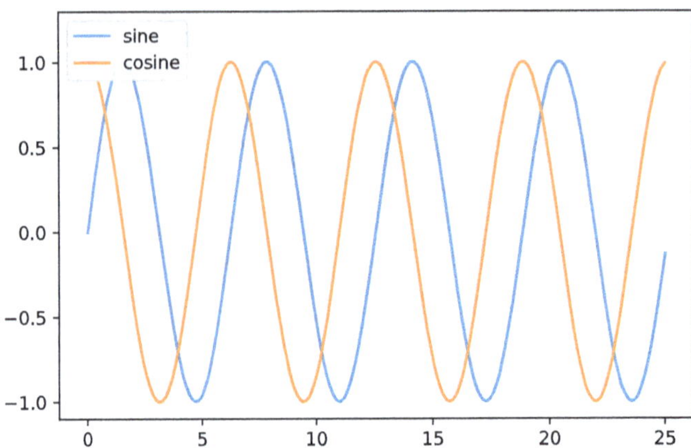

Usually, you don't know in advance how the plot will look. The legend might cover an important part of the plot. In such cases, you can use best as the argument for loc. The next example shows that best finds a good position here:

```python
import numpy as np
import matplotlib.pyplot as plt

X = np.linspace(-2 * np.pi, 2 * np.pi, 70, endpoint=True)
F1, F2 = np.sin(0.5 * X), -3 * np.cos(0.8 * X)
fig, ax = plt.subplots()
fig.set_figheight(2.5)
ax.set_xticks([-2*np.pi, -np.pi, 0, np.pi, 2*np.pi])
ax.set_xticklabels([r'$-2\pi$', r'$-\pi$', '0', r'$+\pi$', r'$+2\pi$'])
ax.set_yticks([-3, -1, 0, +1, 3])
ax.plot(X, F1, label="$sin(0.5x)$")
ax.plot(X, F2, label=r"$-3\cos(0.8x)$")
ax.legend(loc='best')
```

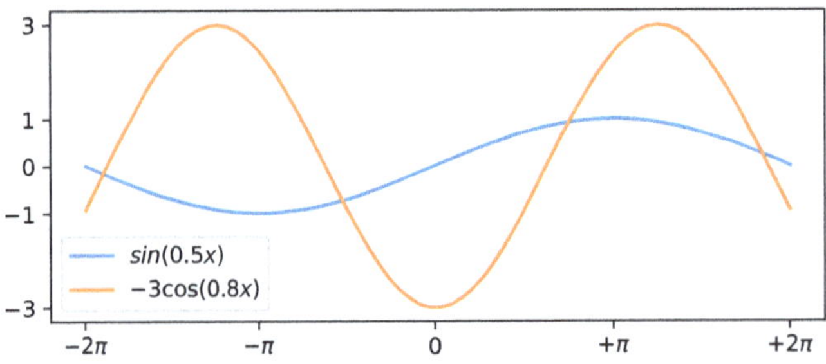

16.2 Annotations

The visualization of functions often requires annotations to highlight important points and regions. For this we use text, labels, and arrows. While axis labels and titles describe the overall figure, the `annotate` method allows targeted hints within the plot. An annotation involves two points: the point being labeled, given by xy, and the position of the text `xytext`, i.e. the left starting point of the text. Both arguments are (x, y) tuples.

We'll show how easily you can add labels in Matplotlib with `annotate` – for example, to mark local maxima and minima of a function. In its simplest form, `annotate` needs two arguments: the text string s and the position xy of the point to label. For the following example you need to download the module `polynomials` (file `polynomials.py`).[1]

```python
from polynomials import Polynomial
import numpy as np
import matplotlib.pyplot as plt


p = Polynomial(1, 0, -12, 0)
p_der = p.derivative()
fig, ax = plt.subplots()
X = np.arange(-5, 5, 0.1)
F = p(X)
F_derivative = p_der(X)
ax.grid()
maximum, minimum = (-2, p(-2)), (2, p(2))
ax.annotate("local maximum", maximum)
ax.annotate("local minimum", minimum)
ax.plot(X, F, label="p")
ax.plot(X, F_derivative, label="derivation of p")
ax.legend(loc='best')
```

---

1 *http://python-kurs.eu/buch/beispiele/polynomials.py*

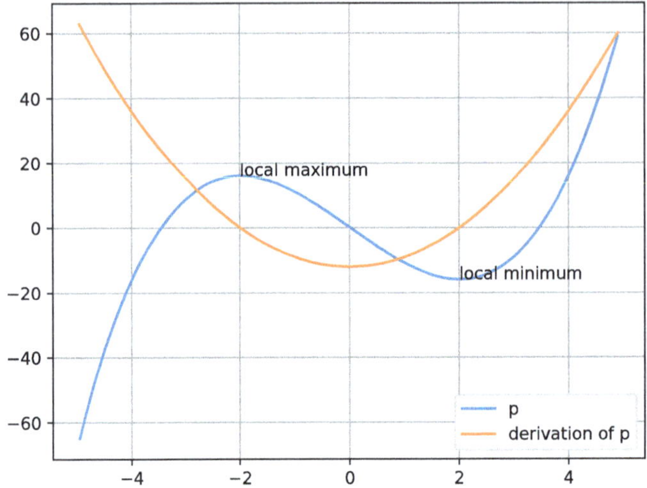

If you're not satisfied with the automatic placement of the text, you can pass a tuple to
the keyword parameter `xytext` to specify where the text should be placed:

```python
from polynomials import Polynomial
import numpy as np
import matplotlib.pyplot as plt


p = Polynomial(1, 0, -12, 0)
p_der = p.derivative()


fig, ax = plt.subplots()
X = np.arange(-5, 5, 0.1)
F = p(X)
F_derivative = p_der(X)
ax.grid()
ax.annotate("local maximum",
            xy=(-2, p(-2)),
            xytext=(-1, p(-2)+35),
            arrowprops=dict(facecolor='orange'))
ax.annotate("local minimum",
            xy=(2, p(2)),
            xytext=(-2, p(2) - 40),
            arrowprops=dict(facecolor='orange', shrink=0.05))
ax.annotate("inflection point",
            xy=(0, p(0)),
            xytext=(-3, -30),
            arrowprops=dict(facecolor='orange', shrink=0.05))
ax.plot(X, F, label="p")
ax.plot(X, F_derivative, label="derivation of p")
ax.legend(loc='best')
```

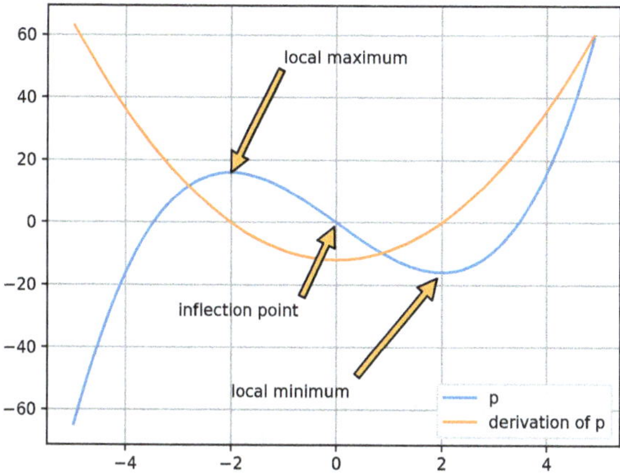

We had to provide several parameters to the `annotate` function.

Parameter	Meaning
xy	Coordinates of the arrow tip
xytext	Coordinates of the text position

In our example, the `xy` and `xytext` positions are given in data coordinates. There are other coordinate systems you can use. The coordinate systems for `xy` and `xytext` can be specified via the string values `xycoords` and `textcoords`. The default is "data":

String value	Coordinate system
figure points	Points from the lower-left corner of the figure
figure pixels	Pixels from the lower-left corner of the figure
figure fraction	0,0 is bottom left and 1,1 is top right in the figure
axes points	Points from the lower-left corner of the axes
axes pixels	Pixels from the lower-left corner of the axes
axes fraction	Fractional: 0,0 is bottom left and 1,1 is top right
data	Use the axes' data coordinate system

You can also customize arrow properties by passing a dictionary of arrow options via the `arrowprops` parameter:

arrowprops key	Description
width	Arrow shaft width in points
headlength	Length occupied by the arrow head
headwidth	Width of the arrowhead base in points
shrink	Move tip and base inwards by a percentage from point and text
**kwargs	Any keyword for `matplotlib.patches.Polygon`, e.g. `facecolor`

Of course, the sine function has "boring" and "interesting" values. Suppose we're interested in the value $3 \cdot \sin\left(3 \cdot \frac{\pi}{4}\right)$.

```python
import numpy as np

print(3 * np.sin(3 * np.pi/4))
```

Output:

```
2.121320343559643
```

The numeric value looks unremarkable, but symbolically it simplifies to $\frac{3}{\sqrt{2}}$. Now we want to mark exactly this point on the graph. We can do this with `annotate`.

```python
import numpy as np
import matplotlib.pyplot as plt
import matplotlib.ticker as ticker

X = np.linspace(-2 * np.pi, 2 * np.pi, 100)
F1, F2 = np.sin(X), 3 * np.sin(X)

fig, ax = plt.subplots()
positions = [np.pi/2 * x for x in range(-4, 5)]
labels = [r'$-2\pi$', r'$-\frac{3\pi}{2}$', r'$-\pi$',
          r'$-\frac{\pi}{2}$', 0, r'$\frac{\pi}{2}$',
          r'$+\pi$', r'$\frac{3\pi}{2}$', r'$+2\pi$']
ax.xaxis.set_major_locator(ticker.FixedLocator(positions))
ax.xaxis.set_major_formatter(ticker.FixedFormatter(labels))
ax.plot(X, F1, label="$sin(x)$")
ax.plot(X, F2, label="$3 sin(x)$")
ax.legend(loc='lower left')
x = 3 * np.pi / 4
# Plot vertical line:
ax.plot([x, x], [-3, 3 * np.sin(x)], color='blue',
        linewidth=2.5, linestyle="--")
# Draw the blue dot:
ax.scatter([x,], [3 * np.sin(x),], 50, color='blue')
text_x, text_y = (3.5, 2.2)
ax.annotate(r'$3\sin(\frac{3\pi}{4})=\frac{3}{\sqrt{2}}$',
            xy=(x, 3 * np.sin(x)),
            xytext=(text_x, text_y),
            arrowprops=dict(facecolor='orange', shrink=0.05),
            fontsize=12)
```

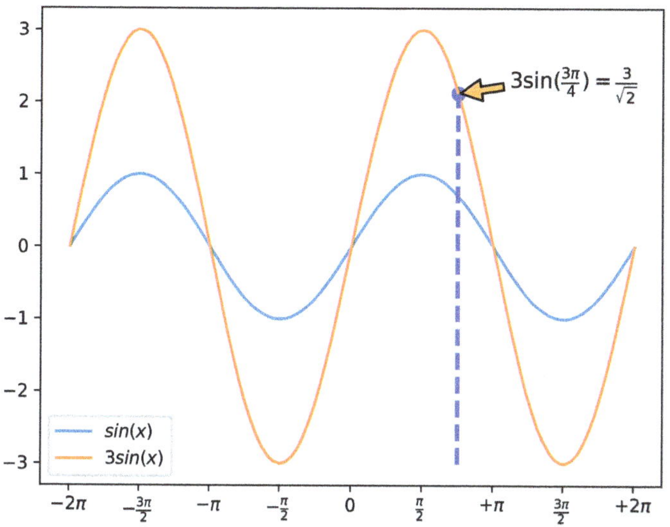

The next example shows variations for annotations and arrows:

```python
import numpy as np
import matplotlib.pyplot as plt


X = np.linspace(-4.1, 3.1, 150, endpoint=True)
F = X**5 + 3 * X**4 - 11 * X**3 - 27 * X**2 + 10 * X + 24


fig, ax = plt.subplots()
ax.plot(X, F)
minimum1 = -1.5264814, -7.051996717492152
minimum2 = 2.3123415793720303, -81.36889464201387
ax.annotate("minima", xy=minimum1, xytext=(-1.5, -50),
            arrowprops=dict(arrowstyle="->",
                connectionstyle="angle3,angleA=0,angleB=-90"))
ax.annotate(" ", xy=minimum2, xytext=(-0.7, -50),
            arrowprops=dict(arrowstyle="->",
                connectionstyle="angle3,angleA=0,angleB=-90"))


maximum1 = -3.35475845886632, 56.963107876630595
maximum2 = .16889828232847673, 24.868343482875485
ax.annotate("maxima", xy=maximum1, xytext=(-1.5, 30),
            arrowprops=dict(arrowstyle="->",
                connectionstyle="angle3,angleA=0,angleB=-90"))
ax.annotate(" ", xy=maximum2, xytext=(-0.6, 30),
            arrowprops=dict(arrowstyle="->",
                connectionstyle="angle3,angleA=0,angleB=-90"))
```

```python
zeroes = -4, -2, -1, 1, 3
for zero in zeroes:
    zero = zero, 0
    ax.annotate(
        "Zeroes", xy=zero, color="orange",
        bbox=dict(boxstyle="round", fc="none", ec="green"),
        xytext=(1, 40),
        arrowprops=dict(
            arrowstyle="->", color="orange",
            connectionstyle="angle3,angleA=0,angleB=-90"
        )
    )
```

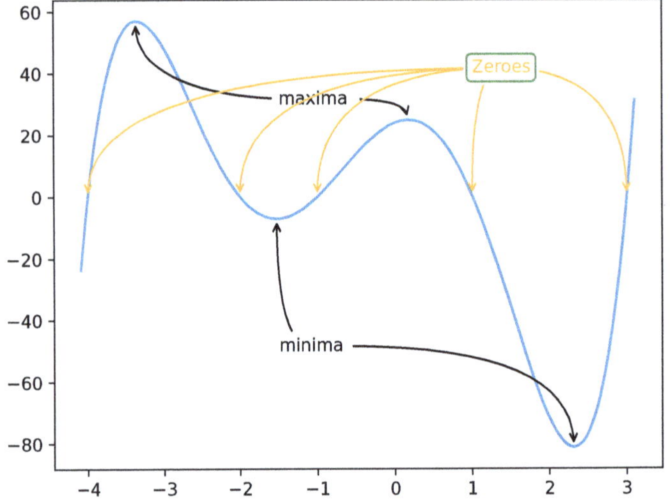

The following program illustrates the basic variants for drawing arrows:

```python
import matplotlib.pyplot as plt


def demo_con_style(ax, connectionstyle):
    x1, y1 = 0.3, 0.2
    x2, y2 = 0.8, 0.6
    ax.plot([x1, x2], [y1, y2], ".")
    ax.annotate("",
                xy=(x1, y1), xycoords='data',
                xytext=(x2, y2), textcoords='data',
                arrowprops=dict(arrowstyle="->", color="0.5",
                                shrinkA=5, shrinkB=5,
                                patchA=None, patchB=None,
                                connectionstyle=connectionstyle))
```

```python
    ax.text(.05, .95, connectionstyle.replace(",", ",\n"),
            transform=ax.transAxes, ha="left", va="top")


fig, axs = plt.subplots(3, 5, figsize=(8, 4.8))
demo_con_style(axs[0, 0], "angle3,angleA=90,angleB=0")
demo_con_style(axs[1, 0], "angle3,angleA=0,angleB=90")
demo_con_style(axs[0, 1], "arc3,rad=0.")
demo_con_style(axs[1, 1], "arc3,rad=0.3")
demo_con_style(axs[2, 1], "arc3,rad=-0.3")
demo_con_style(axs[0, 2], "angle,angleA=-90,angleB=180,rad=0")
demo_con_style(axs[1, 2], "angle,angleA=-90,angleB=180,rad=5")
demo_con_style(axs[2, 2], "angle,angleA=-90,angleB=10,rad=5")
demo_con_style(axs[0, 3],
               "arc,angleA=-90,angleB=0,armA=30,armB=30,rad=0")
demo_con_style(axs[1, 3],
               "arc,angleA=-90,angleB=0,armA=30,armB=30,rad=5")
demo_con_style(axs[2, 3],
               "arc,angleA=-90,angleB=0,armA=0,armB=40,rad=0")
demo_con_style(axs[0, 4], "bar,fraction=0.3")
demo_con_style(axs[1, 4], "bar,fraction=-0.3")
demo_con_style(axs[2, 4], "bar,angle=180,fraction=-0.2")


for ax in axs.flat:
    ax.set(xlim=(0, 1),
           ylim=(0, 1),
           xticks=[],
           yticks=[],
           aspect=1)
fig.tight_layout(pad=0.2)
```

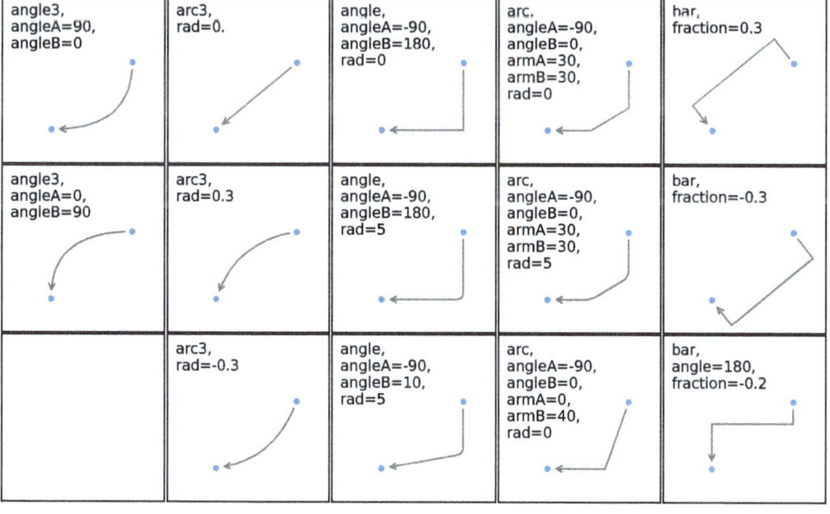

16.3 Exercises

Exercise 1

(Solution: 33.9, Solution 1)

Create a line chart showing the number of units sold for three different products over a year. Use Matplotlib's `legend` function to add the product names as legend labels.

Exercise 2

(Solution: 33.9, Solution 2)

Create a line chart with the monthly temperatures of a given year. Then add annotations that mark the highest and lowest values on the y-axis.

17
Contour Plots

A contour line, or isoline, of a function of two variables is a curve along which the function has a constant value. In essence, it represents a cross-section or projection of the three-dimensional function graph $f(x, y)$ parallel to the x–y plane.

Contour lines are used in disciplines such as geography and meteorology. In cartography, they denote lines that connect points of equal elevation above a reference level – usually mean sea level.

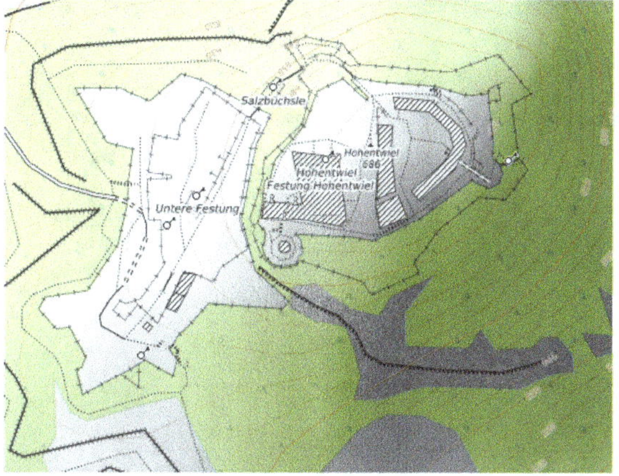

Figure 17.1 Hiking map of Hohentwiel

Contour lines above sea level are called elevation lines, while those below are depth lines. They make it possible to depict terrain structure in two dimensions by showing differences in height.

The adjacent image shows an example of a topographic map with contour lines.[1]

In general, a contour line of a function with two variables is a curve that connects all points with the same function value.

---

1   This map depicts the Hohentwiel fortress near Singen, the largest surviving castle or fortress ruin in Germany, covering about 9 hectares. It sits atop the former Hohentwiel volcano, rising about 260 meters above the city of Singen and offering a unique view across the Hegau region to Lake Constance and the Alps. The map was created by the author using *https://opentopomap.org*.

17.1 Creating a Meshgrid

The purpose of `meshgrid` is to take two one-dimensional arrays – e.g., for x- and y-values – and create a rectangular grid suitable for vectorized evaluation over a surface. To illustrate how `meshgrid` works, we start with the arrays `x_values` and `y_values`. `x_values` contains the values −3, 0, 3, while `y_values` contains −3, −1, 1, 3. We seek a structure that represents all combinations of these pairs, i.e.:

```
(-3, 3) (0, 3) (3, 3)
(-3, 1) (0, 1) (3, 1)
(-3, -1) (0, -1) (3, -1)
(-3, -3) (0, -3) (3, -3)
```

In the coordinate system, these appear as regularly spaced grid nodes:

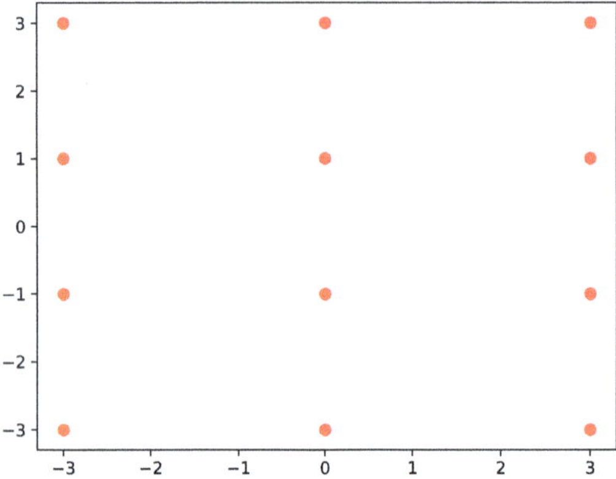

Figure 17.2 Points of a meshgrid

The purpose of NumPy's `meshgrid` function is therefore to generate a rectangular grid, as seen above, from an array of x-values and an array of y-values. To create such a grid from the one-dimensional arrays `x_values` and `y_values`, we need every combination of their values. This is exactly what `meshgrid` does.

```python
import numpy as np

x_values = np.linspace(-3.0, 3.0, 3)
y_values = np.linspace(-3.0, 3.0, 4)
X, Y = np.meshgrid(x_values, y_values)

print(x_values)
print(y_values)
print(X)
print(Y)
```

Output:

```
[-3.  0.  3.]
[-3. -1.  1.  3.]
[[-3.  0.  3.]
 [-3.  0.  3.]
 [-3.  0.  3.]
 [-3.  0.  3.]]
[[-3. -3. -3.]
 [-1. -1. -1.]
 [ 1.  1.  1.]
 [ 3.  3.  3.]]
```

We illustrate what has just been said once again in a diagram:

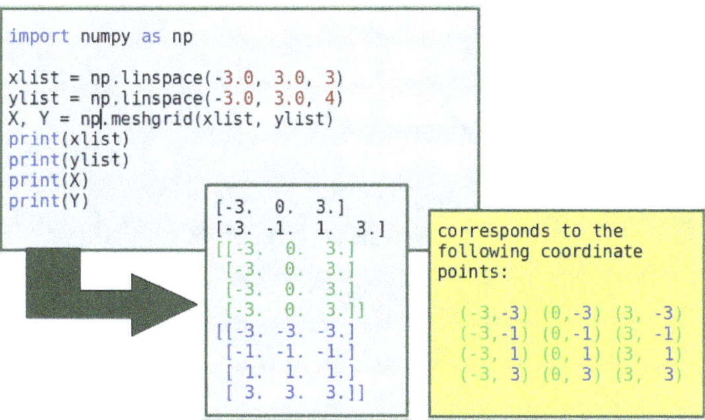

Figure 17.3 How the function meshgrid works

In Diagramm 17.2 we visualized these points using a scatter plot:

```
X, Y = np.meshgrid(x_values, y_values)
fig, ax = plt.subplots()
ax.scatter(X, Y, s=42, color='red')
```

17.2 Functions on Meshgrids

We now take the points of the meshgrid as the domain of a function in two variables.
Consider the function

$$z = \sqrt{x^2 + y^2}$$

– that is, the square root of an elliptic paraboloid. We now compute the function values for the pairs in the meshgrid:

```python
import numpy as np


x_values = np.linspace(-3.0, 3.0, 3)
y_values = np.linspace(-3.0, 3.0, 4)
X, Y = np.meshgrid(x_values, y_values)


Z = np.sqrt(X**2 + Y**2)
print(Z)
```

The result of the code is:

```
[[4.24264069 3.         4.24264069]
 [3.16227766 1.         3.16227766]
 [3.16227766 1.         3.16227766]
 [4.24264069 3.         4.24264069]]
```

From these data, we can produce a contour plot:

```python
import matplotlib.pyplot as plt
fig, ax = plt.subplots()
cp = ax.contour(X, Y, Z)
ax.clabel(cp,
          inline=True,
          fontsize=10)
ax.set_title('Contour Plot')
ax.set_xlabel('x (cm)')
ax.set_ylabel('y (cm)')
```

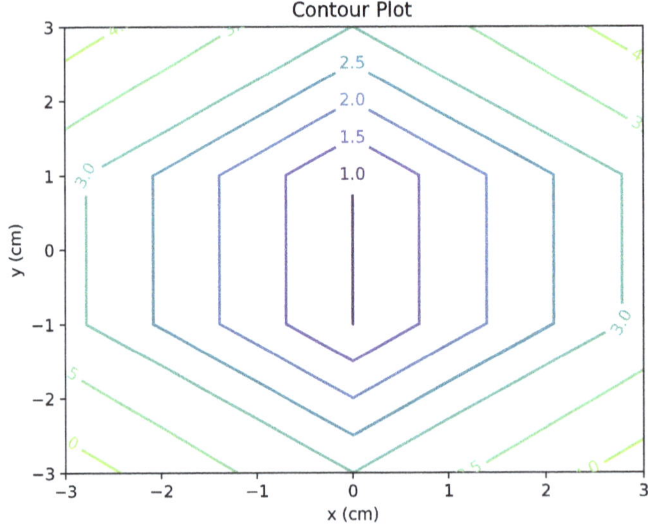

Our contour plot looks blocky because our meshgrid contains only 12 points. We can refine it by increasing the grid density. Replace the lines

```
x_values = np.linspace(-3.0, 3.0, 3)
y_values = np.linspace(-3.0, 3.0, 4)
```

with

```
x_values = np.linspace(-3.0, 3.0, 100)
y_values = np.linspace(-3.0, 3.0, 100)
```

in the previous code to obtain smooth, perfectly rounded contours:

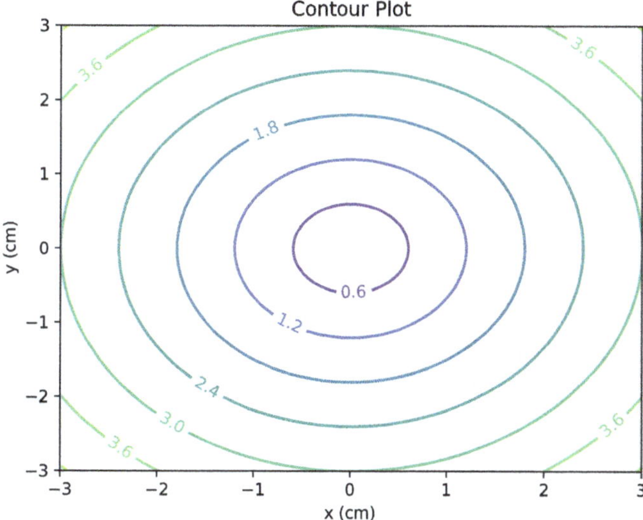

17.3 Contour Without Meshgrid

It is worth looking more closely at the documentation of contour and contourf, especially regarding the parameters X and Y. *"These must both be either 2D arrays of the same shape as Z (e.g., created with meshgrid), or both 1D arrays where len(X) matches the number of columns and len(Y) the number of rows of Z. Both arrays must also be monotonic."*[2]

Thus, we can pass x_values and y_values directly to contour or contourf – meshgrid is not necessary. In our example, the code

```
x_values = np.linspace(-3.0, 3.0, 100)
y_values = np.linspace(-3.0, 3.0, 100)
X, Y = np.meshgrid(x_values, y_values)
Z = np.sqrt(X**2 + Y**2)
```

---

2   Translation from the English help

```python
fig, ax = plt.subplots()
cp = ax.contour(X, Y, Z)
```

can be replaced with:

```python
x_values = np.linspace(-3.0, 3.0, 100)
y_values = np.linspace(-3.0, 3.0, 100)
Z = np.sqrt(x_values.reshape((1, -1))**2 + y_values.reshape((-1, 1))**2)

fig, ax = plt.subplots()
cp = ax.contour(x_values, y_values, Z)
```

We see that to compute Z, we had to reshape x_values and y_values into a row vector
and a column vector, respectively. When adding them, NumPy performs broadcasting
of the row and column vectors.

17.4 Adjusting Line Styles and Colors

So far, we have let Matplotlib automatically choose the line styles and colors. With the
parameters linestyles and colors, we can customize them individually.

We show both a variant with meshgrid and one without.

Variant with meshgrid:

```python
import numpy as np
import matplotlib.pyplot as plt

x_values = np.linspace(-3.0, 3.0, 100)
y_values = np.linspace(-3.0, 3.0, 100)
X, Y = np.meshgrid(x_values, y_values)

Z = np.sqrt(X**2 + Y**2)

fig, ax = plt.subplots()
cp = ax.contour(X, Y, Z,
                colors='black',
                linestyles='dashed')
ax.clabel(cp,
          inline=True,
          fontsize=10)
ax.set_title('Contour Plot')
ax.set_xlabel('x (cm)')
ax.set_ylabel('y (cm)')
```

Variant without `meshgrid`:

```python
import numpy as np
import matplotlib.pyplot as plt


x_values = np.linspace(-3.0, 3.0, 100)
y_values = np.linspace(-3.0, 3.0, 100)
x_values_2D = x_values.reshape((1, -1))**2
y_values_2D = y_values.reshape((-1, 1))**2
Z = np.sqrt(x_values_2D + y_values_2D)


fig, ax = plt.subplots()
cp = ax.contour(x_values, y_values, Z,
                colors='black',
                linestyles='dashed')
ax.clabel(cp,
          inline=True,
          fontsize=10)
ax.set_title('Contour Plot')
ax.set_xlabel('x (cm)')
ax.set_ylabel('y (cm)')
```

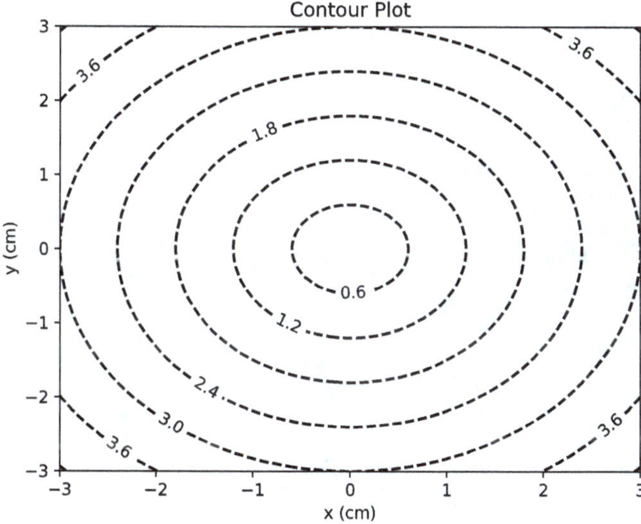

Figure 17.4 Contour plot with dashed lines

17.5 Filled Contours

We can also fill the space between the contour lines with color. For this, we use the
contourf method:

```python
import numpy as np
import matplotlib.pyplot as plt
from matplotlib import cm

x_values = np.linspace(-3.0, 3.0, 100)
y_values = np.linspace(-3.0, 3.0, 100)
X, Y = np.meshgrid(x_values, y_values)
Z = np.sqrt(X**2 + Y**2)

fig, ax = plt.subplots()
ax.set_title('Filled Contour Plot')
ax.set_xlabel('x (cm)')
ax.set_ylabel('y (cm)')
cs = ax.contourf(X, Y, Z, cmap=cm.PuBu_r)
cbar = fig.colorbar(cs)
```

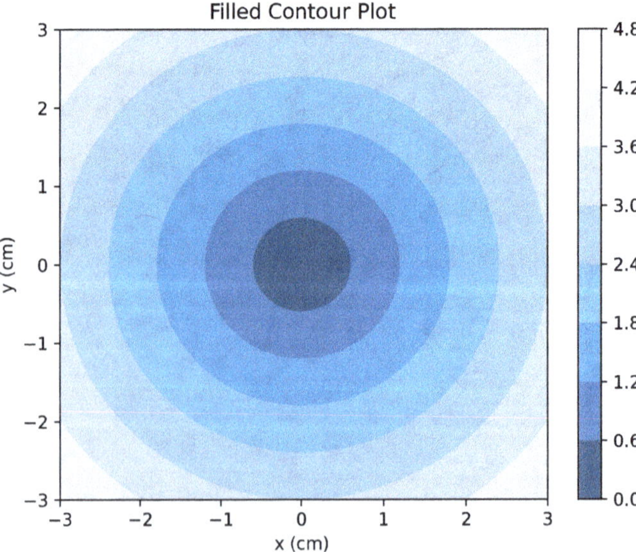

Figure 17.5 Filled contour plot with color scale

17.6 Custom Colors

Of course, we can also define the colors of the filled regions ourselves, as the following example shows:

```python
import numpy as np
import matplotlib.pyplot as plt


x_values = np.linspace(-3.0, 3.0, 100)
y_values = np.linspace(-3.0, 3.0, 100)
X, Y = np.meshgrid(x_values, y_values)
Z = np.sqrt(X**2 + Y**2)


fig, ax = plt.subplots()
contour = ax.contourf(X, Y, Z)
ax.clabel(contour,
          colors='k',
          fmt='%2.1f',
          fontsize=12)
c = ('#ff0000', '#ffA322', '#0054FF', '0.6', 'c', 'm')
contour_filled = ax.contourf(X, Y, Z, colors=c)
fig.colorbar(contour_filled)
ax.set_title('Filled Contour Plot')
ax.set_xlabel('x (cm)')
ax.set_ylabel('y (cm)')
```

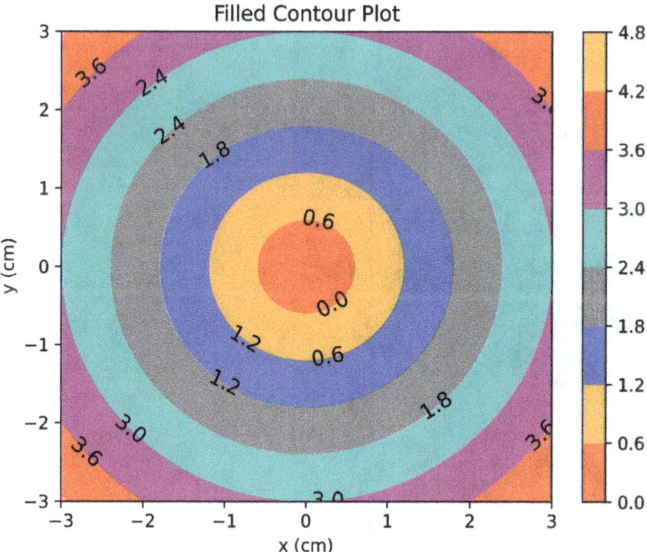

Figure 17.6 Filled contour plot with custom colors

17.7 Levels

The thresholds for contour lines and filled regions are set automatically by `contour` and
`contourf`. They can also be defined manually by passing a list of levels as the fourth
argument. Contour lines are drawn for each value in the list when we use `contour`. If
`contourf` is used, the regions between the level values are filled with color.

```python
import numpy as np
import matplotlib.pyplot as plt


x_values = np.linspace(-3.0, 3.0, 100)
y_values = np.linspace(-3.0, 3.0, 100)
X, Y = np.meshgrid(x_values, y_values)


Z = np.sqrt(X**2 + Y**2)
fig, ax = plt.subplots()


levels = [0.0, 0.2, 0.5, 0.9, 1.5, 2.5, 3.5]
contour = plt.contour(X, Y, Z, levels, colors='k')
ax.clabel(contour,
          colors='k',
          fmt='%2.1f',
          fontsize=12)
contour_filled = ax.contourf(X, Y, Z, levels)
fig.colorbar(contour_filled)


ax.set_title('Filled Contour Plot')
ax.set_xlabel('x (cm)')
ax.set_ylabel('y (cm)')
```

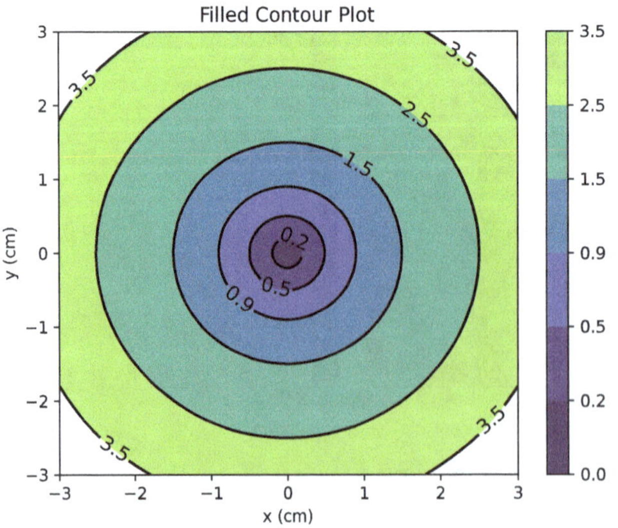

Figure 17.7 Contour plot
with custom contour levels

17.8 Other Grids

We have already introduced NumPy's `meshgrid` function. However, NumPy also contains two other important functions for generating grid-like structures:

- `ogrid`
- `mgrid`

17.8.1 Meshgrid in More Detail

The task of `meshgrid`, as we have seen, is to generate a two-dimensional coordinate matrix from two one-dimensional coordinate vectors. In the general case, one can generate an n-dimensional array from n one-dimensional, array-like structures, allowing vectorized evaluation of n-dimensional vector fields over an n-dimensional grid.

We have already seen how to construct a grid structure using `meshgrid`. For completeness, we show it again here for a grid G with the values $-1, 0, 1$ as x-values and $-2, -1, 0, 1, 2$ as y-values. The $(5, 3)$-grid corresponds to the pairings of the respective components from the arrays X and Y, i.e., the points $P = (X[i], Y[j])$ with $-1 \leq i \leq 2$ and $-2 \leq j \leq 3$.

```python
import matplotlib.pyplot as plt
import numpy as np


x_min, x_max = -1, 2
y_min, y_max = -2, 3
x_values = np.arange(x_min, x_max)
y_values = np.arange(y_min, y_max)
X, Y = np.meshgrid(x_values, y_values)
print(f"{X=}\n{Y=}")
```

After execution we get:

```
X=array([[-1,  0,  1],
       [-1,  0,  1],
       [-1,  0,  1],
       [-1,  0,  1],
       [-1,  0,  1]])
Y=array([[-2, -2, -2],
       [-1, -1, -1],
       [ 0,  0,  0],
       [ 1,  1,  1],
       [ 2,  2,  2]])
```

With a plot, we can make this grid visible:

```
fig, ax = plt.subplots()
ax.scatter(X, Y, s=42, color='red')
```

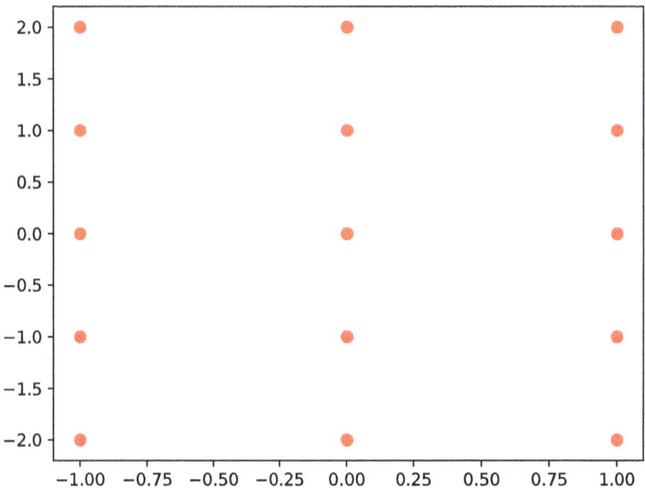

Figure 17.8 Visualization of a two-dimensional grid created with numpy.meshgrid

In the following example, we show that it is also possible – though very cumbersome –
to do this without meshgrid.

```
import numpy as np
x_min, x_max = -1, 2
y_min, y_max = -2, 3
x_values = np.arange(x_min, x_max)
y_values = np.arange(y_min, y_max)

n = len(x_values)
m = len(y_values)
X, Y = np.zeros((m, n), np.int8), np.zeros((m, n), np.int8)
for row in range(m):
    for col in range(n):
        X[row, col] = x_values[col]
        Y[row, col] = y_values[row]
print(f"{X=}\n{Y=}")
```

Output:

```
X=array([[-1,  0,  1],
         [-1,  0,  1],
         [-1,  0,  1],
         [-1,  0,  1],
         [-1,  0,  1]], dtype=int8)
Y=array([[-2, -2, -2],
         [-1, -1, -1],
         [ 0,  0,  0],
         [ 1,  1,  1],
         [ 2,  2,  2]], dtype=int8)
```

17.8.2 mgrid

Unlike meshgrid, mgrid does not take array-like input vectors but is indexed with slice
notation. That's why we use square brackets here – it is not a function call. mgrid
and meshgrid essentially return the same result, but mgrid returns the arrays in the
opposite order compared to meshgrid, i.e., Y first and then X.

```python
import numpy as np

n = 3
Y_mgrid, X_mgrid = np.mgrid[0:n, 0:n]


n = 3
X_meshgrid, Y_meshgrid = np.meshgrid(np.arange(0, n),
                                     np.arange(0, n))


print(X_mgrid == X_meshgrid)
print(Y_mgrid == Y_meshgrid)
```

The output we get is:

```
[[ True  True  True]
 [ True  True  True]
 [ True  True  True]]
[[ True  True  True]
 [ True  True  True]
 [ True  True  True]]
```

17.8.3 ogrid

With `meshgrid` and `mgrid`, the values in the generated matrices are repeated row-wise or column-wise. `ogrid`, on the other hand, returns only the first column (X) and the first row (Y) – a memory-efficient representation of the same ranges.

```python
X_ogrid, Y_ogrid = np.ogrid[-1:2, -2:3]
print(f"{X_ogrid=}\n{Y_ogrid=}")
```

The result follows:

```
X_ogrid=array([[-1],
       [ 0],
       [ 1]])
Y_ogrid=array([[-2, -1,  0,  1,  2]])
```

If full arrays like those from `meshgrid` or `mgrid` are needed, they can easily be generated using broadcasting.

```python
zeilen, spalten = len(X_ogrid), len(Y_ogrid[0])
X = np.zeros((spalten, zeilen)) + X_ogrid.reshape(1, zeilen)
Y = Y_ogrid.reshape(spalten, 1) + np.zeros((spalten, zeilen))
print(f"{X=}\n{Y=}")
```

The code produces the following result:

```
X=array([[-1.,  0.,  1.],
       [-1.,  0.,  1.],
       [-1.,  0.,  1.],
       [-1.,  0.,  1.],
       [-1.,  0.,  1.]])
Y=array([[-2., -2., -2.],
       [-1., -1., -1.],
       [ 0.,  0.,  0.],
       [ 1.,  1.,  1.],
       [ 2.,  2.,  2.]])
```

So far, we have used `ogrid` with a colon `n:m` to produce values with step size 1 between n and m. By appending a third value after another colon, you can specify the number of points between n and m. This value must be a complex number. That means, if you want 10 points, you must write `10j`, i.e., `n:m:10j`.

```python
X_ogrid, Y_ogrid = np.ogrid[2:5:9j, -2:3:5j]
print(f"{X_ogrid=}\n{Y_ogrid=}")
```

This is the result of the code:

```
X_ogrid=array([[2.    ],
       [2.375],
       [2.75 ],
       [3.125],
       [3.5  ],
       [3.875],
       [4.25 ],
       [4.625],
       [5.    ]])
Y_ogrid=array([[-2.    , -0.75,  0.5 ,  1.75,  3.  ]])
```

We use this in the following example. Since `contourf` requires full two-dimensional
arrays like those produced by `meshgrid`, you can also see broadcasting in action:

```python
X_ogrid, Y_ogrid = np.ogrid[-3:3:256j, -3:3:256j]
n, m = len(X_ogrid), len(Y_ogrid[0])
X = np.zeros((m, n)) + X_ogrid.reshape(1, n)
Y = Y_ogrid.reshape(m, 1) + np.zeros((m, n))
Z = (1 - X / 2 + X**5 + Y**3) * np.exp(-X**2 - Y**2)

fig, ax = plt.subplots()
ax.contour(X, Y, Z)
```

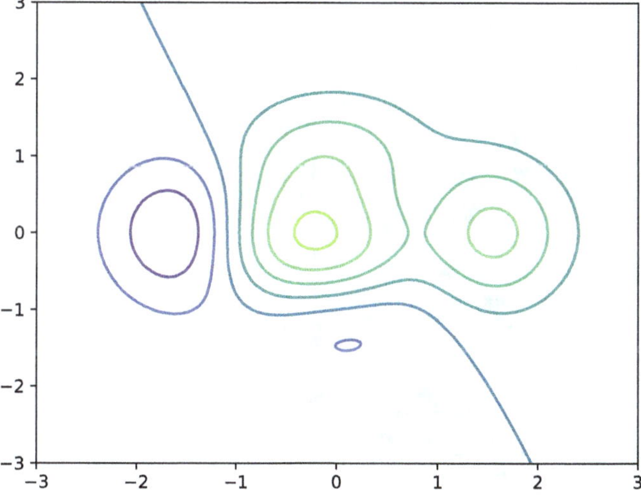

17.9 imshow

With `contour` and `contourf`, we already visualized a projection of the 3D graph of $f(x, y)$ onto the x-y plane. Alternatively, you can use `imshow`. This function displays either PIL images or array-like data and supports the following formats:

- `(m, n)`: scalar data, mapped to colors via a colormap (`cmap`, `norm`, `vmin`, `vmax`).
- `(m, n, 3)`: RGB image (values 0–1 or 0–255).
- `(m, n, 4)`: RGBA image (including transparency).

Here, `m` is the number of rows and `n` the number of columns. Let's now apply `imshow` to our previous example:

```python
X_ogrid, Y_ogrid = np.ogrid[-3:3:256j, -3:3:256j]
n, m = len(X_ogrid), len(Y_ogrid[0])
X = np.zeros((m, n)) + X_ogrid.reshape(1, n)
Y = Y_ogrid.reshape(m, 1) + np.zeros((m, n))
Z = (1 - X / 2 + X**5 + Y**3) * np.exp(-X**2 - Y**2)
plt.imshow(Z)
```

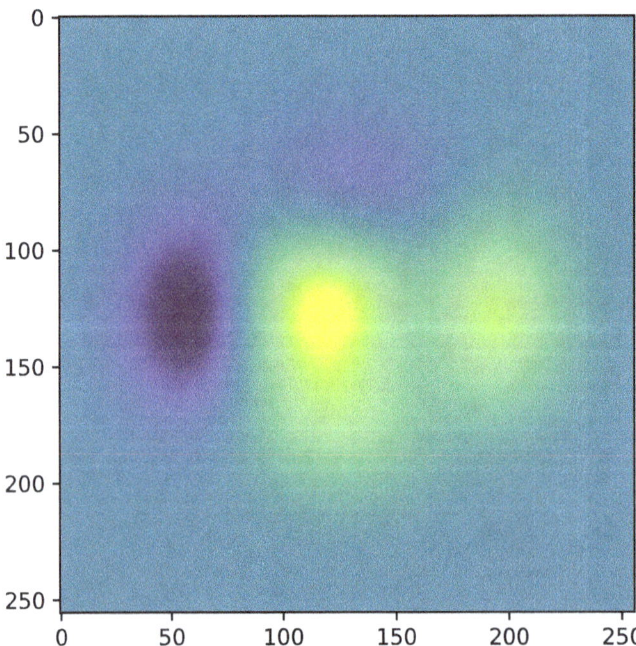

17.10 Exercises

Exercise 1

(Solution: 33.10, Solution 1)

Create a plot of the function

$$z = \sin(x^3) + \cos(y^2)$$

Alternatively, you can use `imshow` to display the data.

Exercise 2

(Solution: 33.10, Solution 2)

This exercise is a little "heartwarming." Simply generate a contour plot for the following function, and you'll see why:

$$x^2 + \left(y - (x^2)^{\frac{1}{5}}\right)^2$$

Exercise 3

(Solution: 33.10, Solution 3)

Fill the contour plot above using `contourf` and experiment with the `cmap` parameter. Possible values include, for example:

```
'Greys', 'Purples', 'Blues', 'Greens', 'Oranges', 'Reds',
'YlOrBr', 'YlOrRd', 'OrRd', 'PuRd', 'RdPu', 'BuPu', 'GnBu',
'PuBu', 'YlGnBu', 'PuBuGn', 'BuGn', 'YlGn', 'viridis',
'plasma', 'inferno', 'magma', 'cividis', 'binary', 'gist_yarg',
'gist_gray', 'gray', 'bone', 'pink', 'spring', 'summer',
'autumn', 'winter', 'cool', 'Wistia', 'hot', 'afmhot',
'gist_heat', 'copper'
```

Exercise 4

(Solution: 33.10, Solution 4)

Create a contour plot for the function

$$\sin(x)^{12} + \cos(10 + xy)\cos(x)$$

18
Histograms and Diagrams

The subject of this chapter is bar charts, column charts, and histograms. We encounter them daily, for example in the media. They provide us with quantitatively based information on a wide variety of topics. Bar and column charts show us clearly where our leading politicians currently stand in the favor or disfavor of the electorate. They also inform us about the conse-

Figure 18.1 Manipulated bar charts

quences of certain behavior: smoking or not smoking, the pros and cons of various activities, income distributions, and so on.

On the one hand, they serve as a source of information to compare our own thinking and behavior statistically with others; on the other hand, by perceiving them, they also change our thinking and behavior in many cases.

In this chapter, however, we are primarily interested in how to create them. We begin with histograms.

What is a histogram? A formal definition could be: It is a graphical representation of a distribution of numerical data. Rectangles of equal width have heights that correspond to the associated frequencies.

18.1 Histograms

A histogram is created by dividing the range of x-values into equally sized adjacent intervals (English: bins). The data are assigned to these intervals, and for each interval a rectangle is drawn whose height corresponds to the frequency.

We now create a histogram from normally distributed random numbers:

```python
import matplotlib.pyplot as plt
import numpy as np

gauss_data = np.random.normal(size=10000)
fig, ax = plt.subplots()
ax.hist(gauss_data)
ax.set_title("Gaussian Histogram")
ax.set_xlabel("Value")
ax.set_ylabel("Frequency")
```

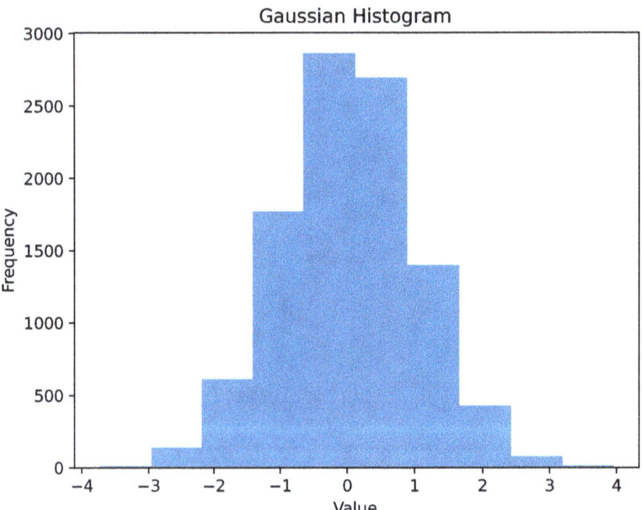

The function `ax.hist` calculates the frequencies, draws the histogram, and returns a tuple (`n`, `bins`, `patches`).

The values from `gauss_data` are sorted into equally sized intervals – so-called "bins". The interval boundaries are calculated automatically by `ax.hist` and returned as the second output value in `bins`.

```python
n, bins, patches = ax.hist(gauss_data)
print("The first three bins: ", bins[0:3])
```

Output:

```
The first three bins:  [-3.72870535 -2.96021206 -2.19171876]
```

n[i] corresponds to the number of values in gauss_data between bins[i] and bins[i+1].

```
print(f"{n}\n{sum(n)=}")
```

Result:

```
[  11.  137.  610. 1768. 2862. 2694. 1399.  428.   77.   14.]
sum(n)=np.float64(10000.0)
```

n is therefore an array containing the frequencies. The last return value of hist is the list patches, which contains the drawn rectangles and their properties. For illustration, we only output the first two elements here:

```
print("patches:", patches)
for i in range(2):
    print(patches[i])
```

The resulting output is:

```
patches: <BarContainer object of 10 artists>
Rectangle(xy=(-3.72871, 0), width=0.768493, height=11, angle=0)
Rectangle(xy=(-2.96021, 0), width=0.768493, height=137, angle=0)
```

Since we are dealing with 10,000 random values here, 10 bins are rather coarse. In the next example, we increase the number of classes by setting the parameter bins=100.

```
ax.hist(gauss_data, bins=100)
```

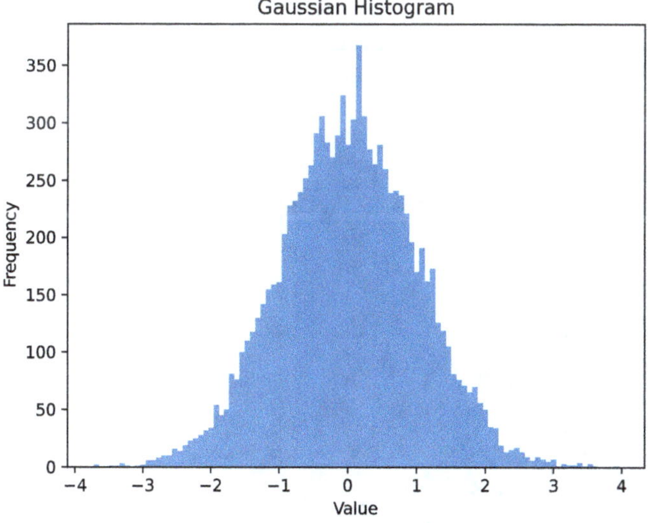

Using `orientation='horizontal'`, the histogram can be displayed sideways:

```
ax.hist(gauss_data, bins=100, orientation="horizontal")
```

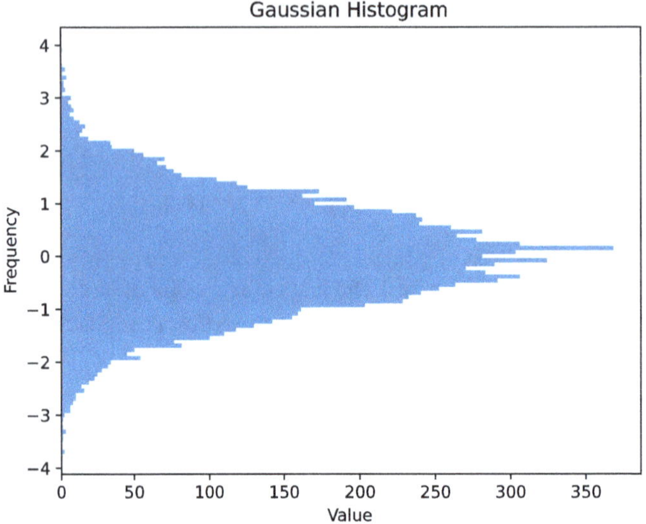

Another important keyword parameter of `hist` is `density`. If it is set to `True`, the first return component – the frequencies – is normalized so that it forms a probability density, i.e., the area under the histogram equals 1.

```
n, bins, patches = ax.hist(gauss_data, bins=100, density=True)
print("Area under the integral: ", np.sum(n * np.diff(bins)))
```

Output:

```
Area under the integral:  1.0
```

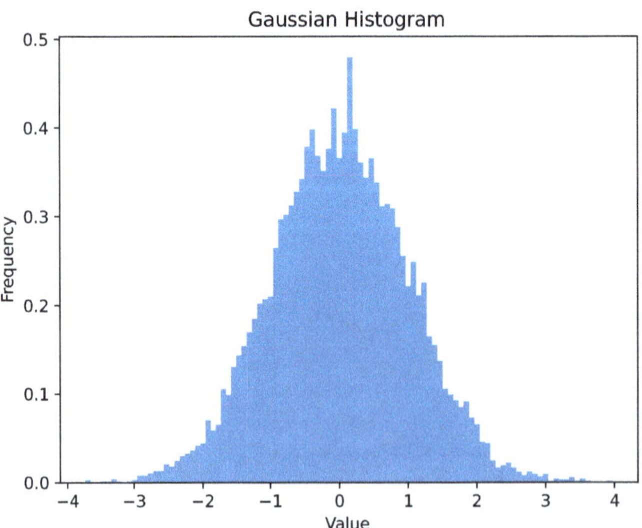

With edgecolor and color, the line color and the fill color can be set:

```
n, bins, patches = ax.hist(gauss_data, bins=100, density=True,
                           edgecolor="#6A2362", color="#33FF82")
```

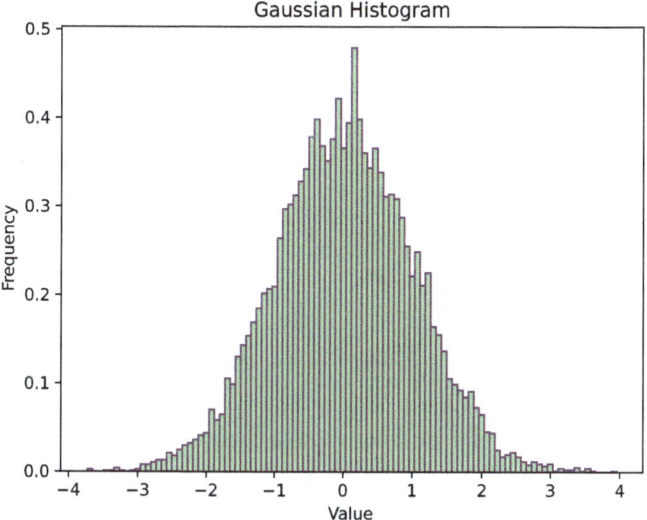

Would you like to see a representation of cumulative values? We can generate a cumulative distribution function by setting the parameter cumulative.

```
ax.hist(gauss_data,
        bins=100,
        density=True,
        stacked=True,
        cumulative=True)
```

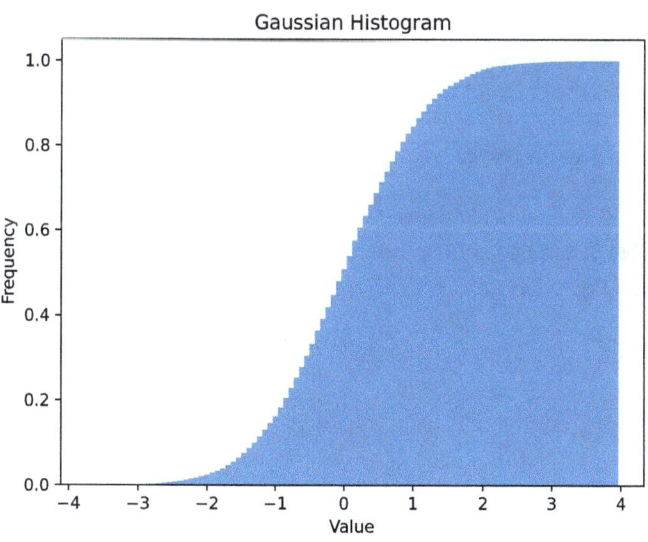

18.2 Column Charts

For the following diagrams, we use the values from the following table.[1]

Continent	Area in million km^2	Percent of land area	Percent of Earth surface	Population in million
Asia	44.4	29.68	8.7	4010
Africa	30.3	20.25	5.9	944
North America	24.9	16.64	4.9	423
South America	17.8	11.90	3.5	381
Antarctica	13.2	8.82	2.6	0.0001
Europe	10.5	7.02	2.1	733
Australia/Oceania	8.5	5.68	1.7	34
Total	149.6	100	29.3	6625

Now we come to one of the most commonly used chart types, which is also well known among non-scientists. The column chart is named because it consists of rectangles standing vertically on the x-axis, rising like columns.

If the width of the columns is very narrow, they are also called bar charts. The width of the rectangles has no mathematical meaning.

```python
import matplotlib.pyplot as plt

continents = ['Asia', 'Africa', 'N-America', 'S-America',
              'Antarctica', 'Europe', 'Australia']
area = (44.4, 30.3, 24.9, 17.8, 13.2, 10.5, 8.5)
bar_width = 0.95
fig, ax = plt.subplots()
ax.set_title('Continents')
ax.set_xlabel('Continents')
ax.set_ylabel('Area in million square kilometres')
ax.bar(continents, area, bar_width, color="green")
ax.tick_params(axis='x', labelsize=8)
ax.set_xticks(continents)
```

If color output is not available, it can be useful to use hatching patterns.[2] The following example shows how this can be achieved:

```python
import matplotlib.pyplot as plt

continents = ['Asia', 'Africa', 'N-America', 'S-America',
              'Antarctica', 'Europe', 'Australia']
area = (44.4, 30.3, 24.9, 17.8, 13.2, 10.5, 8.5)
```

1   *https://de.wikipedia.org/wiki/Kontinent*, Sept. 2022
2   English: "hatchings"

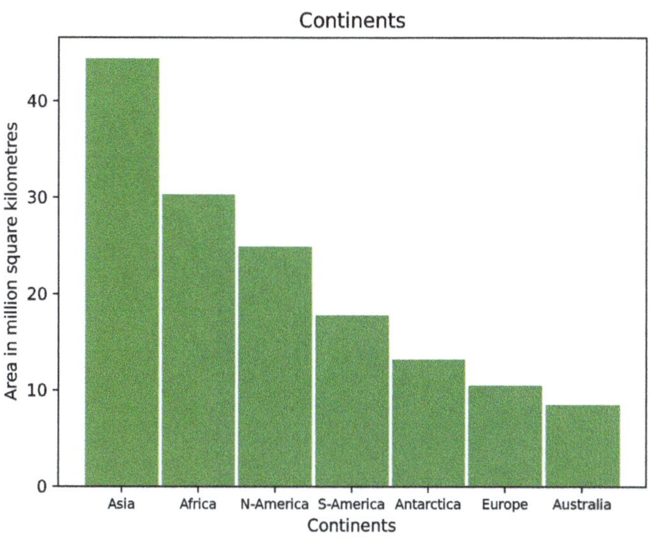


```python
bar_width = 0.95
fig, ax = plt.subplots()
ax.set_title('Continents')
ax.set_xlabel('Continents')
ax.set_ylabel('Area in million square kilometres')
bars = ax.bar(continents, area, bar_width, alpha=0.5)
patterns = ('-', '+', 'x', '*', '.', 'o', 'O', '\\', '-')
for bar, pattern in zip(bars, patterns):
    bar.set_hatch(pattern)
ax.tick_params(axis='x', labelsize=8)
ax.set_xticks(continents)
```

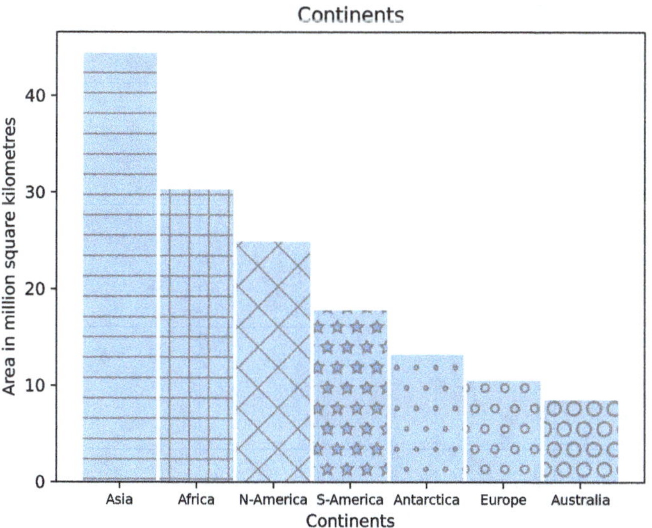

18.3 Bar Charts

Often column charts are incorrectly referred to as bar charts, since they look very similar. In a bar chart, however, the rectangles are oriented horizontally.

In our previous program, we essentially need to replace bar with barh, i.e.,

```python
ax.bar(continents, area, bar_width, color="green")
```

with

```python
ax.barh(continents,
        area,
        align='center',
        color='orange')
```

The new program then looks like this:

```python
import matplotlib.pyplot as plt

continents = ['Asia', 'Africa', 'N-America', 'S-America',
              'Antarctica', 'Europe', 'Australia']
area = (44.4, 30.3, 24.9, 17.8, 13.2, 10.5, 8.5)
fig, ax = plt.subplots()
ax.set_title('Continents')
ax.barh(continents,
        area,
        align='center',
        color='orange')
ax.set_xlabel('Area in million square kilometres')
```

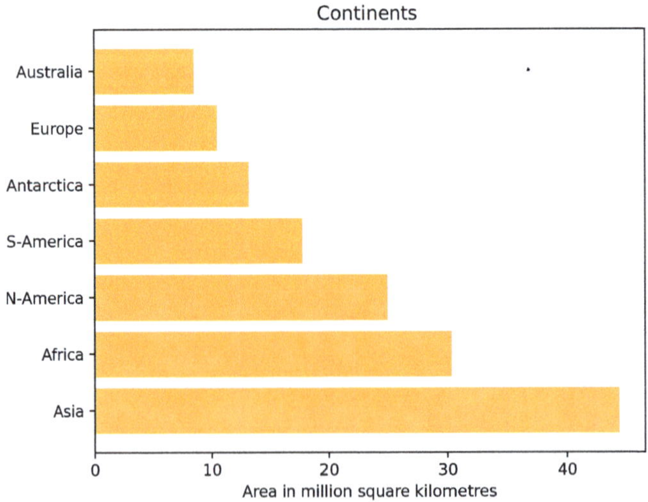

18.4 Grouped Bar Charts

In the previous examples, each x-value corresponded to exactly one y-value – one
bar per x-value. In practice, however, multiple y-values are often assigned to a single
x-value. Such cases can be represented using grouped bar charts.

We begin with a simple example with two values per x-value:

```python
x = np.arange(5)
y1, y2 = [37, 24, 12, 89, 57], [23, 30, 91, 42, 93]
width = 0.40
fig, ax = plt.subplots()
ax.bar(x-0.2, y1, width)
ax.bar(x+0.2, y2, width)
```

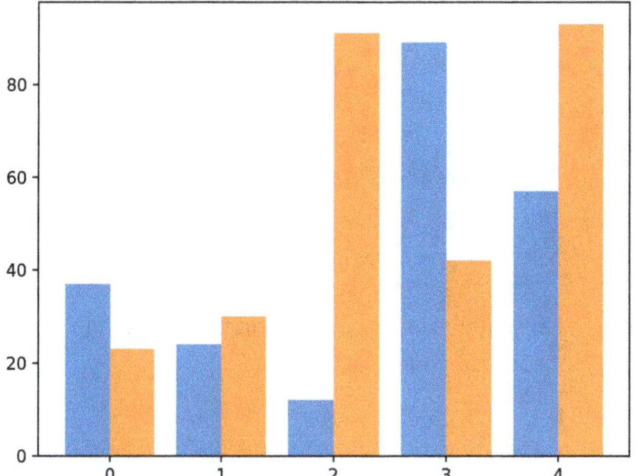

After learning the basic principle of grouped bar charts with artificial numbers, we
now apply it to real data: the areas and population figures of the continents.

```python
import matplotlib.pyplot as plt
import numpy as np
continents = ['Asia', 'Africa', 'N-America', 'S-America',
              'Antarctica', 'Europe', 'Australia']
area = (44.4, 30.3, 24.9, 17.8, 13.2, 10.5, 8.5)
population = (4010, 944, 423, 381, 0.0001, 733, 34)
population_in_10000 = np.array(population) / 100
x = np.arange(len(continents))
width = 0.4
fig, ax = plt.subplots()
ax.set_title('Continents')
ax.set_ylabel('Area in million square kilometres / Pop. in 10,000')
ax.bar(x-0.2, area, width, label="Area")
```

```python
ax.bar(x+0.2, population_in_10000, width, label="Population")
ax.set_xlabel('Area in million square kilometres')
ax.tick_params(axis='x', labelsize=8)
ax.tick_params(axis='y', labelsize=8)
ax.set_xticks(x, continents)
ax.legend()
```

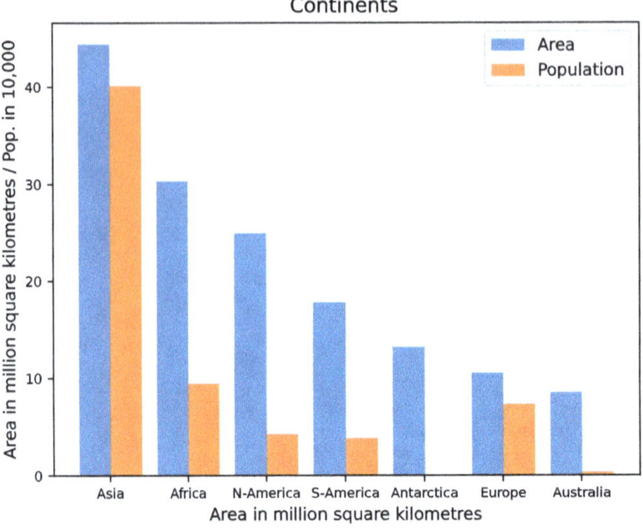

In the following example, we group three data sets. In an imaginary 10th-grade class,
a teacher times three different sprint runs during PE.

```python
import matplotlib.pyplot as plt
import numpy as np

names = ['Emily', 'David', 'Julia',
         'Alexander', 'Leonie', 'Paul']
times = [[14.9, 15.8, 16.2, 14.2, 17.1, 14.2],
         [14.1, 15.2, 15.8, 13.9, 17.6, 14.1],
         [13.7, 17.3, 16.8, 14.5, 17.2, 16.3]]
width = 0.2

fig, ax = plt.subplots()
ticks = np.arange(len(names))
ax.bar(ticks - width, times[0], width, align="center")
ax.bar(ticks , times[1], width, align="center")
ax.bar(ticks + width, times[2], width, align="center")
ax.set_xticks(ticks)
ax.set_xticklabels(names)
ax.set_xlabel("Participants")
ax.set_ylabel("Times")
```

```python
ax.set_title("100-Meter Sprint")
ymin, ymax = 12, 18
ax.set_ylim([ymin, ymax])
ax.legend(["1st Sprint", "2nd Sprint", "3rd Sprint"],
          loc="lower right")
```

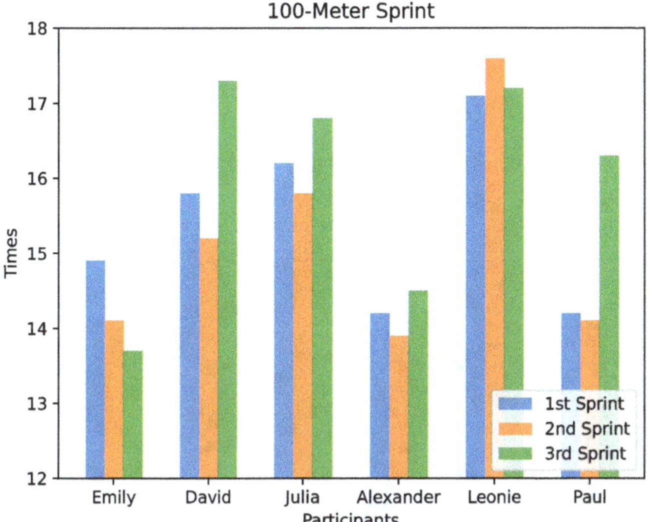

We generalize the previous example by defining a function `grouped_bars`. This allows us to automatically place any number of columns. We demonstrate it with five columns as an example:

```python
def grouped_bars(ax, list_of_values, labels, group_width=0.7):
    ticks = np.arange(len(labels))
    n = len(list_of_values)
    width = group_width / n
    ax.set_xticks(ticks)
    ax.set_xticklabels(labels)
    if n % 2:
        start = (-(n // 2) - (n - 1) % 2) * width
        align = "center"
    else:
        start = (-(n // 2)) * width
        align = "edge"
    for i in range(len(list_of_values)):
        shift = start + i * width
        ax.bar(ticks + shift, list_of_values[i], width, align=align)

names = ['Emily', 'David', 'Julia',
         'Alexander', 'Leonie', 'Paul']
```

```
times = [[14.9, 15.8, 16.2, 14.2, 17.1, 14.2],
         [14.1, 15.2, 15.8, 13.9, 17.6, 14.1],
         [13.7, 17.3, 16.8, 14.5, 17.2, 16.3],
         [14.1, 15.2, 15.8, 13.9, 17.6, 14.1]]

fig, ax = plt.subplots()
grouped_bars(ax, times, names)
ax.set_xlabel("Participants")
ax.set_ylabel("Times")
ymin, ymax = 12, 18
ax.set_ylim([ymin, ymax])
ax.legend(["1st Sprint", "2nd Sprint", "3rd Sprint", "4th Sprint"],
          loc="lower right")
```

18.5 xkcd Mode

In this section, we deal with the xkcd style – named after the website xkcd.com, a webcomic "about romance, sarcasm, math, and language." With this style, plots look humorously hand-drawn.

The command `matplotlib.pyplot.xkcd(scale=1, length=100, randomness=2)` activates sketch mode.

It only affects graphics created afterward – therefore we use a `with` environment.

The parameters control the appearance: `scale` adjusts the wobble amplitude perpendicular to the line, `length` the length along the line, and `randomness` the random deviation.

For optimal results, the font "Humor Sans" should be installed.[3]

```python
import matplotlib.pyplot as plt
import numpy as np
continents = ['Asia', 'Africa', 'N-America', 'S-America',
              'Antarctica', 'Europe', 'Australia']
area = (44.4, 30.3, 24.9, 17.8, 13.2, 10.5, 8.5)

population = (4010, 944, 423, 381, 0.0001, 733, 34)
population_in_10000 = np.array(population) / 100
x = np.arange(len(continents))
width = 0.4

with plt.xkcd(scale=1, length=100, randomness=10):
    fig, ax = plt.subplots()
    ax.set_title('Continents')
    ax.set_ylabel('Area in million square kilometres / Pop. in 10,000')
    ax.bar(x-0.2, area, width, label="Area")
    ax.bar(x+0.2, population_in_10000, width, label="Population")
    ax.set_xlabel('Area in million square kilometres')
    ax.tick_params(axis='x', labelsize=8)
    ax.tick_params(axis='y', labelsize=8)
    ax.set_xticks(x, continents)
    ax.legend()
```

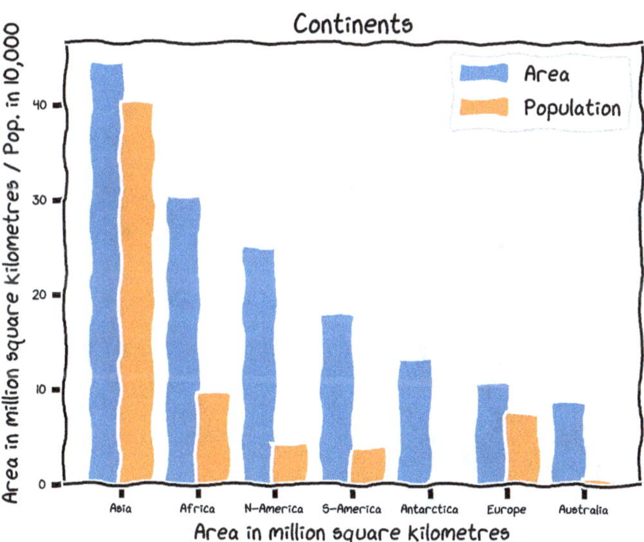

---

3   On Ubuntu: `sudo apt-get install -y fonts-humor-sans`

18.6 Pie Charts

Now we move on to circular charts, known as pie charts. Looking at our first example, it is immediately clear why they are called that. Each slice represents a data category, and its size is proportional to its quantity.

In our first example, we show the popularity of the six most popular programming languages according to TIOBE.[4]

```python
import matplotlib.pyplot as plt

labels = ['Python', 'C++', 'Java', 'C', 'C#', 'SQL', 'others']
sizes = [23.88, 11.37, 10.66, 9.84, 4.12, 3.78]
percent_others = 100 - sum(sizes)    # Share of other languages
sizes.append(percent_others)
# explode specifies how far a slice is pulled out
explode = (0.1, 0.0, 0.3, 0.0, 0, 0, 0)
fig, ax = plt.subplots()
ax.pie(sizes,
        explode=explode,
        labels=labels,
        autopct='%1.1f%%',
        shadow=True,
        startangle=90)
ax.axis('equal')
```

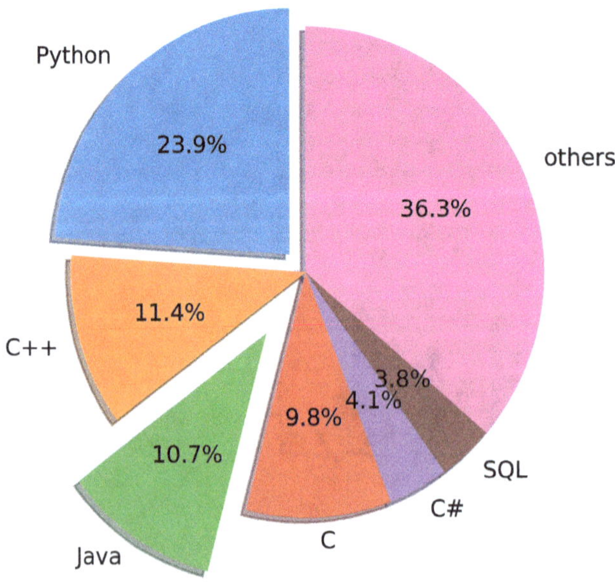

<hr>

4   As of February 2025; see footnote 2 in the introduction to TIOBE

18.7 Stacked Charts

Finally, we introduce stacked area charts. They are sometimes also called "stacked column charts." This type of visualization requires more than one data series. These data series are displayed in a rectangular column, with the individual frequencies shown as differently colored or hatched areas, as in the following example:[5]

```python
import matplotlib.pyplot as plt

year = [1950, 1960, 1970, 1980, 1990, 2000, 2010, 2018]
population_by_continent = {
    'Africa': [228, 284, 365, 477, 631, 814, 1044, 1275],
    'Americas': [340, 425, 519, 619, 727, 840, 943, 1006],
    'Asia': [1394, 1686, 2120, 2625, 3202, 3714, 4169, 4560],
    'Europe': [220, 253, 276, 295, 310, 303, 294, 293],
    'Australia': [12, 15, 19, 22, 26, 31, 36, 39],
}


fig, ax = plt.subplots()
ax.stackplot(year,
             population_by_continent.values(),
             labels=population_by_continent.keys(),
             alpha=0.7)
ax.legend(loc='upper left')
ax.set_title('World Population')
ax.set_xlabel('Year')
ax.set_ylabel('Population in millions')
```

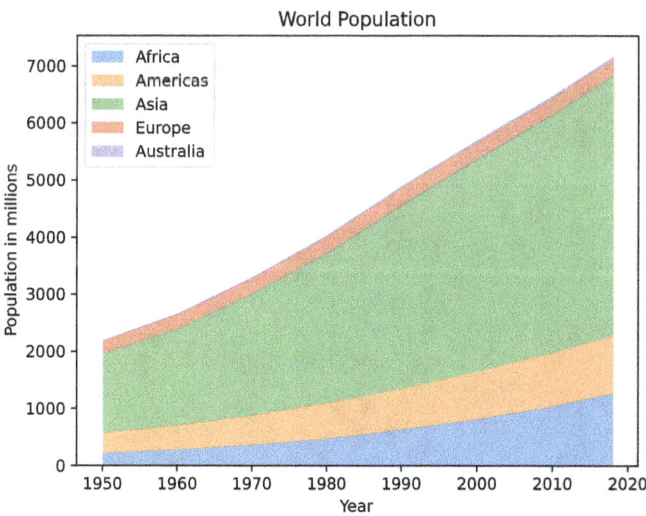

---

5   Data source: "United Nations World Population Prospects (Revision 2019)", *https://population.un.org/ wpp*, license: CC BY 3.0 IGO

18.8 Exercises

Exercise 1

(Solution: 33.11, Solution 1)

In the German federal election in 2025, the following percentage distributions were recorded for the parties:

Table 18.1 Election Results by Party

Party	Vote Share (%)
CDU/CSU	28.6
AfD	20.8
SPD	16.4
Greens	11.6
Left	8.8
BSW	4.9
FDP	4.3
Others	4.7

Create a column chart with these data.

Exercise 2

(Solution: 33.11, Solution 2)

No programming project would be conceivable without coffee. Visualize the coffee consumption of a fictional team:

```
Name Number of coffee cups
Michael 15
Doro 22
Bertie 24
Bea 29
Uli 14
```

Exercise 3

(Solution: 33.11, Solution 3)

In the directory data/eu, there is a file `eu_country_population_surface_gdp.csv`. This file contains the EU countries along with their population, area, and gross domestic product (GDP). Create a bar chart with the GDP values.

Exercise 4

(Solution: 33.11, Solution 4)

Create a grouped bar chart using the available data from Exercise 3.

Exercise 5

(Solution: 33.11, Solution 5)

Create a bar chart using `plt.xkcd()` that resembles the cartoon diagram at the beginning of this chapter.

Part III

Pandas

19
Pandas:Series

Although panda bears are generally considered cute and cuddly, in this chapter we will stay with programming. Pandas is a Python library for data analysis. The name Pandas is derived from the term "panel data". The term originally comes from econometrics and refers to multidimensional datasets with both time and object references. You can also think of such data as a matrix, where the column direction represents the individual dimension and interpolation the row direction represents the time dimension. However, this is already a very specific use case. It is better to see Pandas as a

Figure 19.1 The Pandas team at work

system based on tables, like those used in spreadsheet software such as the well-known program "Excel." A particular strength of Pandas is that it can directly read and write CSV, DSV, and Excel files.

Pandas provides simple and efficient tools for analyzing and manipulating data in Python. It offers numerous methods for cleaning and preparing data, including filling missing values, grouping, merging, transforming, and aggregating.

Together with its visualization capabilities, all these features make Pandas a popular and powerful tool for data analysis that can handle large datasets efficiently. It is sometimes mistakenly assumed that Pandas serves as an alternative to NumPy, SciPy, and Matplotlib. In reality, Pandas is built on top of these libraries. The two primary data structures in Pandas are the `Series`, which is the focus of this chapter, and the `DataFrame`, which will be discussed in Chapter 20 (DataFrame).

19.1 Basics of the Series data structure

A `Series` object can be thought of as a column in an Excel spreadsheet together with its associated index. In other words: A Series is a one-dimensional, array-like object that combines data values with labels. While a NumPy array always uses a zero-based integer index ranging from 0 to the length of the array minus one, a `Series` allows arbitrary, hashable objects to serve as its index.

Both the index and the values of a `Series` should ideally share a uniform data type[1] – for example, only integers, floating-point numbers, or strings.

A `Series` can be viewed as a data structure consisting of two arrays: one that serves as the index (i.e., the labels) and another that contains the data values. In the following example, we create a simple `Series` object by instantiating it with a Python list. Later, we will see that other data structures – such as NumPy arrays or dictionaries – can also be used to create a `Series`.

```python
import pandas as pd
S = pd.Series([11, 28, 72, 3])
print(S)
```

Script output:

```
0    11
1    28
2    72
3     3
dtype: int64
```

---

1   If the values in a `Series` have different types – for example, a mix of numbers and text – then Pandas cannot assign a specific numeric type such as `int64` or `float64`. In such cases, it uses the more general `object` data type internally, which can store arbitrary Python objects. The `object` type is flexible because it allows mixed contents, but this flexibility comes at the cost of performance and memory efficiency. Many operations, especially numeric computations, are much slower with `object`-typed Series than with numerically typed Series. For performance-critical applications, it is therefore advisable to use homogeneous data types whenever possible, particularly when working with large datasets or performing many arithmetic operations.

In this example, we did not specify an index. Nevertheless, the output displays two columns: the right column shows the data values, while the left column represents the index. When no index is provided, Pandas automatically creates a default integer index that starts at 0 and continues sequentially up to 3.

We can access the index and the values of the Series S directly:

```python
print(S.index)
print(S.values)
```

The execution leads to this output:

```
RangeIndex(start=0, stop=4, step=1)
[11 28 72  3]
```

When we compare a Series with a NumPy array, we notice that they share many similarities in structure and behavior.

```python
import numpy as np
X = np.array([11, 28, 72, 3])
print(X)
print(S.values)
# Both have the same type.
print(type(S.values), type(X))
```

The following result is generated:

```
[11 28 72  3]
[11 28 72  3]
<class 'numpy.ndarray'> <class 'numpy.ndarray'>
```

The output shows that both S.values and X are numpy.ndarray objects. This demonstrates that a Series internally uses NumPy arrays to store its data, which explains why many operations on Series objects are highly efficient and similar to those on NumPy arrays.

Up to this point, Series objects do not differ significantly from NumPy ndarrays. This changes when we define Series objects with custom indices:

```python
fruits = ['apples', 'oranges', 'cherries', 'pears']
quantities = [20, 33, 52, 10]
S = pd.Series(quantities, index=fruits)
print(S)
```

The result of the code is:

```
apples      20
oranges     33
cherries    52
pears       10
dtype: int64
```

A major advantage of `Series` objects over `NumPy` arrays becomes apparent here: we can assign arbitrary, user-defined indices to the data values.

When we add two `Series` objects that share the same indices, Pandas automatically aligns them by their index labels and returns a new `Series` object.

The resulting values correspond to the element-wise sums of the matching entries from both `Series` objects.

```python
fruits = ['apples', 'oranges', 'cherries', 'pears']
S = pd.Series([20, 33, 52, 10], index=fruits)
S2 = pd.Series([17, 13, 31, 32], index=fruits)
print(S + S2)
print("Sum of S: ", sum(S))
```

Script output:

```
apples      37
oranges     46
cherries    83
pears       42
dtype: int64
Sum of S:  115
```

The indices do not need to be identical for `Series` objects to be added. The resulting index is the union of both indices. If a label is present in only one of the `Series` objects, the corresponding value in the result is shown as `NaN` (Not a Number).

```python
fruits = ['peaches', 'oranges', 'cherries', 'pears']
fruits2 = ['raspberries', 'oranges', 'cherries', 'pears']

S = pd.Series([20, 33, 52, 10], index=fruits)
S2 = pd.Series([17, 13, 31, 32], index=fruits2)
print(S + S2)
```

The code produces the following result:

```
cherries        83.0
oranges         46.0
peaches          NaN
pears           42.0
raspberries      NaN
dtype: float64
```

NaN stands for "Not a Number," i.e., a value that is undefined or cannot be represented numerically. Such values commonly occur in floating-point computations, for example as the result of invalid or missing numerical operations.

In principle, the indices can also be completely different, as in the following example:

```python
fruits_en = ['apples', 'oranges', 'cherries', 'pears']
fruits_tr = ['elma', 'portakal', 'kiraz', 'armut']


S = pd.Series([20, 33, 52, 10], index=fruits_en)
S2 = pd.Series([17, 13, 31, 32], index=fruits_tr)
print(S + S2)
```

The result follows:

```
apples      NaN
armut       NaN
cherries    NaN
elma        NaN
kiraz       NaN
oranges     NaN
pears       NaN
portakal    NaN
dtype: float64
```

19.2 Access and indexing

You can access individual elements of a `Series` object directly by using its index label:

```python
print(S['apples'])
```

The result of the code is:

```
20
```

Multiple elements can also be accessed at once by passing a list or any array-like object of index labels:

```python
print(S[['apples', 'oranges', 'cherries']])
```

Here is the output:

```
apples     20
oranges    33
cherries   52
dtype: int64
```

Filtering a `Series` with a Boolean array:

```python
print(S[S > 30])
```

After execution we get:

```
oranges    33
cherries   52
dtype: int64
```

Just as in `NumPy`, operations involving scalars or the application of mathematical functions to a `Series` object are also supported:

```python
import numpy as np
print((S + 3) * 4)
print("=======================")
print(np.sin(S))
```

The result is:

```
apples      92
oranges     144
cherries    220
pears       52
dtype: int64
=======================
apples       0.912945
oranges      0.999912
cherries     0.986628
pears       -0.544021
dtype: float64
```

19.3 Value manipulation with apply

```
Series.apply(func, convert_dtype=True, args=(), **kwds)
```

The method applies the function `func` to each element of the `Series`. Depending on the function used, the result may be returned as either a new `Series` object or, in some cases, as a `DataFrame`.

Parameter	Description
func	A function applied either to the entire `Series` (for example, a NumPy function) or elementwise to its values (for example, a standard Python function).
convert_dtype	A Boolean flag. If set to `True` (default), Pandas attempts to determine the most suitable data type (`dtype`) for the elementwise results of the function. If set to `False`, `dtype=object` is used.
args	Positional arguments passed to the function `func`, in addition to the values of the `Series`.
**kwds	Additional keyword arguments passed to the function.

Example:

```python
print(S.apply(np.log))
```

The result appears as follows:

```
apples      2.995732
oranges     3.496508
cherries    3.951244
pears       2.302585
dtype: float64
```

We can also use Python `lambda` functions with the `apply()` method. In the following example, we check the stock levels of each fruit: if fewer than 50 items are available for a given type, the quantity is increased by 10; otherwise, the value remains unchanged.

```python
print(S.apply(lambda x: x if x > 50 else x + 10))
```

The result follows:

```
apples      30
oranges     43
cherries    52
pears       20
dtype: int64
```

19.4 Series from Dictionaries

A Series object can be thought of as an ordered Python dictionary with a fixed length.
A Series can be created directly from a dictionary, using the dictionary's keys as index
labels and its values as the corresponding data. If no index is explicitly specified,
Pandas sorts the dictionary keys alphabetically.

```python
cities = {"London":    8615246,
          "Berlin":    3562166,
          "Madrid":    3165235,
          "Rome":      2874038,
          "Paris":     2273305,
          "Vienna":    1805681,
          "Bucharest": 1803425,
          "Hamburg":   1760433,
          "Budapest":  1754000,
          "Warsaw":    1740119,
          "Barcelona": 1602386,
          "Munich":    1493900,
          "Milan":     1350680}


city_series = pd.Series(cities)
print(city_series)
```

The output shows:

```
London      8615246
Berlin      3562166
Madrid      3165235
Rome        2874038
Paris       2273305
Vienna      1805681
Bucharest   1803425
Hamburg     1760433
Budapest    1754000
Warsaw      1740119
Barcelona   1602386
Munich      1493900
Milan       1350680
dtype: int64
```

19.5 NaN – Missing Data

One common challenge in data analysis is the presence of missing data.

Let's return to the previous example. There, the indices of the `Series` matched the keys of the dictionary from which the object `cities_series` was created. Now suppose we define an index that does not fully overlap with the dictionary keys. We can do this by passing a list or tuple to the `index` keyword argument when creating the `Series`.

In the following example, we provide a list whose elements do not completely match the dictionary keys. As a result, some cities from the dictionary are missing, and for others – such as Stuttgart and Zurich – no data is available. The missing entries are therefore represented as NaN (Not a Number), indicating missing or undefined values.

```python
my_cities = ["London", "Paris", "Zurich", "Berlin",
             "Stuttgart", "Hamburg"]
my_city_series = pd.Series(cities, index=my_cities)
print(my_city_series)
```

Output:

```
London       8615246.0
Paris        2273305.0
Zurich             NaN
Berlin       3562166.0
Stuttgart          NaN
Hamburg      1760433.0
dtype: float64
```

Because of the NaN values, the other population figures are automatically converted to floating-point numbers. In the following example, there are no missing values, so the data type remains integer:

```python
my_cities = ["London", "Paris", "Berlin", "Hamburg"]
my_city_series = pd.Series(cities, index=my_cities)
print(my_city_series)
```

Output:

```
London     8615246
Paris      2273305
Berlin     3562166
Hamburg    1760433
dtype: int64
```

19.5.1 Checking for missing values

We can see that the cities that do not exist in the dictionary are assigned the value NaN. NaN stands for "not a number." In our example it can also be understood as "missing."

Missing values can be identified using the methods `isnull()` and `notnull()`:

```python
my_cities = ["London", "Paris", "Zurich", "Berlin",
             "Stuttgart", "Hamburg"]
my_city_series = pd.Series(cities, index=my_cities)
print(my_city_series.isnull())
```

The code produces the following result:

```
London       False
Paris        False
Zurich        True
Berlin       False
Stuttgart     True
Hamburg      False
dtype: bool
```

Now let's look at `notnull()`, which provides the complementary result to `isnull()`:

```python
print(my_city_series.notnull())
```

```
London        True
Paris         True
Zurich       False
Berlin        True
Stuttgart    False
Hamburg       True
dtype: bool
```

19.5.2 Relation between NaN and None

We also obtain NaN when a value in the dictionary is None. Pandas automatically interprets None as a missing value and converts it to NaN.

```python
d = {"a": 23, "b": 45, "c": None, "d": 0}
S = pd.Series(d)
print(S)
```

The result of the code is:

```
a    23.0
b    45.0
c     NaN
d     0.0
dtype: float64
```

```python
print(pd.isnull(S))
```

The corresponding output can be seen here:

```
a    False
b    False
c     True
d    False
dtype: bool
```

```python
print(pd.notnull(S))
```

The result is:

```
a     True
b     True
c    False
d     True
dtype: bool
```

19.5.3 Filtering missing data

Missing data can be removed from a `Series` using the `dropna()` method. This method
returns a new `Series` that excludes all NaN values:

```python
print(f"my_city_series:\n{my_city_series}")
print(f"my_city_series.dropna():\n{my_city_series.dropna()}")
```

The output shows the Series before and after removing the NaN values:

```
my_city_series:
London       8615246.0
Paris        2273305.0
Zurich             NaN
Berlin       3562166.0
Stuttgart          NaN
```

```
Hamburg       1760433.0
dtype: float64
my_city_series.dropna():
London      8615246.0
Paris       2273305.0
Berlin      3562166.0
Hamburg     1760433.0
dtype: float64
```

19.5.4 Filling missing data

In many cases, we may not want to remove missing data, but rather replace them with meaningful values. Pandas provides several methods for this purpose. The following table summarizes the most commonly used methods for filling missing values in a Series:

Method	Description
fillna()	Explicitly fills missing values, for example with a fixed value or a dictionary of key–value pairs for specific index labels.
ffill()	*Forward fill*: propagates the last valid value forward.
bfill()	*Backward fill*: propagates the next valid value backward.
interpolate()	Estimates missing values by interpolation (for example, linear, polynomial, or spline methods). Requires a numeric or time-based index.

Let us now look at the fillna() method. This method allows us to explicitly replace missing values (NaN) with specified ones.

In the following example, we examine the growth of a baby from birth to the age of 16 months. Measurements were taken at two-week intervals, but some values are missing. In the code below, we use the date_range() method, which we will discuss in more detail in Chapter 30 (Time Series).

```python
import pandas as pd
import numpy as np

groessen = [51, np.nan, 56, np.nan, np.nan, 60, 63, 65, 67,
            69, np.nan, 72, 73, np.nan, 76, 77, 78, 78.5, np.nan,
            80, 81, np.nan, 83, 83.5, 84, np.nan, 85, 85.5, 86]

zeitreihe = pd.date_range("2024-01-01",
                          periods=len(groessen),
                          freq="2W") # 2W -> biweekly time series
wachstum_baby = pd.Series(data=groessen, index=zeitreihe)
print(wachstum_baby.head(6))
```

We obtain this output:

```
2024-01-07    51.0
2024-01-21     NaN
2024-02-04    56.0
2024-02-18     NaN
2024-03-03     NaN
2024-03-17    60.0
Freq: 2W-SUN, dtype: float64
```

The missing values can be filled in various ways, for example with a fixed value such as zero. In the following example, we set the missing values to zero (even though this is not meaningful in practice):

```
filled_constant = wachstum_baby.fillna(0)
```

A more realistic approach is to provide appropriate replacement values. In the next example, specific missing measurements are filled using a dictionary that assigns plausible values to particular dates:

```
specific_fill = wachstum_baby.fillna({
    "2024-01-29": 54, "2024-03-11": 61, "2024-03-25": 62,
    "2024-04-08": 63, "2024-06-17": 79, "2024-07-29": 82,
    "2024-09-09": 84, "2024-10-07": 86, "2024-11-04": 87
})
```

With the `ffill` (forward fill) method, missing values are automatically replaced by the most recent valid value. This approach is useful when it is reasonable to assume that the last known measurement remains valid until the next one:

```
ffilled = wachstum_baby.ffill()
print(ffilled.head(6))
```

The output we get is:

```
2024-01-07    51.0
2024-01-21    51.0
2024-02-04    56.0
2024-02-18    56.0
2024-03-03    56.0
2024-03-17    60.0
Freq: 2W-SUN, dtype: float64
```

With the `bfill` (backward fill) method, missing values are replaced by the next valid
value. This is helpful when one assumes that a future value can already be applied to
a previous point:

```
bfilled = wachstum_baby.bfill()
print(bfilled.head(6))
```

Script output:

```
2024-01-07     51.0
2024-01-21     56.0
2024-02-04     56.0
2024-02-18     60.0
2024-03-03     60.0
2024-03-17     60.0
Freq: 2W-SUN, dtype: float64
```

Interpolation

The `interpolate()` method computes intermediate values (here linear):

```
interpolated = wachstum_baby.interpolate()
print(interpolated.head(6))
```

The output shows:

```
2024-01-07     51.000000
2024-01-21     53.500000
2024-02-04     56.000000
2024-02-18     57.333333
2024-03-03     58.666667
2024-03-17     60.000000
Freq: 2W-SUN, dtype: float64
```

Besides linear interpolation, other methods are available. Some commonly used ones
are summarized in the following table:

Method	Description
polynomial	Polynomial interpolation, for example of degree 2 or 3. Example: `wachstum_baby.interpolate(method='polynomial', order=2)`.
spline	Spline interpolation with a configurable degree specified via the `order` parameter.
barycentric	Barycentric Lagrange interpolation.
pad	Carries forward the previous value (equivalent to `ffill()`).
nearest	Uses the nearest valid value.
quadratic, cubic	Shortcuts for polynomial interpolation of degree 2 or 3.
akima	Smoothing interpolation method (requires `scipy`).

Many of these methods require a numeric or time-based sorted index. For 'polynomial', 'spline', and other advanced methods, scipy is also required.

An example of polynomial interpolation:

```python
interpolated_poly = wachstum_baby.interpolate(method='polynomial',
                                               order=2)
```

19.5.5 Comparison of different interpolation methods

Missing values can be interpolated in different ways. Depending on the nature of the data, the choice of method can significantly affect the result. In this example, we illustrate – using artificial data – how linear interpolation, polynomial interpolation (degree 2), and spline interpolation (degree 3) differ.

```python
y = np.array([1, np.nan, np.nan, 4, 3, np.nan, np.nan, 8, 7, 10])
```

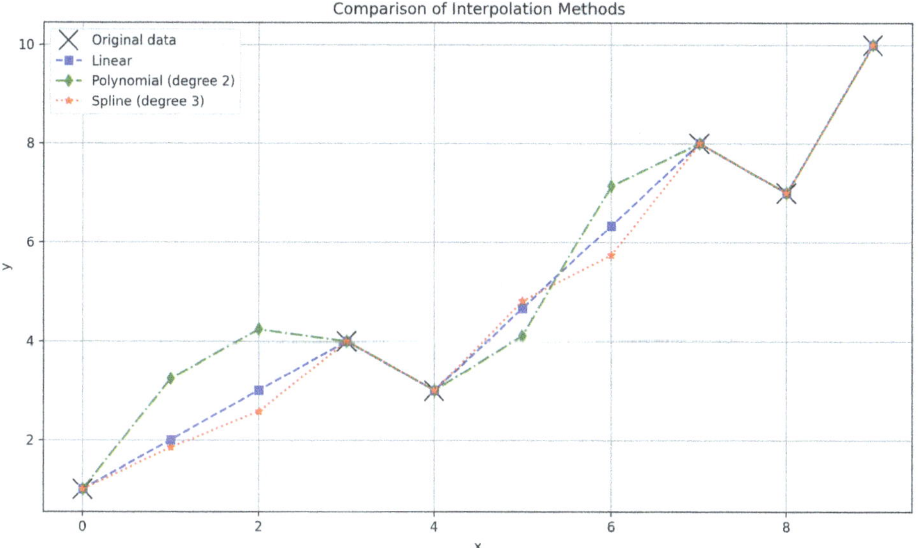

Figure 19.2 Different interpolation methods compared

19.6 Exercises

1. Exercise

(Solution: 33.12, Solution 1)

Define a `Series` object with eight student names as the index. The values should represent their grades between 1 and 10.

2. Exercise

(Solution: 33.12, Solution 2)

Create a second `Series` with the same indices but different grades. Then calculate the average of the two grade series.

Hint: Use `Series.mean()` and `Series.add()` or the operator + to combine both Series.

3. Exercise

(Solution: 33.12, Solution 3)

A temperature sensor measured the outdoor temperature every hour on a hot July day; however, some readings are missing. The measurements were taken from 03:00 to 18:00. The available measurements are as follows:

```python
import numpy as np

temperaturen = [22.0, 23.5, 25.0, 26.8, 28.5, 30.2,
                np.nan, np.nan, 33.8, 33.0, np.nan,
                31.0, 29.5, 28.0, 26.5]
```

Create a `Series` object from this. Then fill in the missing values (NaN) using the methods `bfill()`, `ffill()`, and `interpolate()`.

- Compare the three variants.
- Which method seems most plausible for the course of a day's temperature?
- Justify your decision.

The "true" missing values are: 32.0, 33.5, and 32.2.

20 DataFrame

In Chapter 19 (Pandas:Series), we saw that the data type `Series` logically corresponds to a column with an index in an Excel spreadsheet. In this chapter, we turn to the data type `DataFrame`, which can be viewed as a complete Excel worksheet. In other words, this structure is table-based.

A `DataFrame` consists of an ordered sequence of columns. Each column is internally type-consistent – just like a `Series`[1] – but different columns may contain different data types. For example, one column may contain sales figures as floating-point numbers, while another column may represent years as integers.

	A	B	C
1	Country	City	Population
2	England	London	8615246
3	Germany	Berlin	3562166
4	Spain	Madrid	3165235
5	Italy	Rome	2874038
6	France	Paris	2273305
7	Austria	Vienna	1805681
8	Romania	Bucharest	1803425
9	Germany	Hamburg	1760433
10	Hungary	Budapest	1754000
11	Poland	Warsaw	1740119
12	Spain	Barcelona	1602386
13	Germany	Munich	1493900
14	Italy	Milan	1350680

Figure 20.1 Spreadsheet à la Excel and DataFrames

In addition to columns, a `DataFrame` also includes a row index, which can be used to access or label individual rows.

Each column in a `DataFrame` is internally represented as a `Series` that shares the common index of the entire `DataFrame`. This means that the index of each column is identical to the `DataFrame`'s overall index. This structure makes it easy to work with individual columns as standalone `Series` while preserving their relationship to the full `DataFrame`.

The `DataFrame` type is particularly well suited for working with structured data. Among other things, it excels at:

- reading and analyzing tabular data (e.g., from CSV, Excel, or SQL files);

---

1   We will learn that these are `Series` objects

- processing heterogeneous columns containing numbers, text, or dates;

- filtering, grouping, aggregating, and transforming large datasets;

- merging and joining data from multiple sources.

Pandas provides a wide range of methods that enable intuitive data manipulation. In the following sections, we will explore step by step how to create, access, and modify a DataFrame.

20.1 A first example

In this subsection, we begin with a practical example of working with Pandas. We consider sales data from three fictional retail stores ("shops") that sell different kinds of fruit.

The data are presented in tabular form – just as you might see in a program like Excel. The columns represent the shops, the rows the fruit types, and the cells contain the corresponding sales figures.

We create this table as a DataFrame – the central data structure in Pandas:

```python
import pandas as pd

data = {
    'Shop 1': {'apples': 20, 'pears': 33, 'cherries': 52},
    'Shop 2': {'apples': 17, 'pears': 13, 'cherries': 31},
    'Shop 3': {'apples': 25, 'pears': 41, 'cherries': 38}
}

shops_df = pd.DataFrame(data)
print(shops_df)
```

This output is obtained:

```
          Shop 1  Shop 2  Shop 3
apples        20      17      25
pears         33      13      41
cherries      52      31      38
```

The output shows:

- The products (apples, pears, cherries) appear as the row index on the left.

- The shops (Shop 1, Shop 2, Shop 3) form the column headers.

- The cells contain the sales figures of each fruit type in each shop.

With only a few lines of code, we have created a clear and structured table that we can use immediately. Before we explore how to access individual columns, rows, or cells – and how to filter or modify data – let us first examine the relationship between `DataFrame` and `Series`.

20.2 Relation to Series

In the previous section, we saw how a `DataFrame` can efficiently represent structured data – such as sales figures from several shops. Now we will take a closer look at how a `DataFrame` is structured internally and how it relates to `Series` objects.

A `DataFrame` has both a row and a column index. It can be thought of as a dictionary of `Series` objects that share a common index. Each `Series` is accessed via a key, which corresponds to the column name.

The following example illustrates this relationship by defining three `Series` objects and combining them into a single `DataFrame`:

```python
import pandas as pd

years = range(2014, 2018)
shop1 = pd.Series([2409.14, 2941.01, 3496.83, 3119.55],
                  index=years)
shop2 = pd.Series([1203.45, 3441.62, 3007.83, 3619.53],
                  index=years)
shop3 = pd.Series([3412.12, 3491.16, 3457.19, 1963.10],
                  index=years)
```

What happens if these "shop" `Series` objects are concatenated? Pandas provides a `concat()` function for this purpose:

```python
print(pd.concat([shop1, shop2, shop3]))
```

The processing yields:

```
2014    2409.14
2015    2941.01
2016    3496.83
2017    3119.55
2014    1203.45
2015    3441.62
2016    3007.83
2017    3619.53
2014    3412.12
2015    3491.16
```

```
2016     3457.19
2017     1963.10
dtype: float64
```

The result is probably not what we expected. The reason is that, by default, `concat()` uses `axis=0`. Let us try again with `axis=1`:

```python
shops_df = pd.concat([shop1, shop2, shop3], axis=1)


print(shops_df)
```

Output:

```
            0        1        2
2014  2409.14  1203.45  3412.12
2015  2941.01  3441.62  3491.16
2016  3496.83  3007.83  3457.19
2017  3119.55  3619.53  1963.10
```

But what data type is the result now? `type(shops_df)` returns `DataFrame`. This means that we can transform `Series` objects into `DataFrame` objects through concatenation!

20.3 Manipulating Column Names

Looking at the previously generated `DataFrame`, we notice that the columns are labeled 0, 1, and 2 – not very informative.

```python
print(shops_df.columns)
print(shops_df.columns.values)
```

This follows from the code:

```
RangeIndex(start=0, stop=3, step=1)
[0 1 2]
```

We can see that the `DataFrame` object provides the attribute `columns`, which allows us to access or modify the column labels. Suppose our shops are located in Zurich, Winterthur, and Freiburg. It would be more meaningful to use these city names as column headers. We can assign them directly via the `columns` attribute:

```python
cities = ["Zurich", "Winterthur", "Freiburg"]
shops_df.columns = cities


print(shops_df)
```

Executing the code yields:

```
      Zurich  Winterthur  Freiburg
2014  2409.14     1203.45   3412.12
2015  2941.01     3441.62   3491.16
2016  3496.83     3007.83   3457.19
2017  3119.55     3619.53   1963.10
```

On the other hand, renaming would not have been necessary in our case if the `Series` objects had already been named accordingly. We show this in the following example:

```python
shop1.name = 'Zurich'
shop2.name = 'Winterthur'
shop3.name = 'Freiburg'
shops_df2 = pd.concat([shop1, shop2, shop3], axis=1)
print(shops_df2)
```

In this case, we obtain exactly the same result as before.

20.4 DataFrames from Dictionaries

A `DataFrame` can also be created directly from a Python `dict`. Accessing the columns of a `DataFrame` closely resembles accessing the values of a dictionary: the column name acts as the key, and the column contents represent the corresponding values.

The following dictionary, `cities`, can therefore be directly converted into a `DataFrame`:

```python
cities = {"city": ["London", "Berlin", "Madrid", "Rome",
                   "Paris", "Vienna", "Bucharest", "Hamburg",
                   "Budapest", "Warsaw", "Barcelona",
                   "Munich", "Milan"],
          "population": [8_615_246, 3_562_166, 3165235, 2874038,
                         2273305, 1805681, 1803425, 1760433,
                         1754000, 1740119, 1602386, 1493900,
                         1350680],
          "country": ["England", "Germany", "Spain", "Italy",
                      "France", "Austria", "Romania",
                      "Germany", "Hungary", "Poland", "Spain",
                      "Germany", "Italy"]}
```

```python
city_frame = pd.DataFrame(cities)
print(city_frame)
```

The resulting output is:

```
         city  population  country
0      London     8615246  England
1      Berlin     3562166  Germany
2      Madrid     3165235    Spain
3        Rome     2874038    Italy
4       Paris     2273305   France
5      Vienna     1805681  Austria
6    Bucharest    1803425  Romania
7     Hamburg     1760433  Germany
8    Budapest     1754000  Hungary
9      Warsaw     1740119   Poland
10  Barcelona     1602386    Spain
11     Munich     1493900  Germany
12      Milan     1350680    Italy
```

Nested Dictionaries

Nested `dict` objects can also be directly converted into a `DataFrame`. In this case, the keys of the outer dictionary become the column names, while the keys of the inner dictionaries become the row indices.

In the following example, we use a nested dictionary containing GDP growth rates for several EU countries from 2019 to 2024:[2]

```python
growth = {
   'Belgium':    {'2019': 2.1, '2020': -5.7, '2021': 6.2,
                  '2022': 3.0, '2023': 1.5, '2024': 1.2},
   'Germany':    {'2019': 1.1, '2020': -3.7, '2021': 2.6,
                  '2022': 1.8, '2023': -0.3, '2024': -0.2},
   'France':     {'2019': 1.8, '2020': -7.8, '2021': 6.8,
                  '2022': 2.5, '2023': 0.7, '2024': 1.6},
   'Greece':     {'2019': 1.8, '2020': -9.0, '2021': 8.3,
                  '2022': 5.7, '2023': 2.3, '2024': 2.3},
   'Italy':      {'2019': 0.5, '2020': -9.0, '2021': 6.7,
                  '2022': 4.0, '2023': 0.9, '2024': 0.7}
}


growth_frame = pd.DataFrame(growth)
print(growth_frame)
```

---

2 Source: *https://ec.europa.eu/eurostat/databrowser/view/tec00115/default/table?lang=en*

The processing yields:

```
      Belgium  Germany  France  Greece  Italy
2019      2.1      1.1     1.8     1.8    0.5
2020     -5.7     -3.7    -7.8    -9.0   -9.0
2021      6.2      2.6     6.8     8.3    6.7
2022      3.0      1.8     2.5     5.7    4.0
2023      1.5     -0.3     0.7     2.3    0.9
2024      1.2     -0.2     1.6     2.3    0.7
```

In this representation, the years form the row indices and the country names form the columns. If desired, this representation can be transposed so that the countries appear as rows and the years as columns.

Transposing

The transposition of a `DataFrame` can be done either with the method `transpose()` or with the shorthand T:

```python
print(growth_frame.transpose())  # or: print(growth_frame.T)
```

The result of the code is:

```
         2019  2020  2021  2022  2023  2024
Belgium   2.1  -5.7   6.2   3.0   1.5   1.2
Germany   1.1  -3.7   2.6   1.8  -0.3  -0.2
France    1.8  -7.8   6.8   2.5   0.7   1.6
Greece    1.8  -9.0   8.3   5.7   2.3   2.3
Italy     0.5  -9.0   6.7   4.0   0.9   0.7
```

Adjusting the Row Order

After transposing, we can also adjust the order of the rows (now corresponding to countries):

```python
growth_frame = growth_frame.T
countries = ['Italy', 'Germany', 'Greece', 'Belgium']
growth_frame2 = growth_frame.reindex(countries)
print(growth_frame2)
```

Output:

```
         2019  2020  2021  2022  2023  2024
Italy     0.5  -9.0   6.7   4.0   0.9   0.7
Germany   1.1  -3.7   2.6   1.8  -0.3  -0.2
Greece    1.8  -9.0   8.3   5.7   2.3   2.3
Belgium   2.1  -5.7   6.2   3.0   1.5   1.2
```

20.5 Accessing Columns

You can access the columns of a `DataFrame` directly by label (i.e., using the column
name in square brackets):

```python
print(shops_df['Zurich'])
```

The processing yields:

```
2014      2409.14
2015      2941.01
2016      3496.83
2017      3119.55
Name: Zurich, dtype: float64
```

Each column of a `DataFrame` is internally a `Series` object – both when the DataFrame
is created and when it is accessed later. We can see this when we check the type:

```python
print(type(shops_df['Zurich']))
```

Here is the output:

```
<class 'pandas.core.series.Series'>
```

Pandas also offers a syntactically much simpler way to access columns. Column names
are implemented as properties, which means you can simply append the column name
to the DataFrame with a dot to access it:

```python
print(shops_df.Zurich)
```

The corresponding output can be seen here:

```
2014      2409.14
2015      2941.01
2016      3496.83
2017      3119.55
Name: Zurich, dtype: float64
```

20.6 Row Selection

20.6.1 loc

So far, we have indexed `DataFrame` objects via the columns, i.e. we have only accessed
columns. Now we want to demonstrate how to selectively access rows as well. For this

purpose, Pandas provides two access methods; `loc` (label-based) and `iloc` (position-based).

In the first example, we create a `DataFrame` where the country names serve as the index. We then select all rows with the index 'Germany':

```python
city_frame = pd.DataFrame(cities,
                          columns=['city', 'population'],
                          index=cities['country'])


print(city_frame.loc['Germany'])
```

The resulting output is:

```
            city  population
Germany   Berlin     3562166
Germany  Hamburg     1760433
Germany   Munich     1493900
```

To select multiple index values at once, we pass a list to `loc`:

```python
print(city_frame.loc[['Germany', 'France']])
```

The result appears as follows:

```
            city  population
Germany   Berlin     3562166
Germany  Hamburg     1760433
Germany   Munich     1493900
France     Paris     2273305
```

Of course, rows can also be filtered using conditions. In the following example, we select all cities with more than two million inhabitants:

```python
print(city_frame.loc[city_frame.population > 2_000_000])
```

The corresponding output can be seen here:

```
            city  population
England   London     8615246
Germany   Berlin     3562166
Spain     Madrid     3165235
Italy       Rome     2874038
France     Paris     2273305
```

Multiple conditions can be combined. In the next example, we filter for cities with more than 1.5 million inhabitants *and* whose names contain the letter m:

```
cond1 = city_frame.population > 1_500_000
cond2 = city_frame.city.str.contains('m')


print(city_frame[cond1 & cond2])
```

The result of the code is:

```
             city  population
Italy        Rome     2874038
Germany   Hamburg     1760433
```

In this example, the two conditions are combined using the logical AND operator (&).
Each condition produces a Series of Boolean values (True or False), and the & operator combines them elementwise.

Similarly, you can combine conditions using logical OR (|):

```
cond1 = city_frame.population > 2_500_000
cond2 = city_frame.city.str.contains('m')


print(city_frame[cond1 | cond2])
```

Script output:

```
             city  population
England    London     8615246
Germany    Berlin     3562166
Spain      Madrid     3165235
Italy        Rome     2874038
Germany   Hamburg     1760433
```

Here, we use & (AND) and | (OR) instead of and and or, because the latter work only
with scalar truth values, whereas & and | operate elementwise on Pandas Series.

20.6.2 query

With the query method, row filter conditions can also be expressed as strings – an
alternative and often more readable syntax compared with loc.

In the following example, we again select all rows with the index Germany or France,
but this time using query:

```
print(city_frame.query("index == 'Germany' or index == 'France'"))
```

As in the previous section, we select all rows where the population is greater than two
million – this time using query instead of loc:

```python
print(city_frame.query('population > 2_000_000'))
```

Executing the code yields:

```
          city  population
England  London     8615246
Germany  Berlin     3562166
Spain    Madrid     3165235
Italy      Rome     2874038
France    Paris     2273305
```

In a query expression, external Python variables can also be referenced. To do this, prefix the variable name with the @ symbol:

```python
max_population = 2_000_000
print(city_frame.query('population > @max_population'))
```

We obtain this output:

```
          city  population
England  London     8615246
Germany  Berlin     3562166
Spain    Madrid     3165235
Italy      Rome     2874038
France    Paris     2273305
```

Multiple conditions can be combined with and and or – similar to regular Python expressions:

```python
print(city_frame.query(
        'population > 2_000_000 or city.str.contains("m")',
        engine='python'))
```

After execution we get:

```
          city  population
England  London     8615246
Germany  Berlin     3562166
Spain    Madrid     3165235
Italy      Rome     2874038
France    Paris     2273305
Germany Hamburg     1760433
```

Now with and:

```python
print(city_frame.query(
        'population > 1_500_000 and city.str.contains("m")',
        engine='python'))
```

The processing yields:

```
           city  population
Italy      Rome     2874038
Germany  Hamburg    1760433
```

Note: If a column name contains spaces, it must be enclosed in backticks (`) within a query expression.[3]

```python
df = pd.DataFrame({
    'Primary Color': ['red', 'green', 'blue', 'yellow'],
    'Secondary Color': ['purple', 'green', 'brown', 'yellow']})


print(df.query('`Primary Color` == `Secondary Color`'))
```

The output shows:

```
  Primary Color Secondary Color
1         green           green
3        yellow          yellow
```

20.7 Modification of DataFrames

The DataFrame shown below presents the coffee and tea consumption of a fictional
software team.

```python
import pandas as pd
consumption = pd.DataFrame({'Coffee': [3, 0, 2, 2],
                            'Tea': [0, 4, 2, 0]},
                           index=['Robert', 'Melinda',
                                  'Sarah', 'Karin'])
consumption.index.name = 'Team'
print(consumption)
```

The script returns:

```
         Coffee  Tea
Team
Robert        3    0
Melinda       0    4
Sarah         2    2
Karin         2    0
```

---

3 The English word "backtick" refers to the backward-leaning apostrophe – ` – not to be confused with
   the single quote '!

20.7.1 Inserting Columns

If you want to insert a new column into a `DataFrame`, there are four main approaches:

- Index notation (simple assignment),
- the `insert()` method,
- the `loc` indexer,
- the `assign()` method.

Index Notation

With this method, we specify the new column name as if we were accessing an existing one, and then assign the desired values – that is, we add a new column to the end of the `DataFrame`. In this example, we add a column for the number of cups of cocoa consumed by each team member `DataFrame`:

```python
consumption['Cocoa'] = [1, 2, 0, 0]
print(consumption)
```

This is the result of the code:

```
        Coffee  Tea  Cocoa
Team
Robert       3    0      1
Melinda      0    4      2
Sarah        2    2      0
Karin        2    0      0
```

You can also add multiple columns at once. To do this, pass a list of column names together with a two-dimensional data structure to the parameter `data`:

```python
import pandas as pd
consumption = pd.DataFrame({'Coffee': [3, 0, 2, 2],
                            'Tea': [0, 4, 2, 0]},
                           index=['Robert', 'Melinda',
                                  'Sarah', 'Karin'])
consumption.index.name = 'Team'

data = [[1, 10],
        [2, 12],
        [0, 3],
        [0, 6]]

consumption[['Cocoa', 'Cookies']] = data
print(consumption)
```

What we obtain is:

```
          Coffee  Tea  Cocoa  Cookies
Team
Robert         3    0      1       10
Melinda        0    4      2       12
Sarah          2    2      0        3
Karin          2    0      0        6
```

insert

The indexing method described above is not suitable if a new column should be inserted
at a specific position within the DataFrame rather than appended at the end. In such
cases, the insert() method can be used. The first parameter specifies the insertion
position (as the column index), the second defines the name of the new column, and
the third provides the data source. The data source may also be a single fixed value (a
constant), which will then be used for all rows – for example, 0 for Cocoa:

```python
import pandas as pd
consumption = pd.DataFrame({'Coffee': [3, 0, 2, 2],
                            'Tea': [0, 4, 2, 0]},
                           index=['Robert', 'Melinda',
                                  'Sarah', 'Karin'])
consumption.index.name = 'Team'

consumption.insert(1, 'Cookies', [10, 12, 3, 6])
# The 'Cocoa' column filled with 0 is inserted before 'Cookies'.
consumption.insert(1, 'Cocoa', 0)
print(consumption)
```

After execution we get:

```
          Coffee  Cocoa  Cookies  Tea
Team
Robert         3      0       10    0
Melinda        0      0       12    4
Sarah          2      0        3    2
Karin          2      0        6    0
```

loc

The loc indexer is primarily used to access specific rows or columns by label, as we
have already seen. However, it can also be used to insert new columns or rows into a
DataFrame.

```python
import pandas as pd
consumption = pd.DataFrame({'Coffee': [3, 0, 2, 2],
                            'Tea': [0, 4, 2, 0],
                            'Cocoa': [1, 1, 2, 4]},
                           index=['Robert', 'Melinda',
                                  'Sarah', 'Karin'])
consumption.index.name = 'Team'

# Access a specific row:
print(consumption.loc['Sarah', :])
print('---------------------------------')

# Access a range:
print(consumption.loc[:'Sarah', 'Coffee':'Tea'])
```

The code produces the following result:

```
Coffee    2
Tea       2
Cocoa     2
Name: Sarah, dtype: int64
---------------------------------
         Coffee  Tea
Team
Robert        3    0
Melinda       0    4
Sarah         2    2
```

You can also use the `loc` indexer to add new columns or rows:

```python
import pandas as pd
consumption = pd.DataFrame({'Coffee': [3, 0, 2, 2],
                            'Tea': [0, 4, 2, 0],
                            'Cocoa': [1, 1, 2, 4]},
                           index=['Robert', 'Melinda',
                                  'Sarah', 'Karin'])
consumption.index.name = 'Team'

# Add new column:
consumption.loc[:, 'Cookies'] = [3, 10, 12, 18]

# Add new row:
consumption.loc['Anne'] = [5, 4, 3, 2]
print(consumption)
```

The processing yields:

```
            Coffee  Tea  Cocoa  Cookies
Team
Robert           3    0      1        3
Melinda          0    4      1       10
Sarah            2    2      2       12
Karin            2    0      4       18
Anne             5    4      3        2
```

assign

With the `assign()` method, new columns can be added to a `DataFrame` by passing
both the column name and the corresponding values directly as arguments.

A key difference compared with the `insert()` method is that `assign()` does **not modify the DataFrame in place**. Instead, it returns a **new DataFrame** containing the added
columns, while the original object remains unchanged. In contrast, `insert()` modifies
the existing `DataFrame` directly.

```python
import pandas as pd
consumption = pd.DataFrame({'Coffee': [3, 0, 2, 2],
                            'Tea': [0, 4, 2, 0],
                            'Cocoa': [1, 1, 2, 4]},
                           index=['Robert', 'Melinda',
                                  'Sarah', 'Karin'])
consumption.index.name = 'Team'

consumption = consumption.assign(Cookies=[3, 10, 12, 18])
print(consumption)
```

The result appears as follows:

```
            Coffee  Tea  Cocoa  Cookies
Team
Robert           3    0      1        3
Melinda          0    4      1       10
Sarah            2    2      2       12
Karin            2    0      4       18
```

With `assign()`, it is also possible to create multiple new columns at the same time. A
column can even depend on another column defined in the same `assign()` operation:

```python
import pandas as pd

df = pd.DataFrame({'temp_c': [26, 25, 21]},
                  index=['Zurich', 'Salzburg', 'Hamburg'])
```

```python
df = df.assign(temp_f=lambda x: x['temp_c'] * 9 / 5 + 32,
               temp_k=lambda x: (x['temp_f'] + 459.67) * 5 / 9)

print(df)
```

Within `assign()`, each function (such as the lambda expressions above) receives the current intermediate `DataFrame`, so later columns can depend on those defined earlier in the same call.

The result appears as follows:

```
          temp_c  temp_f  temp_k
Zurich        26    78.8  299.15
Salzburg      25    77.0  298.15
Hamburg       21    69.8  294.15
```

20.7.2 Replacing Columns

Replacing an entire column in a `DataFrame` is straightforward: you simply assign a new list or array of values to the desired column. The number of new values must match the number of rows in the `DataFrame`.

In the following example, we replace the contents of the `Cocoa` and `Coffee` columns:

```python
import pandas as pd
consumption = pd.DataFrame({'Coffee': [3, 0, 2, 2],
                            'Tea': [0, 4, 2, 0],
                            'Cocoa': [1, 1, 2, 4]},
                           index=['Robert', 'Melinda',
                                  'Sarah', 'Karin'])
consumption.index.name = 'Team'

# Replace entire columns
consumption['Cocoa'] = [2, 1, 4, 5]
consumption.Coffee = [3, 3, 2, 3]
print(consumption)
```

The result appears as follows:

```
         Coffee  Tea  Cocoa
Team
Robert        3    0      2
Melinda       3    4      1
Sarah         2    2      4
Karin         3    0      5
```

20.7.3 Replacing Rows

We saw in Section 20.3 how new rows and columns can be added using `loc`. In the following example, we show how existing rows can be selectively replaced using the same method.

We use the `DataFrame` from the previous example and assign new values to the row labeled 'Sarah':

```python
# Replace the row for 'Sarah'
consumption.loc['Sarah'] = [3, 3, 5]
print(consumption)
```

The processing yields:

```
        Coffee  Tea  Cocoa
Team
Robert       3    0      2
Melinda      3    4      1
Sarah        3    3      5
Karin        3    0      5
```

20.7.4 Modifying Individual Values with at and iat

The methods `at` and `iat` provide especially fast access to individual values within a `DataFrame`.

`at` is comparable to `loc`, since both are label-based. In contrast to `loc`, however, `at` is specifically optimized for accessing a single value and is therefore significantly faster when performing many such operations.

In the following example, we increase the number of cups of coffee consumed by `Sarah` by 2:

```python
import pandas as pd
consumption = pd.DataFrame({'Coffee': [3, 0, 2, 5],
                            'Tea': [0, 4, 2, 0],
                            'Cocoa': [1, 1, 2, 4]},
                           index=['Robert', 'Melinda',
                                  'Sarah', 'Karin'])
consumption.index.name = 'Team'

consumption.at['Sarah', 'Coffee'] += 2
print(consumption)
```

Here is the output:

```
         Coffee  Tea  Cocoa
Team
Robert       3    0      1
Melinda      0    4      1
Sarah        4    2      2
Karin        5    0      4
```

iat, on the other hand, uses numerical positions instead of labels. The first number specifies the row position, and the second specifies the column position (both starting from 0). Like at, iat is optimized for single-value access.

In the following example, we access the value in row 3 (corresponding to 'Karin') and column 2 (corresponding to 'Cocoa'):

```python
print(consumption.iat[3, 2])
```

This print() function outputs the value 4, i.e. the entry in the fourth row and third column.

20.8 Changing the Index

If no index is specified when creating a DataFrame, Pandas automatically generates a default index – usually a numeric RangeIndex, as shown in the following example:

```python
cities = ['Berlin', 'Frankfurt', 'Munich']
data = {'City': cities,
        'Max_Temp': [28, 25, 32],
        'Min_Temp': [15, 10, 20]}

df = pd.DataFrame(data)
print(df)
```

After execution we get:

```
        City  Max_Temp  Min_Temp
0     Berlin        28        15
1  Frankfurt        25        10
2     Munich        32        20
```

However, we can also specify an index explicitly when creating a DataFrame. In this case, it makes sense to use the city names as the row index:

```python
df = pd.DataFrame(data, index=cities)
print(df)
```

The result appears as follows:

```
                City  Max_Temp  Min_Temp
Berlin        Berlin        28        15
Frankfurt  Frankfurt        25        10
Munich        Munich        32        20
```

A disadvantage of the example above is that the city names now appear both as the index and as a separate column. This redundancy may be confusing.

Instead, when creating the `DataFrame`, we can specify exactly which columns to include. This is done via the `columns` parameter, to which we pass a list of the desired column names::

```python
df = pd.DataFrame(data,
                  columns=['Min_Temp', 'Max_Temp'],
                  index=cities)
print(df)
```

After execution we get:

```
           Min_Temp  Max_Temp
Berlin           15        28
Frankfurt        10        25
Munich           20        32
```

20.8.1 Reordering Columns and Index

Now we want to reorder the columns and rows of a `DataFrame`. The pandas method `reindex()` can be used for both purposes.

The `reindex()` method takes a new list of indices as an argument and changes the order of the rows in the `DataFrame` accordingly. If a particular index is present in the new list but not in the original `DataFrame`, NaN values are inserted in the corresponding row.

The order of the keys in the list passed to the keyword parameter `columns` also determines the order of the columns in the resulting `DataFrame`.

In the following example, we demonstrate these possibilities:

```python
import pandas as pd

cities = ['Berlin', 'Frankfurt', 'Munich']
data = {'City': cities,
        'Max_Temp': [28, 25, 32],
        'Min_Temp': [15, 10, 20]}
```

```python
df = pd.DataFrame(data,
                  columns=['Min_Temp', 'Max_Temp'],
                  index=cities)

print('Original DataFrame:')
print(df)
df2 = df.reindex(['Berlin', 'Munich', 'Frankfurt'])
print('\nNow with changed index order:')
print(df2)
df3 = df.reindex(['Berlin', 'Munich', 'Frankfurt', 'Konstanz'])
print('\nNow with an additional index value:')
print(df3)
df4 = df.reindex(['Berlin', 'Munich', 'Frankfurt'],
                 columns=['Max_Temp', 'Min_Temp'])
print('\nNow also with changed column order:')
print(df4)
```

What we obtain is:

```
Original DataFrame:
          Min_Temp  Max_Temp
Berlin          15        28
Frankfurt       10        25
Munich          20        32

Now with changed index order:
          Min_Temp  Max_Temp
Berlin          15        28
Munich          20        32
Frankfurt       10        25

Now with an additional index value:
          Min_Temp  Max_Temp
Berlin        15.0      28.0
Munich        20.0      32.0
Frankfurt     10.0      25.0
Konstanz       NaN       NaN

Now also with changed column order:
          Max_Temp  Min_Temp
Berlin          28        15
Munich          32        20
Frankfurt       25        10
```

In summary, `reindex()` provides a simple way to reorder rows or columns and to introduce new index or column labels where needed.

20.8.2 Renaming Columns

Now we want to rename the columns. For this, we use the `DataFrame` method
`rename()`. The method supports the following call signatures:

- `rename(index=index_mapper, columns=columns_mapper, ...)`
- `rename(mapper, axis={'index', 'columns'}, ...)`

In the following example, we rename the columns of our `DataFrame` to more descriptive two-word labels. We set the parameter `inplace` to `True`, so that the `DataFrame` object is changed directly and no new one is created. The default value for the parameter `inplace` is `False`.

```python
df.rename(columns={'Min_Temp': 'Minimum Temperature',
                   'Max_Temp': 'Maximum Temperature'},
          inplace=True)
print(df)
```

The corresponding output can be seen here:

```
          Minimum Temperature  Maximum Temperature
Berlin                     15                   28
Frankfurt                  10                   25
Munich                     20                   32
```

20.8.3 Using a Column as Index

Often, a `DataFrame` already exists, and you may want to use a specific column as the new index. For this purpose, Pandas provides the `set_index` method.

```python
import pandas as pd

cities = ['Berlin', 'Frankfurt', 'Munich']
data = {'City': cities,
        'Max_Temp': [28, 25, 32],
        'Min_Temp': [15, 10, 20]}

df = pd.DataFrame(data)
print(df)

print('DataFrame with City as index:')
df2 = df.set_index('City')
print(df2)
```

The following result is generated:

```
        City  Max_Temp  Min_Temp
0       Berlin        28        15
1    Frankfurt        25        10
2       Munich        32        20
DataFrame with City as index:
           Max_Temp  Min_Temp
City
Berlin           28        15
Frankfurt        25        10
Munich           32        20
```

In the previous example, we saw that the `set_index()` method returns a new `DataFrame` object and does not modify the original one. If you do not want to create a new `DataFrame`, but instead want to set a new index directly for the existing one, you can set the parameter `inplace` to `True`. This will modify the original object in place:

```python
df.set_index('City', inplace=True)
print(df)
```

The corresponding output can be seen here:

```
           Max_Temp  Min_Temp
City
Berlin           28        15
Frankfurt        25        10
Munich           32        20
```

20.9 Sums and Cumulative Sums

With the `sum()` method, you can calculate the sum across all columns of a `DataFrame`. For each numeric column, the column sum is computed:

```python
print(city_frame.sum())
```

However, since in our example there are also columns with non-numeric values, calculating the total sum is only meaningful for certain columns – such as the population numbers.

```python
print(city_frame['population'].sum())
```

The sum of the populations is 33800614.

The cumsum() method calculates cumulative sums – that is, running totals of columns or rows. Each value is replaced by the sum of all previous values, including the current one.

```
x = city_frame["population"].cumsum()


print(x)
```

The result is:

```
England      8615246
Germany     12177412
Spain       15342647
Italy       18216685
France      20489990
Austria     22295671
Romania     24099096
Germany     25859529
Hungary     27613529
Poland      29353648
Spain       30956034
Germany     32449934
Italy       33800614
Name: population, dtype: int64
```

The variable x we just calculated is a Series object containing the cumulative sum. We can assign this Series back to the population column, thereby replacing the original values.

In the following, we use the head() method, which displays only the first five rows – sufficient to illustrate the concept:

```
city_frame['population'] = x
print(city_frame.head())
```

This output is obtained:

```
          city  population
England  London     8615246
Germany  Berlin    12177412
Spain    Madrid    15342647
Italy      Rome    18216685
France    Paris    20489990
```

20.9.1 Empty Columns and Filling Them Later

Pandas allows you to define additional columns when creating a DataFrame – even if
no values are available for them yet. In this case, Pandas automatically fills the cells
with NaN, which serves as a placeholder for missing data.

A typical example: we define a column cum_population, for which we will calculate
values later. Initially, this column contains only NaN values:

```python
# DataFrame with an empty column
city_frame = pd.DataFrame(cities,
                          columns=['country',
                                   'population',
                                   'cum_population'],
                          index=cities['city'])
print(city_frame.head())
```

Script output:

```
        country  population cum_population
London  England     8615246            NaN
Berlin  Germany     3562166            NaN
Madrid    Spain     3165235            NaN
Rome      Italy     2874038            NaN
Paris    France     2273305            NaN
```

Now we fill this column with the cumulative sum of the population numbers:

```python
city_frame['cum_population'] = city_frame['population'].cumsum()
print(city_frame.head())
```

The evaluation yields:

```
        country  population  cum_population
London  England     8615246         8615246
Berlin  Germany     3562166        12177412
Madrid    Spain     3165235        15342647
Rome      Italy     2874038        18216685
Paris    France     2273305        20489990
```

When creating a DataFrame from a dictionary, it is also possible to specify columns that
are not present in the dictionary. In this case, the corresponding cells are automatically
filled with NaN values:

```python
city_frame = pd.DataFrame(cities,
                          columns=["country",
                                   "area",
                                   "population"],
                          index=cities["city"])

print(city_frame.head())
```

The output we get is:

```
        country area  population
London  England NaN     8615246
Berlin  Germany NaN     3562166
Madrid    Spain NaN     3165235
Rome      Italy NaN     2874038
Paris    France NaN     2273305
```

In a further step, the values for the area can be assigned to the `area` column in the form of a list or an array:

```python
# Flächen in qkm:
area = [1572, 891.85, 605.77, 1285, 105.4, 414.6,
        228, 755, 525.2, 517, 101.9, 310.4, 181.8]

city_frame["area"] = area


print(city_frame.head())
```

The code produces the following result:

```
        country     area  population
London  England  1572.00     8615246
Berlin  Germany   891.85     3562166
Madrid    Spain   605.77     3165235
Rome      Italy  1285.00     2874038
Paris    France   105.40     2273305
```

20.10 Sorting

`DataFrame` objects can be sorted according to specific criteria. In the following example, we sort the `DataFrame` by the values in the `area` column – in descending order:

```python
city_frame = city_frame.sort_values(by='area', ascending=False)
print(city_frame)
```

The corresponding output can be seen here:

```
         country     area  population
London   England  1572.00     8615246
Rome       Italy  1285.00     2874038
Berlin   Germany   891.85     3562166
Hamburg  Germany   755.00     1760433
```

```
Madrid      Spain   605.77   3165235
Budapest   Hungary  525.20   1754000
Warsaw      Poland  517.00   1740119
Vienna     Austria  414.60   1805681
Munich     Germany  310.40   1493900
Bucharest  Romania  228.00   1803425
Milan        Italy  181.80   1350680
Paris       France  105.40   2273305
Barcelona    Spain  101.90   1602386
```

You can also sort by multiple columns. The order of the columns in the list determines the sorting priority:

```python
city_frame = city_frame.sort_values(by=['country', 'area'],
                                     ascending=[True, False])
print(city_frame)
```

The corresponding output can be seen here:

```
             country     area  population
Vienna       Austria   414.60     1805681
London       England  1572.00     8615246
Paris         France   105.40     2273305
Berlin       Germany   891.85     3562166
Hamburg      Germany   755.00     1760433
Munich       Germany   310.40     1493900
Budapest     Hungary   525.20     1754000
Rome           Italy  1285.00     2874038
Milan          Italy   181.80     1350680
Warsaw        Poland   517.00     1740119
Bucharest    Romania   228.00     1803425
Madrid         Spain   605.77     3165235
Barcelona      Spain   101.90     1602386
```

The index of a DataFrame can also be sorted:

```python
city_frame = city_frame.sort_index()
print(city_frame)
```

The processing yields:

```
             country    area  population
Barcelona      Spain  101.90     1602386
Berlin       Germany  891.85     3562166
Bucharest    Romania  228.00     1803425
Budapest     Hungary  525.20     1754000
Hamburg      Germany  755.00     1760433
```

```
London      England   1572.00        8615246
Madrid        Spain    605.77        3165235
Milan         Italy    181.80        1350680
Munich      Germany    310.40        1493900
Paris        France    105.40        2273305
Rome          Italy   1285.00        2874038
Vienna      Austria    414.60        1805681
Warsaw       Poland    517.00        1740119
```

20.11 Exercises

1. Exercise

(Solution: 33.13, Solution 1)

Create a `DataFrame` object from the following data:

```
Vienna    country             Austria
          area                  414.6
          population          1805681
Hamburg   country             Germany
          area                    755
          population          1760433
Berlin    country             Germany
          area                 891.85
          population          3562166
Zurich    country         Switzerland
          area                  87.88
          population           378884
dtype: object
```

2. Exercise

(Solution: 33.13, Solution 2)

Swap the indices of the previous Series.

3. Exercise

(Solution: 33.13, Solution 3)

Create a `DataFrame` whose index consists of first names and which contains two columns: one for weight (in kilograms) and one for height (in meters).

Then calculate the Body Mass Index (BMI) for each person and extract all rows where the BMI falls within the normal range – that is, between 18.5 and 25.

Use the following formula:

$$\text{BMI} = \frac{W}{H^2}$$

where W denotes weight (in kilograms) and H denotes height (in meters).

4. Exercise

(Solution: 33.13, Solution 4)

Output the rows whose names contain a lowercase "i".

5. Exercise

(Solution: 33.13, Solution 5)

Add a column with the BMI to the `DataFrame` created in Exercise 3.

6. Exercise

(Solution: 33.13, Solution 6)

Output the `DataFrame` created in the last exercise, sorted in descending order by BMI.

7. Exercise

(Solution: 33.13, Solution 7)

Now output all rows whose BMI values lie between 18.5 and 23 and whose first names contain an "a".

8. Exercise

(Solution: 33.13, Solution 8)

Create a `DataFrame` with an index consisting of month names and column names corresponding to first names. Now fill the columns with random integers between 120 and 200.

9. Exercise

(Solution: 33.13, Solution 9)

Invert the `DataFrame` you just created so that the index consists of the first names, and the column labels correspond to the month names.

21 Styling

21.1 Introduction

Plain text is clear and easy to read, but it can sometimes lack emphasis and clarity – especially when dealing with complex or extensive content. Highlighting text using different fonts and colors helps draw the reader's attention, emphasize important points, and improve readability. Visual distinctions such as **bold**, *italics*, and color coding can highlight key information, enhance understanding, and increase user engagement. However, excessive use of these elements can lead to visual clutter and reduced readability – balance is key.

Figure 21.1 Styling a Panda

The previous section presented the content in plain form; the next illustrates the same text with visual emphasis.

Plain text is clear and easy to read but can sometimes lack **emphasis** and **clarity**, especially with complex or extensive content.

By contrast, **highlighted text**, *different fonts*, and colors help **draw the reader's attention**, emphasize key points, and improve **readability**.

✓The use of **bold**, *italics*, and color coding can **highlight important information**, improve comprehension, and enhance **user engagement**.

✎However, **overuse** of these elements can create **clutter** and reduce **readability** – **balance is essential**!

The focus of this chapter in the Pandas tutorial is now clear: just as we can apply formatting to text for better legibility, we can also style a DataFrame to make it visually clearer and more readable – without modifying the underlying data.

In programming, including Python development, a fundamental best practice is the separation of raw data (logic) from its presentation (styling or rendering). This principle applies broadly, from web development to data analysis and backend design.

In Pandas, we follow the same principle by keeping the raw data separate from its presentation. This ensures that the data remains precise, computationally usable, and can be flexibly formatted without altering its structure.

21.2 Separating Data and Presentation

- **Preserving data integrity:** The underlying numerical values remain unchanged, preventing rounding errors or data distortion.
  Example: A value is stored internally as 1234.5678 rather than as the formatted string "1,234.57 EUR".

- **Ensuring computational compatibility:** Calculations such as sums, averages, or statistical analyses require pure numeric data.
  Example: If "$100.50" is stored as a string, Pandas cannot compute the total correctly.

- **Flexibility in presentation:** Formatting can be adapted dynamically for different use cases such as reports, dashboards, or user-specific views.
  Example: Displaying "50%" is visually helpful but internally the value is stored as 0.5 for calculations.

- **Improved maintainability:** If display requirements change (for example, from USD to EUR), only the presentation logic needs to be adjusted – not the underlying data.

21.3 The .style Property

Pandas provides a powerful .style property that enables visually appealing formatting of DataFrame objects – particularly useful in Jupyter notebooks and reports. The .style property allows dynamic formatting and visualization without changing the raw data. It improves readability through number formatting, color gradients, and highlights, while the underlying calculations remain unaffected.

21.3.1 Basic Formatting with `.format`

Let's start with the `format()` method of the `.style` property. It controls how values are displayed in a `DataFrame` without modifying the actual data.

The following example formats the numerical values in column B to two decimal places:

```python
import pandas as pd

df = pd.DataFrame({'A': [1, 2, 3],
                   'B': [4.1234, 5.5678, 6.91011]})

# Apply formatting: round column 'B' to two decimal places
styled_df = df.style.format({'B': "{:,.2f}"})
styled_df   # Display in Jupyter Notebook
```

`styled_df` will be rendered as a formatted HTML table only in a Jupyter environment (e.g., JupyterLab or Jupyter Notebook) if it appears as the last line of a code cell.

	A	B
0	1	4.12
1	2	5.57
2	3	6.91

Additional examples of common formatting specifiers:

Table 21.1 Formatting specifiers and their effects

Specifier	Effect	Example (`"{:.2f}".format(123.456)`)
`.0f`	Round to 0 decimal places	123
`.2f`	Round to 2 decimal places	123.46
`.2%`	Convert to percent with 2 decimal places	12345.60%

21.4 Maximum Values in Rows and Columns

In the previous example, we highlighted the maximum value in each `DataFrame` column. However, highlighting the maximum values in each row would not be meaningful there, since the data was heterogeneous – it would make little sense to compare within a row attributes such as a name, weight, height, and IQ.

To demonstrate a case where row-wise highlighting *is* meaningful, let's consider a more suitable dataset. The parameter axis determines the direction of the operation: row-wise (axis=1) or column-wise (axis=0).

```python
import pandas as pd

df = pd.DataFrame({
    'Monday': [8.5, 7.2, 9.0, 6.8, 8.3],
    'Tuesday': [7.4, 8.1, 6.5, 9.2, 7.0],
    'Wednesday': [8.0, 9.3, 7.7, 8.1, 6.9],
    'Thursday': [6.2, 8.4, 9.1, 7.3, 8.5],
    'Friday': [7.3, 6.8, 8.2, 7.6, 9.1]
}, index=['Alice', 'Bob', 'Charlie', 'David', 'Emma'])

# Highlight the maximum value in each row
styled_df = df.style.highlight_max(axis=1, color='orange')
styled_df
```

Output in Jupyter Notebook:

	Monday	Tuesday	Wednesday	Thursday	Friday
Alice	8.500000	7.400000	8.000000	6.200000	7.300000
Bob	7.200000	8.100000	9.300000	8.400000	6.800000
Charlie	9.000000	6.500000	7.700000	9.100000	8.200000
David	6.800000	9.200000	8.100000	7.300000	7.600000
Emma	8.300000	7.000000	6.900000	8.500000	9.100000

Now, we highlight the longest workday *per weekday* by using axis=0 instead:

```python
styled_df = df.style.highlight_max(axis=0, color='orange')
styled_df
```

Output in Jupyter Notebook:

	Monday	Tuesday	Wednesday	Thursday	Friday
Alice	8.500000	7.400000	8.000000	6.200000	7.300000
Bob	7.200000	8.100000	9.300000	8.400000	6.800000
Charlie	9.000000	6.500000	7.700000	9.100000	8.200000
David	6.800000	9.200000	8.100000	7.300000	7.600000
Emma	8.300000	7.000000	6.900000	8.500000	9.100000

21.5 Applying a Color Gradient

The method `.background_gradient()` applies a color gradient to each cell based on its numeric value. A colormap (`cmap`) from `matplotlib` is used for this purpose. Internally, the data is first normalized and then mapped to a color scale.

```
styled_df = df.style.background_gradient(cmap='Blues')
styled_df
```

Output in Jupyter Notebook:

	Monday	Tuesday	Wednesday	Thursday	Friday
Alice	8.500000	7.400000	8.000000	6.200000	7.300000
Bob	7.200000	8.100000	9.300000	8.400000	6.800000
Charlie	9.000000	6.500000	7.700000	9.100000	8.200000
David	6.800000	9.200000	8.100000	7.300000	7.600000
Emma	8.300000	7.000000	6.900000	8.500000	9.100000

Step-by-Step Logic Behind Gradient Coloring

1. **Normalization of values**
   - The values in each column are scaled between 0 and 1.
   - The smallest value becomes 0 (lightest color), the largest value becomes 1 (darkest color).
2. **Application of the colormap (`cmap='Blues'`)**
   - A Matplotlib colormap maps normalized values to colors.
   - Smaller values receive lighter shades of blue.
   - Larger values receive darker shades of blue.
3. **Rendering the colors**
   - Each cell background is colored according to its mapped value.

By default, `background_gradient()` normalizes data column-wise (`axis=0`). To scale row-wise, set `axis=1`.

Experimenting with Different cmap Values

By changing the `cmap` parameter, different color schemes can be applied:

- **'Blues'** – shades of blue (neutral, calm)
- **'Greens'** – shades of green (fresh, positive)
- **'Oranges'** – shades of orange (warm, energetic)

- **'Purples'** – shades of purple (elegant, creative)
- **'Reds'** – shades of red (intense, urgent)
- **'Greys'** – shades of gray (neutral, subtle)

21.5.1 Applying Bar Charts Inside Cells

The `.style.bar()` method in `Pandas` allows embedding horizontal bar charts directly inside `DataFrame` cells to visually represent numerical values. This provides an
intuitive, at-a-glance comparison across categories.

- **Row-wise** (`axis=1`) – bars represent values relative to other entries in the same
  row.
- **Column-wise** (`axis=0`) – bars represent values relative to other entries in the same
  column.

This method is particularly useful for highlighting variations in working hours, performance metrics, or any set of numeric comparisons within a dataset.

```python
import pandas as pd

df = pd.DataFrame({
    'Monday': [8.5, 5.2, 9.8, 6.1, 7.3],
    'Tuesday': [6.4, 8.7, 7.1, 9.0, 5.6],
    'Wednesday': [7.8, 9.5, 5.9, 8.3, 6.7],
    'Thursday': [5.6, 7.2, 9.3, 6.8, 8.9],
    'Friday': [9.1, 6.5, 8.0, 7.6, 9.4]
}, index=['Alice', 'Bob', 'Charlie', 'David', 'Emma'])

# Each column with its own bar scale
styled_columnwise_bar = df.style.bar(color='lightblue', axis=0)

# Each row with its own bar scale
styled_rowwise_bar = df.style.bar(color='lightgreen',
                                  width=90,
                                  axis=1)

styled_rowwise_bar
```

Output in a Jupyter Notebook:

	Monday	Tuesday	Wednesday	Thursday	Friday
Alice	8.500000	6.400000	7.800000	5.600000	9.100000
Bob	5.200000	8.700000	9.500000	7.200000	6.500000
Charlie	9.800000	7.100000	5.900000	9.300000	8.000000
David	6.100000	9.000000	8.300000	6.800000	7.600000
Emma	7.300000	5.600000	6.700000	8.900000	9.400000

The next example demonstrates the use of additional parameters:

```python
import pandas as pd

data = {
    'January': [5000, -2000, 3000, -1000, 2600],
    'February': [-1500, 4000, -2500, 500, -1100],
    'March': [3000, -1800, 6200, -700, 1000],
    'April': [-2200, 5000, -1200, 1000, 3500]
}

index = ['Nimbus Corp', 'Quantum Dynamics', 'Aurora Ventures',
         'Vertex Solutions', 'Orion Enterprises']

df = pd.DataFrame(data, index=index)

styled_df = df.style.bar(
    color=('red', 'green'),   # Red for negative, green for positive
    align='zero',             # Center on zero; options: 'left', 'mid'
    width=80,                 # Maximum width 80%
    axis=0                    # Column-wise bar charts
)
styled_df
```

Output in a Jupyter Notebook:

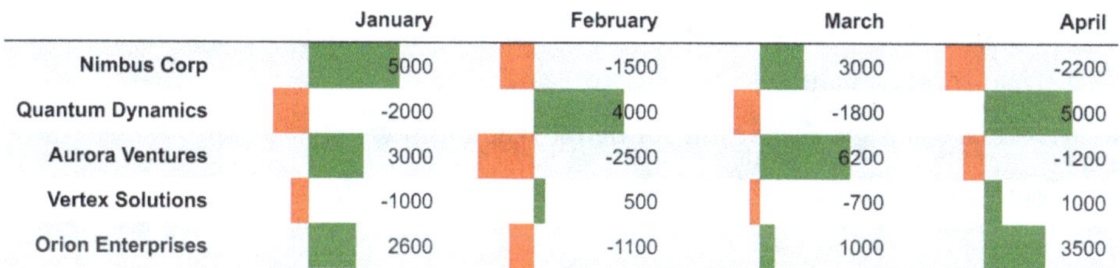

	January	February	March	April
Nimbus Corp	5000	-1500	3000	-2200
Quantum Dynamics	-2000	4000	-1800	5000
Aurora Ventures	3000	-2500	6200	-1200
Vertex Solutions	-1000	500	-700	1000
Orion Enterprises	2600	-1100	1000	3500

21.6 Exercises

Exercise 1

(Solution: 33.14, Solution 1)

Apply the following styles to the `DataFrame` below:

- Profits (positive values) in green, losses (negative values) in red.
- Yellow background for column headers and row index.
- Format numbers with a thousands separator.

```
df = pd.DataFrame({
    'Zurich': [15600, -4500, 13400],
    'Frankfurt': [-2400, 18200, -3200],
    'Hamburg': [10200, 9800, 7500],
    'Munich': [12000, -1000, -2000]
}, index=['January', 'February', 'March'])
```

Exercise 2

(Solution: 33.14, Solution 2)

A pandas DataFrame contains the monthly revenues (in euros) for four retail stores:
Berlin, Paris, Rome, and Madrid. The goal is to improve readability and visually highlight performance trends through styling.

- Load the given DataFrame.

- Apply **conditional formatting**:

    - **Successful months** (≥ €10,000): green background.

    - **Low revenue** (€5,000–€9,999): yellow background.

    - **Losses** (< €5,000): red background with bold text.

- Style headers:

    - **Column headers** (store names): blue background, white bold text.

    - **Row headers** (months): light gray background.

- Format revenue values:

    - Add a thousands separator for better readability.

```
import pandas as pd

df = pd.DataFrame({
    'Berlin': [12500, 8700, 3000, 15500, 9200, 4500],
    'Paris': [9800, 11200, 14000, 5000, 6800, 7100],
    'Rome': [6200, 3500, 10500, 9600, 4200, 15000],
    'Madrid': [11000, 13400, 8500, 7800, 12500, 9000]
}, index=['January', 'February', 'March',
          'April', 'May', 'June'])


print(df.to_string())
```

22

File Processing

Pandas with its powerful data structures "Series" and "DataFrame" would be merely a nice toy without its powerful capabilities to read and write data of various formats from files. Of course, one could also process files using Python's built-in input/output without additional modules, but then the code would be cumbersome to write, and not efficient enough. Pandas, therefore, offers high-level functionality for all important data formats to read and write them. For example, it provides functions for reading JSON, HTML, HDF5, Feather, SAS, and SQL formats.

In this chapter, however, we will only deal with "MS Excel" and CSV files, since these are the most

Figure 22.1 Pandas playing with files

important and most frequently used data formats. We will see that one can easily convert these file formats into DataFrames and just as easily save DataFrames in these file formats.

22.1 DSV / CSV Files

In everyday language, the terms "CSV" and "DSV" are often used synonymously. Strictly speaking, however, CSV is a special case of the DSV format.

A DSV file stores structured, tabular data in which each line represents a row and the column values are separated by a predefined delimiter. This delimiter can be freely chosen (e.g., tabs, semicolons, or pipe characters) but must remain consistent within a file. The term DSV stands for "Delimiter Separated Values."

CSV, by definition, uses commas as delimiters ("Comma Separated Values"). In German-speaking countries, commas are commonly used as decimal separators, so semicolons or tabs are often used instead. Such files are therefore technically DSV rather than CSV.

In practice, however, both terms are used interchangeably, including in Pandas, where "CSV" is commonly used to refer to any delimiter-separated file.

The file exchange_rates_eu_us_tr_ch.csv in directory data1 is a DSV file that uses a tab (\t) as delimiter.[1]

22.1.1 Reading CSV and DSV Files

Pandas provides the method read_csv to read CSV files.

```python
import pandas as pd


fname = "data1/exchange_rates_eu_us_tr_ch.csv"
exchange_rates = pd.read_csv(fname, sep="\t")
print(exchange_rates.tail(5))   # print only the last 5 rows
```

This is the result of the code:

```
    year       CHF       TRY  USD       EUR
18  2018  0.977892  4.828370    1  0.846773
19  2019  0.993709  5.673819    1  0.893276
20  2020  0.938965  7.008605    1  0.875506
21  2021  0.913846  8.850408    1  0.845494
22  2022  0.954940  16.570000   1  0.949624
```

As we have seen, read_csv automatically uses the first line as headers, i.e. column names. We can also assign arbitrary other names to the columns. For this, the first line must be skipped, which we achieve by setting the parameter header to 0, and assigning a list of column names to the parameter names. Additionally, we use the parameter index_col to make the first column of the CSV file, i.e. the years, the index:

```python
import pandas as pd


fname = "data1/exchange_rates_eu_us_tr_ch.csv"
column_names = ['year', 'CH', 'TR', 'US', 'EU']
exchange_rates = pd.read_csv(fname,
                             sep="\t",
                             header=0,
                             index_col=0,
                             names=column_names)
print(exchange_rates.head(4))
```

---

1   Data from *OECD Data* (*https://data.oecd.org*), February 13, 2023.

Executing the code yields:

```
            CH          TR  US          EU
year
2000  1.688843  0.625219   1  1.082705
2001  1.687615  1.225588   1  1.116533
2002  1.558607  1.507226   1  1.057559
2003  1.346651  1.500885   1  0.884048
```

If we pass a filename to the function `read_csv`, pandas automatically opens and closes the file. Beyond that, it is also possible to pass a file handle. In this case, we must either explicitly close the file with `close` or use `with`.

```python
import pandas as pd


fname = "data1/exchange_rates_eu_us_tr_ch.csv"
with open(fname) as fh:
    exchange_rates = pd.read_csv(fh, sep="\t", index_col=0)
    print(exchange_rates.head(4))
```

Output:

```
            CHF         TRY  USD          EUR
year
2000  1.688843  0.625219    1  1.082705
2001  1.687615  1.225588    1  1.116533
2002  1.558607  1.507226    1  1.057559
2003  1.346651  1.500885    1  0.884048
```

22.1.2 Writing CSV Files

A Simple Example

In the following simple example, we create a DataFrame and save it using the method `to_csv` in the file "`persons.csv`":

```python
import pandas as pd
data = [('Michelle', 175, 'Munich'),
        ('Lisa', 172, 'Mannheim'),
        ('Finn', 178, 'Freiburg')]


df = pd.DataFrame(data)
df.columns = ['Name', 'Height', 'Place of residence']
df.to_csv("data/persons.csv")
```

The CSV file generated by the program above looks like this:

```
,Name,Height,Place of residence
0,Michelle,175,Munich
1,Lisa,172,Mannheim
2,Finn,178,Freiburg
```

It is striking that the header line begins with a comma. We also see that each data line begins with a number corresponding to the automatically generated index of the DataFrame. Reading this file can lead to an unintended effect:

```python
import pandas as pd
df = pd.read_csv('data/persons.csv')
print(df)
```

The corresponding output can be seen here:

```
   Unnamed: 0      Name  Height Place of residence
0           0  Michelle     175             Munich
1           1      Lisa     172           Mannheim
2           2      Finn     178           Freiburg
```

We get an unwanted column Unnamed: 0, which represents the automatically generated index that was saved to the file. To avoid this, there are two solutions: When reading, one should have set the parameter index_col to the value 0, i.e.

```python
df = pd.read_csv('data/persons.csv', index_col=0)
print(df)
```

Executing the code yields:

```
       Name  Height Place of residence
0  Michelle     175             Munich
1      Lisa     172           Mannheim
2      Finn     178           Freiburg
```

The second solution is error prevention, i.e., making sure when saving that the automatically generated index is not saved at all. For this, to_csv offers the optional parameter index. If set to False, the index is not saved:

```python
df.to_csv("data/persons_2.csv", index=False)
```

The file now looks as desired:

```
Name,Height,Place of residence
Michelle,175,Munich
Lisa,172,Mannheim
Finn,178,Freiburg
```

Now we can read it without worrying about the index:

```python
df = pd.read_csv('data/persons_2.csv')
print(df)
```

Here is the output:

```
       Name  Height Place of residence
0  Michelle     175             Munich
1      Lisa     172          Mannheim
2      Finn     178          Freiburg
```

More Extensive Example

We can write DataFrames to CSV files with the method `to_csv`. We demonstrate this
with an example. First, however, we generate data that we will then write out. In
directory `data1` there are the two files

- `countries_male_population.csv` and
- `countries_female_population.csv`

which contain the male and female population numbers of countries, respectively. We
will create a new file with the sum of both, i.e. the total population. To limit the number
of columns shown in the output, we adjust Pandas' display option.

```python
column_names = ["Country"] + list(range(2003, 2013))
male_pop = pd.read_csv("data1/countries_male_population.csv",
                       header=None,
                       index_col=0,
                       names=column_names)

female_pop = pd.read_csv("data1/countries_female_population.csv",
                         header=None,
                         index_col=0,
                         names=column_names)


population = male_pop + female_pop
print(population.head(4))
```

This output is obtained:

```
              2003      2004   ...      2011      2012
Country                          ...
Australia  19872646  20091504  ...  22620554  22683573
Austria     8067289   8140122  ...   8404252   8443018
Belgium    10355844  10396421  ...  10366843  11035958
Canada     31361611  31372587  ...  33927935  34492645

[4 rows x 10 columns]
```

In the file `countries_total_population1.csv` in directory `data1` we save the population DataFrame we just created:

```python
population.to_csv("data1/countries_total_population1.csv")
```

We now want to create a DataFrame and corresponding file containing all information, i.e. both female and male population as well as the total population. For this, we concatenate the three DataFrames:

```python
pop_complete = pd.concat([population, male_pop, female_pop],
                         keys=["total", "male", "female"])
```

To better understand the result of the concatenation, we now print only the interesting indices:

```python
print(pop_complete.iloc[[0, 1, 2, 29, 30, 31, 59, 60, 61]])
```

This follows from the code:

```
                            2003        2004   ...        2011        2012
       Country                            ...
total  Australia        19872646    20091504   ...    22620554    22683573
       Austria           8067289     8140122   ...     8404252     8443018
       Belgium          10355844    10396421   ...    10366843    11035958
       United States   288774226   290810719   ...   309989078   312232049
male   Australia         9873447     9990513   ...    11260747    11280804
       Austria           3909120     3949825   ...     4095337     4118035
       United States   141957038   143037260   ...   152449134   153596908
female Australia         9999199    10100991   ...    11359807    11402769
       Austria           4158169     4190297   ...     4308915     4324983

[9 rows x 10 columns]
```

We now want to swap the hierarchical index, so that for each country, all population information appears together. The method `swaplevel()` exchanges the order of the hierarchical index levels, which we then sort with `sort_index()`:

```
df = pop_complete.swaplevel()
df.sort_index(inplace=True)
print(df.head(4))
```

The output we get is:

```
                         2003        2004    ...       2011       2012
Country                                      ...
Australia female      9999199    10100991    ...   11359807   11402769
          male        9873447     9990513    ...   11260747   11280804
          total      19872646    20091504    ...   22620554   22683573
Austria   female      4158169     4190297    ...    4308915    4324983


[4 rows x 10 columns]
```

```
df.to_csv("data1/countries_total_population2.csv")
```

22.1.3 Example with a Non-Standard CSV File

In the previous examples we dealt with relatively simple CSV files. Often, real-world files contain irregularities that make processing more difficult. At this point, it would make sense to solve the second exercise at the end of this chapter as preparation for the following example.

The file `bundeslaender_2021.csv` deviates from the standard CSV format: the first line contains a heading, the last one a source reference – both do not belong to the actual data. With the parameters `skiprows=1` and `skipfooter=1` these can be skipped. Since `skipfooter` is only supported by the Python engine, `engine='python'` must also be set.[2]

The file contains further peculiarities:

- In the population columns, spaces are used as thousand separators.

- Area values use a comma as decimal separator and are partly enclosed in quotes.

These deviations can be handled with the parameter `converters`. It expects a dictionary, whose keys are the column indices and whose values are functions that are applied to the respective cell contents.

The task is to read the file and then create two new columns: one column with the respective total population, i.e. the sum of female and male inhabitants. Additionally, a column with the population density. The columns with the data for female and male population should be removed, which is done with `drop`:

---

[2] `ParserWarning`: *Falling back to the 'python' engine because the 'c' engine does not support skipfooter...*

```python
import pandas as pd

def comma_string2float(s):
    """Convert a comma number string to float."""
    return float(s.replace(',', '.'))

def remove_spaces(str_int):
    """Remove spaces from a number string and convert to int."""
    return int(str_int.replace(' ', ''))

states = pd.read_csv('data1/bundeslaender_2021.csv',
                     skiprows=1,
                     skipfooter=1,
                     engine='python',
                     converters={1: comma_string2float,
                                 2: remove_spaces,
                                 3: remove_spaces},
                     sep=",")

total = states['Inhabitants female'] + states['Inhabitants male']
states['Population'] = total
states['Density'] = total / states['Area']
states.drop(['Inhabitants male', 'Inhabitants female'],
            axis=1, inplace=True)
print(states)
```

We obtain this output:

```
                             State      Area  Population      Density
0                Baden-Wuerttemberg  35747.82    11124642   311.197774
1                          Bavaria   70541.57    13176989   186.797501
2                           Berlin    891.12     3677472  4126.797738
3                      Brandenburg  29654.35     2537868    85.581643
4                           Bremen    419.62      676463  1612.084743
5                          Hamburg    755.09     1853935  2455.250368
6                            Hesse  21115.64     6295017   298.121061
7   Mecklenburg-Western Pomerania  23295.45     1611160    69.162004
8                     Lower Saxony  47709.82     8027031   168.246935
9            North Rhine-Westphalia  34112.44    17924591   525.456139
10           Rhineland-Palatinate  19858.00     4106485   206.792477
11                        Saarland   2571.11      982348   382.071557
12                          Saxony  18449.93     4043002   219.133731
13                   Saxony-Anhalt  20459.12     2169253   106.028656
14             Schleswig-Holstein  15804.30     2922005   184.886708
15                       Thuringia  16202.39     2108863   130.157526
```

This can be solved much more elegantly when reading the data by using the parameters decimal and thousands of read_csv. This eliminates the need for custom converter functions. The previous solution merely served to show how one can work with converters.

```python
import pandas as pd

states = pd.read_csv('data1/bundeslaender_2021.csv',
                     skiprows=1,
                     skipfooter=1,
                     engine='python',
                     decimal=',',
                     thousands=' ')

total = states['Inhabitants female'] + states['Inhabitants male']
states['Population'] = total
states['Density'] = total / states['Area']
states.drop(['Inhabitants male', 'Inhabitants female'],
            axis=1, inplace=True)
print(states)
```

Note:

- decimal=',' indicates that a comma is used as decimal separator.

- thousands=' ' ensures that spaces as thousand separators are correctly recognized and removed.

After execution we get:

```
                          State       Area  Population       Density
0             Baden-Wuerttemberg   35747.82    11124642    311.197774
1                        Bavaria   70541.57    13176989    186.797501
2                         Berlin     891.12     3677472   4126.797738
3                    Brandenburg   29654.35     2537868     85.581643
4                         Bremen     419.62      676463   1612.084743
5                        Hamburg     755.09     1853935   2455.250368
6                          Hesse   21115.64     6295017    298.121061
7   Mecklenburg-Western Pomerania   23295.45     1611160     69.162004
8                  Lower Saxony   47709.82     8027031    168.246935
9          North Rhine-Westphalia   34112.44    17924591    525.456139
10          Rhineland-Palatinate   19858.00     4106485    206.792477
11                      Saarland    2571.11      982348    382.071557
12                        Saxony   18449.93     4043002    219.133731
13                  Saxony-Anhalt   20459.12     2169253    106.028656
14            Schleswig-Holstein   15804.30     2922005    184.886708
15                     Thuringia   16202.39     2108863    130.157526
```

22.2 Reading and Writing JSON Files

Reading and writing JSON files is analogous to handling CSV files. In the following program we create a DataFrame object, write it to a JSON file, and then read it back in:

```python
import pandas as pd


shops = pd.DataFrame({'Basel': {'apples': 44, 'oranges': 61},
                      'Zurich': {'apples': 32, 'oranges': 89},
                      'Constance': {'apples': 93, 'oranges': 17}})


# Save to JSON file:
shops.to_json('shops.json')

# Read the file just written:
shops2 = pd.read_json('shops.json')
print(shops2)
```

The result appears as follows:

```
         Basel  Zurich  Constance
apples      44      32         93
oranges     61      89         17
```

22.3 Reading and Writing Excel Files

It is also possible to read and write Microsoft Excel files.

We will use a simple Excel document to demonstrate Pandas' reading capabilities. The document "sales.xls" contains two sheets, one named 'week1' and the other 'week2'. An Excel file can be read with the function read_excel. We show this with the following Python program:

```python
with pd.ExcelFile("data1/sales.xls") as excel_file:
    sheet = pd.read_excel(excel_file)
    print(sheet)
```

The script returns:

```
     Weekday         Sales
0     Monday  123432.980000
1    Tuesday  122198.650200
2  Wednesday  134418.515220
3   Thursday  131730.144916
4     Friday  128173.431003
```

Of the two sheets of the file "sales.xls" we have only read one with `read_excel`. An Excel file, which may consist of many sheets, can be read with all sheets as follows:

```python
document = {}
with pd.ExcelFile("data1/sales.xls") as excel_file:
    for sheet_name in excel_file.sheet_names:
        document[sheet_name] = excel_file.parse(sheet_name)

    for sheet_name in document:
        print("\n" + sheet_name + ":\n", document[sheet_name])
```

The result follows:

```
week1:
        Weekday          Sales
0        Monday  123432.980000
1       Tuesday  122198.650200
2     Wednesday  134418.515220
3      Thursday  131730.144916
4        Friday  128173.431003

week2:
        Weekday          Sales
0        Monday  223277.980000
1       Tuesday  234441.879000
2     Wednesday  246163.972950
3      Thursday  241240.693491
4        Friday  230143.621590
```

22.4 Exercises

1. Exercise

(Solution: 33.15, Solution 1)

The file "countries_population.csv" is a CSV file that contains the population numbers of all countries (July 2014). The delimiter is a space, and commas separate the thousand positions in numbers. Read the file into a DataFrame and then output the first five rows of the DataFrame.

2. Exercise

(Solution: 33.15, Solution 2)

- Read the CSV file bundeslaender.txt. Create a new file with the column names 'state', 'area', 'female', 'male', 'population', and 'density', i.e. inhabitants per square kilometer.
- Output all rows with an area greater than 30000 and a population greater than 10000.
- Output all rows whose density is greater than 30000.

3. Exercise

(Solution: 33.15, Solution 3)

In directory data1 there is a file person_data.txt with personal data. Each line has the following structure:

```
FirstName LastName Height Weight Gender
```

Read the file into a DataFrame.

Then create a new column with the BMI (Body Mass Index) and add it as the last column to the DataFrame.

It holds:

$$BMI = \frac{w}{h^2}$$

4. Exercise

(Solution: 33.15, Solution 4)

The file usedcars.csv contains cars of a fictitious used car dealer. However, his prices are written with a comma as decimal separator, and the thousand places are separated with spaces.

```
Brand;Model;Purchase price;Sale price
Volkswagen;Golf;8 500,00;12 000,00
Toyota;Yaris;9 999,99;14 500,00
BMW;3 Series;18 500,50;24 999,00
Mercedes-Benz;C-Class;22 000,00;29 999,99
```

Then save the values in a new file named usedcars2.csv. The delimiter should be commas, and the values should use a point as decimal separator.

23

Pandas: groupby

In this chapter, we deal with a very important functionality, namely groupby. It is not particularly complicated, but it is not immediately intuitive and is sometimes perceived as difficult – quite unjustly, as we will see. It is very useful to become familiar with groupby, as it allows many problems to be solved much more elegantly and efficiently. Without groupby, the corresponding code is often unnecessarily long, unclear, and less performant.

Figure 23.1 Child sorting wooden blocks

The Pandas groupby operation combines splitting the object, applying a function, and then combining the results. We can split a DataFrame object into groups according to various criteria – both row- and column-wise, for example by using the parameter axis.

groupby can be applied to Pandas Series objects and DataFrame objects! How this works we will learn in this tutorial with many small, practical examples.

"Apply" here means:
- filtering the data,
- transforming the data, or
- aggregating the data.

Anyone with SQL experience will recognize in Pandas' groupby an equivalent to the SQL statement GROUP BY.

23.1 Groupby with Series

To demonstrate the use of groupby on Series objects, we first create an example with a non-unique index. Our goal is to construct a Series whose index values occur multiple times. For this, we use the list fruits as the basis for the index. To actually create duplicates, the variable num_values must be greater than the length of the list fruits.

This artificially generated Series then serves as a simple and manageable dataset to illustrate the grouping behavior of groupby.

```python
import pandas as pd
import numpy as np


num_values = 9
# Generate random values for the Series values:
values = np.random.randint(1, 20, num_values)
fruits = ["Bananas", "Oranges", "Apples", "Clementines"]
fruits_index = np.random.choice(fruits, num_values)


series = pd.Series(values, index=fruits_index)
print(series)
```

This is the result of the code:

```
Clementines    13
Bananas        11
Bananas        13
Clementines    15
Clementines     4
Clementines    10
Bananas         5
Clementines     5
Apples         10
dtype: int64
```

Now let's see what happens when we apply groupby to the Series object we just created:

```python
grouped = series.groupby(series.index)
print(grouped)
```

Output:

```
<pandas.core.groupby.generic.SeriesGroupBy object at 0x71f3481fb590>
```

When we apply groupby to the index of the Series object, we obtain a SeriesGroupBy object. This object is iterable: in each iteration we get a tuple consisting of an index label and a sub-series. The sub-series contains all values with the respective label.

```python
for fruit, subseries in grouped:
    print(f"===== {fruit} =====")
    print(subseries)
```

After execution we get:

```
===== Apples =====
Apples    10
dtype: int64
===== Bananas =====
Bananas    11
Bananas    13
Bananas     5
dtype: int64
===== Clementines =====
Clementines    13
Clementines    15
Clementines     4
Clementines    10
Clementines     5
dtype: int64
```

A similar result could also be achieved with a loop and manual filtering, as the following
example shows:

```python
for fruit in set(series.index):
    print(f"===== {fruit} =====")
    print(series[fruit])
```

The result of the code is:

```
===== Clementines =====
Clementines    13
Clementines    15
Clementines     4
Clementines    10
Clementines     5
dtype: int64
===== Bananas =====
Bananas    11
Bananas    13
Bananas     5
dtype: int64
===== Apples =====
10
```

However, this manual approach is neither particularly clear nor efficient, since a new filtering pass is carried out in each iteration. It is also more error-prone and harder to extend for more complex tasks. Therefore, using groupby is clearly the better choice.

23.2 How groupby Works

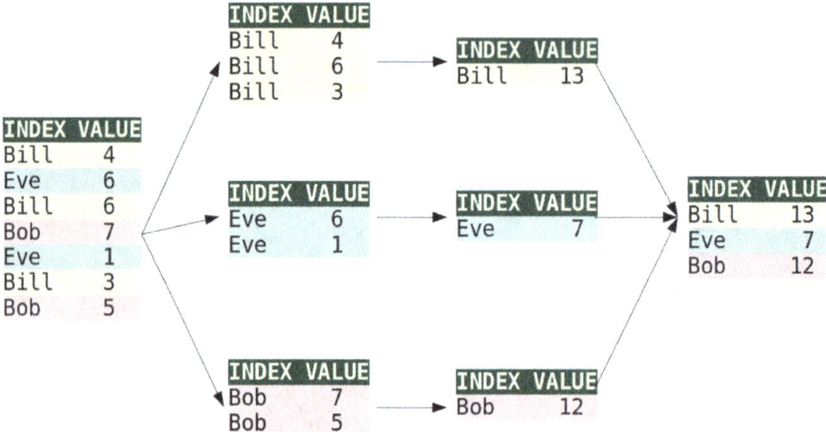

Figure 23.2 How groupby works

We have already explained the basic functionality of groupby in the previous chapter. Here, we will briefly summarize it again and visualize it using the graphic above.

The use of groupby typically involves three steps:

- **Split**: Divide the data into groups, for example, based on identical index values.

- **Apply**: Apply a function to each group, such as sum, mean, or a custom function.

- **Combine**: Merge the results into a new object.

In the first step, the existing Series object is split into several sub-objects according to a criterion (here the index). This corresponds to the output of the for loop in the following example. Then the function sum() is applied to each sub-object. In the final step, the results are combined into a new Series object.

```
import pandas as pd

s = pd.Series([4, 6, 6, 7, 1, 3, 5],
              index=["Bill", "Eve", "Bill",
                     "Bob", "Eve", "Bill", "Bob"])
```

```python
groupby_res = s.groupby(s.index)
for index, group in groupby_res:
    print("\nIndex: ", index)
    print(group)

print("\nCombined result:")
print(s.groupby(s.index).sum())
```

We obtain this output:

```
Index:  Bill
Bill    4
Bill    6
Bill    3
dtype: int64

Index:  Bob
Bob    7
Bob    5
dtype: int64

Index:  Eve
Eve    6
Eve    1
dtype: int64

Combined result:
Bill    13
Bob     12
Eve      7
dtype: int64
```

23.3 GroupBy with DataFrames

Having examined the basic functionality of `groupby` with a `Series` object, we now want to show how grouping works with `DataFrames` – and what additional possibilities arise.

We begin with a very simple `DataFrame` that has three columns: the first column, `Name`, contains names; the second column, `Coffee`, shows the number of cups of coffee consumed; and the third column, `Tea`, shows the number of cups of tea consumed.

```python
import pandas as pd
beverages = pd.DataFrame({'Name': ['Robert', 'Melinda', 'Brenda',
                                    'Sarah', 'Melinda', 'Robert',
                                    'Melinda', 'Brenda', 'Sarah'],
                          'Coffee': [3, 0, 2, 2, 0, 2, 0, 1, 3],
                          'Tea':    [0, 4, 2, 0, 3, 0, 3, 2, 0]})

print(beverages)
```

The processing yields:

```
      Name  Coffee  Tea
0   Robert       3    0
1  Melinda       0    4
2   Brenda       2    2
3    Sarah       2    0
4  Melinda       0    3
5   Robert       2    0
6  Melinda       0    3
7   Brenda       1    2
8    Sarah       3    0
```

The total number of cups of coffee drunk can be calculated very easily. We simply sum the column `Coffee`:

```python
print(beverages['Coffee'].sum())
```

Script output:

```
13
```

We can also calculate the total number of coffee and tea cups:

```python
print(beverages[['Coffee', 'Tea']].sum())
```

The resulting output is:

```
Coffee    13
Tea       14
dtype: int64
```

Up to this point, we haven't needed `groupby`. Looking again at the `DataFrame`, we can see that some names occur more than once. It is therefore interesting to find out how many cups of coffee and tea each person has consumed in total.

For this we apply `groupby` to the column `Name`. Then we sum the grouped values with `sum()`:

```
result = beverages.groupby(['Name']).sum()
print(result)
```

The script returns:

```
         Coffee  Tea
Name
Brenda        3    4
Melinda       0   10
Robert        5    0
Sarah         5    0
```

The names now form the index of the resulting `DataFrame`:

```
print(result.index)
```

What we obtain is:

```
Index(['Brenda', 'Melinda', 'Robert', 'Sarah'], dtype='object', name='Name
 ↪  ')
```

Instead of sums, we can also calculate the average number of cups of coffee and tea:

```
print(beverages.groupby(['Name']).mean())
```

The result follows:

```
         Coffee      Tea
Name
Brenda      1.5  2.000000
Melinda     0.0  3.333333
Robert      2.5  0.000000
Sarah       2.5  0.000000
```

23.3.1 GroupBy with Function

Let's consider a `DataFrame` that contains the working hours of several developers across the days of the week. The names form the index, and the columns contain the hours worked from Monday to Sunday.

To analyze the data more specifically, we group the individual days into two categories: `Weekday` and `Weekend`. For this purpose, we define a function that classifies each day accordingly and apply it to the columns. This allows us to analyze the working hours grouped by day type.

```python
import numpy as np
names = ('Ortwin', 'Mara', 'Siegrun', 'Sylvester', 'Metin',
         'Adeline', 'Utz', 'Susan', 'Gisbert', 'Senol')

data = {'Mon': np.array([0, 9, 2, 3, 7, 3, 9, 2, 4, 9]),
        'Tue': np.array([2, 6, 3, 3, 5, 5, 7, 7, 1, 0]),
        'Wed': np.array([6, 1, 1, 9, 4, 0, 8, 6, 8, 8]),
        'Thu': np.array([1, 8, 6, 9, 9, 4, 1, 7, 3, 2]),
        'Fri': np.array([3, 5, 6, 6, 5, 2, 2, 4, 6, 5]),
        'Sat': np.array([8, 4, 8, 2, 3, 9, 3, 4, 9, 7]),
        'Sun': np.array([0, 8, 7, 8, 9, 7, 2, 0, 5, 2])}

data_df = pd.DataFrame(data, index=names)
print(data_df)
```

The evaluation yields:

```
           Mon  Tue  ...  Sat  Sun
Ortwin       0    2  ...    8    0
Mara         9    6  ...    4    8
Siegrun      2    3  ...    8    7
Sylvester    3    3  ...    2    8
Metin        7    5  ...    3    9
Adeline      3    5  ...    9    7
Utz          9    7  ...    3    2
Susan        2    7  ...    4    0
Gisbert      4    1  ...    9    5
Senol        9    0  ...    7    2

[10 rows x 7 columns]
```

Next, we define a function, `is_weekend`, that classifies the columns (weekdays) into
the categories `Weekday` and `Weekend`:

```python
def is_weekend(day):
    if day in {'Sat', 'Sun'}:
        return "Weekend"
    else:
        return "Weekday"
```

We then group the transposed table using this function:

```python
for category, df in data_df.T.groupby(is_weekend):
    print(df.T)
```

The following result is generated:

```
              Mon   Tue   ...   Thu   Fri
Ortwin          0     2   ...     1     3
Mara            9     6   ...     8     5
Siegrun         2     3   ...     6     6
Sylvester       3     3   ...     9     6
Metin           7     5   ...     9     5
Adeline         3     5   ...     4     2
Utz             9     7   ...     1     2
Susan           2     7   ...     7     4
Gisbert         4     1   ...     3     6
Senol           9     0   ...     2     5

[10 rows x 5 columns]
              Sat   Sun
Ortwin          8     0
Mara            4     8
Siegrun         8     7
Sylvester       2     8
Metin           3     9
Adeline         9     7
Utz             3     2
Susan           4     0
Gisbert         9     5
Senol           7     2
```

Finally, we sum all columns within each category:

```
print(data_df.T.groupby(is_weekend).sum().T)
```

This output is obtained:

```
              Weekday   Weekend
Ortwin             12         8
Mara               29        12
Siegrun            18        15
Sylvester          30        10
Metin              30        12
Adeline            14        16
Utz                27         5
Susan              26         4
Gisbert            22        14
Senol              24         9
```

23.3.2 Example with File

Figure 23.3 Five professions – one responsibility

The folder `data` contains a file named `donations.txt` with the following data:[1]

```
firstname,surname,city,job,income,donations
Sophie,Dubois,Lyon,Politician,244400,2512
Luca,Schneider,Zurich,Student,16800,336
Anton,Lefèvre,Brussels,Manager,508200,3037
Hannah,van Dijk,Amsterdam,Engineer,116900,1479
Marco,Rossi,Milan,Musician,57700,1142
Johannes,Fischer,Munich,Engineer,109300,1592
Elena,Moretti,Florence,Student,12500,250
Clara,Meier,Basel,Engineer,128700,1984
David,Lambert,Brussels,Politician,161300,822
Theo,Bernard,Luxembourg,Engineer,129000,2159
```

The task is now to calculate the donations as the sum for each professional group and
then also set them in relation to income.

```python
data = pd.read_csv('data/donations.txt',
                   usecols=['job', 'income', 'donations'])
data_sum = data.groupby(['job']).sum()
data_sum.sort_values(by='donations', inplace=True)
print(data_sum)
```

---

1   All entries in this file are synthetically generated, and any resemblance to real persons is purely coinci-
    dental.

The following result is generated:

```
            income  donations
job
Student     372900        7458
Musician   1448700       24376
Engineer   2067200       25564
Politician 4118300       30758
Manager   12862600       87475
```

Next, we calculate the donations in relation to income.

```python
data_sum['relative'] = data_sum.donations * 100 / data_sum.income
data_sum.sort_values(by='relative', inplace=True)
print(data_sum)
```

The result is:

```
            income  donations  relative
job
Manager   12862600      87475  0.680072
Politician 4118300      30758  0.746862
Engineer   2067200      25564  1.236649
Musician   1448700      24376  1.682612
Student     372900       7458  2.000000
```

We can see that those with the lowest income in our file, i.e. the students, donate the
most generously!

23.4 Exercises

1. Exercise

(Solution: 33.16, Solution 1)

Calculate the average prices for the products of the following DataFrame:

```python
import pandas as pd


d = {"products": ["Oppilume", "Dreaker", "Lotadilo",
                  "Crosteron", "Wazzasoft", "Oppilume",
                  "Dreaker", "Lotadilo", "Wazzasoft"],
     "colours": ["blue", "blue", "blue",
                 "green", "blue", "green",
                 "green", "green", "red"],
     "customer_price": [2345.89, 2390.50, 1820.00,
                        3100.00, 1784.50, 2545.89,
                        2590.50, 2220.00, 2084.50],
```

```
                    "non_customer_price": [2445.89, 2495.50, 1980.00,
                                           3400.00, 1921.00, 2645.89,
                                           2655.50, 2140.00, 2190.00]}

    product_prices = pd.DataFrame(d)


print(product_prices)
```

Result:

```
     products colours  customer_price  non_customer_price
0    Oppilume    blue         2345.89             2445.89
1     Dreaker    blue         2390.50             2495.50
2    Lotadilo    blue         1820.00             1980.00
3   Crosteron   green         3100.00             3400.00
4   Wazzasoft    blue         1784.50             1921.00
5    Oppilume   green         2545.89             2645.89
6     Dreaker   green         2590.50             2655.50
7    Lotadilo   green         2220.00             2140.00
8   Wazzasoft     red         2084.50             2190.00
```

2. Exercise

(Solution: 33.16, Solution 2)

Calculate the sum of the prices by color.

3. Exercise

(Solution: 33.16, Solution 3)

Read the file `project_times.txt` from the directory `data1`. The lines of this file contain, comma-separated: the date, the programmer's name, the project name, and the time the programmer spent on the project.

Calculate the total time spent per day on all projects.

4. Exercise

(Solution: 33.16, Solution 4)

Create a DataFrame with the total time all programmers spent per day on a project.

5. Exercise

(Solution: 33.16, Solution 5)

Calculate the monthly total time spent per project.

6. Exercise

(Solution: 33.16, Solution 6)

Calculate the monthly times of the individual programmers regardless of the projects.

7. Exercise

(Solution: 33.16, Solution 7)

Arrange the DataFrame with a MultiIndex consisting of the date and the project names. The columns should be the programmers' names, and the column data the time the programmers spent on the projects.

```
                      time
programmer            Antonie  Elise  Fatima  Hella  Mariola
date        project
2020-01-01  BIRDY     NaN      NaN    NaN     1.50   1.75
            NSTAT     NaN      NaN    0.25    NaN    1.25
            XTOR      NaN      NaN    NaN     1.00   3.50
2020-01-02  BIRDY     NaN      NaN    NaN     1.75   2.00
            NSTAT     0.5      NaN    NaN     NaN    1.75
```

Replace the NaN values with 0.

8. Exercise

(Solution: 33.16, Solution 8)

You receive a dataset df containing information about book sales in several bookstores. This is an order journal: each time a bookstore places an order, a new entry is added to the journal. Therefore, bookstores can appear multiple times in the dataset.

Each row describes a sales transaction with the following columns:

- **Customer**: Name of the bookstore
- **Item**: Title of the purchased book
- **Qty**: Number of copies purchased
- **Price**: Price per copy in euros

A journal could, for example, look like this:

```
       Customer  Qty                                  Item   Price
       Pagewise    6 Functional Programming with Python   39.99
    Paper & Ink    7              Introduction to Python 3   24.99
    Paper & Ink    5              Introduction to Python 3   24.99
       Pagewise    5              Introduction to Python 3   24.99
       Bookmark    5              Python Basics | eLearning   99.00
    Book Island    9              Python Basics | eLearning   99.00
    Book Island    1              Introduction to Python 3   24.99
    Book Island    6              Python Basics | eLearning   99.00
       Pagewise    5 Functional Programming with Python   39.99
    Paper & Ink    5              Python Basics | eLearning   99.00
       Pagewise    2 Functional Programming with Python   39.99
       Pagewise    8                    Numerical Python   29.99
  Chapter & Co.    9              Introduction to Python 3   24.99
    Paper & Ink    5              Python Basics | eLearning   99.00
```

Calculate the **total revenue per bookstore** (Customer) and additionally assign each
bookstore one of the following revenue categories:

- **low**: less than 15 % of the total order sum

- **medium**: at least 15 % but less than 25 %

- **high**: at least 25 % of the total order sum

24
Pivot Tables

Pivot tables are a powerful tool for presenting, restructuring, and analyzing data in different ways. The underlying original tables remain unchanged. Pivot tables serve to condense large datasets into a manageable form and analyze them in a targeted way. This process is usually associated with some loss of information – though often this is explicitly desired.

The name *pivot* comes from the idea of turning your data to view it from different angles – just as a window pivots on its hinge. That's why we chose a matching image for this chapter.

Figure 24.1 Window with Pivot Element

Pivot tables are used exclusively for analyzing and visualizing data – they cannot be used to extend or directly edit the database.

In 1991, the California company Brio Technology released a product called *DataPivot*. This was probably the first time the term "pivot" was used in today's context.

24.1 Pivot Function in Pandas

DataFrame objects in Pandas are also tables. This object type also provides a `pivot` method, which can be used as described above. The pivot function is used to reshape a given DataFrame into another form.

The function is called with the three arguments `index`, `columns`, and `values`. The values of these parameters correspond to column names of the DataFrame to be re-shaped. We can illustrate this with an example. We begin with a DataFrame `df` with four columns A, B, C and D. The call

```python
df2 = df.pivot(index='A', columns='B', values='C')
```

makes the elements of A the index, those of B the column labels – i.e., one and two – and the elements of C are used as values. The call

```python
df3 = df.pivot(index='A', columns='B', values=['C', 'D'])
```

uses all four columns of `df`. The difference is that now columns C and D are both used as values. This produces a hierarchical column structure, because we must assign the values of C and of D to the columns one and two:

```python
import pandas as pd

d = {'A': ['red', 'green', 'blue', 'red', 'green', 'blue'],
     'B': ['one', 'two', 'one', 'two', 'one', 'two'],
     'C': [345, 325, 898, 989, 23, 143],
     'D': [1, 2, 3, 4, 5, 6]}

df = pd.DataFrame(d)
print(df)
print('\n==============\n')
df2 = df.pivot(index='A',
               columns='B',
               values='C')
print(df2)
print('\n==============\n')
df3 = df.pivot(index='A',
               columns='B',
               values=['C', 'D'])
print(df3)
```

The output we get is:

```
       A      B    C  D
0    red    one  345  1
1  green    two  325  2
2   blue    one  898  3
3    red    two  989  4
4  green    one   23  5
5   blue    two  143  6


==============
```

```
B      one  two
A
blue   898  143
green   23  325
red    345  989
```

```
==============
```

```
          C        D
B      one  two one two
A
blue   898  143   3   6
green   23  325   5   2
red    345  989   1   4
```

The following example does not introduce any new concept. We just use more concrete
values and names to demonstrate again:

```python
import pandas as pd

d = {"Products": ["Product1", "Product1", "Product2", "Product3"],
     "Colors": ["blue", "green", "blue", "green"],
     "DiscountPrice": [2345.89, 2390.50, 1820.00, 3100.00],
     "Price": [2445.89, 2495.50, 1980.00, 3400.00]}

df = pd.DataFrame(d)
print(df)
```

What we obtain is:

```
   Products Colors  DiscountPrice    Price
0  Product1   blue        2345.89  2445.89
1  Product1  green        2390.50  2495.50
2  Product2   blue        1820.00  1980.00
3  Product3  green        3100.00  3400.00
```

Now we apply the pivot function:

```python
df2 = df.pivot(index='Products',
               columns='Colors',
               values='Price')
print(df2)
```

The script returns:

```
Colors        blue   green
```

```
Products
Product1  2445.89  2495.5
Product2  1980.00     NaN
Product3      NaN  3400.0


df3 = df.pivot(index='Products',
               columns='Colors',
               values=['DiscountPrice', 'Price'])
print(df3)
```

The result of the code is:

```
          DiscountPrice               Price
Colors             blue   green        blue    green
Products
Product1        2345.89  2390.5     2445.89   2495.5
Product2        1820.00     NaN     1980.00      NaN
Product3            NaN  3100.0         NaN   3400.0


print(df3["Price"]["blue"])
print(df3.columns)
```

The corresponding output can be seen here:

```
Products
Product1    2445.89
Product2    1980.00
Product3        NaN
Name: blue, dtype: float64
MultiIndex([('DiscountPrice',   'blue'),
            ('DiscountPrice', 'green'),
            (        'Price',   'blue'),
            (        'Price', 'green')],
           names=[None, 'Colors'])
```

24.2 Pivot Call Without Values for values

If the values parameter is omitted, and the input DataFrame contains additional
columns that are not used as the index or column labels, those remaining columns
are automatically used as the values in the resulting DataFrame:

```python
import pandas as pd

d = {"Products": ["Product1", "Product1", "Product2", "Product3"],
     "Colors": ["blue", "green", "blue", "green"],
     "DiscountPrice": [2345.89, 2390.50, 1820.00, 3100.00],
     "Price": [2445.89, 2495.50, 1980.00, 3400.00]}

df = pd.DataFrame(d)
print(df)

df_pivot = df.pivot(index='Products', columns='Colors')
print(f"\n\n{df_pivot}")
```

The resulting output is:

```
   Products Colors  DiscountPrice    Price
0  Product1   blue        2345.89  2445.89
1  Product1  green        2390.50  2495.50
2  Product2   blue        1820.00  1980.00
3  Product3  green        3100.00  3400.00


          DiscountPrice           Price
Colors             blue   green    blue   green
Products
Product1        2345.89  2390.5  2445.89  2495.5
Product2        1820.00     NaN  1980.00     NaN
Product3            NaN  3100.0      NaN  3400.0
```

24.3 The Function pivot_table in Pandas

The method `pivot_table` is closely related to `pivot` but offers greater flexibility. In particular, `pivot_table` allows applying aggregation functions, which makes it better suited than `pivot` for many analytical tasks.

With `pivot`, each combination of index and column must correspond to exactly one value. By contrast, `pivot_table` can handle combinations that occur multiple times. In such cases, Pandas uses the `mean` by default, but you can specify other aggregation functions such as `sum`, `min`, `max`, or `count`.

`pivot_table` is typically used with the following parameters:

- index: column(s) to use as row index,

- columns: column(s) to use as column headers,

- values: column(s) whose values should be aggregated,
- aggfunc: aggregation function (e.g. mean, sum, count).

The following example shows the use of pivot_table to calculate the average price per product and color:

```python
import pandas as pd

d = {"Products": ["Product1", "Product1", "Product2", "Product3", "
    Product2"],
     "Colors": ["blue", "green", "blue", "green", "blue"],
     "Price": [2445.89, 2495.50, 1980.00, 3400.00, 2100.00]}

df = pd.DataFrame(d)

table = pd.pivot_table(df,
                       index='Products',
                       columns='Colors',
                       values='Price',
                       aggfunc='mean')

print(table)
```

In this example, the average prices (aggfunc='mean') are calculated for each combination of product and color. Since Product2 occurs twice with the color "blue," the mean is automatically calculated there.

pivot_table is thus particularly useful when data should be grouped, aggregated, or condensed – similar to pivot tables in spreadsheet programs.

After execution we get:

```
Colors          blue    green
Products
Product1  2445.89   2495.5
Product2  2040.00      NaN
Product3      NaN   3400.0
```

24.4 Pivoting on the Titanic Data

In 2023, "Titanic" – one of the most successful movies of all time – celebrated its 25th anniversary. In the following example, we'll work with the Titanic passenger dataset. Using this data, we can even check whether the two main characters, Jack Dawson (Leonardo DiCaprio) and Rose DeWitt Bukater (Kate Winslet), actually existed and

were listed among the passengers. The dataset[1] is stored in the directory `data1` under
the name `titanic3.xls`. Let's read the data and inspect the column names:

```python
import pandas as pd


data = pd.read_excel('data1/titanic3.xls')
print(f"The column names:{data.columns}\ndata:\n{data[:4]}\n")
```

The code produces the following result:

```
The column names:Index(['pclass', 'survived', 'name', 'sex', 'age', 'sibsp
↪ ', 'parch', 'ticket',
       'fare', 'cabin', 'embarked', 'boat', 'body', 'home.dest'],
      dtype='object')
data:
   pclass  survived  ...   body                        home.dest
0       1         1  ...    NaN                      St Louis, MO
1       1         1  ...    NaN  Montreal, PQ / Chesterville, ON
2       1         0  ...    NaN  Montreal, PQ / Chesterville, ON
3       1         0  ...  135.0  Montreal, PQ / Chesterville, ON

[4 rows x 14 columns]
```

In the following table we explain the column names:

Column name	Explanation
pclass	Passenger class (1 = 1st class, 2 = 2nd class, 3 = 3rd class)
survived	Survival indicator (1 = survived, 0 = did not survive)
name	Full name of the passenger
sex	Sex of the passenger (male/female)
age	Age in years
sibsp	Number of siblings and/or spouses aboard
parch	Number of parents and/or children aboard
ticket	Ticket number
fare	Ticket fare
cabin	Cabin identifier
embarked	Port of embarkation: C = Cherbourg, Q = Queenstown, S = Southampton
boat	Lifeboat number (if the passenger survived)
body	Body identification number (if the passenger did not survive)

---

1   We use the dataset provided by Kaggle, available at
    https://www.kaggle.com/datasets/vinicius150987/titanic3?resource=download

Let's start by calculating the survival rate by gender using `pivot_table()`.

```python
rate = data.pivot_table('survived', index='sex')
print(rate.round(2))
```

This output is obtained:

```
        survived
sex
female      0.73
male        0.19
```

We can also calculate the survival rates using `groupby`:

```python
print(data.groupby('sex')[['survived']].mean())
```

This follows from the code:

```
        survived
sex
female  0.727468
male    0.190985
```

Things get more interesting when, in addition to grouping by sex, the booked class is also taken into account:

```python
print(data.pivot_table('survived', index='sex', columns='pclass'))
```

This is the result of the code:

```
pclass         1         2         3
sex
female  0.965278  0.886792  0.490741
male    0.340782  0.146199  0.152130
```

We can achieve the same result with `groupby`, but this requires the knowledge of multi-level indexing introduced in Chapter 27 (Multi-level Indexing):

```python
x = data.groupby(['sex', 'pclass'])['survived'].mean().unstack()
print(x)
```

The resulting output is:

```
pclass         1         2         3
sex
female  0.965278  0.886792  0.490741
male    0.340782  0.146199  0.152130
```

Finally, let's analyze survival rates across different age groups. For this, we use the method cut introduced in Chapter 26 (Binning):

```python
age = pd.cut(data['age'], [0, 20, 40, 60, 80])
df = data.pivot_table('survived',
                      ['sex', age],
                      'pclass',
                      observed=False)
print(df.round(2))
```

The output we get is:

```
pclass                    1     2     3
sex     age
female  (0, 20]        0.94  0.96  0.52
        (20, 40]       0.97  0.88  0.46
        (40, 60]       0.98  0.81  0.27
        (60, 80]       0.83   NaN  1.00
male    (0, 20]        0.60  0.46  0.20
        (20, 40]       0.42  0.08  0.17
        (40, 60]       0.31  0.04  0.06
        (60, 80]       0.07  0.17  0.00
```

Finally, a fun question: Did Jack Dawson and Rose DeWitt Bukater really exist, and were they actually on the Titanic? To avoid missing entries due to slight spelling variations, we'll search for their first and last names (or parts of them) using `str.contains()` with a regular expression:

```python
df = data[['name', 'survived']]
res = df[data.name.str.contains('Rose|Witt|Jack|Dawson')]
print(res)
```

This is the result of the code:

```
                                          name  survived
40                      Brewe, Dr. Arthur Jackson         0
242                  Rosenbaum, Miss. Edith Louise         1
243    Rosenshine, Mr. George ("Mr George Thorne")         0
612                      Aks, Mrs. Sam (Leah Rosen)         1
1298                   Wittevrongel, Mr. Camille         0
```

24.5 Exercises

1. Exercise

(Solution: 33.17, Solution 1)

The file `country_sales.csv` in the `data1` directory contains sales data for fictional products sold in Germany, Switzerland, and Austria. Create a pivot table with the sales figures as the values, the countries as the index, and the products as the columns.

2. Exercise

(Solution: 33.17, Solution 2)

Using the Titanic dataset, create a DataFrame that shows the survival rate by gender and by port of embarkation.

25

Handling NaN

NaN was officially introduced by the IEEE Standard for Floating-Point Arithmetic (IEEE 754). This is a technical standard for floating-point calculations, established in 1985 by the "Institute of Electrical and Electronics Engineers" (IEEE) – years before Python existed, and even more years before Pandas was introduced. The standard was designed to solve problems found in many floating-point implementations, which had made

Figure 25.1 Handling NaN

them difficult to use in a simple and cross-platform way.

The standard added NaN to the arithmetic formats – sets of binary and decimal floating-point data.

25.1 'nan' in Python

Python without Pandas also knows NaN values. We can create them with `float()`:

```python
n1 = float("nan")
n2 = float("Nan")
n3 = float("NaN")
n4 = float("NAN")
print(n1, n2, n3, n4)
print(type(n1))
```

Here is the result of the code:

```
nan nan nan nan
<class 'float'>
```

The capitalization of "nan" does not matter – `float()` interprets all case variations as NaN.

nan has also been part of the `math` module since Python 3.5:

```python
import math
n1 = math.nan
print(n1)
print(math.isnan(n1))
```

The result is:

```
nan
True
```

Warning: Do not perform comparisons between "NaN" values and regular numeric values. According to the IEEE 754 standard, all comparisons with NaN return `False`, including comparisons between two NaN values. Sorting also fails because NaN is not orderable:

```python
print(n1 == n2)
print(n1 == 0)
print(n1 == 100)
print(n2 < 0)
```

This is the result of the code:

```
False
False
False
False
```

25.2 NaN in Pandas

In this section, we will look at how to handle NaN values in Pandas in a meaningful way. We will analyze a file with temperature measurements that occasionally contains NaN values.

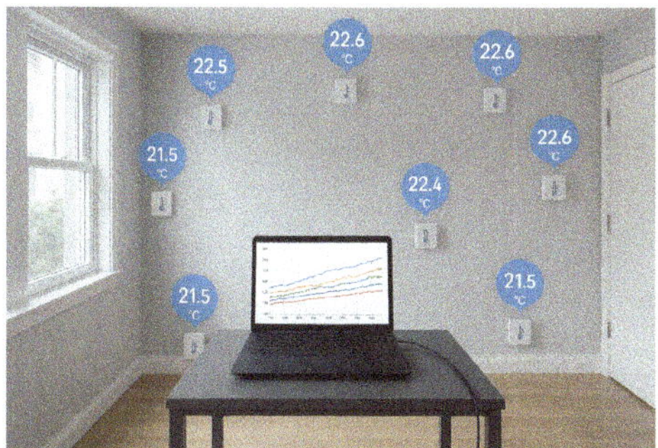

Figure 25.2 Temperature sensors

But before we work with NaN values, let's first process a file without any NaNs. The file `temperatures.csv` contains the temperatures of six sensors, measured every 15 minutes between 6:00 a.m. and 7:15 p.m.

The data from this file can be read with the `read_csv` function:

```python
import pandas as pd

df = pd.read_csv("data1/temperatures.csv",
                 sep=";",
                 index_col=0,
                 decimal=",")
print(df.head())
```

We obtain this output:

```
          sensor1  sensor2  ...  sensor5  sensor6
time                        ...
06:00:00     23.3     22.7  ...     22.5     22.6
06:15:00     23.5     23.5  ...     23.5     23.7
06:30:00     23.6     24.1  ...     23.0     23.2
06:45:00     23.8     23.5  ...     23.7     23.6
07:00:00     24.0     23.9  ...     23.0     24.3

[5 rows x 6 columns]
```

We want to calculate the average temperature for each measurement time. For this we can use the DataFrame method `mean`. When `mean` is used without parameters, the columns are aggregated. While this is not what we want, it is still interesting, because it gives us the average across the entire measurement day.

```python
print(df.mean())
```

Result:

```
sensor1    28.775926
sensor2    28.757407
sensor3    28.840741
sensor4    29.187037
sensor5    28.181481
sensor6    28.437037
dtype: float64
```

What we actually want is the average temperature across all six sensors. For this, we set the parameter `axis` to 1, which tells Pandas to compute the mean across the columns (i.e., row-wise):

```python
average_temp_series = df.mean(axis=1)
print(average_temp_series[:8])  # the first 8 rows
```

The result appears as follows:

```
time
06:00:00    22.933333
06:15:00    23.533333
06:30:00    23.666667
06:45:00    23.900000
07:00:00    24.083333
07:15:00    24.116667
07:30:00    24.283333
07:45:00    24.116667
dtype: float64
```

Since we only need this aggregated temperature for the following steps, we remove the original sensor columns. We obtain the column names first and then drop them from the DataFrame:

```python
sensors = df.columns.values
# remove all sensor columns:
df = df.drop(sensors, axis=1)
print(df[:5])
```

The evaluation yields:

```
Empty DataFrame
Columns: []
Index: [06:00:00, 06:15:00, 06:30:00, 06:45:00, 07:00:00]
```

Now we add the average temperatures as a new column `temperature` to the DataFrame:

```python
df = df.assign(temperature=average_temp_series)

# alternatively:
# df.loc[:, "temperature"] = average_temp_series


print(df[:5])
```

Result:

```
          temperature
time
06:00:00     22.933333
06:15:00     23.533333
06:30:00     23.666667
06:45:00     23.900000
07:00:00     24.083333
```

25.2.1 Example with NaNs

Let's imagine that the file `temperatures.csv` contained NaN values in the sensor columns. A NaN value means that the device was unable to provide a measurement at that moment.

Since we don't have such a file, we will create one artificially for practice. We will use the values from `temperatures.csv` to generate a DataFrame, then randomly insert NaN values into this structure:

```python
temp_df = pd.read_csv("data1/temperatures.csv",
                      sep=";",
                      index_col=0,
                      decimal=",")
```

Now we assign NaN values randomly to the DataFrame. For this we use the `where` method of DataFrames. When applied as `df.where(cond, other_df)`, it returns an object with the same shape as `df`, whose values come from `df` wherever the condition is True, otherwise from `other_df`.

Before continuing with our temperature example, let us first demonstrate the behavior of where on simple examples:

```python
s = pd.Series(range(5))
print(s.where(s > 1))
```

This follows from the code:

```
0    NaN
1    NaN
2    2.0
3    3.0
4    4.0
dtype: float64

import numpy as np

A = np.random.randint(1, 30, (4, 2))

df = pd.DataFrame(A, columns=['Foo', 'Bar'])
m = df % 2 == 0
df.where(m, -df, inplace=True)
print(df)
```

The result appears as follows:

```
    Foo   Bar
0    22    22
1   -27    -1
2    22    -1
3    -5    20
```

For our temperature example we need a DataFrame nan_df that contains only NaN values but has the same shape as temp_df. We then use this in the where method. In addition, we need a DataFrame df_bool with boolean conditions. We create it by generating random values between 0 and 1 and checking random_df < 0.8. This yields df_bool with about 80% True values:

```python
random_df = pd.DataFrame(np.random.random(size=(54, 6)),
                         columns=temp_df.columns.values,
                         index=temp_df.index)
nan_df = pd.DataFrame(np.nan,
                      columns=temp_df.columns.values,
                      index=temp_df.index)
df_bool = random_df < 0.8

print(df_bool[:5])
```

This is the result of the code:

```
          sensor1  sensor2  ...  sensor5  sensor6
time                        ...
06:00:00     True     True  ...     True     True
06:15:00    False     True  ...     True     True
06:30:00     True    False  ...     True     True
06:45:00     True     True  ...     True     True
07:00:00     True     True  ...     True    False

[5 rows x 6 columns]
```

Now we have everything to create our DataFrame with incomplete measurements using where, and then save it to a file temperatures_with_NaN.csv with to_csv:

```python
disturbed_data = temp_df.where(df_bool, nan_df)

disturbed_data.to_csv("data1/temperatures_with_NaN.csv")
print(disturbed_data[:10])
```

Result:

```
          sensor1  sensor2  ...  sensor5  sensor6
time                        ...
06:00:00     23.3     22.7  ...     22.5     22.6
06:15:00      NaN     23.5  ...     23.5     23.7
06:30:00     23.6      NaN  ...     23.0     23.2
06:45:00     23.8     23.5  ...     23.7     23.6
07:00:00     24.0     23.9  ...     23.0      NaN
07:15:00     24.2     24.2  ...     24.5     23.9
07:30:00     24.4      NaN  ...     23.7     24.1
07:45:00     24.5      NaN  ...      NaN     23.9
08:00:00     24.7     24.6  ...     24.4     24.4
08:15:00     24.9     24.8  ...     25.0     25.2

[10 rows x 6 columns]
```

25.3 Using dropna()

First we read the incomplete measurements with read_csv:

```python
import pandas as pd
df2 = pd.read_csv("data1/temperatures_with_NaN.csv",
                  sep=",",
                  decimal=".",
                  index_col=0)
```

dropna is a DataFrame method. When used without arguments, it returns an object
where every row containing NaN values has been removed:

```python
cleansed_df2 = df2.dropna()
print(cleansed_df2)
```

This is the result of the code:

```
          sensor1   sensor2   ...   sensor5   sensor6
time                          ...
06:00:00     23.3      22.7   ...      22.5      22.6
06:45:00     23.8      23.5   ...      23.7      23.6
07:15:00     24.2      24.2   ...      24.5      23.9
08:00:00     24.7      24.6   ...      24.4      24.4
08:15:00     24.9      24.8   ...      25.0      25.2
09:00:00     25.8      26.3   ...      24.9      25.1
09:30:00     26.7      27.2   ...      25.9      26.4
10:30:00     29.4      28.4   ...      29.2      28.8
10:45:00     30.1      29.9   ...      28.7      29.5
12:15:00     32.8      32.7   ...      31.2      31.4
12:45:00     32.4      31.6   ...      30.8      32.8
13:45:00     31.7      32.3   ...      30.0      32.0
16:15:00     29.9      29.6   ...      29.3      30.6
16:45:00     29.6      30.4   ...      28.1      30.2
18:00:00     28.8      29.0   ...      29.1      29.2
18:30:00     28.5      28.1   ...      27.3      27.3

[16 rows x 6 columns]
```

dropna can also be used to remove all columns that contain any NaN values, by setting
the parameter axis=1. As we saw earlier, the default is axis=0. If every sensor column
contains NaN values, then all columns will be removed:

```python
cleansed_df2 = df2.dropna(axis=1)
print(cleansed_df2[:5])
```

Script output:

```
Empty DataFrame
Columns: []
Index: [06:00:00, 06:15:00, 06:30:00, 06:45:00, 07:00:00]
```

Now we change the task: we are only interested in rows that contain at most two
NaN values, i.e. at least four valid measurements. The parameter thresh is ideal here.
thresh is set to the minimum number of non-NaN values required. Since we have six
sensors per row, with thresh=4 we ensure that at least 4 values are not NaN:

```
cleansed_df2 = df2.dropna(thresh=4, axis=0)
print(cleansed_df2[:7])
```

The result of the code is:

```
          sensor1  sensor2  ...  sensor5  sensor6
time                        ...
06:00:00     23.3     22.7  ...     22.5     22.6
06:30:00     23.6      NaN  ...     23.0     23.2
06:45:00     23.8     23.5  ...     23.7     23.6
07:00:00     24.0     23.9  ...     23.0      NaN
07:15:00     24.2     24.2  ...     24.5     23.9
07:30:00     24.4      NaN  ...     23.7     24.1
07:45:00     24.5      NaN  ...      NaN     23.9

[7 rows x 6 columns]
```

Next we compute the averages again, but this time from cleansed_df2, i.e. the
DataFrame from which all rows with too many NaNs have been removed:

```
average_temp_series = cleansed_df2.mean(axis=1)
sensors = cleansed_df2.columns.values
df = cleansed_df2.drop(sensors, axis=1)

df = df.assign(temperature=average_temp_series)
print(df[:6])
```

The output we get is:

```
          temperature
time
06:00:00    22.933333
06:30:00    23.525000
06:45:00    23.900000
07:00:00    23.875000
07:15:00    24.116667
07:30:00    24.280000
```

25.4 Exercises

Exercise 1

(Solution: 33.18, Solution 1)

In this chapter we used the DataFrame `disturbed_data` with corrupted temperature measurements. We filtered it by allowing only rows with at most one NaN. Now create a slightly more fault-tolerant DataFrame, allowing at most two NaN values.

Exercise 2

(Solution: 33.18, Solution 2)

Now create a DataFrame that contains only one column with the average values.

26
Binning

26.1 Introduction

Binning is a statistical technique used in data preprocessing and data preparation. It refers to forming classes or categories from an ordered set of values by dividing them into intervals, usually according to their magnitude. The aim is to create clearer, more interpretable categories from detailed individual numbers. These intervals are called "bins", and each bin is represented by a label, often referred to as an interval label.

Typical use cases include grouping age, weight, or income into classes. Instead of considering each exact value separately, contiguous ranges of values are combined into meaningful categories.

Figure 26.1 Illustration of the binning concept

As an example, suppose we want to predict purchasing behavior for an online shop based on age. Two issues arise: First, there will be no or too few samples for certain ages – for example, for 82-year-olds. Second, management is not particularly interested in 82-year-olds as such, but rather in how purchasing behavior differs across age groups, such as 18–25 or 25–40. Statistically, you would not expect different purchasing behavior between, say, 31- and 32-year-olds. Therefore, we split our data into age groups. Figuratively, you can imagine each group as a "bucket" – hence the term *binning*, which means "to put into a container" but also "to group". Binning is therefore a form of quantizing the data.

The divisions (bins) do not have to be numeric. Categories may be of any type – for example "dogs", "cats", "hamsters", and so on.

Binning is also used in image processing to reduce data volume by combining adjacent pixels into single pixels. This is known as $k \times k$ binning, because regions of $k \times k$ pixels are reduced to one pixel.

26.2 Binning with Pandas

The Pandas module provides powerful functionality for grouping data. We begin with the cut function.

26.2.1 Binning with cut

The help text states that you can use cut when you need to segment and sort data values into bins. It further says: "This function is also useful for converting a continuous variable into a categorical variable. For example, cut can convert ages into groups of age ranges. It supports dividing into an equal number of bins or using a specified set of bins."

In the following examples, we present this function with its most important parameters:

```python
import pandas as pd

ages = [32, 17,  29, 48, 71, 55, 59, 19, 21]

age_categories = pd.cut(ages, bins=[0, 21, 35, 65, 100])
print(age_categories)
```

This is the result of the code:

```
[(21, 35], (0, 21], (21, 35], (35, 65], (65, 100], (35, 65], (35, 65], (0,
↪    21], (0, 21]]
Categories (4, interval[int64, right]): [(0, 21] < (21, 35] < (35, 65] <
↪    (65, 100]]
```

The result of cut() is a categorical object:

```python
print(type(age_categories))
```

The result of the code is:

```
<class 'pandas.core.arrays.categorical.Categorical'>
```

Each "bin" corresponds to a category. The categories are described using mathematical interval notation. (0, 21] means that this bin contains values between 0 (exclusive) and 21 (inclusive). Mathematically, this is a half-open interval: the right endpoint is inclusive, the left endpoint is not. Sometimes this is called a half-closed interval.

It is not apparent from the printed categories that the age_categories object also contains the frequencies within each interval. You can obtain the counts with value_counts:

```
print(age_categories.value_counts())
```

The result of the code is:

```
(0, 21]       3
(21, 35]      2
(35, 65]      3
(65, 100]     1
Name: count, dtype: int64
```

Boundary behavior and NaN values

If a value lies outside the defined bins, cut() returns NaN:

```
ages = [32, 101]
age_categories = pd.cut(ages, bins=[0, 21, 35, 65, 100])
print(age_categories)
```

Here is the output:

```
[(21.0, 35.0], NaN]
Categories (4, interval[int64, right]): [(0, 21] < (21, 35] < (35, 65] <
↪  (65, 100]]
```

With the parameter include_lowest=True you can control whether the lowest boundary is included:

```
print(pd.cut(ages, bins=[0, 21, 35, 65, 100], include_lowest=True))
```

What we obtain is:

```
[(21.0, 35.0], NaN]
Categories (4, interval[float64, right]): [(-0.001, 21.0] < (21.0, 35.0] <
↪   (35.0, 65.0] <
                                          (65.0, 100.0]]
```

Disable labels

Often you may want numeric group codes instead of interval labels. Use `labels=False`:

```
pd.cut(ages, bins=[0, 21, 35, 65, 100], labels=False)
```

26.2.2 Creating an `IntervalIndex` object

With `pd.IntervalIndex.from_tuples` you can create an `IntervalIndex`. The following shows how to create an `IntervalIndex` from a list of tuples, each representing an interval:

```python
import pandas as pd

intervals = [(0, 1), (1, 3), (3, 5), (5, 8)]

interval_index = pd.IntervalIndex.from_tuples(intervals)

print(interval_index)
```

This follows from the code:

```
IntervalIndex([(0, 1], (1, 3], (3, 5], (5, 8]], dtype='interval[int64,
↪  right]')
```

We see that the intervals are open on the left and closed on the right. With the parameter `closed`, you control whether endpoints are inclusive or exclusive:

- `'left'`: left side closed and right side open
- `'right'`: (default) left side open and right side closed
- `'both'`: both sides closed
- `'neither'`: both sides open

As an example, we set `closed` to "left":

```python
import pandas as pd

intervals = [(0, 1), (1, 3), (3, 5), (5, 8)]
interval_index = pd.IntervalIndex.from_tuples(intervals, closed="left")
print(interval_index)
```

The result of the code is:

```
IntervalIndex([[0, 1), [1, 3), [3, 5), [5, 8)], dtype='interval[int64,
↪  left]')
```

26.2.3 More about `pd.cut`

In our `pd.cut` example, we set the parameter `bins` to a list describing the scalar edges of the intervals. The `cut()` function can handle three different representations for bins:

- Integer value: specifies the number of equal-width bins over the range of values x. The range of x (the input array to be grouped) is extended by 0.1% on each side to include minimum and maximum values.
- Sequence of scalars: defines the bin edges, allowing unequal bin widths. The range of x is not extended.
- `IntervalIndex`: specifies the exact bins to use. Note that an `IntervalIndex` used for bins must not contain overlapping intervals.

We now show an example of using cut with an `IntervalIndex`:

```
import pandas as pd
ages = [32, 17, 29, 48, 71, 55, 59, 19, 21]
intervals = [(0, 21), (21, 35), (35, 65), (65, 100)]

interval_index = pd.IntervalIndex.from_tuples(intervals)
age_categories = pd.cut(ages, bins=interval_index)
print(age_categories)
```

The corresponding output can be seen here:

```
[(21, 35], (0, 21], (21, 35], (35, 65], (65, 100], (35, 65], (35, 65], (0,
↪    21], (0, 21]]
Categories (4, interval[int64, right]): [(0, 21] < (21, 35] < (35, 65] <
↪    (65, 100]]
```

As a final example, we use an integer for the `bins` parameter. This integer specifies the number of bins into which the values are grouped:

```
import pandas as pd
ages = [32, 17, 29, 48, 71, 55, 59, 19, 21]

num_bins = 4
age_categories = pd.cut(ages, bins=num_bins)
print(age_categories)
```

The result follows:

```
[(30.5, 44.0], (16.946, 30.5], (16.946, 30.5], (44.0, 57.5], (57.5, 71.0],
↪    (44.0, 57.5], (57.5, 71.0], (16.946, 30.5], (16.946, 30.5]]
Categories (4, interval[float64, right]): [(16.946, 30.5] < (30.5, 44.0] <
↪    (44.0, 57.5] <
                                        (57.5, 71.0]]
```

26.2.4 Memory optimization with Categorical

Categorical data can be stored more efficiently by declaring it as `Categorical`. This is a special data structure for features that have only a limited number of possible values – such as colors, countries, product categories, or grades.

Using `Categorical` saves memory especially when a DataFrame contains many repetitions of the same values. In the following example, we compare the memory usage of a regular object dtype with a `Categorical`:

```python
import pandas as pd

# Example DataFrame with strings (object dtype)
df_object = pd.DataFrame({'Column': ['A', 'B', 'C'] * 100000})
print(df_object.memory_usage(deep=True))

# Example DataFrame with categorical dtype
df_categorical = pd.DataFrame({'Column': pd.Categorical(['A', 'B', 'C'] *
    100000)})
print(df_categorical.memory_usage(deep=True))
```

Output:

```
Index            132
Column     15000000
dtype: int64
Index            132
Column       300258
dtype: int64
```

As the output shows, the `Categorical` version uses significantly less memory because repeated values are internally encoded as integers and stored only once. For large datasets with many repetitions, this is an effective optimization approach.

26.2.5 Binning with labels

You can also assign labels to the groups (bins), as in the following example:

```python
import pandas as pd

# List of students and their grades
students = ['Anna', 'Bob', 'Charlie', 'Dave', 'Emma', 'Frank']
grades = [1.4, 2.4, 1.5, 1.4, 3.4, 1.8]
```

```python
df = pd.DataFrame({'Student': students, 'Grade': grades})

# Create grade groups:
bins = [0, 1.5, 2.5, 5]
labels = ['magna cum laude', 'cum laude', 'rite']
grade_groups = pd.cut(x=df['Grade'], bins=bins, labels=labels)

df['Grade group'] = grade_groups

print(df)
```

We obtain this output:

```
    Student  Grade        Grade group
0      Anna    1.4  magna cum laude
1       Bob    2.4        cum laude
2   Charlie   1.5  magna cum laude
3      Dave    1.4  magna cum laude
4      Emma    3.4             rite
5     Frank    1.8        cum laude
```

26.3 Exercises

Exercise 1

(Solution: 33.19, Solution 1)

Given the following list of incomes (in thousand euros):

Create a binning categorization with the following intervals:

- 0–30 k€
- 30–60 k€
- 60–90 k€

Exercise 2

(Solution: 33.19, Solution 2)

Given a list of students and their exam grades (scale: 1 = very good to 5 = poor):

```python
students = ['Anna', 'Bob', 'Charlie', 'Dave', 'Emma', 'Frank']
grades = [1.4, 2.4, 1.5, 1.4, 3.4, 1.8]
```

Create a DataFrame with the columns `Student` and `Grade`. Then perform binning to divide the grades into the following three groups with appropriate labels:

- `magna cum laude` for grades from 0 up to and including 1.5
- `cum laude` for grades up to and including 2.5
- `rite` for all grades above that up to a maximum of 5.0

Add the result as a new column `Grade group` to the DataFrame and print it.

27
Multi-level Indexing

27.1 Introduction

In the previous chapters, we encountered various indices in Pandas Series and DataFrame examples. All of them were single-level. While this is sufficient for many applications, some scenarios require more structure.

Consider sales figures for several branches of a retail chain by year, or a software company tracking working hours by employee and project. Such data can be stored in a DataFrame, but not as a Series. With a multi-level (hierarchical) index, this becomes possible. For example, branches and years, or projects and team members, can form primary and secondary index levels, allowing DataFrame structures to be represented as Series objects.

Figure 27.1 Software team at work

If the company also distinguishes between "regular" and "irregular" hours (e.g. night or weekend work), a three-level index can be used.

In general, hierarchical indices allow n-dimensional data to be represented with `Series` and `DataFrame` objects without relying on external structures.

In this chapter we show:

- what multi-level indices are,
- how to create and use them, and
- how to switch between `DataFrame`s and `Series` with `stack` and `unstack`.

27.2 Multi-level indexed Series objects

Multi-level indices are available for both `Series` and `DataFrame` objects in Pandas. They make it possible to efficiently handle higher-dimensional data within the otherwise one- or two-dimensional Pandas structures. This hierarchical indexing provides a flexible way to map, store, and analyze complex data – all within familiar Pandas objects. In the following example we consider a fictitious software team – not necessarily one from the early 20th century as in our slightly surreal chapter illustration – working on three projects with the codenames `LOON`, `BOAL`, and `KLF`. For each combination of project and team member we record the hours worked. The index consists of two levels: the project name and the person's name.

```python
import pandas as pd

projects = ['LOON', 'LOON', 'LOON',
            'BOAL', 'BOAL', 'BOAL',
            'KLF', 'KLF', 'KLF']
team = ['Anna', 'Ben', 'Carla',
        'Anna', 'Ben', 'Carla',
        'Anna', 'Ben', 'Carla']

index = [projects, team]
data = [68, 50, 68, 66, 57, 61, 52, 64, 55]

hours = pd.Series(data, index=index)
print(hours)
```

Result:

```
LOON  Anna     68
      Ben      50
      Carla    68
BOAL  Anna     66
      Ben      57
      Carla    61
KLF   Anna     52
      Ben      64
      Carla    55
dtype: int64
```

As we can see from the example, multi-level indexing in Pandas can be realized by passing a list of lists when creating a `Series` or a `DataFrame`. In our example, the index has two levels: project names and team members.

The two lists `projects` and `team` each contain nine entries, i.e. they are of equal length. Pandas interprets the structure

```
index = [projects, team]
```

as a two-dimensional indexing, where each entry in the `Series` is assigned to a pair (`Project, Person`). Internally this becomes a so-called `MultiIndex`.

One can think of it as a table with two columns: the first contains the project names, the second the associated persons. Each combination forms a unique index entry.

The result is a hierarchically indexed `Series`, where both levels can be accessed – either together or separately (e.g. grouped by project or by person).

Notice that the team member names repeat in the second list: 'Anna', 'Ben', and 'Carla' each occur three times – once per project. This is intentional: the combination of project (first list) and person (second list) forms a unique key for each row.

Pandas uses this structure to generate a `MultiIndex`, where the values from the two lists are combined pairwise into a hierarchical index entry. In our example, each of the nine values in the Series is assigned to a unique combination of project and team member.

27.3 Multi-level indexing through list multiplication

In this section we show a particularly compact and elegant way to create a hierarchical index. We use two lists: one for the projects and one for the team members. Together, these two lists form the two levels of a multi-level index:

```python
import pandas as pd

projects = ['LOON'] * 3 + ['BOAL'] * 3 + ['KLF'] * 3
team = ['Anna', 'Ben', 'Carla'] * 3

index = [projects, team]
```

Pandas interprets this structure as a pairing of entries in the two lists. The result is a so-called `MultiIndex`, where each combination of project and person is used as a unique index entry. This allows a clear representation of, for example, project hours or task allocations in a hierarchically structured `Series`:

```python
data = [68, 50, 68, 66, 57, 61, 52, 64, 55]
hours = pd.Series(data, index=index)
print(hours)
```

The result follows:

```
LOON  Anna      68
      Ben       50
      Carla     68
BOAL  Anna      66
      Ben       57
      Carla     61
KLF   Anna      52
      Ben       64
      Carla     55
dtype: int64
```

Note: This method is especially readable and avoids repetitions in code. However, it only works if both lists are of equal length – otherwise Pandas raises an error.

27.4 Other ways of creating indices
With `from_tuples()`: manual pair creation

The method `MultiIndex.from_tuples()` expects a list of tuples, in which each combination of index values is explicitly specified. In our example we combine all project–person pairs using a list comprehension:

```python
import pandas as pd

projects = ['LOON', 'BOAL', 'KLF']
team = ['Anna', 'Ben', 'Carla']
data = [68, 50, 68, 66, 57, 61, 52, 64, 55]

# List of tuples (Project, Person)
tuples = [(proj, name) for proj in projects for name in team]

multi_index = pd.MultiIndex.from_tuples(
    tuples, names=['Project', 'Person'])

hours = pd.Series(data, index=multi_index)

print(hours)
```

The evaluation yields:

```
Project  Person
LOON     Anna      68
         Ben       50
         Carla     68
BOAL     Anna      66
         Ben       57
         Carla     61
KLF      Anna      52
         Ben       64
         Carla     55
dtype: int64
```

Advantage: This method is very flexible – even incomplete combinations or arbitrary pairings can be represented.

With `from_product()`: full Cartesian product

If every possible combination of two levels should be included in the index, the method `from_product()` is suitable. It automatically creates the Cartesian product of two (or more) lists:

```python
hours = pd.Series(data,
                  index=pd.MultiIndex.from_product(
                      [projects, team],
                      names=['Project', 'Person']))


print(hours)
```

The following result is generated:

```
Project  Person
LOON     Anna      68
         Ben       50
         Carla     68
BOAL     Anna      66
         Ben       57
         Carla     61
KLF      Anna      52
         Ben       64
         Carla     55
dtype: int64
```

Advantage: `from_product()` is particularly compact and ideal for fully structured data with a uniform layout.

Which method to choose?

- `from_product()` is the first choice if the data model covers all combinations of two (or more) categories.
- `from_tuples()` is better suited if only certain combinations are needed or if they are distributed irregularly.

Both methods produce identical index structures – as long as the underlying pairs are the same. The choice therefore mainly depends on the structure of the data and the desired level of control over the index combinations.

27.5 Access methods

In the following we see how to access data organized with a multi-level index. As an example we again use our `Series` object `hours`, which records the working hours of a team on different projects:

```python
print(hours['LOON'])
```

Here is the result of the code:

```
Person
Anna     68
Ben      50
Carla    68
dtype: int64
```

Accessing individual values

The number of hours for a specific person in a project can be queried in two ways:

```python
print(hours['BOAL']['Carla'])
print(hours['BOAL', 'Carla'])
```

The output we get is:

```
61
61
```

Accessing sub-levels (e.g. all projects for a person)

With slicing you can target a specific hierarchy level. For example, all projects for a certain person can be queried:

```python
print(hours[:, 'Carla'])
```

The output we get is:

```
Project
LOON    68
BOAL    61
KLF     55
dtype: int64
```

Accessing selected combinations

If you only want to access certain projects (not all) and certain people, you need loc:

```python
print(hours.loc[['BOAL', 'LOON'], 'Carla'])
print(hours.loc[['BOAL', 'LOON'], ['Carla', 'Ben']])
```

The evaluation yields:

```
Project  Person
BOAL     Carla     61
LOON     Carla     68
dtype: int64
Project  Person
BOAL     Carla     61
         Ben       57
LOON     Carla     68
         Ben       50
dtype: int64
```

Access to multiple *top* levels

If access should be restricted only to the top index level (e.g. certain projects), this can be done directly:

```python
print(hours[['BOAL', 'LOON']])
```

The following result is generated:

```
Project  Person
BOAL     Anna      66
         Ben       57
         Carla     61
LOON     Anna      68
         Ben       50
         Carla     68
dtype: int64
```

Accessing index levels (`index.levels`)

With `index.levels` you can access the hierarchy levels of the index. The result is a
`FrozenList`:

```python
for i in range(len(hours.index.levels)):
    if i == 0:
        print('Top hierarchy level:')
    elif i == 1:
        print('Lower hierarchy level:')
    print(hours.index.levels[i])
```

This follows from the code:

```
Top hierarchy level:
Index(['BOAL', 'KLF', 'LOON'], dtype='object', name='Project')
Lower hierarchy level:
Index(['Anna', 'Ben', 'Carla'], dtype='object', name='Person')
```

Slicing with range specifications

As soon as a (`MultiIndex`) is sorted, range queries (label slicing) can also be used:

```python
hours = hours.sort_index()
print('Hours listing with sorted index:')
print(hours)

print('\nWith slicing:')
print(hours['BOAL':'KLF'])
```

Script output:

```
Hours listing with sorted index:
Project  Person
BOAL     Anna       66
         Ben        57
         Carla      61
KLF      Anna       52
         Ben        64
         Carla      55
LOON     Anna       68
         Ben        50
         Carla      68
dtype: int64

With slicing:
Project  Person
BOAL     Anna       66
         Ben        57
         Carla      61
KLF      Anna       52
         Ben        64
         Carla      55
dtype: int64
```

27.6 Three-level indices

So far we have seen how to create a `Series` with a two-level index – for example by passing a list of two lists or by using a `MultiIndex`. But hierarchical indices are not limited to two levels.

We now extend our previous example by another level. Let us imagine that we want to break down the project hours of our team members into "regular working hours" and "irregular working hours"[1].

```python
import pandas as pd

projects = ['LOON', 'BOAL', 'KLF']
team = ['Anna', 'Ben', 'Carla']
work_type = ['regular', 'irregular']
data = [56, 14, 56, 14, 59, 8,
        60, 24, 55, 6, 54, 25,
        52, 5, 60, 23, 55, 25]
```

---

1   That is, night work, weekend work, and so on

```
multi_index = pd.MultiIndex.from_product(
                    [projects, team, work_type],
                    names=['Project', 'Person', 'Work type'])
hours = pd.Series(data, index=multi_index)
print(hours)
```

The corresponding output can be seen here:

```
Project  Person  Work type
LOON     Anna    regular     56
                 irregular   14
         Ben     regular     56
                 irregular   14
         Carla   regular     59
                 irregular    8
BOAL     Anna    regular     60
                 irregular   24
         Ben     regular     55
                 irregular    6
         Carla   regular     54
                 irregular   25
KLF      Anna    regular     52
                 irregular    5
         Ben     regular     60
                 irregular   23
         Carla   regular     55
                 irregular   25
dtype: int64
```

With the following statement we obtain, for each project member, the number of hours
for project LOON that were performed within regular working hours:

```
print(hours['LOON', :, 'regular'])
```

Output:

```
Person
Anna    56
Ben     56
Carla   59
dtype: int64
```

Now let's look at the hours performed during regular working time, broken down by
project and for all team members:

```
print(hours[:, :, 'regular'])
```

Output:

```
Project  Person
LOON     Anna      56
         Ben       56
         Carla     59
BOAL     Anna      60
         Ben       55
         Carla     54
KLF      Anna      52
         Ben       60
         Carla     55
dtype: int64
```

27.7 Relation to DataFrames

Some may have wondered whether the previously introduced multi-indexed `Series` can also be represented as a DataFrame. A DataFrame is inherently two-dimensional, while `Series` objects are only one-dimensional – unless they have a multi-level index.

Let us return to the example from Section 27.6. The goal is to create a DataFrame in which the first index level ("Project") becomes the row index and the second index level ("Person") becomes the columns.

We show two possible approaches:

- Manual construction with iteration and `pd.concat`
- Using the `unstack` method

27.7.1 Manual approach with pd.concat

The following code shows how to iteratively transform a `Series` object with a two-level index into a DataFrame. Note that the parameter `sort` in `concat` must be set explicitly:

```python
hours_df = pd.DataFrame([], index=index[0][::3])


for person in index[1][:3]:
    hours_df = pd.concat([hours_df,
                          hours[:, person]],
                         axis=1,
                         sort=True)


hours_df.columns = index[1][:3]
print(hours_df)
```

The evaluation yields:

```
        Anna  Ben  Carla
BOAL     66   57     61
KLF      52   64     55
LOON     68   50     68
```

If the parameter `sort=False` is set, the order of projects is preserved:

```python
hours_df = pd.DataFrame([], index=index[0][::3])


for person in index[1][:3]:
    hours_df = pd.concat([hours_df,
                          hours[:, person]],
                         axis=1,
                         sort=False)


hours_df.columns = index[1][:3]
print(hours_df)
```

Result:

```
        Anna  Ben  Carla
LOON     68   50     68
BOAL     66   57     61
KLF      52   64     55
```

27.7.2 unstack and stack

The conversion of a multi-indexed `Series` into a `DataFrame` can be achieved much
more elegantly with the `unstack` method than with manual iteration. The method
`unstack` moves one level of the index into the column axis, thereby automatically
creating a `DataFrame`. The prerequisite is that the `Series` object has a hierarchical
index (`MultiIndex`).

The reverse operation – converting a `DataFrame` back into a `Series` – is possible with
the `stack` method.

`unstack` offers two optional parameters:
- `level` specifies which level of the multi-index should be moved into the column
  axis. The default value is `-1`, meaning the innermost level of the index is used –
  in our example the team members. If `level=0` is set, the project names appear as
  column headings, and the team members remain in the index.
- `fill_value` specifies which value is used in place of missing data (NaN). The default
  is None, i.e. missing values remain unchanged.

```python
hours_df = hours.unstack()
print('Default value -1 was used for level:')
print(hours_df)


hours_df = hours.unstack(level=0)
print('\nResult for level=0:')
print(hours_df)
```

The result appears as follows:

```
Default value -1 was used for level:
      Anna  Ben  Carla
BOAL    66   57     61
KLF     52   64     55
LOON    68   50     68


Result for level=0:
       BOAL  KLF  LOON
Anna     66   52    68
Ben      57   64    50
Carla    61   55    68
```

The `DataFrame` method `stack` corresponds to the inverse function of `unstack`, i.e. it turns a `DataFrame` object back into a multi-indexed `Series` object:

```python
print(hours_df.stack())
```

The code produces the following result:

```
Anna   BOAL    66
       KLF     52
       LOON    68
Ben    BOAL    57
       KLF     64
       LOON    50
Carla  BOAL    61
       KLF     55
       LOON    68
dtype: int64
```

The use of `unstack` becomes particularly interesting when a `Series` object has more than two index levels. In the following example we work with a four-level index containing information about different products from companies:

```python
import numpy as np
companies = ['Wirth GbR', 'NAN AG']
items = ['Table', 'Chair']
colors = ['white', 'brown']
materials = ['Wood', 'Plastic']
m_index = pd.MultiIndex.from_product(
                [companies, items, colors, materials],
                names=['Company', 'Product', 'Color', 'Material'])

prices = np.random.randint(10000, 25000, (len(m_index),)) / 100
products = pd.Series(prices, index=m_index)
print(products)
```

Here is the result of the code:

```
Company     Product  Color  Material
Wirth GbR   Table    white  Wood          136.36
                            Plastic       226.20
                     brown  Wood          167.99
                            Plastic       149.95
            Chair    white  Wood          192.74
                            Plastic       115.45
                     brown  Wood          159.93
                            Plastic       186.03
NAN AG      Table    white  Wood          197.33
                            Plastic       178.71
                     brown  Wood          249.29
                            Plastic       240.71
            Chair    white  Wood          238.23
                            Plastic       233.93
                     brown  Wood          173.04
                            Plastic       164.53
dtype: float64
```

We now use the unstack method without parameters, i.e. the parameter level defaults
to -1. This means that the innermost index, the Material index, is used for the column
names of the DataFrame object:

```python
products_df = products.unstack()
print(products_df)
```

The output shows:

```
Material                        Plastic     Wood
Company     Product Color
NAN AG      Chair   brown       164.53   173.04
                    white       233.93   238.23
            Table   brown       240.71   249.29
                    white       178.71   197.33
Wirth GbR   Chair   brown       186.03   159.93
                    white       115.45   192.74
            Table   brown       149.95   167.99
                    white       226.20   136.36
```

Alternatively, you can explicitly specify which index level should become columns. For example, if you want `Color` as columns, set `level=2`:

```
df = products.unstack(level=2)
print(df)
```

This is the result of the code:

```
Color                           brown    white
Company     Product Material
NAN AG      Chair   Plastic     164.53   233.93
                    Wood        173.04   238.23
            Table   Plastic     240.71   178.71
                    Wood        249.29   197.33
Wirth GbR   Chair   Plastic     186.03   115.45
                    Wood        159.93   192.74
            Table   Plastic     149.95   226.20
                    Wood        167.99   136.36
```

Multiple levels can also be unpacked into columns simultaneously. In the following example `Company` and `Product` together become column headers:

```
df = products.unstack(level=(0, 1))
print(df)
```

Output:

```
Company             Wirth GbR            NAN AG
Product             Table    Chair       Table    Chair
Color Material
brown Plastic       149.95   186.03      240.71   164.53
      Wood          167.99   159.93      249.29   173.04
white Plastic       226.20   115.45      178.71   233.93
      Wood          136.36   192.74      197.33   238.23
```

27.8 Swapping multi-level indices

It is possible to swap the levels of a multi-level index with the `swaplevel` method.
You can swap two levels at a time. By default, the innermost levels are swapped. The
default call behavior of `swaplevel` looks like this:

```
swaplevel(i=-2, j=-1, copy=True)
```

We demonstrate this with our previous example:

```
products_swapped = products.swaplevel()
products_swapped.sort_index(inplace=True)
print(products_swapped)
```

After execution we get:

```
Company     Product  Material  Color
NAN AG      Chair    Plastic   brown    231.96
                               white    220.89
                     Wood      brown    207.91
                               white    133.04
            Table    Plastic   brown    115.78
                               white    183.69
                     Wood      brown    100.69
                               white    112.19
Wirth GbR   Chair    Plastic   brown    142.38
                               white    201.32
                     Wood      brown    241.21
                               white    243.62
            Table    Plastic   brown    187.36
                               white    203.19
                     Wood      brown    102.30
                               white    217.84
dtype: float64
```

We now swap the two top levels by setting i and j to 0 and 1:

```
products_swapped = products.swaplevel(0, 1)
products_swapped.sort_index(inplace=True)
print(products_swapped)
```

What we obtain is:

```
Product  Company      Color  Material
Chair    NAN AG       brown  Plastic     231.96
                             Wood        207.91
                      white  Plastic     220.89
                             Wood        133.04
         Wirth GbR    brown  Plastic     142.38
                             Wood        241.21
                      white  Plastic     201.32
                             Wood        243.62
Table    NAN AG       brown  Plastic     115.78
                             Wood        100.69
                      white  Plastic     183.69
                             Wood        112.19
         Wirth GbR    brown  Plastic     187.36
                             Wood        102.30
                      white  Plastic     203.19
                             Wood        217.84
dtype: float64
```

27.9 Exercises

Exercise 1

(Solution: 33.20, Solution 1)

Convert the following dictionary into a `Series` with a two-level index, where the country names form the primary index and the years the secondary index:

```python
growth_rates = {("Germany", 2019): 1.05,
                ("Germany", 2020): -4.56,
                ("Germany", 2021): 2.79,
                ("Switzerland", 2019): 1.24,
                ("Switzerland", 2020): -2.52,
                ("Switzerland", 2021): 3.72,
                ("Austria", 2019): 1.49,
                ("Austria", 2020): -6.74,
                ("Austria", 2021): 4.48}
```

Exercise 2

(Solution: 33.20, Solution 2)

Swap the multi-level index of the `Series` created in the previous exercise, so that the years form the primary index and the countries the secondary index.

Exercise 3

(Solution: 33.20, Solution 3)

Write a Python program that creates the following Series object:

```
City        Category
Vienna      Country        Austria
            Area           414.6
            Population     1_805_681
Hamburg     Country        Germany
            Area           755.0
            Population     1_760_433
Berlin      Country        Germany
            Area           891.85
            Population     3_562_166
Zurich      Country        Switzerland
            Area           87.88
            Population     378_884
dtype: object
```

Exercise 4

(Solution: 33.20, Solution 4)

Swap the indices in the Series object you just created.

Exercise 5

(Solution: 33.20, Solution 5)

Convert the Series object created in Exercise 3 into a DataFrame object.

Exercise 6

(Solution: 33.20, Solution 6)

As in the previous exercise, convert the Series object created in Exercise 3 into a DataFrame object. This time, however, the city names should become column names, and Population, Area, and Country should form the index.

Exercise 7

(Solution: 33.20, Solution 7)

Read the file colors_tab.csv in the directory data1 and transform the loaded DataFrame object so that we have a two-level index with the color as the primary index and the intensity as the secondary index. The columns should correspond to the location, i.e. outside and inside. This is best achieved using pivoting, see Chapter 24. Pivot Tables

28
Data Visualization with Pandas

28.1 Introduction

Data visualization refers to the representation of data in a pictorial or graphical format. It is rarely a good idea to present scientific or business data purely in text or as tables of numbers to the target audience. A well-chosen visualization supports decision-makers in understanding complex relationships and identifying new patterns or

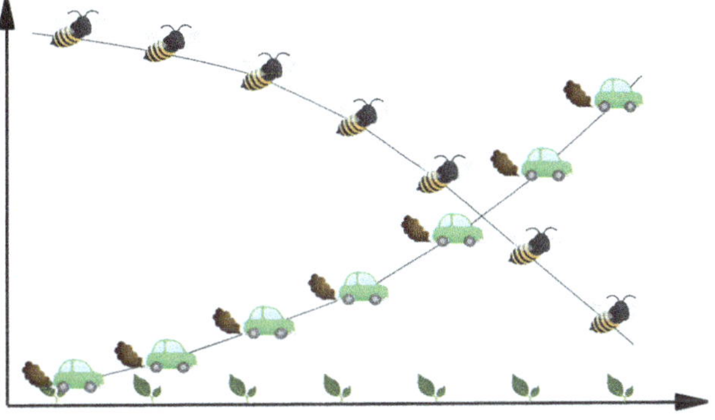

Figure 28.1 Cars and Bees

trends. This makes communication of the information more efficient and the data more tangible. In other words, complex data becomes more accessible and understandable. For example, numerical data can be represented graphically in scatter plots, line charts, column and bar charts, as well as pie charts. Such graphics can be enhanced with additional elements like legends, axis labels, or highlights to increase clarity.

Although all of this can already be achieved with Matplotlib, it is a low-level tool. That means many visualizations require relatively high effort or complex code. Pandas, on the other hand, provides its own functionality to make visualization easier to implement. Nevertheless, Pandas visualization tools are built on top of Matplotlib.

This chapter provides a practical overview of visualization possibilities with Pandas – starting with line charts, followed by bar and pie charts, and extending to area plots. Special cases such as secondary axes, multiple y-axes, or converting text values into numerical data are also covered.

28.2 Line Charts in Pandas

28.2.1 Series

Both `Series` and `DataFrame` objects in Pandas have an integrated `plot()` function that allows data to be visualized quickly. In the following example, a simple line chart is created for a `Series` object.

```python
import pandas as pd

data = [16.2, 16.6, 17.0, 17.3, 17.7, 18.0, 18.3, 18.5,
        18.3, 18.2, 17.9, 17.3, 19.1, 19.3, 19.5, 19.8,
        19.8, 20.0, 20.2, 20.4, 20.6, 20.8, 21.0, 21.2,
        21.3, 21.5, 21.7, 21.8, 22.0, 22.3]
s = pd.Series(data, index=range(100, 250, 5))
s.plot()
```

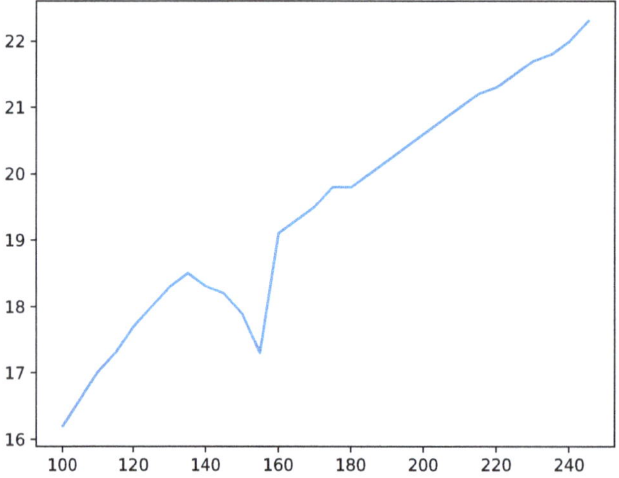

If you want to save a plot, you can use `savefig`. However, we need a `figure` object, which we obtain from the `AxesSubplot` object (the return value of `plot`) using `get_figure`:

```python
plot = s.plot()
fig = plot.get_figure()
fig.savefig('../MatplotlibImages/seriesPlot.pdf')
```

It is possible to suppress the use of the index by setting the parameter `use_index` to
`False`:

```
s.plot(use_index=False)
```

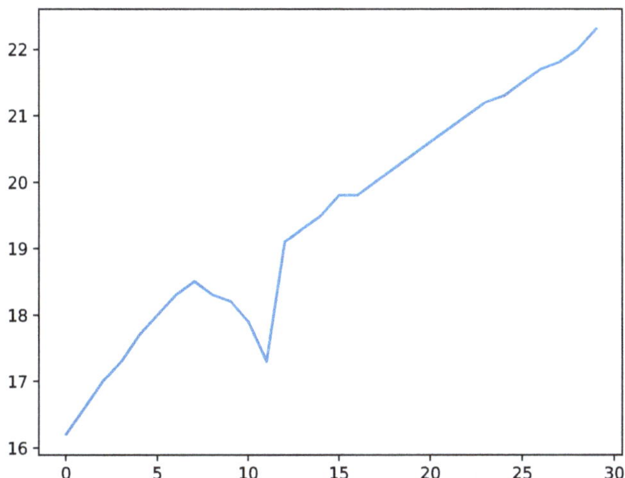

We now experiment with a `Series` object that has an index of alphabetic values:

```
fruits = ['apples', 'oranges', 'cherries', 'pears']
quantities = [20, 33, 52, 10]
fruits = pd.Series(quantities, index=fruits)
fruits.plot()
```

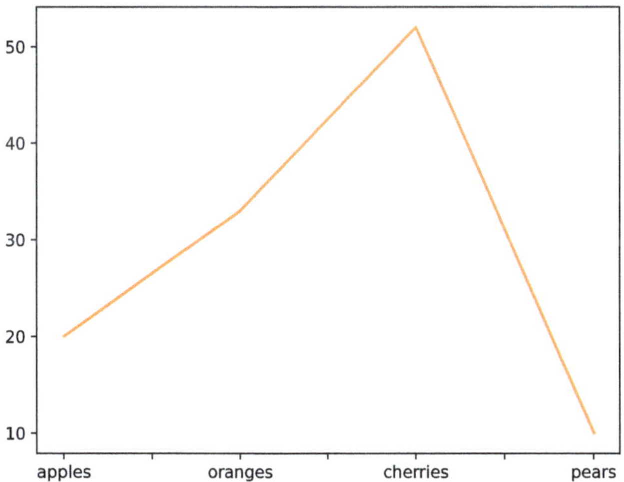

Of course, in this case (categorical data) a line chart makes little sense, since the data
does not describe a continuous function. Here it is better to use, for example, a column,
bar, or pie chart. We will demonstrate this later in the chapter.

28.2.2 DataFrames

Naturally, Pandas also allows plotting of DataFrames. We demonstrate this with an
example. We construct a `DataFrame` object from the monthly temperature and precipitation data of the island of Crete. We then generate a line chart for this `DataFrame`:

```python
months = ["January", "February", "March", "April", "May", "June",
          "July", "August", "September", "October", "November",
          "December"]
max_temp = [17, 16, 17, 19, 23, 25, 28, 28, 27, 24, 21, 18]
avg_temp = [14, 13, 14, 17, 20, 24, 26, 27,
            25, 22, 19, 15]
min_temp = [10, 9, 11, 14, 18, 22, 25, 26, 24, 19, 15, 12]
precip_mm = [296, 278, 117, 79, 74, 24, 1, 27, 72, 155,
             110, 283]

crete_dict = {"Maximum": max_temp,
              "Average": avg_temp,
              "Minimum": min_temp,
              "Precipitation": precip_mm}

crete_df = pd.DataFrame(crete_dict, index=months)
print(crete_df.head(5))
```

The output we get is:

```
          Maximum  Average  Minimum  Precipitation
January        17       14       10            296
February       16       13        9            278
March          17       14       11            117
April          19       17       14             79
May            23       20       18             74
```

We now generate the line chart for the DataFrame:

```python
crete_df.plot()
```

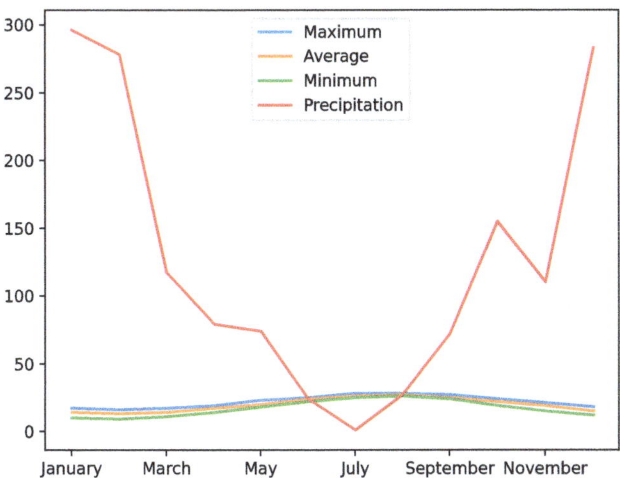

After looking at the plot, the axis labeling is not ideal yet. First, the x-axis has no label, and second, the y-axis is used for both temperatures (in °C) and precipitation (in mm). Because precipitation spans a much larger numerical range, the temperature curves are visually compressed and hard to distinguish.

As a first step, we improve readability by rotating the month labels:

```
rotation = 80   # rotate month labels by 80 degrees
crete_df.plot(xticks=range(len(crete_df.index)),
              rot=rotation)
```

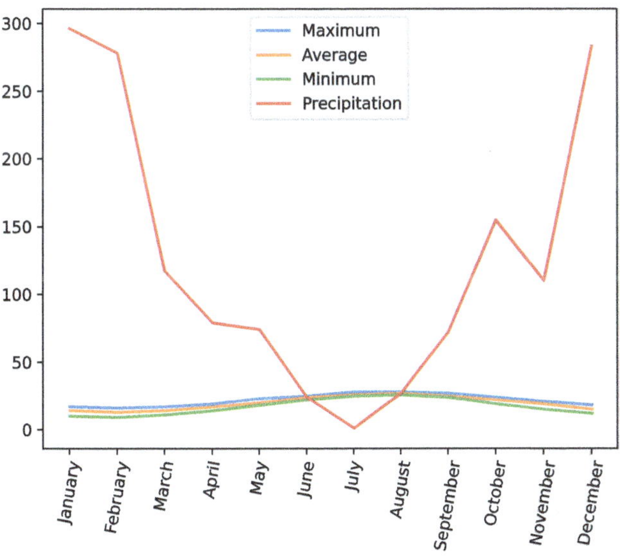

Here, the tick positions on the x-axis are set explicitly to match the number of months. The labels themselves come from the DataFrame index. The rot parameter rotates the tick labels; without rotation, the month names would overlap and become unreadable.

Even with rotated labels, temperature values are still difficult to read because precipitation dominates the scale. A simple remedy is to plot temperatures and precipitation in separate charts.

We start with the temperature columns and add a y-axis label via ylabel:

```python
temps = crete_df[['Minimum', 'Maximum', 'Average']]
temps.plot(xticks=range(len(crete_df.index)),
           rot=rotation,
           ylabel='Temperature in Celsius',
           title='Annual Temperatures on Crete')
```

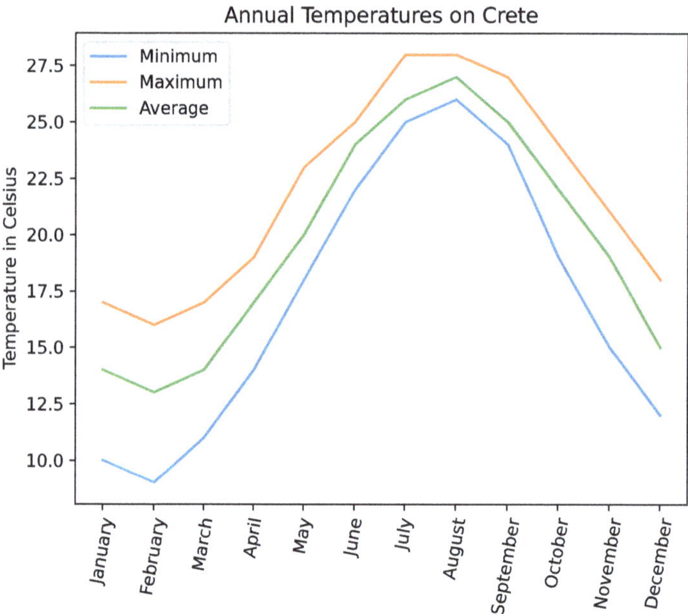

The precipitation plot can be created in the same way:

```python
rain = crete_df['Precipitation']
rain.plot(xticks=range(len(crete_df.index)),
          rot=rotation,
          ylabel='Precipitation (mm)',
          title='Annual Precipitation on Crete')
```

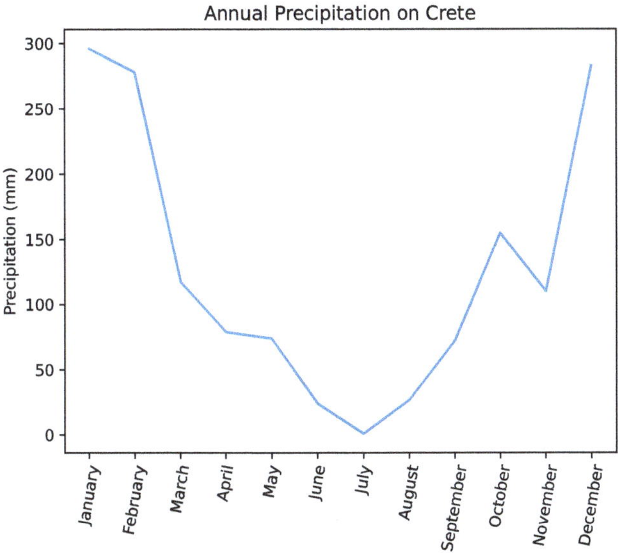

28.2.3 Secondary Axes (Twin Axes)

Another common approach is to use a secondary y-axis so that temperatures and precipitation can be shown in a single chart. We first plot the temperature series on the left axis and then create a second axis for precipitation using twinx().

```python
ax = crete_df['Maximum'].plot(xticks=range(len(crete_df.index)),
                              figsize=(3.5, 3.5),
                              use_index=True,
                              title='Annual Climate on Crete',
                              rot=60)

crete_df['Average'].plot(ax=ax,
                         xticks=range(len(crete_df.index)),
                         use_index=True,
                         rot=60)
crete_df['Minimum'].plot(ax=ax,
                         xticks=range(len(crete_df.index)),
                         use_index=True,
                         rot=60)

ax2 = ax.twinx()
crete_df['Precipitation'].plot(ax=ax2, style="r-")
```

```
ax.set_ylabel('Temperature in Celsius')
ax.set_xlabel('Months')
ax2.set_ylabel('Precipitation (mm)')


ax.legend(['Maximum', 'Average', 'Minimum'], loc=2)
ax2.legend(loc=1)
```

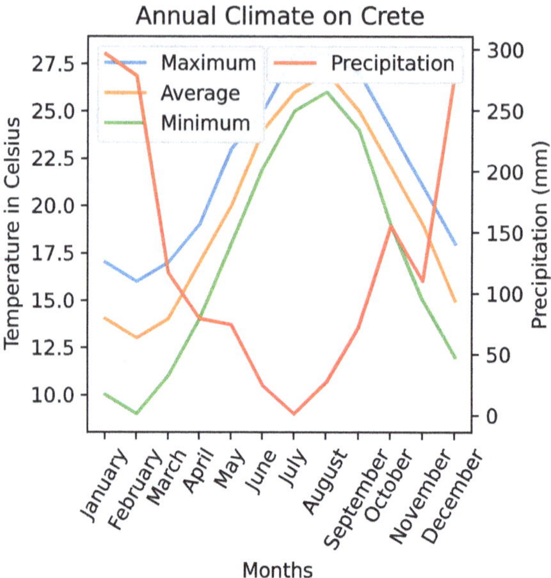

28.2.4 Multiple Y-Axes

It is also possible to add more axes. Since our `crete_df` DataFrame does not yet contain
another column to plot, we first add a new column with the average daily sunshine
hours.

```
sunshine = [5, 4, 8, 9, 10, 12, 12, 12, 9, 8, 9, 5]
crete_dict = {"Maximum": max_temp,
              "Average": avg_temp,
              "Minimum": min_temp,
              "Precipitation": precip_mm,
              "Sunshine": sunshine}
crete_df = pd.DataFrame(crete_dict, index=months)


temp = crete_df['Average']
ax = temp.plot(xticks=range(len(crete_df.index)),
               figsize=(5, 3),
               style="g-",
```

```python
                use_index=True,
                title='Annual Climate on Crete',
                rot=60)

ax_rain, ax_sun = ax.twinx(), ax.twinx()
crete_df['Precipitation'].plot(ax=ax_rain, style="r-")
crete_df['Sunshine'].plot(ax=ax_sun, style="b-")
ax.set_ylabel('Temperature')
ax.set_xlabel('Months')
ax_rain.set_ylabel('Precipitation in mm')
ax_sun.set_ylabel('Sunshine hours per day')
ax_rain.spines['right'].set_position(('axes', 1.0))
ax_sun.spines['right'].set_position(('axes', 1.15))
ax.legend(['Temperature'],
          loc='upper left',
          bbox_to_anchor=(0.0, 1.0),
          frameon=False)
ax_rain.legend(loc='upper left',
               bbox_to_anchor=(0.0, 0.94),
               frameon=False)
ax_sun.legend(loc='upper left',
              bbox_to_anchor=(0.0, 0.88),
              frameon=False)
```

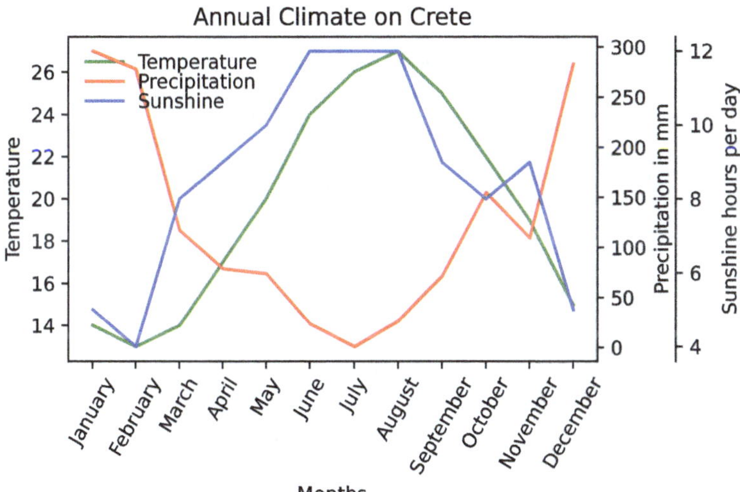

28.2.5 Converting String Columns to Floats

Next, we examine a ranking of programming languages. In the directory data1, the file
tiobe_programming_language_usage_jun2025.csv contains this ranking, collected
and prepared by TIOBE in June 2025. The file content is shown below. The percentage
column includes strings with a percent sign. We can handle (or remove) this using the
read_csv function. To do so, we define a converter function and pass it to read_csv
via the converters parameter:

```python
import pandas as pd

def strip_percentage_sign(x):
    return float(x.strip('%'))

data_path = "data1/"
fname = "tiobe_programming_language_usage_jun2025.csv"
progs = pd.read_csv(data_path + fname,
                    quotechar="'",
                    index_col=2,
                    converters={'Ratings': strip_percentage_sign,
                                'Change': strip_percentage_sign},
                    delimiter=r",")

print(progs[:12])  # output of the top 12 programming languages
rotation = 82
progs['Ratings'].plot(xticks=range(len(progs.index)),
                      use_index=True,
                      rot=rotation)
```

Script output:

	Jun 2024	Jun 2025	Ratings	Change
Language				
Python	1	1	25.87	10.48
C++	2	2	10.68	0.65
C	3	3	9.47	0.24
Java	4	4	8.84	0.44
C#	5	5	4.69	-1.96
JavaScript	6	6	3.21	-0.11
Go	7	7	2.28	0.35
Visual Basic	8	9	2.20	0.54
Object Pascal	9	11	2.15	0.62
Fortran	10	10	1.86	0.33
Ada	11	25	1.70	0.91
SQL	12	8	1.55	-0.21

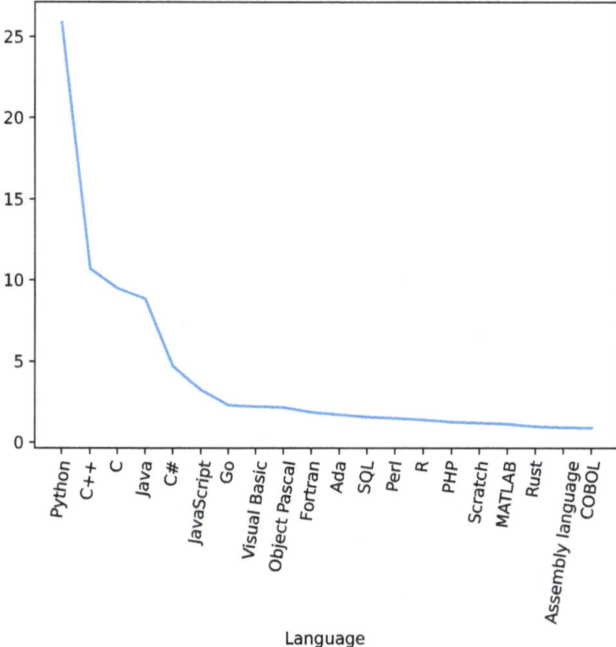

28.3 Bar Charts in Pandas

Creating bar charts with Pandas is just as easy as creating line charts. To do so, we simply add the keyword parameter kind to the plot call and set its value to bar.

28.3.1 A Simple Example

```
import pandas as pd

data = [100, 120, 140, 180, 200, 210, 214]
s = pd.Series(data, index=range(len(data)))

s.plot(kind="bar", rot=0)
```

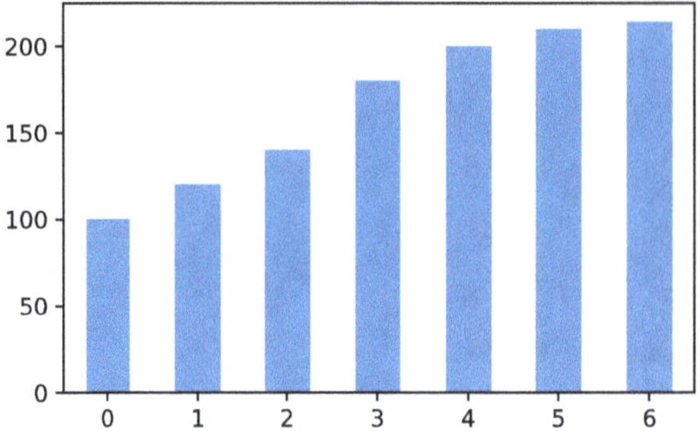

28.3.2 Bar Chart for Programming Language Usage

We now return to the programming language ranking example. This time, we generate a bar chart of the ten most widely used programming languages:

```python
top10 = progs[:10]
top10['Ratings'].plot(kind="bar",
                      title='TIOBE Index June 2025',
                      ylabel='Percent')
```

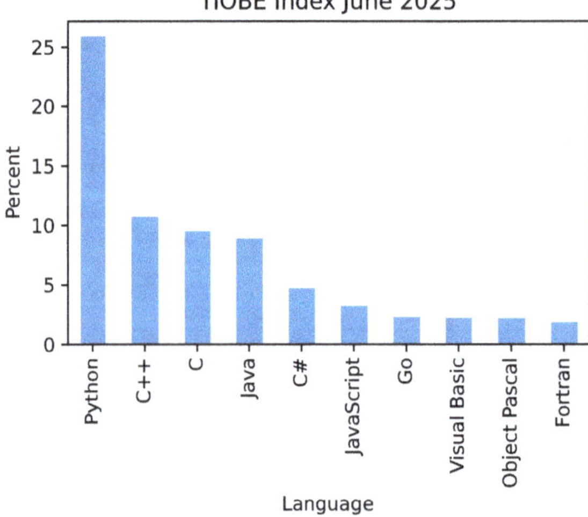

Now let's also display an additional bar with the percentage changes compared to the previous year:

```
df = top10[['Ratings', 'Change']]
plot = df.plot(kind="bar",
               title='TIOBE Index June 2025',
               ylabel='Percent')
```

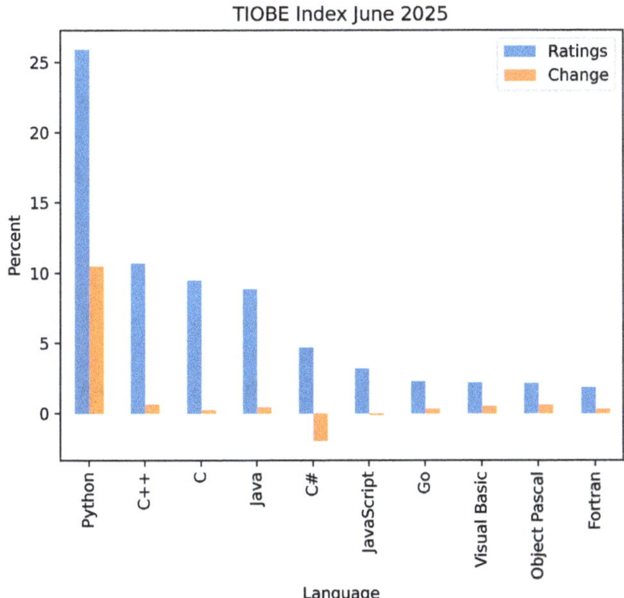

We can also display the ratings for 2024 and 2025 directly side by side. To do so, we first calculate the ratings for 2024:

```
progs["Ratings2024"] = progs["Ratings"] - progs["Change"]
# New DataFrame with both years
ratings_df = progs[["Ratings2024", "Ratings"]][:6].copy()
ratings_df.columns = ["2024", "2025"]


ratings_df = ratings_df.sort_values("2025", ascending=False)


ax = ratings_df.plot(kind="bar",
                     rot=45,
                     color=["lightgray", "steelblue"],
                     figsize=(10, 5))


ax.set_ylabel("Percent")
ax.set_title("TIOBE Rankings 2024 vs. 2025")
fig = ax.get_figure()
fig.tight_layout()
```

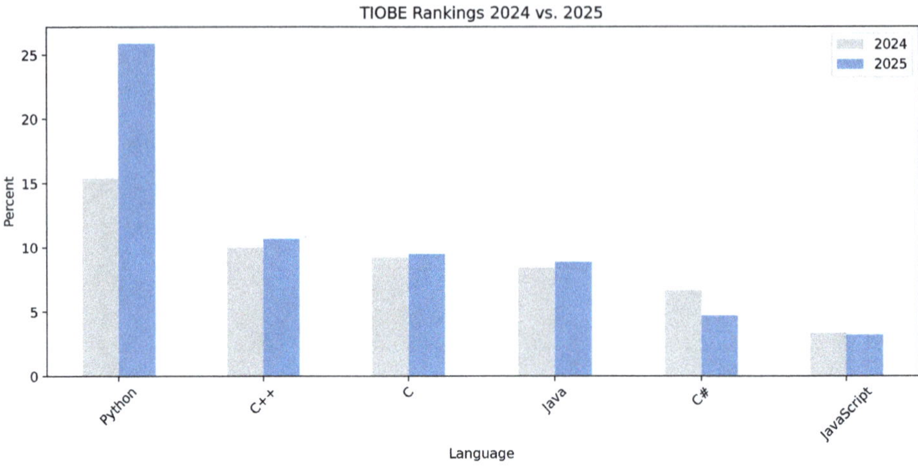

28.3.3 Coloring a Bar Chart

It is possible to color the bars individually by passing a list of color values to the `color` keyword parameter:

```python
my_colors = ['b', 'r', 'c', 'y', 'g', 'm']
progs['Ratings'][:6].plot(kind="bar",
                          color=my_colors,
                          title='TIOBE Index June 2025',
                          ylabel='Percent')
```

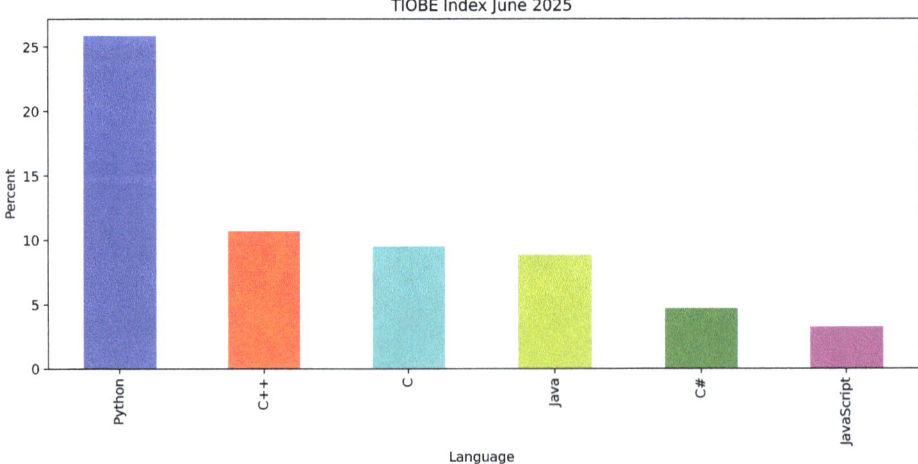

28.4 Pie Charts in Pandas

28.4.1 A Simple Example

```python
import pandas as pd

fruits = ['apples', 'pears', 'cherries', 'bananas']
series = pd.Series([20, 30, 40, 10],
                   index=fruits,
                   name='Fruits')
series.plot.pie(figsize=(6, 6))
```

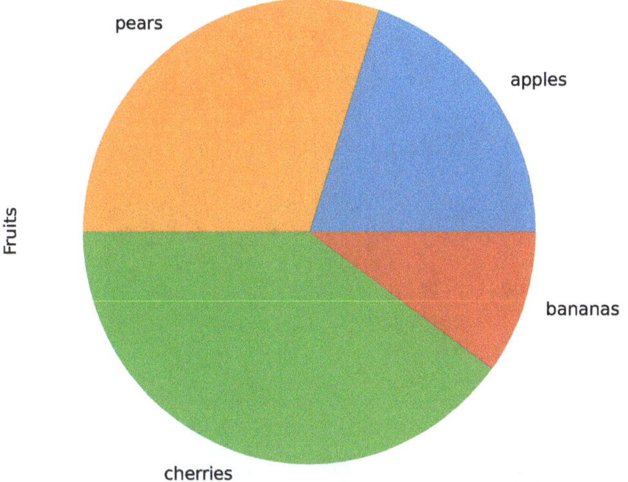

The pie chart above resembles a cake, and like a cake, you can pull out individual "slices." This can be achieved using the `explode` parameter. It accepts an array-like structure (tuple or list) that specifies the offset from the center. The default values are 0, meaning the slices remain in place:

```python
import pandas as pd
fruits = ['apples', 'pears', 'cherries', 'bananas']

series = pd.Series([20, 30, 40, 10],
                   index=fruits,
                   name='Fruits')
explode = [0, 0.10, 0.40, 0.5]
series.plot.pie(figsize=(6, 6),
                explode=explode)
```

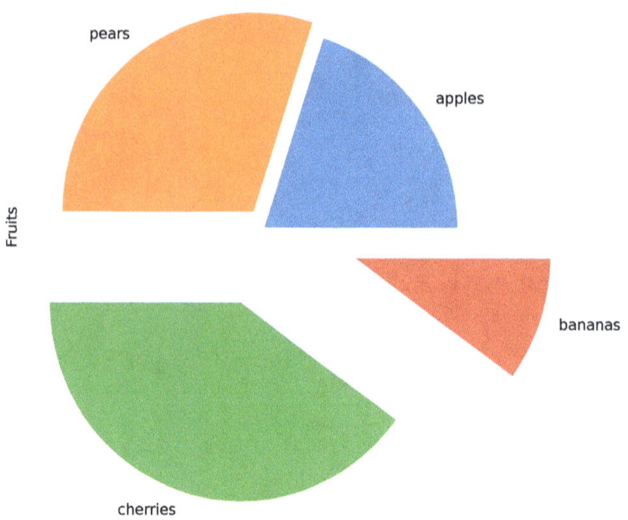

Now let's also look at the pie chart for the six most important programming languages:

```python
my_colors = ['b', 'r', 'c', 'y', 'g', 'm']
explode = [0.2, 0.0, 0.0, 0.0, 0.0, 0.0]
progs['Ratings'][:6].plot(kind="pie",
                          explode=explode,
                          colors=my_colors,
                          autopct='%1.1f%%',
                          title='TIOBE Index June 2025',
                          ylabel='Percent')
```

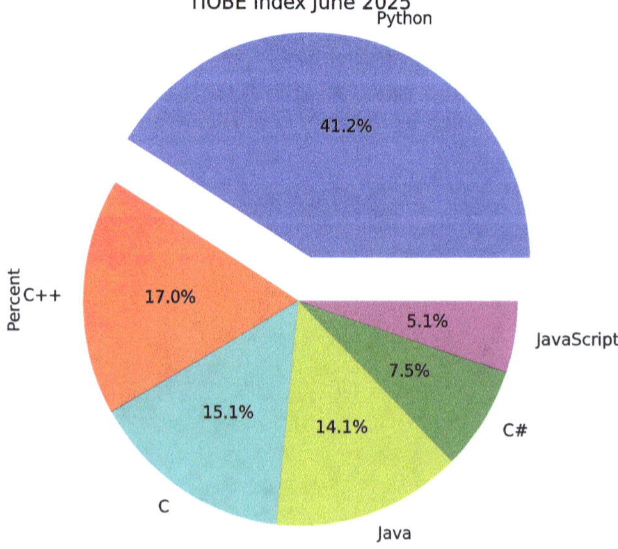

28.5 Area Plot with area

```python
import pandas as pd

path = 'data1/'
sales = pd.read_csv(path + "sales.csv",
                    index_col=0)
print(sales)
# calculate cumulative sums:
sales['ProductA'] = sales['ProductA'].cumsum()
sales['ProductB'] = sales['ProductB'].cumsum()
sales['ProductC'] = sales['ProductC'].cumsum()
sales['ProductD'] = sales['ProductD'].cumsum()

sales.plot(kind='area',
           xticks=range(len(sales.index)))
```

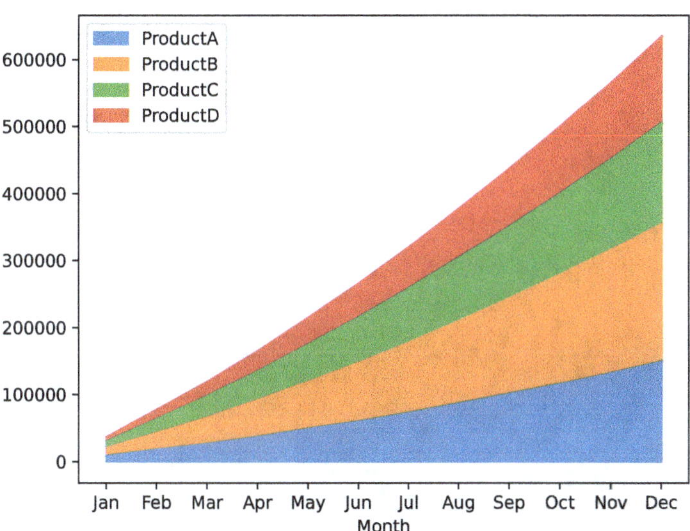

28.6 Exercises

Exercise 1

(Solution: 33.21, Solution 1)

The file `data1/exchange_rates_eu_us_tr_ch.csv` is a CSV file containing the average yearly exchange rates of the Euro, Swiss Franc, and Turkish Lira against the US Dollar since 2000.

- Plot the trend without the Turkish Lira.
- Plot in a separate chart the trend of the Dollar versus the Turkish Lira.

Exercise 2

(Solution: 33.21, Solution 2)

The file `data1/drinks_january2023.csv` is a CSV file containing the number of cups of tea and coffee consumed in one month. Aggregate these by person and generate a grouped bar plot.

29

Time and Date

29.1 Introduction

No matter the programming language, as soon as it comes to calendar dates and times, problems arise. Problems with processing calendar data are due in part to the many variants used in written language, e.g. June 14, 2025, Jun. 14, 2025, 14.06.2025, 14/06/2025, 06/14/2025, and so on. A format many probably did not miss is `2018-12-24`. This is actually the officially used format. The DIN 5008 standard, which defines writing and formatting rules for text processing, states that for numeric date notation only the international date format according to ISO 8601 is permitted, namely `YYYY-MM-DD`.[1]

Figure 29.1 Pandas playing with clocks.

Python provides extensive functionality for working with date and time data. The standard libraries include the following modules:

- `time`
- `calendar`
- `datetime`

---

[1] Standards Committee for Information Technology and Applications (NIA), Working Committee NA 043-03-01 AA "Text Processing"

These modules contain classes for handling both simple and complex time and date information.

The `datetime` class in particular plays a central role when working with time series in Pandas.

29.2 Python Standard Modules for Time Data

The most important Python modules for working with date and time values are `time`, `calendar`, and `datetime`.

The `datetime` module provides a variety of classes, methods, and functions for working with dates, times, and time intervals. The most important classes are:

- The `date` class represents dates in the range of years 1 to 9999.
- An instance of the `datetime` class combines date and time in one object.
- The `time` class represents time objects without a date component.
- The `timedelta` class is used to calculate differences between two time or date values.
- The `tzinfo` class allows definition of time zone information for time and date objects.

We start with the `date` object.

29.2.1 The date Class

```python
from datetime import date

x = date(1993, 12, 14)
print(x)
```

The execution leads to this output:

```
1993-12-14
```

We can instantiate date objects between January 1, 0001 and December 31, 9999. The attributes `min` and `max` can be used to check this:

```python
from datetime import date

print(date.min)
print(date.max)
```

The corresponding output can be seen here:

```
0001-01-01
9999-12-31
```

We can apply various methods to the date object. The proleptic Gregorian ordinal is returned by the toordinal method. The proleptic Gregorian calendar extends the Gregorian calendar backwards beyond its introduction in 1582. In this ordinal numbering, day 1 corresponds to January 1 of the year 1:

```
x = date(1, 1, 1)   # January 1, 1
print(x.toordinal())
x = date(1, 1, 2)   # January 2, 1
print(x.toordinal())
x = date(2020, 5, 1)   # May 1, 2020
print(x)
print(x.toordinal())
```

The execution leads to this output:

```
1
2
2020-05-01
737546
```

From an ordinal, the date can be recalculated using the class method fromordinal:

```
print(date.fromordinal(726952))
```

This is the result of the code:

```
1991-04-30
```

If you want to know the weekday of a given date, this can be calculated with the weekday method. weekday returns numbers between 0 (Monday) and 6 (Sunday):

```
print(x.weekday())
```

The corresponding output can be seen here:

```
4
```

```
print(date.today())
```

The execution leads to this output:

```
2026-02-01
```

Via attributes, we can access the day, month, and year of a date object:

```python
print(x.day)
print(x.month)
print(x.year)
```

The code produces the following result:

```
1
5
2020
```

29.2.2 The time Class

The time class is organized in the same way as the date class.

```python
from datetime import time

t = time(15, 6, 23)
print(t)
```

We obtain this output:

```
15:06:23
```

The possible times are between:

```python
print(time.min)
print(time.max)
```

The result appears as follows:

```
00:00:00
23:59:59.999999
```

Accessing hour, minute, and second:

```python
print(t.hour, t.minute, t.second)
```

The resulting output is:

```
15 6 23
```

Each component of a time object can be changed using replace():

```python
t = t.replace(hour=11, minute=59)
print(t)
```

The result follows:

```
11:59:23
```

We can generate a date string in C-style, corresponding to the `ctime` function in C:

```
print(x.ctime())
```

This follows from the code:

```
Fri May  1 00:00:00 2020
```

29.3 The datetime Class

The `datetime` module provides us with functions and methods for manipulating date and time objects. It also provides functionality for arithmetic operations on date and time objects, such as addition and subtraction. Another focus of the implementation is on extracting attributes.

There are two types of date and time objects:

- naive
- aware

If a time object is "naive," it does not contain information for comparison or localization with respect to other date or time objects. The semantics of whether the "naive" object corresponds to a particular time zone (such as UTC, local time, etc.) are embedded in the program's logic.

On the other hand, an "aware" object has information about the time zone. Thus it can be localized relative to other "aware" objects.

How can one determine if a `datetime` object t is "aware"?

t is "aware" if `t.tzinfo` is not None and `t.tzinfo.utcoffset(t)` is not None. Both conditions must be satisfied.

Conversely, the object t is "naive" if `t.tzinfo` or `t.tzinfo.utcoffset(t)` is None.

Let us create a `datetime` object:

```
from datetime import datetime
t = datetime(2017, 4, 19, 16, 31, 0)
print(t)
```

Executing the code yields:

```
2017-04-19 16:31:00
```

t is "naive," because the following expression evaluates to True:

```python
print(t.tzinfo is None)
```

We obtain this output:

```
True
```

We create an "aware" datetime object of the current date. For this we need the pytz module. pytz is a module that provides the "Olson time zone database" in Python. The Olson time zones are almost completely supported by this module.

```python
from datetime import datetime
import pytz
t = datetime.now(pytz.utc)
```

We see that both t.tzinfo and t.tzinfo.utcoffset(t) are not None, and thus t is an "aware" object:

```python
print(t.tzinfo, t.tzinfo.utcoffset(t))
```

Here is the result of the code:

```
UTC 0:00:00
```

```python
from datetime import datetime, timedelta as delta
ndays = 15
start = datetime(1991, 4, 30)
dates = [start - delta(days=x) for x in range(0, ndays)]
print(dates)
```

The script returns:

```
[datetime.datetime(1991, 4, 30, 0, 0), datetime.datetime(1991, 4, 29, 0,
↪ 0), datetime.datetime(1991, 4, 28, 0, 0), datetime.datetime(1991, 4,
↪ 27, 0, 0), datetime.datetime(1991, 4, 26, 0, 0), datetime.datetime
↪ (1991, 4, 25, 0, 0), datetime.datetime(1991, 4, 24, 0, 0), datetime.
↪ datetime(1991, 4, 23, 0, 0), datetime.datetime(1991, 4, 22, 0, 0),
↪ datetime.datetime(1991, 4, 21, 0, 0), datetime.datetime(1991, 4, 20,
↪ 0, 0), datetime.datetime(1991, 4, 19, 0, 0), datetime.datetime(1991,
↪ 4, 18, 0, 0), datetime.datetime(1991, 4, 17, 0, 0), datetime.datetime
↪ (1991, 4, 16, 0, 0)]
```

29.4 Difference Between Times

Let's see what happens when we subtract `datetime` objects:

```python
from datetime import datetime

delta = datetime(1993, 12, 14) - datetime(1991, 4, 30)
print(delta, type(delta))
```

Output:

```
959 days, 0:00:00 <class 'datetime.timedelta'>
```

The result of subtracting two `datetime` objects is a `timedelta` object. With the at-tribute days, we can read out the difference in days:

```python
print(delta.days)
```

Output:

```
959
```

```python
t1 = datetime(2017, 1, 31, 14, 17)
t2 = datetime(2015, 12, 15, 16, 59)
delta = t1 - t2
print(delta.days, delta.seconds)
```

Executing the code yields:

```
412 76680
```

It is possible to subtract or add a `timedelta` object (in days) from another `datetime` object to calculate a new `datetime` object:

```python
from datetime import datetime, timedelta
d1 = datetime(1991, 4, 30)
d2 = d1 + timedelta(10)
print(d2)
print(d2 - d1)

d3 = d1 - timedelta(100)
print(d3)
d4 = d1 - 2 * timedelta(50)
print(d4)
```

This is the result of the code:

```
1991-05-10 00:00:00
10 days, 0:00:00
1991-01-20 00:00:00
1991-01-20 00:00:00
```

Similarly, `timedelta` objects can also be added to or subtracted from `datetime` objects in days and minutes:

```python
from datetime import datetime, timedelta
d1 = datetime(1991, 4, 30)
d2 = d1 + timedelta(10, 100)
print(d2)
print(d2 - d1)
```

This is the result of the code:

```
1991-05-10 00:01:40
10 days, 0:01:40
```

29.4.1 Converting datetime Objects to Strings

The simplest way to represent a `datetime` object as a string is the `str` method.

```python
s = str(d1)
print(s)
```

The script returns:

```
1991-04-30 00:00:00
```

29.4.2 Conversion with strftime

The method call `datetime.strftime(format)` returns a string representing the time and date, but according to an explicitly defined format:

```python
print(d1.strftime('%Y-%m-%d'))
print("Weekday: " + d1.strftime('%a'))
print("Weekday written out: " + d1.strftime('%A'))

# Weekday as a decimal number, 0 corresponds to Sunday
# and 6 corresponds to Saturday
print("Weekday as decimal: " + d1.strftime('%w'))
```

The result follows:

```
1991-04-30
Weekday: Di
Weekday written out: Dienstag
Weekday as decimal: 2
```

Formatting months:

```python
# Day of month as decimal with leading zero.
# 01, 02, ..., 31
print(d1.strftime('%d'))

# Month as locale's abbreviated name
# Jan, Feb, ..., Dec (en_US);
# Jan, Feb, ..., Dez (de_DE)
print(d1.strftime('%b'))

# Full month name (locale-dependent)
# January, February, ..., December (en_US);
# Januar, Februar, ..., Dezember (de_DE)
print(d1.strftime('%B'))

# Month as decimal number with leading zero.
# 01, 02, ..., 12
print(d1.strftime('%m'))
```

This follows from the code:

```
30
Apr
April
04
```

29.5 Output in Local Language

We have already seen that date output was in English. The following shows a date in
the way most common in the United Kingdom:

```python
from datetime import datetime, timedelta
d1 = datetime(1993, 12, 14)

print(d1.strftime('%d %B %Y'))
```

```python
print("Numbers only:")
print(d1.strftime('%d/%m/%Y'))
print("US style:")
print(d1.strftime('%m/%d/%Y'))

print(f"It was a {d1.strftime('%A'):s}")
```

The result is:

```
14 Dezember 1993
Numbers only:
14/12/1993
US style:
12/14/1993
It was a Dienstag
```

A frequently asked question is how to produce this output in the local language. First, it is important to import the `locale` module:

```python
from datetime import datetime, timedelta
import locale

# Switch to German:
locale.setlocale(locale.LC_ALL, 'de_DE.utf8')
d1 = datetime(1993, 12, 14)

print(d1.strftime('%d. %B %Y'))

print("Numbers only:")
print(d1.strftime('%d.%m.%Y'))

print(f"On {d1.strftime('%d.%m.%Y'):s} it was a {d1.strftime('%A'):s}")
```

This follows from the code:

```
14. Dezember 1993
Numbers only:
14.12.1993
On 14.12.1993 it was a Dienstag
```

Note:

The locale-specific output of the examples above only works if `de_DE.utf8` and `fr_FR.utf8` are installed on the operating system. On Ubuntu, these can be installed as follows:

```
sudo locale-gen fr_FR.UTF-8
```

and

```
sudo locale-gen de_DE.UTF-8
```

29.6 Creating datetime Objects from Strings

We can use `strptime` to create new `datetime` objects from strings that contain date and time. The arguments of `strptime` are the string to be parsed and the format specification:

```python
from datetime import datetime
t = datetime.strptime("30 12 1999", "%d %m %Y")
print(t)
```

The following result is generated:

```
1999-12-30 00:00:00
```

```python
dt = "2007-03-04T21:08:12"
dt = datetime.strptime(dt, '%Y-%m-%dT%H:%M:%S')
print(dt)
```

This output is obtained:

```
2007-03-04 21:08:12
```

```python
import locale
locale.setlocale(locale.LC_ALL, 'en_US.UTF-8')

dt = '12/24/1957 4:03:29 AM'
dt = datetime.strptime(dt, '%m/%d/%Y %I:%M:%S %p')
print(dt)
```

Executing the code yields:

```
1957-12-24 04:03:29
```

On a Linux machine we can generate an English date string using the command
`LC_ALL=en_EN.utf8 date`:

```python
dt = 'Wed Apr 12 20:29:53 GMT 2017'
dt = datetime.strptime(dt, '%a %b %d %H:%M:%S %Z %Y')
print(dt)
```

The output shows:

```
2017-04-12 20:29:53
```

Although `datetime.strptime()` is a simple way to parse a date with a known format,
it can be cumbersome to create a new specification for every new date format.

For parsing, the use of the `dateutil.parser` method is preferable:

```python
from dateutil.parser import parse

print(parse('2011-01-03'))
```

The result appears as follows:

```
2011-01-03 00:00:00
```

```python
print(parse('Wed Apr 12 20:29:53 CEST 2017'))
```

The evaluation yields:

```
2017-04-12 20:29:53+02:00
```

30
Time Series

30.1 Introduction

In this chapter we now focus on time series, i.e. the time series functionality of the Pandas module. These are essentially just a special variant of the Series data type, which we have already discussed extensively. This data type can also be used to represent time series. In general, a time series is understood to be a series or sequence of data points that are arranged in chronological order. Typically, the intervals between the values of a time series are equidistant.

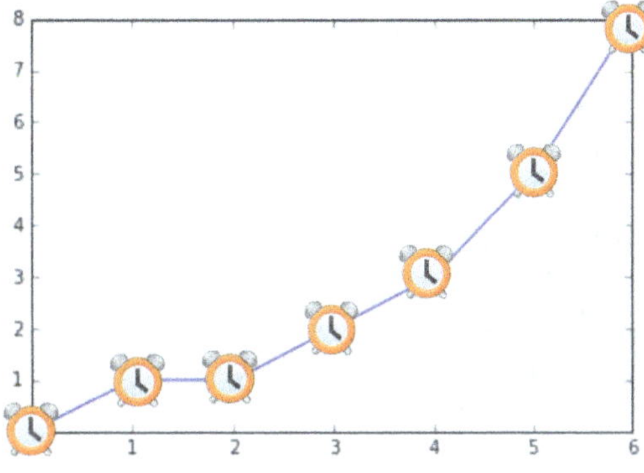

Figure 30.1 Time Series

All measured data that are associated with a specific point in time can be regarded as a time series. Measurements may be irregular, but in most cases they have a fixed frequency or regularity. For example, data may be collected every 5 milliseconds, every 10 seconds, or every hour. Line charts are frequently used to visualize time series.

In this chapter, we introduce the Pandas tools that can be used to process time series. The focus is particularly on working with large time series and modifying them in a targeted manner.

30.2 Time Series and Python

We can define a Pandas Series whose index consists of a sequence of timestamps:

```python
import numpy as np
import pandas as pd
from datetime import datetime, timedelta as delta

ndays = 10
start = datetime(2018, 12, 1)
dates = [start - delta(days=x) for x in range(0, ndays)]

values = [25, 50, 15, 67, 70, 9, 28, 30, 32, 12]

ts = pd.Series(values, index=dates)
print(ts)
```

What we obtain is:

```
2018-12-01    25
2018-11-30    50
2018-11-29    15
2018-11-28    67
2018-11-27    70
2018-11-26     9
2018-11-25    28
2018-11-24    30
2018-11-23    32
2018-11-22    12
dtype: int64
```

We determine the type of the time series we just created:

```python
print(type(ts))
```

The execution leads to this output:

```
<class 'pandas.core.series.Series'>
```

What we have created is a time series, because it is based on the Pandas Series object.
What does the index of this time series look like? We can see it here:

```python
print(ts.index)
```

We obtain this output:

```
DatetimeIndex(['2018-12-01', '2018-11-30', '2018-11-29', '2018-11-28',
               '2018-11-27', '2018-11-26', '2018-11-25', '2018-11-24',
               '2018-11-23', '2018-11-22'],
              dtype='datetime64[ns]', freq=None)
```

We create another time series:

```
values2 = [32, 54, 18, 61, 72, 19, 21, 33, 29, 17]


ts2 = pd.Series(values2, index=dates)
```

It is possible to perform arithmetic operations on time series, just as with other Series objects. As an example, we add the two time series created above:

```
print(ts + ts2)
```

The result appears as follows:

```
2018-12-01     57
2018-11-30    104
2018-11-29     33
2018-11-28    128
2018-11-27    142
2018-11-26     28
2018-11-25     49
2018-11-24     63
2018-11-23     61
2018-11-22     29
dtype: int64
```

Arithmetic mean of the two Series objects:

```
print((ts + ts2) / 2)
```

The result is:

```
2018-12-01    28.5
2018-11-30    52.0
2018-11-29    16.5
2018-11-28    64.0
2018-11-27    71.0
2018-11-26    14.0
2018-11-25    24.5
2018-11-24    31.5
2018-11-23    30.5
2018-11-22    14.5
dtype: float64
```

This can also be done with Series objects that have different indices.

```python
import pandas as pd
from datetime import datetime, timedelta as delta

ndays = 10
start = datetime(2018, 6, 1)
dates = [start - delta(days=x) for x in range(0, ndays)]
start2 = datetime(2018, 5, 28)
dates2 = [start2 - delta(days=x) for x in range(0, ndays)]
values = [25, 50, 15, 67, 70, 9, 28, 30, 32, 12]
values2 = [32, 54, 18, 61, 72, 19, 21, 33, 29, 17]
ts = pd.Series(values, index=dates)
ts2 = pd.Series(values2, index=dates2)
print(ts + ts2)
```

Output:

```
2018-05-19      NaN
2018-05-20      NaN
2018-05-21      NaN
2018-05-22      NaN
2018-05-23     31.0
2018-05-24    104.0
2018-05-25     91.0
2018-05-26     46.0
2018-05-27     63.0
2018-05-28    102.0
2018-05-29      NaN
2018-05-30      NaN
2018-05-31      NaN
2018-06-01      NaN
Freq: D, dtype: float64
```

30.3 Creating Date Ranges

The date_range() method from the Pandas module can be used to create a timestamp
index:

```python
import pandas as pd

date_range = pd.date_range('12/24/1970', '01/03/1971')
print(date_range)
```

The evaluation yields:

```
DatetimeIndex(['1970-12-24', '1970-12-25', '1970-12-26',
               '1970-12-27', '1970-12-28', '1970-12-29',
               '1970-12-30', '1970-12-31', '1971-01-01',
               '1971-01-02', '1971-01-03'],
              dtype='datetime64[ns]', freq='D')
```

We passed a start date and an end date to the `date_range` method. It is also possible to specify only a start or only an end date. In that case, however, the number of periods must be specified using the keyword parameter `periods`:

```python
date_range = pd.date_range(start='12/24/1970', periods=7)
print(date_range)
```

Here is the output:

```
DatetimeIndex(['1970-12-24', '1970-12-25', '1970-12-26',
               '1970-12-27', '1970-12-28', '1970-12-29',
               '1970-12-30'],
              dtype='datetime64[ns]', freq='D')
```

```python
date_range = pd.date_range(end='12/24/1970', periods=7)
print(date_range)
```

Here is the result of the code:

```
DatetimeIndex(['1970-12-18', '1970-12-19', '1970-12-20',
               '1970-12-21', '1970-12-22', '1970-12-23',
               '1970-12-24'],
              dtype='datetime64[ns]', freq='D')
```

For the above dates, it is also possible to display the weekdays:

```python
print(date_range.day_of_week)
```

What we obtain is:

```
Index([4, 5, 6, 0, 1, 2, 3], dtype='int32')
```

Here, 0 represents Monday, 1 represents Tuesday, and so on.

It is also possible to create date ranges that include only business days. For this, the keyword parameter `freq` must be set to B:

```python
date_range = pd.date_range('2017-04-07', '2017-04-13', freq="B")
print(date_range)
```

The evaluation yields:

```
DatetimeIndex(['2017-04-07', '2017-04-10', '2017-04-11',
               '2017-04-12', '2017-04-13'],
              dtype='datetime64[ns]', freq='B')
```

In the next example, we generate a date range that contains the month ends between two points in time. We can see that the year 2016 had February 29, because it was a leap year:

```python
date_range = pd.date_range('2016-02-25', '2016-07-02', freq="ME")
print(date_range)
```

Executing the code yields:

```
DatetimeIndex(['2016-02-29', '2016-03-31', '2016-04-30',
               '2016-05-31', '2016-06-30'],
              dtype='datetime64[ns]', freq='ME')
```

In the following case, the string "W-Mon" indicates that the frequency of the date range should be weekly and that the dates should fall on Mondays within the range. The "W" stands for "weekly", and the "Mon" part indicates that the dates should be aligned to Mondays.

```python
dr = pd.date_range('2017-02-05', '2017-04-13', freq="W-Mon")
print(dr)
```

What we obtain is:

```
DatetimeIndex(['2017-02-06', '2017-02-13', '2017-02-20',
               '2017-02-27', '2017-03-06', '2017-03-13',
               '2017-03-20', '2017-03-27', '2017-04-03',
               '2017-04-10'],
              dtype='datetime64[ns]', freq='W-MON')
```

Further abbreviations:

Alias	Description
B	business day frequency
C	custom business day frequency (experimental)
D	calendar day frequency
W	weekly frequency
M	month end frequency
BM	business month end frequency
MS	month start frequency

Alias	Description
BMS	business month start frequency
Q	quarter end frequency
BQ	business quarter end frequency
QS	quarter start frequency
BQS	business quarter start frequency
A	year end frequency
BA	business year end frequency
AS	year start frequency
BAS	business year start frequency
H	hourly frequency
T	minutely frequency
S	secondly frequency
L	milliseconds
U	microseconds

30.4 Date Ranges with Time Components

With the following command, we output the hourly times from March 18 to March 19:

```python
import pandas as pd
date_range = pd.date_range('2023-03-18', '2023-03-19', freq='h')
print(date_range)
```

Here is the result of the code:

```
DatetimeIndex(['2023-03-18 00:00:00',
               '2023-03-18 01:00:00',
               '2023-03-18 02:00:00',
               '2023-03-18 03:00:00',
               '2023-03-18 04:00:00',
               '2023-03-18 05:00:00',
               '2023-03-18 06:00:00',
               '2023-03-18 07:00:00',
               '2023-03-18 08:00:00',
               '2023-03-18 09:00:00',
               '2023-03-18 10:00:00',
               '2023-03-18 11:00:00',
               '2023-03-18 12:00:00',
               '2023-03-18 13:00:00',
               '2023-03-18 14:00:00',
```

```
                    '2023-03-18 15:00:00',
                    '2023-03-18 16:00:00',
                    '2023-03-18 17:00:00',
                    '2023-03-18 18:00:00',
                    '2023-03-18 19:00:00',
                    '2023-03-18 20:00:00',
                    '2023-03-18 21:00:00',
                    '2023-03-18 22:00:00',
                    '2023-03-18 23:00:00',
                    '2023-03-19 00:00:00'],
                  dtype='datetime64[ns]', freq='h')
```

In the following case, we obtain a time series from 11:00 a.m. to 10:30 p.m. at intervals of 90 minutes, starting on the current day:

```python
# Creates a time series on the current date from 11:00 to 22:30
# with a 90-minute interval between timestamps
time_range = pd.date_range("11:00", "22:30", freq="90min")
print(time_range)
```

Result:

```
DatetimeIndex(['2026-02-01 11:00:00',
                '2026-02-01 12:30:00',
                '2026-02-01 14:00:00',
                '2026-02-01 15:30:00',
                '2026-02-01 17:00:00',
                '2026-02-01 18:30:00',
                '2026-02-01 20:00:00',
                '2026-02-01 21:30:00'],
              dtype='datetime64[ns]', freq='90min')
```

30.5 Exercises

Exercise 1

(Solution: 33.22, Solution 1)

How many Wednesdays are there between February 5 and May 17 in 2023?

Exercise 2

(Solution: 33.22, Solution 2)

How many Fridays were there between June 1, 1998 and April 1, 2023 that fell on the thirteenth day of a month?

Part IV

Applications

31
Image Processing Techniques

31.1 Introduction

Photography has never been as easy and inexpensive as it is today. All you need is a mobile phone. That is all that is necessary to take and view a picture. Taking photos is practically free. Just one generation ago, amateur photographers and real artists needed special and often expensive equipment, and the cost per picture was anything but free. We take photos to preserve great moments – pickled memories ready to be opened at will in the future.

Similar to pickling food, we must pay attention to the right "preservatives." Of course, the mobile phone also offers us a wide range of image

Figure 31.1 Charlie Cubism

editing software, but as soon as we want or need to edit a large number of photos, we need other tools. This is where programming and of course Python come in. Python and its modules such as NumPy, SciPy, Matplotlib and other specialized modules provide the optimal functionality to cope with the flood of images.

This chapter does not provide a systematic introduction to image processing, but rather covers selected fundamentals and techniques of image manipulation. The focus is mainly on the modules NumPy, Matplotlib, and SciPy.

31.2 Loading and Displaying Images

The following examples use two image files[1] – `flute_player.png` and `firebird.png`
– which are stored locally in this project directory.

```python
import matplotlib.pyplot as plt
import matplotlib.image as mpimg


image = mpimg.imread("images/flute_player.png")
plt.axis("off")              # Hide axes
plt.imshow(image)
```

In the next example we show the image `firebird.png`, which depicts a firebird rising
from the flames of destruction – against the same background as the previous image.
In addition, we analyze the structure of the image array using `.shape`:

```python
import matplotlib.pyplot as plt
import matplotlib.image as mpimg


firebird = mpimg.imread("images/firebird.png")
rows, cols, channels = firebird.shape
print(f"{rows=}, {cols=}, {channels=}")
print("Color values of some pixels (RGB):")
for row, col in [(50, 50), (100, 150), (200, 300)]:
    print(f"Pixel at ({row}, {col}): {firebird[row, col]}")
```

---

1   Both images are taken from the author's self-conceived music video *Firebird's Return – A Musical Vision
    of Peace After War* (music, video and concept: © Bernd Klein). Available at: *https://www.youtube.com/
    watch?v=S0ap2PfZ5I8*.

```python
print(f'{firebird.dtype=}')
print(f'{type(firebird)=}')
plt.axis("off")
plt.imshow(firebird)
```

The processing yields:

```
rows=1150, cols=2047, channels=4
Color values of some pixels (RGB):
Pixel at (50, 50): [0.16862746 0.1882353  0.16078432 1.        ]
Pixel at (100, 150): [0.16862746 0.19607843 0.16862746 1.        ]
Pixel at (200, 300): [0.18039216 0.21176471 0.16862746 1.        ]
firebird.dtype=dtype('float32')
type(firebird)=<class 'numpy.ndarray'>
```

As the output shows, the image is a three-dimensional NumPy array. The dimensions represent:

- number of rows (image height),
- number of columns (image width), and
- number of color channels (e.g., 3 for RGB or 4 for RGBA).

The color channels contain per-pixel values either in the range 0 - 255 (type `uint8`) or between 0.0 - 1.0 (type `float32`). Matplotlib can display both formats. PNG files with 3 channels are classic RGB images, while a fourth channel (A for Alpha) contains transparency information.

31.3 Histograms of Color Values

For this subsection we use the image `stellisee.png`.

```python
import matplotlib.pyplot as plt

img = plt.imread('images/stellisee.png')
print(img[0]) # values of the first row

plt.axis("off")
plt.imshow(img)
```

The result appears as follows:

```
[[0.20784314 0.6313726  0.88235295]
 [0.20784314 0.6313726  0.88235295]
 [0.20784314 0.6313726  0.88235295]
 ...
 [0.1882353  0.58431375 0.8509804 ]
 [0.1882353  0.58431375 0.8509804 ]
 [0.1882353  0.58431375 0.8509804 ]]
```

The values in `img[0]` show that the image is stored as an array of floating-point numbers (`float32`) in the range `[0, 1]`. This is because `plt.imread` by default loads images as normalized RGB values.

In contrast, `Image.open` from the PIL package provides image data as integers of type `uint8` in the range `[0, 255]`.

To illustrate the structure of the image, we extract a single color channel – in this case the blue channel:

```python
blue_img = img[:, :, 2] # extract blue channel
print(blue_img[0]) # values of the first row

plt.axis("off")
plt.imshow(blue_img)
plt.colorbar()
```

The corresponding output can be seen here:

```
[0.88235295 0.88235295 0.88235295 ... 0.8509804  0.8509804  0.8509804 ]
```

imshow uses the `viridis` colormap by default for 2D data, which displays grayscale values in color. For a classic grayscale representation, you can instead specify `cmap="gray"`.

Sometimes we want to assess or adjust the contrast of an image or of a particular color channel. Histograms are a helpful tool for analyzing the distribution of pixel values, which can support targeted contrast adjustments. The following code produces histograms for each color channel using the function `hist` from `matplotlib.pyplot`:

```python
import matplotlib.pyplot as plt

img = plt.imread('images/stellisee.png')
fig, ax = plt.subplots(1, 3, sharey=True)
colors = ['Red', 'Green', 'Blue']
for i in range(3):
    # extract the i-th color channel:
    channel = img[:, :, i]
    # convert 2D channel to 1D array:
    values = channel.ravel()
    ax[i].hist(values,
               bins=256,
               range=(0.0, 1.0),
               fc='k',
               ec='k')
    ax[i].set_title(colors[i] + ' Values')
```

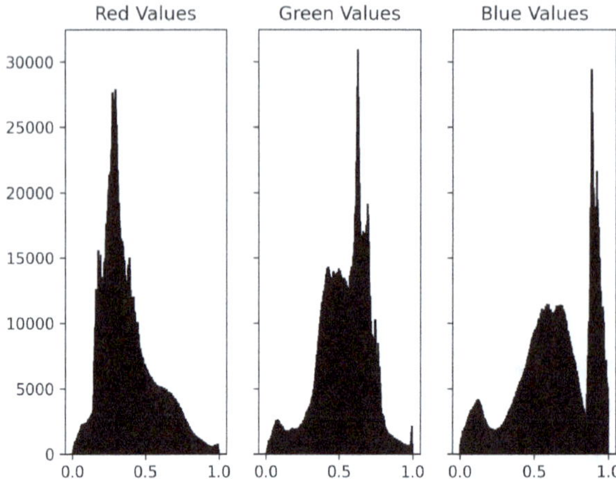

31.4 Image Cropping

Using the slicing operator, a specific section of an image can be extracted. In the following example we crop the Matterhorn from the Stellisee image:

```
stellisee[min_row:max_row, min_col:max_col]
```

This operation returns a view, not a copy, meaning the data is shared with the original array. Changes to the cropped section therefore also affect the original image. To avoid this, you can explicitly create a copy:

```
stellisee[min_row:max_row, min_col:max_col].copy()
```

```
stellisee = plt.imread('images/stellisee.png')
min_row, max_row, min_col, max_col = 100, 300, 700, 1000
matterhorn = stellisee[min_row:max_row, min_col:max_col]
```

We reuse the code above in the next example, where we also display the cropped image section.

31.5 Geometric Transformations

We can apply geometric transformations to images such as reflections and rotations. In the following example we use `np.flipud` to flip the cropped Matterhorn image vertically (i.e., upside down). We then rotate the image by 35 degrees using `ndimage.rotate` from the module `scipy.ndimage`.

However, this rotation introduces a small problem: due to interpolation, pixel values in the result can be slightly greater than 1, although the original image was in the range [0, 1]. To correct this, we use `np.clip` to restrict all pixel values to the valid range [0, 1].

Finally, we show how to rotate the image without changing the original dimensions by setting the parameter `reshape` to `False`. The following code performs all transformations and shows the original image, the vertically flipped version, the rotated image with altered shape, and the rotated image with preserved shape.

```python
import numpy as np
import matplotlib.pyplot as plt
from scipy import ndimage


img = plt.imread('images/stellisee.png')
min_row, max_row, min_col, max_col = 100, 300, 700, 1000
matterhorn = img[min_row: max_row, min_col: max_col]
upside_down = np.flipud(matterhorn.copy())


rotated_matterhorn = ndimage.rotate(matterhorn.copy(), 35)
print(f"{rotated_matterhorn.min()=}")
print(f"{rotated_matterhorn.max()=}")


min_value, max_value = 0, 1
rotated_matterhorn = np.clip(rotated_matterhorn,
                             a_min=min_value,
                             a_max=max_value)
rotated_no_reshape = ndimage.rotate(matterhorn.copy(),
                                    35,  # rotation in degrees
                                    reshape=False)
rotated_no_reshape = np.clip(rotated_no_reshape,
                             a_min=min_value,
                             a_max=max_value)
print(f'{matterhorn.shape=}')
print(f'{upside_down.shape=}')
print(f'{rotated_matterhorn.shape=}')
print(f'{rotated_no_reshape.shape=}')


rows, cols = 2, 2
fig, ax = plt.subplots(rows, cols)
[ax[i, j].axis('off') for i in range(2) for j in range(2)]
ax[0, 0].imshow(matterhorn)
ax[0, 0].set_title('Matterhorn')
```

```
ax[0, 1].imshow(upside_down)
ax[0, 1].set_title('Upside Down')

ax[1, 0].imshow(rotated_matterhorn)
ax[1, 0].set_title('Rotation 35 Degrees')

ax[1, 1].imshow(rotated_no_reshape)
ax[1, 1].set_title('Keep Shape')
fig.tight_layout()
```

This output is obtained:

```
rotated_matterhorn.min()=np.float32(0.0)
rotated_matterhorn.max()=np.float32(1.0428782)
matterhorn.shape=(200, 300, 3)
upside_down.shape=(200, 300, 3)
rotated_matterhorn.shape=(336, 360, 3)
rotated_no_reshape.shape=(200, 300, 3)
```

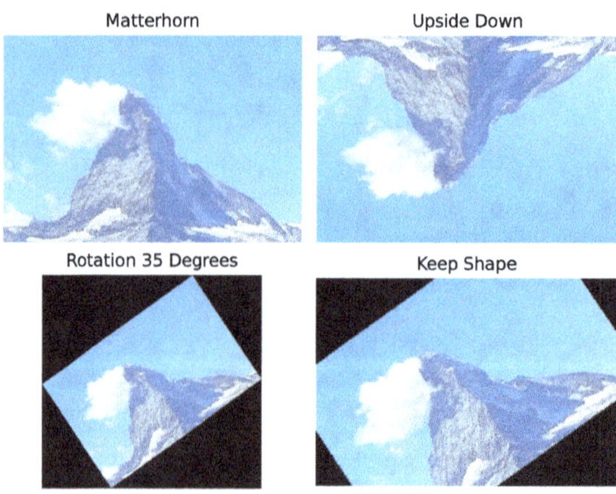

31.6 Filtering

Manual Application of generic_filter

Now we filter images with the function `generic_filter` from the module `scipy.ndimage`. This function makes it possible to apply any function to a local neighborhood of each pixel:

```
generic_filter(input, function, size=None)
```

Here, `input` refers to the array (i.e., the image) to be filtered. `function` is a user-defined or built-in function (e.g., `np.mean`, `np.max`), which is applied to local neighborhoods, and `size` defines the shape of this window.

We demonstrate this with a simple number array:

```python
import numpy as np
from scipy import ndimage

arr = np.array([[11, 12, 13, 14],
                [21, 22, 23, 24],
                [31, 32, 33, 34]], dtype=np.float64)

n, m = 3, 3
result = ndimage.generic_filter(arr, np.mean, size=(n, m))
print(result)
```

The code produces the following result:

```
[[14.66666667 15.33333333 16.33333333 17.        ]
 [21.33333333 22.         23.         23.66666667]
 [28.         28.66666667 29.66666667 30.33333333]]
```

The figure on the right shows how `generic_filter` works in the default boundary mode `reflect`. For better illustration we use integers, but internally floating-point numbers are used. The `reflect` mode mirrors boundary values outward to simulate edge behavior when the filter window extends beyond the border. This helps to avoid artificial edges at the image boundaries during filtering.

The new rows above and below are mirrored in the same way. If we set `size=(3, 3)`, a 3×3 window is centered around each pixel. If no neighboring values are available at the edges, filling is performed according to the chosen mode. To instead fill with a constant value, you can set `mode='constant'` and specify a cval.

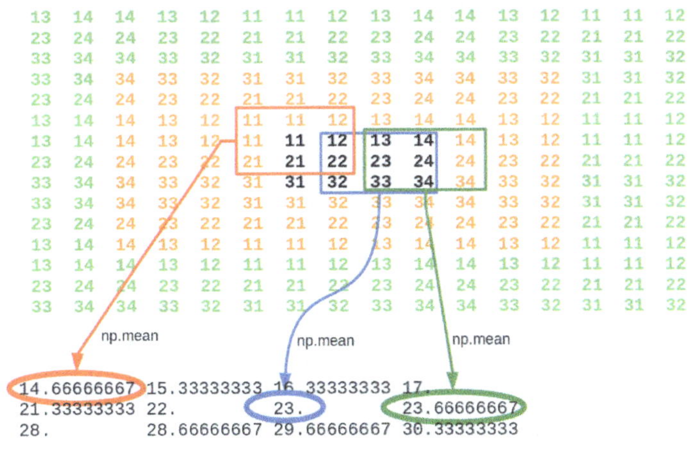

Figure 31.2 `generic_filter` in mode reflect

Manual Replication of generic_filter

To better understand how scipy.ndimage.generic_filter handles image boundaries in reflect mode, we implement this behavior manually in Python. This allows
us to observe how padding and the sliding window behave at the edges of an array.

The function reflect_filter takes a two-dimensional NumPy array and applies a
user-defined function (e.g., np.mean or np.max) to each neighborhood defined by the
window size. The edges are padded by symmetric reflection – corresponding to the
behavior of reflect in SciPy's filter functions.

```python
import numpy as np

def reflect_filter(arr, func, size=(3, 3)):
    """
    Apply a function to a sliding window over an array
    with half-symmetric 'reflect' padding at the edges.

    Parameters:
        arr : 2D NumPy array
        func : function to apply (e.g. np.mean, np.max)
        size : (rows, cols) - filter window size

    Returns:
        result : 2D array with the same shape as the input
    """
    assert arr.ndim == 2, "Only 2D arrays are supported"

    pad_y = size[0] // 2  # vertical padding
    pad_x = size[1] // 2  # horizontal padding

    # Apply symmetric padding
    padded = np.pad(arr, ((pad_y, pad_y),
                          (pad_x, pad_x)),
                        mode='symmetric')
    # Prepare result array
    result = np.empty_like(arr)
    # Slide window over each element
    for i in range(arr.shape[0]):
        for j in range(arr.shape[1]):
            window = padded[i:i+size[0], j:j+size[1]]
            result[i, j] = func(window)

    return result
```

Now we apply our own filter to an example array:

```python
arr = np.array([[11, 12, 13, 14],
                [21, 22, 23, 24],
                [31, 32, 33, 34]], dtype=np.float64)


manual = reflect_filter(arr, np.mean, size=(3, 3))

# For comparison: SciPy implementation
from scipy import ndimage
scipy_result = ndimage.generic_filter(arr,
                                       np.mean,
                                       size=(3, 3),
                                       mode='reflect')

# Print both results and their difference
print("Manual result:\n", manual)
print("SciPy result:\n", scipy_result)
```

This is the result of the code:

```
Manual result:
 [[14.66666667 15.33333333 16.33333333 17.         ]
 [21.33333333 22.          23.          23.66666667]
 [28.          28.66666667 29.66666667 30.33333333]]
SciPy result:
 [[14.66666667 15.33333333 16.33333333 17.         ]
 [21.33333333 22.          23.          23.66666667]
 [28.          28.66666667 29.66666667 30.33333333]]
```

As the output shows, both methods produce identical results. This confirms that our
manual implementation correctly reproduces the behavior of SciPy's `reflect` mode,
which mirrors edge values half-symmetrically.

Explanation of Modes in `generic_filter`

The parameter mode in `generic_filter` determines how the array is extended at the
boundaries. The available options are:

```
'reflect'  -> d c b a | a b c d | d c b a   (half-symmetric)
'constant' -> k k k k | a b c d | k k k k   (fills with "cval")
'nearest'  -> a a a a | a b c d | d d d d   (repeats edge values)
'mirror'   -> d c b   | a b c d | c b a     (fully symmetric)
'wrap'     -> a b c d | a b c d | a b c d   (cyclic/wrap-around)
```

Filtering an Image Section

Now we apply `generic_filter` to the Matterhorn section of our image, using a 3×3×3 mean filter:

```python
import numpy as np
import matplotlib.pyplot as plt
from scipy import ndimage

img = plt.imread('images/stellisee.png')
matterhorn = img[100:300, 700:1000].copy()

filtered_img = ndimage.generic_filter(matterhorn,
                                       np.mean,
                                       size=(3, 3, 3))

plt.imshow(filtered_img)
```

Larger Filters and Other Functions

Now we increase the neighborhood to 7×7 and replace `np.mean` with `np.max`. This change has a much stronger effect: the image appears brighter and coarser, as the maximum pixel values of each neighborhood dominate the result. Such filters are useful for enhancing bright structures and suppressing dark details.

```python
filtered_img = ndimage.generic_filter(matterhorn,
                                       np.max,
                                       size=(7, 7, 3))

plt.imshow(filtered_img)
```

31.7 Lightening and Toning Images

We now travel to the Netherlands, the homeland of Rembrandt, Vincent van Gogh, Hieronymus Bosch, and many other great artists. In the following example, we use a photograph of traditional Dutch windmills.[2]

In this section, we also revisit a concept from classical painting: the artistic technique of **lightening** or **toning** colors to influence mood, clarity, or emphasis.

```python
import matplotlib.pyplot as plt
import matplotlib.image as mpimg

windmills = mpimg.imread('images/windmills.png')
plt.axis("off")
plt.imshow(windmills)
```

Lightening the Image

We now want to **lighten** the image, which means mixing the original colors with white. This increases overall brightness and can improve visibility or create a lighter mood.

To do this, we define a Python function called `brighten`, which takes two parameters: the image and a percentage value. If `percent` is set to 0, the image remains unchanged. A value of 1 produces a completely white image. This works by moving every pixel value toward 1 (white), effectively blending the image with white.

```python
import numpy as np
import matplotlib.pyplot as plt
import matplotlib.image as mpimg
```

---

[2]　The photograph was taken by the author in Kinderdijk, a village in the Netherlands about 15 km east of Rotterdam and 50 km from The Hague. Kinderdijk has been a UNESCO World Heritage Site since 1997.

```python
def brighten(imag, percent):
    """

    imag: image to be brightened
    percent: value between 0 (no change)
             and 1 (completely white)
    """

    brightened_imag = imag + (np.ones(imag.shape) - imag) * percent
    return brightened_imag

windmills = mpimg.imread('images/windmills.png')
brightened_windmills = brighten(windmills, 0.8)
plt.axis("off")
plt.imshow(brightened_windmills)
```

Darkening Images by Scaling Pixel Values

In painting, a color is darkened by mixing it with black. In digital image processing, we achieve a similar effect by multiplying all pixel values by a factor between 0 and 1. A factor of 1 leaves the image unchanged, while a factor of 0 produces a completely black image.

For demonstration we define a function darken. It takes an image and a percentage value that determines how much the image is darkened:

```python
import matplotlib.pyplot as plt
import matplotlib.image as mpimg

def darken(imag, percent):
    """

    imag: the image to darken
    percent: a value between 0 (no change)
             and 1 (completely black)
    """

    darkened_imag = imag * (1 - percent)
    return darkened_imag
```

```python
windmills = mpimg.imread('images/windmills.png')
darkened_windmills = darken(windmills, 0.4)
plt.axis("off")
plt.imshow(darkened_windmills)
```

Applying a Horizontal Gradient

We define a function `horizontal_gradient` to generate a smooth brightness gradient across the image. This function produces a horizontal gradient that we can multiply with the image. If `reverse=False` (default), the image gradually becomes brighter from left to right. With `reverse=True` it becomes darker instead.

```python
import numpy as np
import matplotlib.pyplot as plt
import matplotlib.image as mpimg


def horizontal_gradient(image, reverse=False):
    """
    Creates a horizontal gradient for RGB images.
    reverse=False: dark to bright (left to right)
    reverse=True: bright to dark
    """
    width = image.shape[1]
    ramp = np.linspace(0, 1, width) if not reverse else np.linspace(1, 0,
        width)
    return np.dstack((ramp, ramp, ramp))  # Shape: (1, width, 3)


windmills = mpimg.imread('images/windmills.png')[:, :, :3]  # remove alpha
gradient = horizontal_gradient(windmills, reverse=False)
result = windmills * gradient
plt.axis("off")
plt.imshow(result)
```

Now we reverse the gradient direction. The image then becomes darker from left to right:

```python
horizontal_rev = horizontal_gradient(windmills, reverse=True)
```

Applying a Vertical Gradient

We now write a function `vertical_gradient` to create a vertical brightness gradient. If `reverse=False` (default), the image becomes darker from top to bottom. If `True`, the opposite happens.

```python
import numpy as np
import matplotlib.pyplot as plt
import matplotlib.image as mpimg


def vertical_gradient(image, reverse=False):
    """
    Creates a vertical gradient for RGB images.
    reverse=False: bright to dark (top to bottom)
    reverse=True: dark to bright
    """
    height = image.shape[0]
    ramp = np.linspace(1, 0, height) if not reverse else np.linspace(0, 1,
        height)
    ramp = ramp[:, np.newaxis]  # column vector
    gradient = np.dstack([ramp] * 3)  # Shape: (height, 1, 3)
    return gradient
```

```python
windmills = mpimg.imread('images/windmills.png')[:, :, :3]
v_gradient = vertical_gradient(windmills)
result = windmills * v_gradient
plt.axis("off")
plt.imshow(result)
```

Now we test the function with `reverse=True` to invert the gradient:

```python
vertical_brush = vertical_gradient(windmills, reverse=True)
```

Selective Channel Manipulation

So far we have modified all three color channels equally. Now we want to manipulate
the channels of an image separately. For demonstration we use a grayscale image of
Charlie Chaplin:

```python
import matplotlib.pyplot as plt
import matplotlib.image as mpimg

charlie = mpimg.imread('images/Chaplin.png')
plt.gray()
plt.imshow(charlie)
```

It is a grayscale image, as the following pixel values show:

```python
print(charlie[468:470, 275:280])
```

After execution we get:

```
[[0.4392157  0.29803923 0.28627452 0.32156864 0.34509805]
 [0.5529412  0.3882353  0.30980393 0.30980393 0.33333334]]
```

To apply color effects, we create a pseudo-color image by stacking three copies with
np.dstack. Before stacking, we scale each copy differently – for red, green, and blue:

```python
import numpy as np
R = charlie * 0.1
G = charlie * 0.9
B = charlie * 0.5
colored = np.dstack((R, G, B))
plt.imshow(colored)
```

Alternatively, we could have used `np.stack` to replicate the grayscale image across all three channels:

```
colored = np.stack((charlie,) * 3, axis=2)
```

Then we multiply the result directly with a vector `[0.1, 0.9, 0.5]`, which is applied to all pixels:

```python
import numpy as np
colored = np.stack((charlie,) * 3, axis=2)
colored *= [0.1, 0.9, 0.5]
plt.imshow(colored)
```

Experiments with Color Mapping

We now conduct a small experiment in which we apply different color mappings to a grayscale image of Charlie Chaplin. In the first part, we multiply the RGB channels by random factors to generate pseudo-colors:

```python
import numpy as np
import matplotlib.pyplot as plt
import matplotlib.image as mpimg

charlie = mpimg.imread('images/Chaplin.png')
colored = np.dstack((charlie, charlie, charlie))  # grayscale to RGB

X = [(1, (1, 0.0, 0.3)),
     (2, (0.5, 0.4, 0)),
     (3, (0, 1, 0.3)),
     (4, (0, 0.0, 1)),
     ((5, 8), (0, 0.3, 1)),
```

```
        (6, (1, 0, 1)),
        (7, (0.0, 1, 0.1)),
        (9, (0, 0.5, 0.5)),
        (10, (0, 0.5, 1)),
        (11, (0.2, 0.6, 0)),
        (12, (0.3, 1, 1))]

fig = plt.figure(figsize=(6, 5))
nrows, ncols = 4, 3

for plot_number, factor in X:
    sub = fig.add_subplot(nrows, ncols, plot_number)
    sub.set_xticks([])
    sub.set_yticks([])
    new_img = colored * np.random.random((3,))
    sub.imshow(new_img)
```

In the second part, we apply standard Matplotlib colormaps to the grayscale image.
Each subimage uses a different color scale from the `plt.cm.datad` directory:

```
import numpy as np
import matplotlib.pyplot as plt
import matplotlib.image as mpimg

charlie = mpimg.imread('images/Chaplin.png')
cmaps = set(plt.cm.datad.keys())
```

```python
X = [1, 2, 3, 4, (5, 8), 6, 7, 9, 10, 11, 12]
fig = plt.figure()
nrows, ncols = 4, 3

for plot_number in X:
    sub = fig.add_subplot(nrows, ncols, plot_number)
    sub.set_xticks([])
    sub.set_yticks([])
    sub.imshow(charlie, cmap=cmaps.pop())
```

31.8 Tiling

The function np.tile, which we will use below, is best explained with the following diagram:

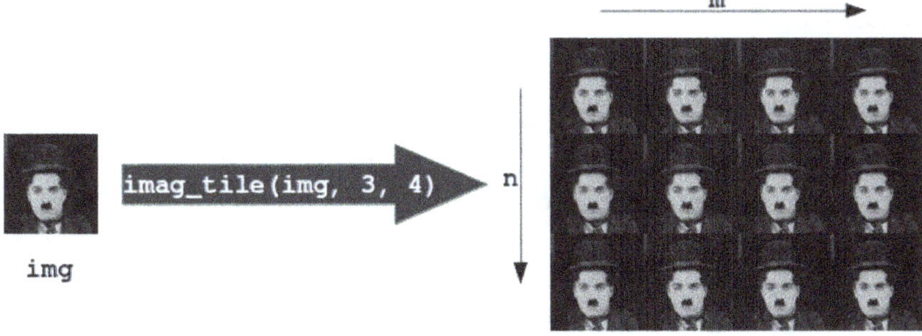

The function call `np.tile(img, (n, m, 1))` creates a tiled image by repeating the image "img" as follows:

- *m* times horizontally, then the resulting image row is repeated *n* times vertically. The third value 1 refers to the color dimension.

In the following code we use an image with four decoration elements:

```python
import matplotlib.pyplot as plt
import matplotlib.image as mpimg
import numpy as np

basic_pattern = mpimg.imread('images/decorators_b2.png')
decorators_img = np.tile(basic_pattern, (3, 4, 1))
plt.axis("off")
plt.imshow(decorators_img)
```

31.9 Watermarking with `np.where`

A watermark is a feature embedded in a medium – mostly in images or documents – that traditionally serves to mark authorship, control distribution, or increase forgery protection. This technique is known from paper documents such as banknotes or official certificates, but also from the digital world, e.g. stock photos overlaid with semi-transparent logos.

In the examples shown here, however, the watermark is not primarily used to prevent unauthorized use but as a design element. The overlay of symbols – such as an "@" sign or a cello silhouette – creates visual effects that aesthetically alter the image without completely covering it. Nevertheless, with small adjustments, the shown techniques can be extended toward protective applications: for example, permanent but subtle logo overlays or the insertion of invisible watermarks that can only be detected computationally. Thus, the original function of the watermark – protection and traceability – is only one step away from the creative use pursued here.

Now we load the symbol for the watermark – an image with an at-sign ('@'):

To combine both images pixel by pixel, we adjust the shape of the at-image to the decorators image:

```python
at_img = mpimg.imread('images/at_sign.png')
# Adjust shape to the decorators image
at_img = at_img[:decorators_img.shape[0],
                :decorators_img.shape[1]]
```

Now we combine all three elements:

1. the original image,

2. its darkened version, and

3. the shape of the watermark.

For this we use np.where:

- In regions where the watermark is bright (above a threshold), we keep the original image.
- Otherwise, we show the darkened version.

```
img_deco_at = np.where(at_img > [0.1, 0.1, 0.1],
                       decorators_img,
                       darkened_img)
```

```
plt.axis("off")
plt.imshow(img_deco_at)
```

31.10 Another Example of Watermarking with np.where

As a second example of the previously introduced watermarking technique, we combine two images: a color photo of a dancing couple (dancers.png) and a grayscale silhouette of a cello (cello_bw.png). The following figure shows both source images side by side:

dancers.png – Dancing couple

Cello silhouette

First we load and inspect the shapes of the two images:

```python
import matplotlib.image as mpimg
import matplotlib.pyplot as plt
import numpy as np

cello = mpimg.imread("images/cello_bw.png")
dancers = mpimg.imread("images/dancers.png")

print(f"{cello.shape=}")
print(f"{dancers.shape=}")
```

The resulting output is:

```
cello.shape=(1536, 1024, 3)
dancers.shape=(1024, 1536, 3)
```

Since the cello image has a shape of (1536, 1024, 3), this corresponds to a height
of 1536 and a width of 1024 pixels. To adapt it to the format of the dancers image, we
transpose the first two axes – height and width – changing the shape to (1024, 1536,
3). The color information (RGB) remains unchanged.

```python
cello_transposed = np.transpose(cello, (1, 0, 2))
dancers_tinted = dancers * 0.5   # darkened background
watermarked = np.where(cello_transposed > (0.2, 0.2, 0.2),
                       dancers,
                       dancers_tinted)
plt.axis("off")
plt.imshow(watermarked)
```

Because the watermark covers the central area of the image, we now create a subtler and visually more appealing version. For this we shrink the cello and place it upright in the lower right corner of the image:

```python
from scipy.ndimage import zoom

# Scale cello image proportionally to target height
target_height = 400
height, width, colors = cello.shape
scaling_factor = target_height / height
resized_cello = zoom(cello,
                     (scaling_factor, scaling_factor, 1),
                     order=1)  # bilinear interpolation

# Create empty mask with light background
cello_mask = np.ones(dancers.shape, dtype=np.float32) * [0.9176, 0.9176,
    0.9098]

# Insert resized cello in bottom right corner
cw, ch, _ = resized_cello.shape
mw, mh, _ = cello_mask.shape
cello_mask[mw - cw:, mh - ch:] = resized_cello

# Apply watermark by conditional combination
watermarked = np.where(cello_mask > (0.2, 0.2, 0.2),
                       dancers,
                       dancers_tinted)
plt.axis("off")
plt.imshow(watermarked)
```

31.11 Exercises

Exercise 1

(Solution: 33.23, Solution 1)

In the `images` directory you will find the images `weg_und_weide.png`, `ostsee.png` and `regiestuhl.png`. Create a new image where, whenever a pixel in `regiestuhl.png` is black or dark gray, the corresponding pixel from `ostsee.png` is used, otherwise the corresponding pixel from `weg_und_weide.png`.

Exercise 2

(Solution: 33.23, Solution 2)

In the `images` directory there is a picture `bench.jpg` with a bench in a green meadow.[3]

- Cut out the bench.
- Create a new image in which the bench is painted over with a green area.
- Create another image in which the image is mirrored horizontally.

```python
import matplotlib.pyplot as plt
img = plt.imread('images/bench.jpg')
#plt.axis("off")
plt.imshow(img)
```

---

3   The bench is located in Singen at the Hohentwiel, the author's residence

32
Financial Management with Pandas

In this chapter, we won't introduce new concepts; instead, we will practice what we have already learned by working through two practical and engaging case studies. The chapter title – Financial Management – might sound a bit grand. In reality, however, it is "just" about the implementation of two simple yet very important use cases:

- budget book
- Income and expenditure statement

Figure 32.1 Cash flow

Both examples deal with the topic of money management – in the first case in a private context, in the second in a business context (including VAT). A common feature is that the underlying data comes from files, which are read and processed with Pandas.

32.1 Budget Book

The first example deals with simple expense and income tables for private use. Some say that if you want to manage money successfully, you need to track income and expenses precisely. Monitoring cash flow is important to better understand your financial situation. You need to know exactly how much comes in and how much goes out. Typically, a budget book is used, in which all income and expenses are recorded. This article does not aim to convince anyone of the necessity of doing this. Rather, the main focus is on the possibilities Python and Pandas offer for programming the necessary tools. We will demonstrate methods to analyze a budget book.

32.1.1 Budget Book with CSV File

In this subsection, we show how personal income and expenses can be analyzed with Python and Pandas – assuming the data is stored in a CSV file. In the next section, we will then look at a more extensive example tailored to the needs of small businesses.

CSV files have proven to be a simple and effective format for data storage – especially in combination with Python and Pandas. They offer several practical advantages:

- They can be easily opened and edited with common spreadsheet programs such as Excel or LibreOffice.

- As a text-based format, they are easy to create, human-readable, and can be version-controlled with tools such as Git.

- CSV files can be read directly and efficiently with Python – particularly conveniently with the Pandas library (see Chapter 22, "File Processing").

To analyze the data of our fictional budget book, we first need to read it from the CSV file. With the Pandas library, this is particularly easy. The following code reads the file `budget_book.csv` and outputs the contents as a DataFrame:

```python
import pandas as pd
transactions = pd.read_csv("budget_book.csv",
                index_col="Date")


print(transactions)
```

The result is:

```
                 Description    Category   Expenses    Income
Date
2025-08-01      Frank Salary      Income       0.00   5020.00
2025-08-02      Laura Salary      Income       0.00   5095.25
2025-08-03      Supermarket         Food     145.35      0.00
2025-08-04              Rent         Rent    1290.00      0.00
2025-08-05       Electricity    Utilities     88.76      0.00
2025-08-06             Water    Utilities     62.10      0.00
2025-08-07         Sarah Gym       Health     39.00      0.00
2025-08-08      Loan Payment         Loan    1287.43      0.00
2025-08-09            Cinema      Culture     28.00      0.00
2025-08-12    Frank Side Job       Income      0.00    720.00
2025-08-15    Home Insurance    Insurance    170.25      0.00
2025-08-20       Supermarket         Food     167.89      0.00
2025-08-25        Restaurant       Dining     112.40      0.00
2025-09-01      Frank Salary       Income      0.00   5020.00
2025-09-02      Laura Salary       Income      0.00   5095.25
2025-09-03       Supermarket         Food     151.60      0.00
2025-09-04              Rent         Rent    1290.00      0.00
```

2025-09-05	Electricity	Utilities	90.12	0.00
2025-09-06	Sarah Gym	Health	49.00	0.00
2025-09-08	Loan Payment	Loan	1287.43	0.00
2025-09-09	Streaming	Leisure	14.99	0.00
2025-09-10	Health Insurance	Insurance	340.00	0.00
2025-09-12	Laura Bonus	Income	0.00	500.00
2025-09-15	Theater	Culture	72.00	0.00
2025-09-18	Car Insurance	Insurance	285.00	0.00
2025-09-20	Supermarket	Food	162.40	0.00
2025-09-22	Tennis Club	Leisure	45.00	0.00
2025-09-25	Pizzeria	Dining	57.00	0.00
2025-10-01	Frank Salary	Income	0.00	5020.00
2025-10-02	Laura Salary	Income	0.00	5095.25
2025-10-03	Supermarket	Food	139.50	0.00
2025-10-03	Cinema	Culture	28.00	0.00
2025-10-04	Rent	Rent	1290.00	0.00
2025-10-05	Electricity	Utilities	92.03	0.00
2025-10-05	Liability Insurance	Insurance	48.60	0.00
2025-10-06	Water	Utilities	63.50	0.00
2025-10-07	Sarah Gym	Health	49.00	0.00
2025-10-08	Loan Payment	Loan	1287.43	0.00
2025-10-10	Vacation	Travel	850.00	0.00
2025-10-12	Concert Tickets	Leisure	120.00	0.00
2025-10-15	Supermarket	Food	177.70	0.00
2025-10-20	Furniture	Home	620.00	0.00
2025-10-22	Frank Project	Income	0.00	980.00
2025-10-25	Restaurant	Dining	124.20	0.00

What can we do with the DataFrame generated from the CSV file? Or put differently:
what information are Frank and Laura interested in? Naturally, they want to know
the account balance. They want to know the total income and also the total expenses.
The balances of their expenses and income can be easily calculated by applying the
function sum to the DataFrame transactions[['Expenses', 'Income']] object:

```python
print(transactions[['Expenses', 'Income']].sum())
```

Executing the code yields:

```
Expenses    12125.68
Income      32545.75
dtype: float64
```

What other insights can be gained from the data? For example, Frank and Laura might
want to know what they are spending their money on. An analysis of expenses by
category provides valuable insights. This can be implemented easily with Pandas –
using groupby and sum:

```
columns = ['Category', 'Expenses']
# Expenses without the income:
expenses = transactions[columns][transactions['Expenses'] > 0]
total_expenses = expenses.groupby('Category').sum()
print(total_expenses)
```

This way, they can see at a glance how much they spent on rent, food, or leisure.
The execution leads to this output:

```
               Expenses
Category
Culture          128.00
Dining           293.60
Food             944.44
Health           137.00
Home             620.00
Insurance        843.85
Leisure          179.99
Loan            3862.29
Rent            3870.00
Travel           850.00
Utilities        396.51
```

Income and expenses can also be displayed as bar charts:

```
ax = total_expenses.plot.bar(y="Expenses", rot=90)
```

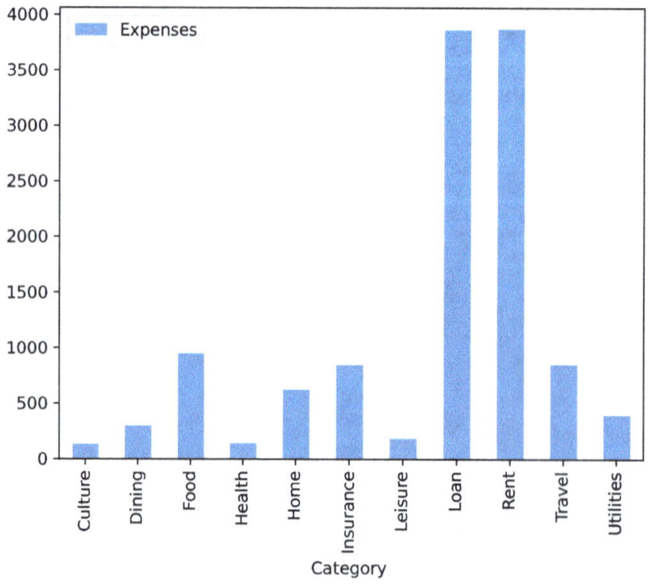

Pie charts are even more suitable in this case:

```
ax = total_expenses.plot.pie(y="Expenses")
ax.legend(loc="upper left", bbox_to_anchor=(1.5, 1))
```

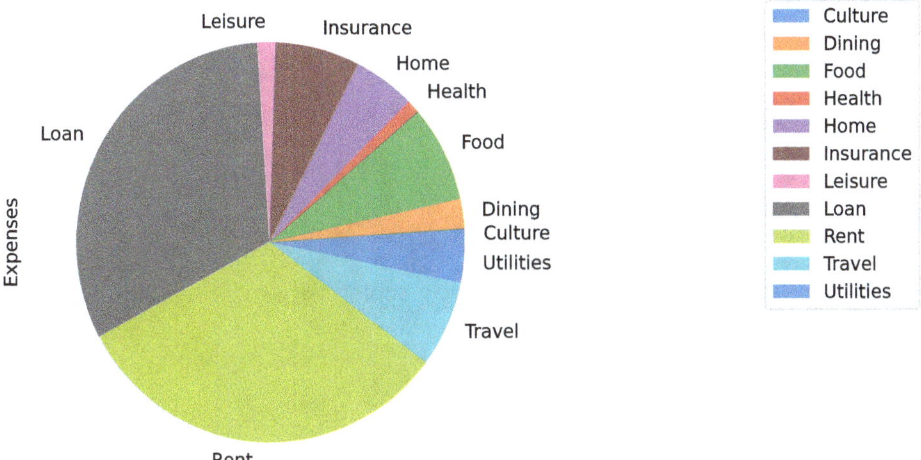

32.1.2 Excel budget book with Chart of Accounts

If you imagine having to constantly type in category names such as "Food" or "Entertainment," it quickly becomes clear that this is both cumbersome and error-prone, as typos can easily creep into the expense and income journal. It is therefore a good idea to use account numbers for the categories. Each account number corresponds to an account description. The account descriptions correspond to what we previously called "categories." We now want to create an Excel file from the data used so far, which contains two sheets. The first sheet contains the mapping of account descriptions (categories) to account numbers. For our example, we want to use the following mappings:

Table 32.1 Account Descriptions and Numbers

Account Description	Account Number
Credit	200
Insurance	201
Food	202
Culture	203
Travel	204

Account Description	Account Number
Health	205
Housing	206
Clothing	207
Communication	208
Entertainment	209
Utilities	210
Rent	211
Leisure	220
Income	400

We can implement this as a Python dictionary mapping categories to account numbers:

```python
category2account = {
    "Credit": "200",
    "Insurance": "201",
    "Food": "202",
    "Culture": "203",
    "Travel": "204",
    "Health": "205",
    "Housing": "206",
    "Clothing": "207",
    "Communication": "208",
    "Entertainment": "209",
    "Utilities": "210",
    "Rent": "211",
    "Leisure": "220",
    "Income": "400"}
```

In the next step, we add the account numbers as a new column in our transactions
DataFrame. To do this, we use the mapping table category2account (from categories
to account numbers) and apply the Pandas method .map to the column Category.

```python
chart_of_accounts = transactions['Category'].map(category2account)
# Insert as column with index 2:
transactions.insert(loc=2, column='Acc', value=chart_of_accounts)
# Delete the 'Category' column:
transactions.drop('Category', axis=1, inplace=True)

print(transactions[:7])
```

The corresponding output can be seen here:

```
             Description  Acc  Expenses   Income
Date
2025-08-01  Frank Salary  400      0.00  5020.00
2025-08-02  Laura Salary  400      0.00  5095.25
2025-08-03   Supermarket  202    145.35     0.00
2025-08-04          Rent  211   1290.00     0.00
2025-08-05   Electricity  210     88.76     0.00
2025-08-06         Water  210     62.10     0.00
2025-08-07     Sarah Gym  205     39.00     0.00
```

We will also save this DataFrame object in our Excel file as a separate sheet. Thus, this Excel file contains two sheets: one named "Journal," in which the entries are listed chronologically, and another mapping account numbers to account descriptions named "Chart of Accounts."

```python
account_numbers = pd.Series(category2account.keys(),
                            index=category2account.values())
account_numbers.name = "Account Description"


with pd.ExcelWriter('budget_book_with_chart_of_accounts.xlsx') as writer:
    account_numbers.to_excel(excel_writer=writer,
                             index_label="Account Number",
                             sheet_name="Chart of Accounts")
    transactions.to_excel(excel_writer=writer,
                          sheet_name="Journal")
```

32.1.3 Analysis of the Excel budget book

Now we have everything in a form where additional entries can be made and evaluations can be carried out. With this, we have created the foundation for an income and expenditure statement. In the next step, we show how to reuse these data in the same way as in the simpler version. First, we read the Excel file:

```python
import pandas as pd


with pd.ExcelFile('budget_book_with_chart_of_accounts.xlsx') as xl:
    print(xl.sheet_names)
    chart_of_accounts = xl.parse('Chart of Accounts', index_col=0)
    journal = xl.parse('Journal', index_col=0)

print(chart_of_accounts[:5])
print(journal[:6])
```

The output we get is:

```
['Chart of Accounts', 'Journal']
                Account Description
Account Number
200                         Credit
201                      Insurance
202                           Food
203                        Culture
204                         Travel
             Description    Acc  Expenses    Income
Date
2025-08-01  Frank Salary  400.0      0.00   5020.00
2025-08-02  Laura Salary  400.0      0.00   5095.25
2025-08-03   Supermarket  202.0    145.35      0.00
2025-08-04          Rent  211.0   1290.00      0.00
2025-08-05   Electricity  210.0     88.76      0.00
2025-08-06         Water  210.0     62.10      0.00
```

We now generate a pie chart from the data grouped by categories:

```python
# replace account number with account descriptions:
journal['Acc'] = journal['Acc'].map(chart_of_accounts['Account Description
    '])
category_sums = journal.groupby('Acc').sum()
expenses = category_sums['Expenses']
expenses = expenses[expenses > 0] # exclude income

ax = expenses.plot.pie(autopct='%1.1f%%',
                   startangle=90,
                   pctdistance=0.8,  # percentage labels inside
                   labeldistance=1.1,  # category labels outside
                   textprops={'fontsize': 8}
                   )
ax.set_ylabel('')
ax.set_title('Expenses by Category')
```

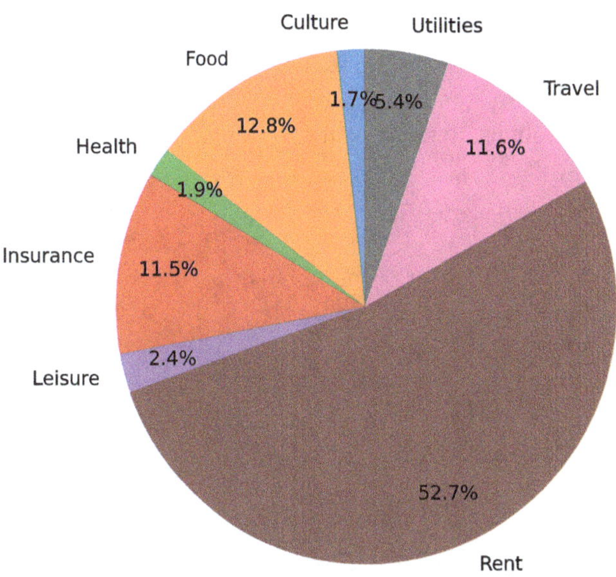

32.2 Income and expenditure statement

In this section, we use a *cash-based income and expenditure statement* as a practical example for demonstrating how pandas and Python can be applied to financial data analysis and visualization. In a cash-based system, income and expenses are recorded when funds are actually received or paid, rather than when they are accrued. Changes in inventory are not taken into account.

Such simplified forms of profit determination are used in many countries, particularly by freelancers, sole proprietors, and small businesses that are not required to maintain double-entry bookkeeping. One concrete example is the *income surplus statement* (EÜR), which is prescribed by tax law in Germany and Austria for certain categories of taxpayers. Switzerland applies a comparable simplified bookkeeping approach for microenterprises under its current accounting legislation. While the legal details differ by jurisdiction, the underlying accounting principle is essentially the same.

Our primary goal is to demonstrate how pandas and Python can be used to organize, analyze, and visualize income and expense data. In particular, we show how cash flows can be monitored and summarized, and how tax-related aggregates can be computed programmatically. While the presented algorithms may serve as a starting point for practical applications, they must always be adapted to the specific legal and tax context in which they are used.

32.2.1 Journal File

As the basis for our income surplus statement, we use an Excel document with two tables: one with the current entries, i.e., income and expenses in chronological order (we refer to this table as the journal), and the second table containing the mappings of account numbers to account descriptions. In the following, we read this Excel file into two DataFrame objects:

```python
import pandas as pd


with pd.ExcelFile("income_statement_2025.xlsx") as xl:
    chart_of_accounts = xl.parse("Chart of Accounts",
                                 index_col=0)
    journal = xl.parse("Journal",
                       index_col=0)


print("The first seven rows of 'journal':\n", journal[:7])
print("\nChart of accounts\n", chart_of_accounts[:8])
```

The result is:

```
The first seven rows of 'journal':
             Acc  DocuNumber             Description  TaxRate      Gross
Date
2025-04-02  4402  8983233038           Zurkan, Cologne       19    4105.98
2025-04-02  2010    57550799    Bengelmann, Souvenirs       19   -1890.00
2025-04-02  2200    14989004                 Salaries        0  -17478.23
2025-04-02  2500    12766279     Gas Station, Gasoline       19     -89.40
2025-04-02  4400  3733462359         EnergyCom, Hamburg       19    4663.54
2025-04-02  4402  7526058231       Enoigo, Strasbourg       19    2412.82
2025-04-05  4402  1157284466        Qbooks, Frankfurt        7    2631.42

Chart of accounts
            Description
Acct
4400      Location Munich
4401   Location Frankfurt
4402       Location Berlin
2010             Souvenirs
2020              Clothing
2030           Other Items
2050                 Books
2100             Insurance
```

32.2.2 Analysis and Visualization of the Data

There are many ways to analyze these data. For example, we can summarize all accounts:

```python
account_sums = journal[["Acc", "Gross"]].groupby("Acc").sum()
print(account_sums)
```

Executing the code yields:

```
          Gross
Acc
2010    -4090.00
2020   -10500.80
2030    -1350.00
2050     -900.00
2100     -612.00
2200   -69912.92
2300   -18791.92
2400    -1597.10
2500      -89.40
2600     -492.48
2610     -561.00
4400    37771.84
4401    69610.35
4402    61593.99
```

Now we want to visualize the data using circle diagrams, usually called pie charts. In English, they are referred to as "pie charts". However, we have a small problem: pie charts cannot contain negative values. This can be quickly fixed. We can divide the accounts into income accounts and expense accounts. This also corresponds more closely to what we actually want to see.

We first create one DataFrame for income and one for expenses. After generating the expense sums, we multiply the result by -1 to make the values positive:

```python
income = account_sums[account_sums["Gross"] > 0]
expenses = account_sums[account_sums["Gross"] < 0] * -1

print("---- Income -----")
print(income)
print("---- Expenses  -----")
print(expenses)
```

The result of the code is:

```
---- Income -----
          Gross
Acc
4400   37771.84
4401   69610.35
4402   61593.99
---- Expenses  -----
          Gross
Acc
2010    4090.00
2020   10500.80
2030    1350.00
2050     900.00
2100     612.00
2200   69912.92
2300   18791.92
2400    1597.10
2500      89.40
2600     492.48
2610     561.00
```

Now we create a pie chart showing the revenues:

```python
ax = income.plot(y='Gross',
                 title='Revenues',
                 kind="pie")
ax.legend(bbox_to_anchor=(0.5, 0.5),
          loc="upper left")
```

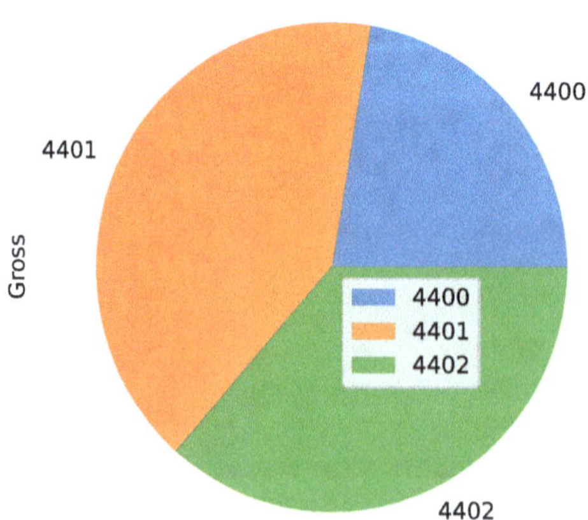

Now we create the corresponding pie chart for the expenses. This time, we display the account descriptions together with their numbers in parentheses instead of showing only the numbers. To keep the chart readable, we focus on the six largest expense accounts.

```python
# Build mapping: "Description (Account number)"
account_map = {
    num: f"{desc} ({num})"
    for num, desc in zip(chart_of_accounts.index,
                         chart_of_accounts['Description'])}

# Select only the 6 largest expenses
top6 = expenses.nlargest(6, 'Gross').copy()

# Replace account numbers with "Description (Number)"
top6.index = top6.index.map(account_map)

ax = top6.plot(
    y='Gross',
    kind='pie',
    title='Top 6 Expenses',
    autopct='%1.1f%%',
    legend=False,
    ylabel=''
)

# Optional: legend outside
ax.legend(bbox_to_anchor=(1.05, 1), loc='upper left')
```

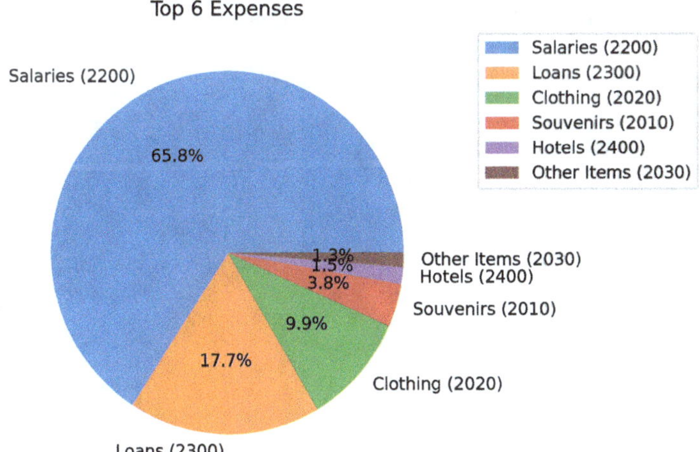

Now we proceed analogously but place the labels only in the legend. This time, we again include all expense accounts:

```python
ax = expenses.plot(y='Gross',
                   title='Expenses',
                   kind="pie",
                   labels=[''] * len(expenses))


ax.legend(bbox_to_anchor=(0.5, 0.5),
          labels=expenses.index)
```

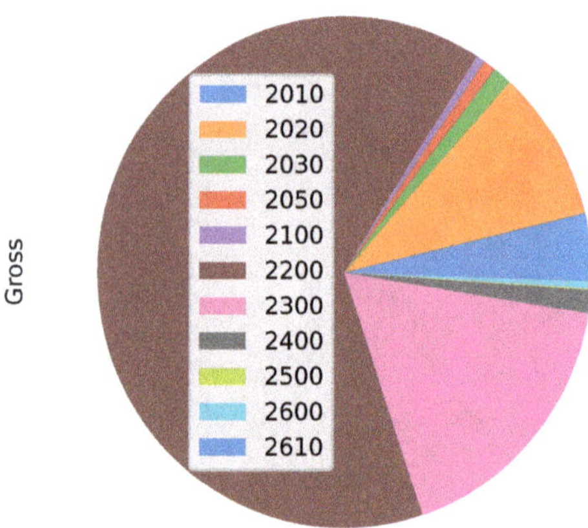

Now we use the account names instead of account numbers for the revenues:

```python
descriptions = chart_of_accounts["Description"].loc[income.index]

ax = income.plot(y='Gross',
                 title='Revenues',
                 labels=descriptions,
                 kind="pie")
ax.legend(bbox_to_anchor=(0.5, 0.5),
          labels=descriptions,
          loc="upper left")
```

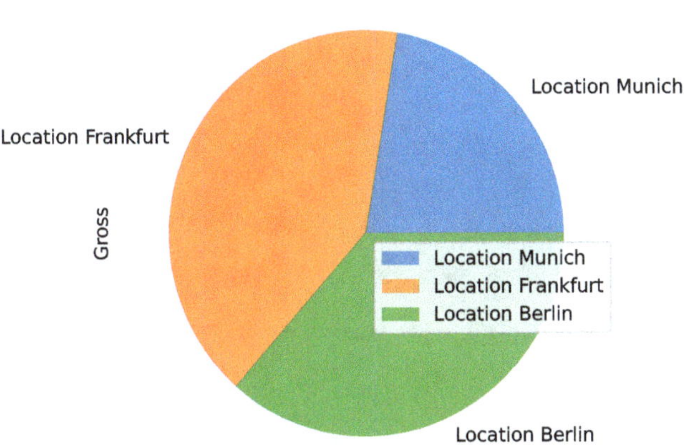


```python
descriptions = chart_of_accounts["Description"].loc[expenses.index]

ax = expenses.plot(y='Gross',
                   title='Expenses',
                   kind="pie",
                   labels=[''] * len(expenses))

ax.legend(loc="lower left",
          labels=descriptions)
```

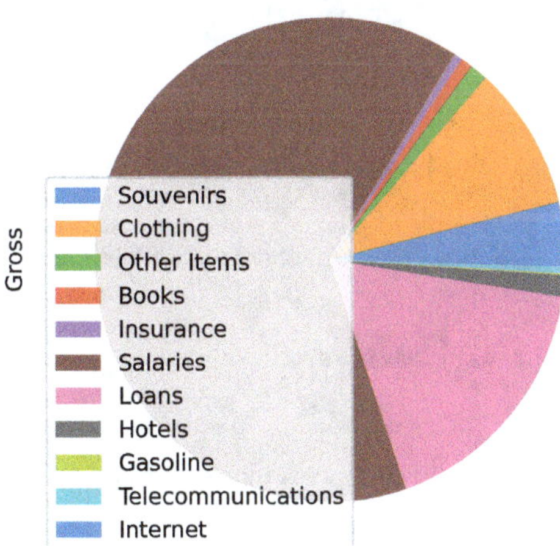

32.2.3 Tax Totals

We now want to calculate the tax totals. For this purpose, we use the column TaxRate,
which contains the VAT rate. We define a function tax_totals, which calculates VAT
totals by tax rate from a journal DataFrame:

```python
import pandas as pd


def tax_totals(journal_df, months=None):
    """Return a DataFrame with turnover and VAT totals.
    If months is given as a number or list, only the
    turnover of the corresponding months is considered.
    Example: tax_totals(df, months=[3, 6]) means only
    months 3 (March) and 6 (June)."""

    if months:
        if isinstance(months, int):
            month_cond = journal_df.index.month == months
        elif isinstance(months, (list, tuple)):
            month_cond = journal_df.index.month.isin(months)
        positive = journal_df["Gross"] > 0
        output_vat = journal_df[positive & month_cond]
        negative = journal_df["Gross"] < 0
        input_vat = journal_df[negative & month_cond]
    else:
        output_vat = journal_df[journal_df["Gross"] > 0]
        input_vat = journal_df[journal_df["Gross"] < 0]

    output_vat = output_vat[["TaxRate", "Gross"]].groupby("TaxRate").sum()
    output_vat.rename(columns={"Gross": "Turnover gross"},
                inplace=True)
    output_vat.index.name = 'Tax rate'

    input_vat = input_vat[["TaxRate", "Gross"]].groupby("TaxRate").sum()
    input_vat.rename(columns={"Gross": "Expenses gross"},
                inplace=True)
    input_vat.index.name = 'Tax rate'

    taxes = pd.concat([input_vat, output_vat], axis=1)
    taxes.insert(1,
            column="Input VAT",
            value=(taxes["Expenses gross"] * taxes.index / 100).round
                (2))
    taxes.insert(3,
            column="Output VAT",
            value=(taxes["Turnover gross"] * taxes.index / 100).round
                (2))
```

```
    return taxes.fillna(0)
```

We read the data again from the Excel file and compute the tax totals by tax rate using the function `tax_totals` with `journal` as the argument:

```python
with pd.ExcelFile("income_statement_2025.xlsx") as xl:
    chart_of_accounts = xl.parse("Chart of Accounts",
                                 index_col=0)
    journal = xl.parse("Journal",
                       index_col=0)


totals = tax_totals(journal)
print(totals)
```

The output shows:

```
          Expenses gross  Input VAT  Turnover gross  Output VAT
Tax rate
0              -90102.20      -0.00         8334.43        0.00
7               -3847.10    -269.30        11240.71      786.85
19             -14948.32   -2840.18       149401.04    28386.20
```

The tax totals for the month of May are calculated as follows:

```python
totals = tax_totals(journal, months=5)
print(totals)
```

The code produces the following result:

```
          Expenses gross  Input VAT  Turnover gross  Output VAT
Tax rate
0              -22411.53      -0.00            0.00        0.00
7                -900.00     -63.00            0.00        0.00
19               -145.00     -27.55        31328.98     5952.51
```

Now we calculate the taxes for April through June:

```python
totals = tax_totals(journal, months=[4, 5, 6])
print(totals)
```

The corresponding output can be seen here:

```
          Expenses gross  Input VAT  Turnover gross  Output VAT
Tax rate
0              -67690.67      -0.00         8334.43        0.00
7               -2139.10    -149.74        11240.71      786.85
19              -8748.32   -1662.18       102960.24    19562.45
```

Part V

Solutions to the Exercises

33

Solutions to the Exercises

33.1 Solutions to Chapter 5 (Creation and Structure of Arrays)

Solution to Exercise 1

We can create a one-dimensional array as follows:

```python
import numpy as np
arr = np.array([3, 8, 12, 18, 7, 11, 30])
```

Solution to Exercise 2

We obtain the odd indices by selecting every second element starting from the first element.

```python
odd_elements = arr[1::2]
```

Solution to Exercise 3

We obtain the reverse order by specifying a negative step size (step) in the slice operator.

```python
reverse_order = arr[::-1]
```

Solution to Exercise 4

The output is 200, because the slice operator in NumPy provides views, not copies.

Solution to Exercise 5

We can create a two-dimensional array as follows:

```
mat = np.array([[11, 12, 13, 14],
                [21, 22, 23, 24],
                [31, 32, 33, 34]])
```

Solution to Exercise 6

Here we specify the negative step size (`step`) in the slice operator for the second dimension.

```
mat[::, ::-1]
```

Solution to Exercise 7

To swap the rows, we must use the slice operator for the first dimension – the second dimension can be ignored.

```
mat[::-1]
```

Solution to Exercise 8

Now we must use the slice operators for both dimensions.

```
mat[::-1, ::-1]
```

Solution to Exercise 9

To cut off the first and last row and column, we specify 1 for `start` and `-1` for `stop` in both dimensions.

```
mat[1:-1, 1:-1]
```

33.2 Solutions to Chapter 6 (Data Type Object: dtype)

Solution to Exercise 1

```python
import numpy as np

mytype = [('product_id', np.int32), ('price', np.float64)]

products = np.array([(34765, 603.76),
                     (45765, 439.93),
                     (99661, 344.19),
                     (12129, 129.39)], dtype=mytype)

print(f'Product IDs: {products["product_id"]}')
print(f'First row: {products[0]}')
print(f'Third product price: {products[2]["price"]}')
```

The execution leads to this output:

```
Product IDs: [34765 45765 99661 12129]
First row: (34765, 603.76)
Third product price: 344.19
```

Solution to Exercise 2

```python
sales = np.array([3, 5, 2, 1])

revenues = products["price"] * sales

print("Revenue per item: ", revenues)
print("Total revenue: ", revenues.sum())
```

The following result is generated:

```
Revenue per item:  [1811.28 2199.65  688.38  129.39]
Total revenue:  4828.700000000001
```

Solution to Exercise 3

```python
time_type = np.dtype([('h', int),
                      ('min', int),
                      ('sec', int)])
```

```python
times = np.array([(11, 38, 5),
                  (14, 56, 0),
                  (3, 9, 1)], dtype=time_type)
print(times)
print(times['h'])
print(times['min'])
print(times['sec'])
```

The output we get is:

```
[(11, 38, 5) (14, 56, 0) ( 3,  9, 1)]
[11 14  3]
[38 56  9]
[5 0 1]
```

From the dtype structure above, we can also create a two-dimensional array where
the columns correspond to hours, minutes, and seconds:

```python
times_stacked = np.column_stack((times['h'],
                                 times['min'],
                                 times['sec']))


print(times_stacked)
```

Script output:

```
[[11 38  5]
 [14 56  0]
 [ 3  9  1]]
```

Solution to Exercise 4

```python
import numpy as np

hms = [('hour', int), ('minute', int), ('second', int)]
time_temp_type = np.dtype([('time', hms), ('temperature', float)])

time_temp_data = np.array([((11, 42, 17), 20.8),
                           ((13, 19, 3), 23.2),
                           ((14, 50, 29), 24.6)],
                          dtype=time_temp_type)

print(time_temp_data)
print(time_temp_data['time'])
print(time_temp_data['time']['hour'])
print(time_temp_data['temperature'])
```

The evaluation yields:

```
[((11, 42, 17), 20.8) ((13, 19,  3), 23.2) ((14, 50, 29), 24.6)]
[(11, 42, 17) (13, 19,  3) (14, 50, 29)]
[11 13 14]
[20.8 23.2 24.6]
```

Solution to Exercise 5

```python
with open("time_temp.csv", "w") as file:
    for row in time_temp_data:
        # Access ('hour', 'minute', 'second'):
        time_vals = [f"{val:02d}" for val in row[0]]
        time_str = ":".join(time_vals)
        temperature = row[1]
        file.write(f"{time_str},{temperature}\n")
```

We can display the generated file in a Linux shell[1]:

```
$cat time_temp.csv
```

Executing the code yields:

```
11:42:17,20.8
13:19:03,23.2
14:50:29,24.6
```

33.3　Solutions to Chapter 7 (Combining and Reshaping Arrays)

Solution to Exercise 1

```python
import numpy as np

# Create 5 arrays
list_of_arrays = []
for i in range(5):
    arr = np.arange(i * 100, i * 100 + 24).reshape(4, 3, 2)
    list_of_arrays.append(arr)
```

1　On Windows, the type command can be used.

```python
# Stack along axis 0
result = np.concatenate(list_of_arrays, axis=0)

print("Stacked array:")
print(result)

print("Shape of stacked array:", result.shape)
```

This follows from the code:

```
Stacked array:
[[[  0    1]
  [  2    3]
  [  4    5]]

 [[  6    7]
  [  8    9]
  [ 10   11]]

 [[ 12   13]
  [ 14   15]
  [ 16   17]]

 [[ 18   19]
  [ 20   21]
  [ 22   23]]

 [[100 101]
  [102 103]
  [104 105]]

 [[106 107]
  [108 109]
  [110 111]]

 [[112 113]
  [114 115]
  [116 117]]

 [[118 119]
  [120 121]
  [122 123]]

 [[200 201]
  [202 203]
  [204 205]]
```

```
[[206 207]
 [208 209]
 [210 211]]

[[212 213]
 [214 215]
 [216 217]]

[[218 219]
 [220 221]
 [222 223]]

[[300 301]
 [302 303]
 [304 305]]

[[306 307]
 [308 309]
 [310 311]]

[[312 313]
 [314 315]
 [316 317]]

[[318 319]
 [320 321]
 [322 323]]

[[400 401]
 [402 403]
 [404 405]]

[[406 407]
 [408 409]
 [410 411]]

[[412 413]
 [414 415]
 [416 417]]

[[418 419]
 [420 421]
 [422 423]]]
Shape of stacked array: (20, 3, 2)
```

Solution to Exercise 2

```python
import numpy as np

colors = np.array([1, 2, 3])   # Red, Green, Blue
# Color pattern repeated four times:
row = np.tile(colors, 4)
print("Row:", row)


mosaic = np.tile(row, (5, 1))
print("Mosaic:\n", mosaic)
print("Shape:", mosaic.shape)


# Create rotated mosaic:
rotated = np.array([np.roll(row, -i) for i in range(5)])
print("Rotated mosaic:\n", rotated)
```

We obtain this output:

```
Row: [1 2 3 1 2 3 1 2 3 1 2 3]
Mosaic:
 [[1 2 3 1 2 3 1 2 3 1 2 3]
 [1 2 3 1 2 3 1 2 3 1 2 3]
 [1 2 3 1 2 3 1 2 3 1 2 3]
 [1 2 3 1 2 3 1 2 3 1 2 3]
 [1 2 3 1 2 3 1 2 3 1 2 3]]
Shape: (5, 12)
Rotated mosaic:
 [[1 2 3 1 2 3 1 2 3 1 2 3]
 [2 3 1 2 3 1 2 3 1 2 3 1]
 [3 1 2 3 1 2 3 1 2 3 1 2]
 [1 2 3 1 2 3 1 2 3 1 2 3]
 [2 3 1 2 3 1 2 3 1 2 3 1]]
```

33.4 Solutions to Chapter 8 (Numerical Operations on NumPy Arrays)

Solution to Exercise 1

```python
B = np.array([1, 2, 3])
print(B.shape)
B = B[np.newaxis, :]
```

```python
print(B.shape)
B = np.concatenate((B, B, B)).transpose()
print(B.shape)
B = B[:, np.newaxis]
print(B.shape)
print(B)
```

Here is the output:

```
(3,)
(1, 3)
(3, 3)
(3, 1, 3)
[[[1 1 1]]

 [[2 2 2]]

 [[3 3 3]]]
```

Solution to Exercise 2

```python
A = np.random.randint(-10, 10, (3, 4))
print(A)
print("Row minima: ")
print(np.min(A, axis=1))
print("Column minima: ")
print(np.min(A, axis=0))
print("Absolute minimum: ")
print(np.min(A))
```

This is the result of the code:

```
[[ 7  7  0 -4]
 [ 2  9  2 -3]
 [ 0  7  4  7]]
Row minima:
[-4 -3  0]
Column minima:
[ 0  7  0 -4]
Absolute minimum:
-4
```

Solution to Exercise 3

The accumulate method of the ufunc np.add computes the cumulative sum over an array. The solution looks like this:

```python
import numpy as np


steps = np.array([3000, 4500, 4000, 5000, 3500, 6000, 5500])
cumulative_steps = np.add.accumulate(steps)


print("Cumulative steps: ", cumulative_steps)
```

The result appears as follows:

```
Cumulative steps:  [ 3000  7500 11500 16500 20000 26000 31500]
```

Solution to Exercise 4

To calculate the total costs for each combination of product and order quantity, we use the function np.outer, which computes the outer product of two arrays. In this case, we multiply unit prices with quantities to obtain a cost matrix.

```python
import numpy as np

# Unit prices for 4 different products:
prices = np.array([10.0, 15.0, 25.0, 50.0])

# Order quantities from 5 different customers
quantities = np.array([1, 2, 3, 4, 5])
cost_matrix = np.outer(prices, quantities)

print(f"Cost matrix:\n{cost_matrix}")
```

This is the result of the code:

```
Cost matrix:
[[ 10.  20.  30.  40.  50.]
 [ 15.  30.  45.  60.  75.]
 [ 25.  50.  75. 100. 125.]
 [ 50. 100. 150. 200. 250.]]
```

33.5 Solutions to Chapter 9 (Statistics and Probability)

Solution to Exercise 1

```python
from random import randint

results = [randint(1, 6) for _ in range(10000)]
even_rolls = [x for x in results if x % 2 == 0]
greater_than_two = [x for x in results if x > 2]
combined = [x for x in results if x % 2 == 0 and x > 2]

print(len(even_rolls) / len(results))
print(len(greater_than_two) / len(results))
print(len(combined) / len(results))
```

This output is obtained:

```
0.5064
0.6753
0.3435
```

Solution to Exercise 2

We first write the function `process_file` to process the data from the file:

```python
def process_file(filename):
    """ process_file -> (universities,
                         enrollments,
                         total_students)
        universities: list of university names
        enrollments: corresponding list of enrollment numbers
        total_students: across all universities
    """

    universities = []
    enrollments = []
    with open(filename) as file:
        total_students = 0
        file.readline()  # skip header
        for line in file:
            parts = line.split('\t')
            university_name = parts[1].strip()
```

```python
        number_of_students = int(parts[-1].replace(',', ''))
        universities.append(university_name)
        enrollments.append(number_of_students)
        total_students += number_of_students

    return (universities, enrollments, total_students)
```

Let us run the function and check the result:

```python
universities, enrollments, total_students = \
    process_file("universities_uk.txt")


print("Enrolled students at British universities\n")
print(f"{'University':40} | {'Students':>12}")
print("-" * 55)


for i, university in enumerate(universities[:10]):
    # Use "." as thousands separator:
    number = f"{enrollments[i]:,}".replace(",", ".")
    print(f"{university:40} | {number:>12}")


print(f"{'... etc.':40} |           ...")
print("-" * 55)
print(f"{'Total':40} | {total_students:12,}".replace(",", "."))
```

The result of the code is:

```
Enrolled students at British universities

University                               |     Students
-------------------------------------------------------
Open University in England               |      123.490
University of Manchester                 |       37.925
University of Nottingham                 |       33.270
Sheffield Hallam University              |       33.100
University of Birmingham                 |       32.335
Manchester Metropolitan University       |       32.160
University of Leeds                      |       30.975
Cardiff University                       |       30.180
University of South Wales                |       29.195
University College London                |       28.430
... etc.                                 |          ...
-------------------------------------------------------
Total                                    |    2.299.380
```

We want to enroll a virtual student at a random university:

```python
import random


# Make a random selection
print(random.choices(universities,
                     weights=enrollments,  # does not need to be
                         normalized
                     k=1)[0])
```

The processing yields:

```
University of Salford
```

The task was to "enroll" 100,000 fictional students. This can be implemented using `random.choices`, where the probability for each university is proportional to its actual enrollment number.

```python
import random
from collections import Counter
from pprint import pprint  # nice output


n = 100_000    # corresponds to 100,000 enrollments
results = random.choices(universities,
                         weights=enrollments,
                         k=n)


counter = Counter(results)

# Output the 20 most frequent universities:
pprint(counter.most_common(20), indent=2, width=70)
```

Output:

```
[ ('Open University in England', 5500),
  ('University of Manchester', 1617),
  ('University of Nottingham', 1479),
  ('Manchester Metropolitan University', 1413),
  ('Sheffield Hallam University', 1387),
  ('University of Birmingham', 1374),
  ('Cardiff University', 1345),
  ('University of Leeds', 1339),
  ('University of South Wales', 1250),
  ('University College London', 1245),
  ('University of Plymouth', 1240),
  ('University of Glasgow', 1237),
  ('Northumbria University', 1201),
```

```
("King's College London", 1189),
('Nottingham Trent University', 1186),
('University of Sheffield', 1179),
('University of Edinburgh', 1171),
('University of the West of England', 1164),
('Ulster University', 1146),
('Coventry University', 1127)]
```

Solution to Exercise 3

At the beginning, all 11 Amazons are equally likely to be drawn. The total number of possible combinations of 4 different Amazons is:

$$\binom{11}{4} = 330$$

There is exactly one combination in which all four desired Amazons (Iocaste, Medousa, Sophronia, and Andromeda) are drawn. The probability at the start is therefore about 0.3%, as the calculation shows:

$$P = \frac{1}{\binom{11}{4}} = \frac{1}{330} \approx 0.00303$$

We are looking for the earliest point in time (in days) at which the probability that exactly the four desired Amazons (Iocaste, Medousa, Sophronia, and Andromeda) are selected through a random draw exceeds `target_probability`.

To solve the exercise:

At the beginning, all 11 Amazons have the same probability of being drawn. The initial probabilities are therefore: $p_i = \frac{1}{11}$ for $i = 1, \ldots, 11$

Each day the probability distribution changes according to the following rule:

- For the first 7 Amazons (index 0 to 6): $p_i \leftarrow \left(1 - \frac{1}{13}\right) \cdot p_i$
- For the last 4 Amazons (index 7 to 10): $p_i \leftarrow \left(1 + \frac{1}{12}\right) \cdot p_i$

After every update step, the probability distribution is renormalized to ensure that the sum of all probabilities equals 1:

$$\sum_{i=0}^{10} p_i = 1$$

On each day, a combination of 4 different Amazons is drawn *without replacement*. The probability that *exactly the four desired Amazons* (indices 7 to 10) are drawn is very small, but it increases each day due to the probability shift.

This probability is estimated using a Monte Carlo simulation:

1. For each day, use the current probability distribution p.
2. Draw 10,000 samples, each time selecting 4 Amazons without replacement.
3. Count how often exactly the set $\{7, 8, 9, 10\}$ (the four desired Amazons) is drawn.
4. The relative frequency yields the empirical probability.

The algorithm stops as soon as this probability is greater than or equal to the target probability.

```python
import numpy as np

amazons = ["Airla", "Barbara", "Eos", "Glykeria", "Hanna", "Helen",
           "Agathangelos", "Iocaste", "Medousa", "Sophronia", "Andromeda"]

desired_indices = {7, 8, 9, 10}  # indices of the desired Amazons

def normalize(p):
    """Normalize a probability distribution."""
    return p / p.sum()

def update_probabilities(p):
    """Update probabilities according to the daily rule."""
    delta = np.zeros_like(p)
    # First 7 lose 1/13 of their probability each
    delta[:7] -= p[:7] / 13
    # Last 4 gain 1/12 of their probability each
    delta[7:] += p[7:] / 12
    p_new = p + delta
    # Normalize to avoid numerical drift
    return normalize(p_new)

def simulate_day(p, trials=10000):
    """Simulate one day's draw with the given distribution."""
    success = 0
    for _ in range(trials):
        drawn = np.random.choice(len(p), size=4, replace=False, p=p)
        if set(drawn) == desired_indices:
            success += 1
    return success / trials

p = np.full(11, 1/11)   # start probabilities
print("Probability of drawing the king's desired Amazons:")
days = 0
target_probability = 0.99
while True:
    prob = simulate_day(p, trials=10000)
    if days % 5 == 0:   # print only every 5 days
        print(f"{days+1:2d} day(s): probability = {prob:.4f}")
    if prob >= target_probability:
        break
    p = update_probabilities(p)
    days += 1
```

```python
print(f"\nAfter {days+1} day(s), the desired Amazons are drawn with a "
      f"probability greater than or equal to "
      f"{int(target_probability * 100)}%.")
```

After execution we get:

```
Probability of drawing the king's desired Amazons:
 1 day(s): probability = 0.0030
 6 day(s): probability = 0.0251
11 day(s): probability = 0.1244
16 day(s): probability = 0.3292
21 day(s): probability = 0.5865
26 day(s): probability = 0.7712
31 day(s): probability = 0.8864
36 day(s): probability = 0.9495
41 day(s): probability = 0.9759
46 day(s): probability = 0.9880


After 48 day(s), the desired Amazons are drawn with a probability greater
↪   than or equal to 99%.
```

33.6 Solutions to Chapter 10 (Boolean Masking and Indexing)

Solution to 1. Exercise

```python
import numpy as np
A = np.array([3, 4, 6, 10, 24, 89, 45, 43, 46, 99, 100])

div3 = A[A % 3 != 0]
print(f"Elements of A not divisible by 3:\n{div3}")

div5 = A[A % 5 == 0]
print(f"Elements of A divisible by 5:\n{div5}")

div35 = A[(A % 3 == 0) & (A % 5 == 0)]
print(f"Elements of A divisible by both 3 and 5:\n{div35}")

A[A % 3 == 0] = 42
print(f"All values of A divisible by 3 have been set to 42:\n{A}")
```

The code produces the following result:

```
Elements of A not divisible by 3:
[   4  10  89  43  46 100]
Elements of A divisible by 5:
[ 10  45 100]
Elements of A divisible by both 3 and 5:
[45]
All values of A divisible by 3 have been set to 42:
[ 42   4  42  10  42  89  42  43  46  42 100]
```

Solution to 2. Exercise

With a Boolean mask, you can selectively include or exclude numbers from an array. In this exercise, you should use the *Sieve of Eratosthenes* to find all prime numbers below 100. To do this, first mark all numbers as "potentially prime," and then systematically strike out all multiples of primes.

```python
import numpy as np


is_prime = np.ones((100,), dtype=bool)
is_prime[:2] = 0    # 0 and 1 are not prime numbers

# Strike out multiples of numbers (Sieve of Eratosthenes):
nmax = int(np.sqrt(len(is_prime)))
for i in range(2, nmax):
    is_prime[2 * i::i] = False


print(np.nonzero(is_prime))
```

The output shows:

```
(array([ 2,  3,  5,  7, 11, 13, 17, 19, 23, 29, 31, 37, 41, 43,
       47, 53, 59, 61, 67, 71, 73, 79, 83, 89, 97]),)
```

Solution to 3. Exercise

The function np.where conditionally replaces all outliers with np.nan. The conditions are combined using logical OR |.

```python
import numpy as np
```

```
values = np.array([22.1, -77.5, 18.4, 999.0,
                   25.6, -12.3, 58.9, 120.0])
filtered = np.where((values < -50) | (values > 60), np.nan, values)
print(filtered)
```

This output is obtained:

```
[ 22.1    nan  18.4    nan  25.6 -12.3  58.9    nan]
```

33.7 Solutions to Chapter 13 (Object-Oriented Plotting)

Solution to Exercise 1

```python
import matplotlib.pyplot as plt

days = ['Mon', 'Tue', 'Wed', 'Thu', 'Fri', 'Sat', 'Sun']
minutes = [30, 42, 35, 50, 45, 60, 40]  # jogging times in minutes

fig, ax = plt.subplots()
ax.plot(days, minutes, marker='o', linestyle='-', color='tab:blue')
ax.set_xlabel('Day of the week')
ax.set_ylabel('Jogging time (minutes)')
ax.set_title('Jogging over seven days')
ax.grid(True)   # grid lines
```

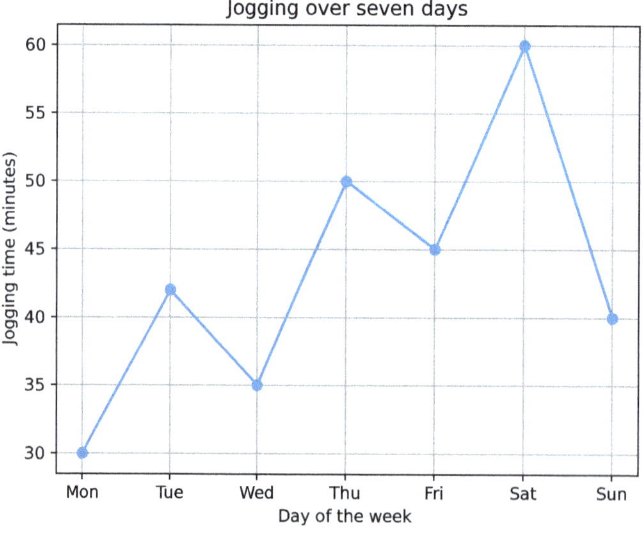

Figure 33.1 Solution diagram: jogging time per weekday

Solution to Exercise 2

```python
import matplotlib.pyplot as plt

days = list(range(1, 9))
city_a = [21, 23, 24, 25, 26, 27, 29, 30]
city_b = [18, 20, 22, 23, 25, 28, 31, 33]

fig, ax = plt.subplots()
ax.plot(days, city_a, label='City A',
        color='blue',  linestyle='-', marker='o')

ax.plot(days, city_b, label='City B',
        color='red', linestyle='--',  marker='x')
ax.set_xlabel('Day')
ax.set_ylabel('Temperature in degrees Celsius')
ax.set_title('Daily high temperatures in two cities')
ax.legend() # add legend
```

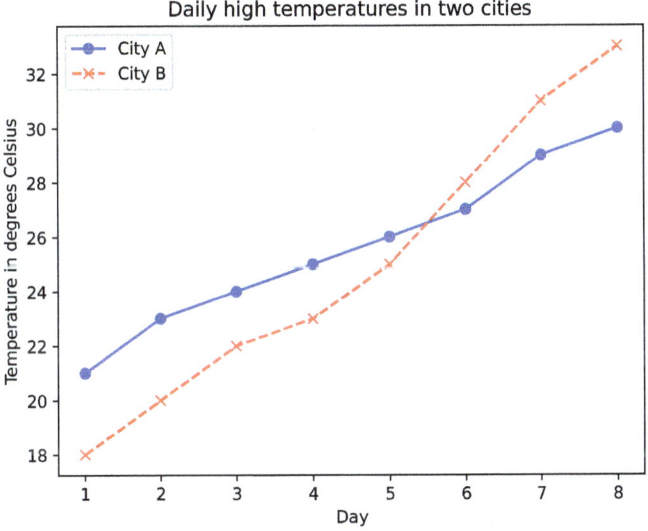

Figure 33.2 Temperature course in City A and City B over eight days

Solution to Exercise 3

```python
import numpy as np
import matplotlib.pyplot as plt

np.random.seed(1)
# Random data for lemons (less sweet, very sour)
sweet_lemons = np.random.normal(loc=2.0, scale=0.5, size=15)
sour_lemons = np.random.normal(loc=8.0, scale=0.6, size=15)
# Random data for oranges (sweeter, less sour)
sweet_oranges = np.random.normal(loc=7.0, scale=0.6, size=14)
sour_oranges = np.random.normal(loc=4.0, scale=0.5, size=14)

fig, ax = plt.subplots()
ax.scatter(sweet_lemons, sour_lemons, c='gold',
           label='Lemons', s=200, edgecolor='black', alpha=0.8)
ax.scatter(sweet_oranges, sour_oranges, c='orange',
           label='Oranges', s=200, edgecolor='black', alpha=0.8)
ax.set_xlabel('Sweetness')
ax.set_ylabel('Sourness')
ax.set_title('Sweetness vs. Sourness for lemons and oranges')

ax.set_xlim(0, 10) # adjust axis range
ax.set_ylim(0, 10) # adjust axis range
ax.legend()
```

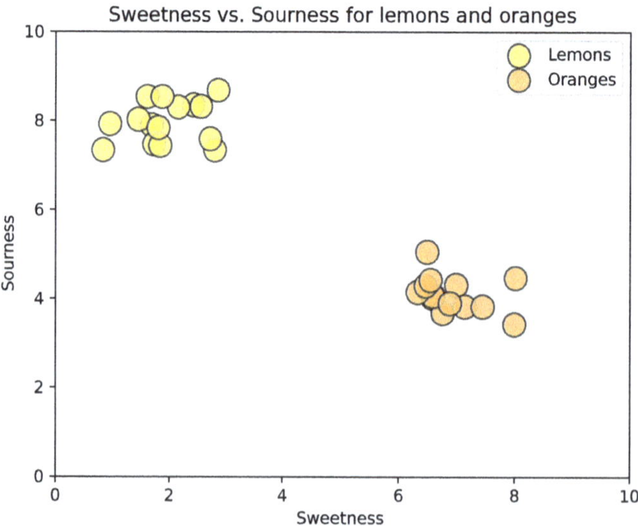

Figure 33.3 Sweetness and sourness of lemons and oranges compared

33.8 Solutions to Chapter 14 (Multiple Plots and Dual Axes)

Solution to 1. Exercise

```python
import matplotlib.pyplot as plt
fig = plt.figure(figsize=(2, 3))
X = [(1, 2, 1), (3, 2, 2), (3, 2, 4), (3, 2, 6)]
for nrows, ncols, plot_number in X:
    plt.subplot(nrows, ncols, plot_number)
    plt.xticks([])
    plt.yticks([])

fig.savefig('../MatplotlibImages/chapter15solution1.pdf')
```

Solution to 2. Exercise

```python
import matplotlib.pyplot as plt
fig = plt.figure(figsize=(2, 3))
X = [(4, 2, 1), (4, 2, 2), (4, 2, 3), (4, 2, 5), (4, 2, (4, 6)), (4, 1, 4)
    ]
plt.subplots_adjust(bottom=0, left=0, top=0.975, right=1)
for nrows, ncols, plot_number in X:
    plt.subplot(nrows, ncols, plot_number)
    plt.xticks([])
    plt.yticks([])

fig.savefig('../MatplotlibImages/chapter15solution2.pdf')
```

Solution to 3. Exercise

```python
import matplotlib.gridspec as gridspec
import matplotlib.pyplot as pl

pl.figure(figsize=(2, 3))
G = gridspec.GridSpec(4, 2)

fontsize = 12
alpha = 0.5
axes_1 = pl.subplot(G[0, 0])
pl.xticks(())
pl.yticks(())
pl.text(0.5, 0.5, 'area 1', ha='center',
        va='center', size=fontsize, alpha=alpha)

axes_2 = pl.subplot(G[0, 1])
pl.xticks(())
pl.yticks(())
pl.text(0.5, 0.5, 'area 2', ha='center',
        va='center', size=fontsize, alpha=alpha)

axes_3 = pl.subplot(G[1, 0])
pl.xticks(())
pl.yticks(())
pl.text(0.5, 0.5, 'area 3', ha='center',
        va='center', size=fontsize, alpha=alpha)

axes_4 = pl.subplot(G[2, 0])
pl.xticks(())
pl.yticks(())
pl.text(0.5, 0.5, 'area 4', ha='center',
        va='center', size=fontsize, alpha=alpha)
```

```python
axes_5 = pl.subplot(G[1:3, 1])
pl.xticks(())
pl.yticks(())
pl.text(0.5, 0.5, 'area 5', ha='center',
        va='center', size=fontsize, alpha=alpha)

axes_6 = pl.subplot(G[3, :])
pl.xticks(())
pl.yticks(())
pl.text(0.5, 0.5, 'area 6', ha='center',
        va='center', size=fontsize, alpha=alpha)

pl.tight_layout()
pl.savefig('../MatplotlibImages/chapter15solution3.pdf')
```

33.9 Solutions to Chapter 16 (Legends and Annotations)

Solution to Exercise 1

```python
import matplotlib.pyplot as plt

# Data for the three products
product1 = [66, 62, 55, 50, 30, 35, 40, 45, 50, 55, 60, 65]
product2 = [5, 10, 17, 24, 27, 40, 50, 62, 45, 50, 55, 60]
product3 = [14, 25, 30, 35, 36, 45, 50, 55, 59, 65, 75, 82]

# X-axis labels
months = ['Jan', 'Feb', 'Mar', 'Apr', 'May', 'Jun',
          'Jul', 'Aug', 'Sep', 'Oct', 'Nov', 'Dec']
```

```python
fig, ax = plt.subplots()
ax.plot(months, product1, label='Product 1')
ax.plot(months, product2, label='Product 2')
ax.plot(months, product3, label='Product 3')
ax.legend()
```

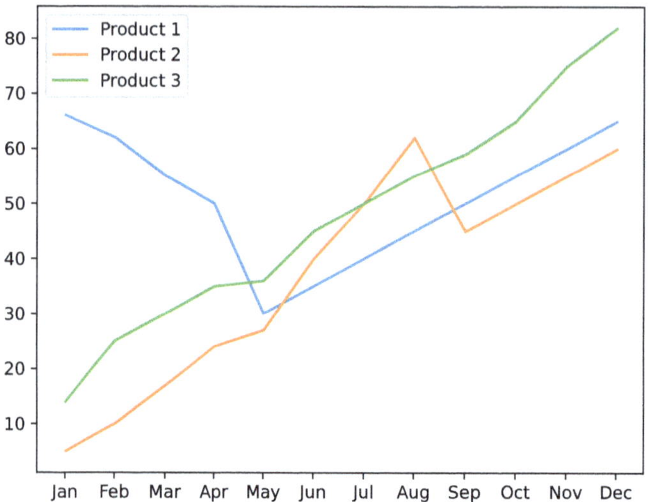

Solution to Exercise 2

```python
import matplotlib.pyplot as plt

months = ['Jan', 'Feb', 'Mar', 'Apr', 'May', 'Jun',
          'Jul', 'Aug', 'Sep', 'Oct', 'Nov', 'Dec']
temperatures = [4, 6, 9, 12, 17, 20, 23, 24, 19, 14, 9, 5]

fig, ax = plt.subplots()
ax.plot(months, temperatures, color='green')
ax.set_xlabel('Month')
ax.set_ylabel('Temperature in degrees Celsius')

temp_max, index_max = max(zip(temperatures, range(len(months))))
temp_min, index_min = min(zip(temperatures, range(len(months))))
ax.annotate(f'Highest value: {temp_max} in degrees Celsius',
            xy=(index_max, temp_max),
            xytext=(index_max-7, temp_max-1),
            arrowprops=dict(facecolor='orange', shrink=0.05))
ax.annotate(f'Lowest value: {temp_min} in degrees Celsius',
```

```
xy=(index_min, temp_min),
xytext=(index_min+4, temp_min+8),
arrowprops=dict(facecolor='orange', shrink=0.05))
```

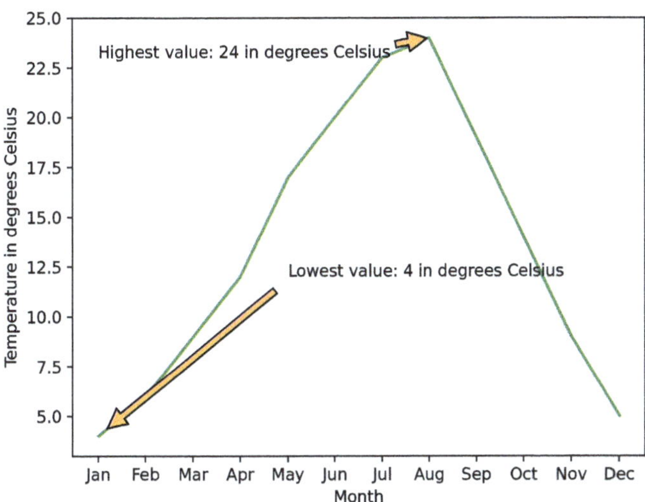

33.10 Solutions to Chapter 17 (Contour Plots)

Solution to Exercise 1

```python
import numpy as np
import matplotlib.pyplot as plt
from matplotlib import cm

def sin2d(x, y):
    return np.sin(x**3) + np.cos(y**2)

X, Y = np.meshgrid(np.linspace(0, 5 * np.pi, 200),
                   np.linspace(0, 5 * np.pi, 200))
Z = sin2d(X, Y)

fig, ax = plt.subplots()
ax.set_title('Exercise 1: Contour Plots')
cs = ax.contourf(X, Y, Z, cmap=cm.PuBu_r)
cbar = fig.colorbar(cs)
```

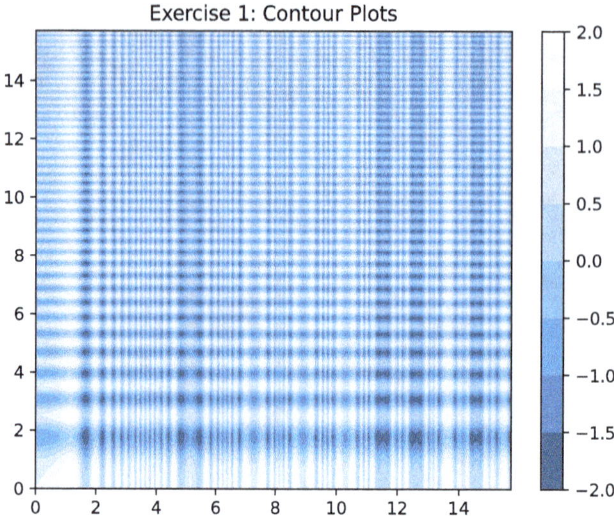

An alternative solution using `imshow`:

```python
import numpy as np
import matplotlib.pyplot as plt


def sin2d(x, y):
    return np.sin(x**3) + np.cos(y**2)


X, Y = np.meshgrid(np.linspace(0, 5 * np.pi, 200),
                   np.linspace(0, 5 * np.pi, 200))
Z = sin2d(X, Y)
plt.imshow(Z, origin='lower')
```

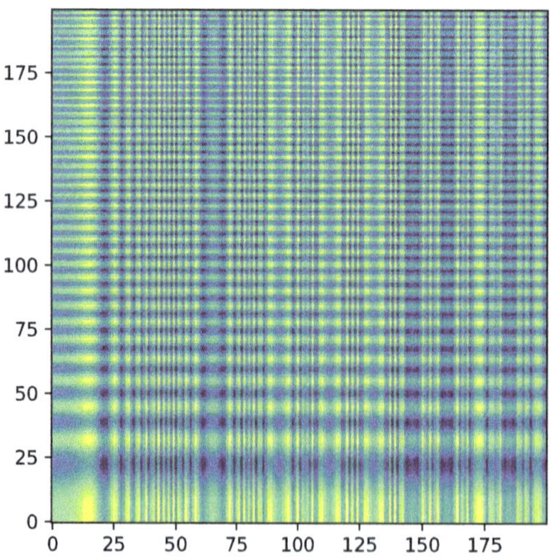

Solution to Exercise 2

```python
import matplotlib.pyplot as plt
import numpy as np

y, x = np.ogrid[-1:2:100j, -1:1:100j]
z = x**2 + (y - ((x**2) ** (1.0 / 5)))**2

fig, ax = plt.subplots()
ax.contour(x.ravel(), y.ravel(), z, [1], colors='red')
ax.axis('equal')
```

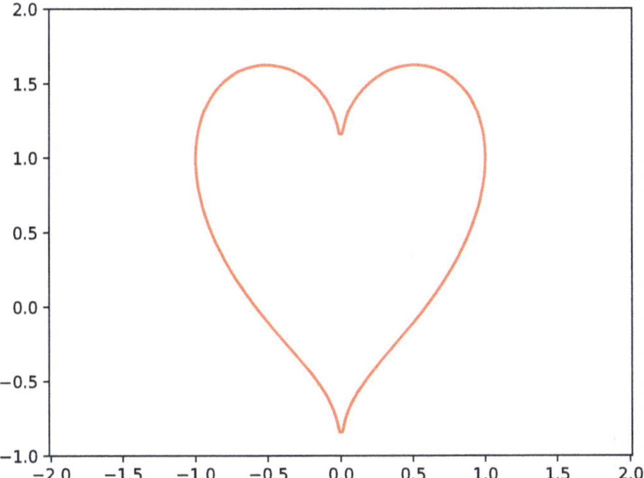

Solution to Exercise 3

```python
import matplotlib.pyplot as plt
import numpy as np

y, x = np.ogrid[-4:5:100j, -4:4:100j]
z = x**2 + (y - ((x**2) ** (1.0 / 5)))**2

fig, ax = plt.subplots()
ax.contourf(x.ravel(), y.ravel(), z,
            levels=np.linspace(0, 10, 10), cmap='Reds')
ax.axis('equal')
```

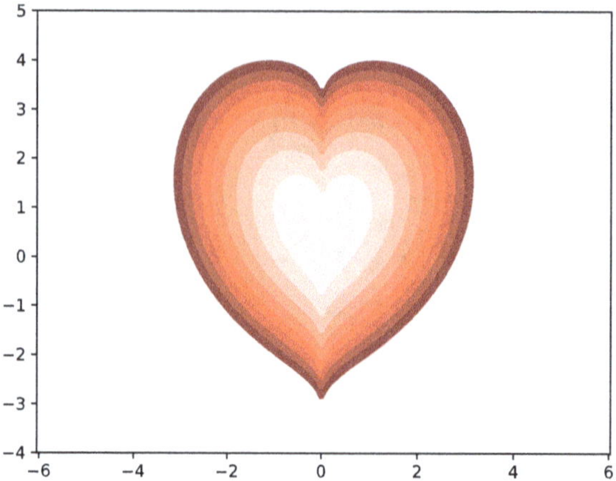

Solution to Exercise 4

```python
import numpy as np
import matplotlib.pyplot as plt
start, stop, n_values = -8, 8, 800
x_vals = np.linspace(start, stop, n_values)
y_vals = np.linspace(start, stop, n_values)
X, Y = np.meshgrid(x_vals, y_vals)
Z = np.sin(X) ** 12 + np.cos(10 + Y*X) * np.cos(X)

fig, ax = plt.subplots()
contour_filled = ax.contourf(X, Y, Z, 39, cmap="RdGy")
fig.colorbar(contour_filled)
ax.set_title('Contour Plot')
ax.set_xlabel('x (cm)')
ax.set_ylabel('y (cm)')
```

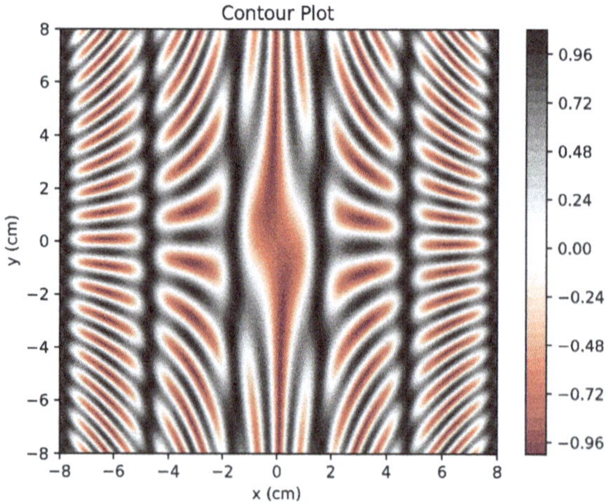

33.11 Solutions to Chapter 18 (Histograms and Diagrams)

Solution to Exercise 1

```python
import matplotlib.pyplot as plt

parties = ["SPD", "CDU/CSU", "Greens", "FDP", "AfD", "Left", "Others"]
shares = [25.7, 24.1, 14.8, 11.5, 10.3, 4.9, 8.7]
colors = ['red', 'black', 'green', 'yellow', 'blue', 'magenta', 'grey']

plt.figure(figsize=(8, 5))
plt.bar(parties, shares, color=colors)
plt.ylabel("Percent")
plt.title("Federal Election 2025 - Vote Shares")
plt.grid(axis='y', linestyle='--', alpha=0.7)
```

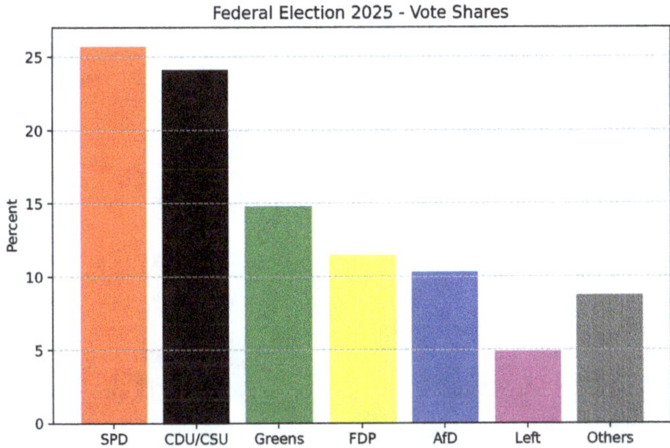

Solution to Exercise 2

```python
import numpy as np
import matplotlib.pyplot as plt

fig, ax = plt.subplots()

people = ('Michael', 'Doro', 'Bertie', 'Bea', 'Uli')
y_pos = np.arange(len(people))
consumption = (15, 22, 24, 29, 14)

ax.barh(y_pos, consumption, align='center',
        color='brown', ecolor='black')
```

```python
ax.set_yticks(y_pos)
ax.set_yticklabels(people)
ax.invert_yaxis()  # labels from top to bottom
ax.set_xlabel('Consumption')
ax.set_title('Coffee Consumption')
```

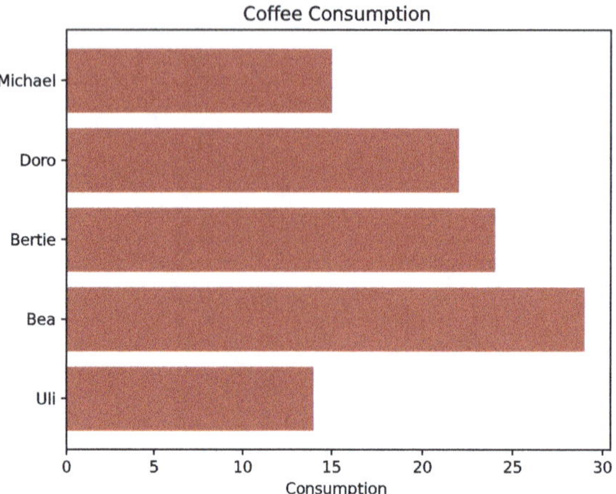

Solution to Exercise 3

```python
import matplotlib.pyplot as plt
import numpy as np


fname = 'data/eu/eu_country_population_surface_gdp.csv'
eu_data = np.loadtxt(fname,
                     delimiter=',',
                     skiprows=4,
                     dtype=[('country', '|U14'),
                            ('pop', int),
                            ('area', float),
                            ('gdp', int)])


bar_width = 0.95
fig, ax = plt.subplots()
ax.set_title('GDP per Capita in PPS')
ax.tick_params(axis='y', labelsize=7)
ax.barh(eu_data['country'],
        eu_data['gdp'],
        align='center',
        color='orange')
ax.set_xlabel('Gross Domestic Product')
```

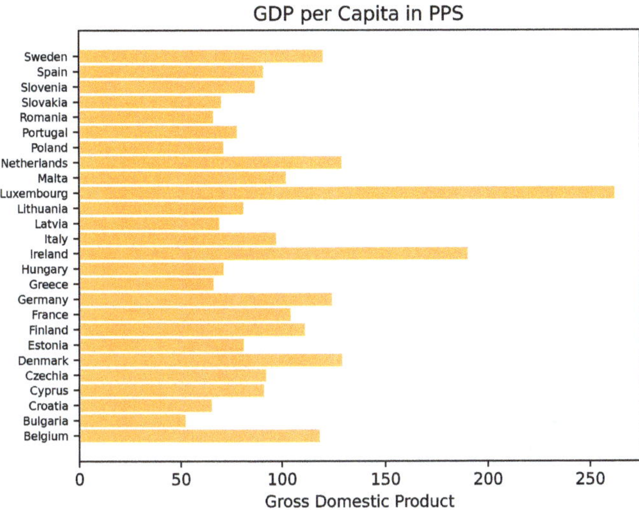

Solution to Exercise 4

```python
import matplotlib.pyplot as plt
import numpy as np

fname = 'data/eu/eu_country_population_surface_gdp.csv'
eu_data = np.loadtxt(fname,
                     delimiter=',',
                     skiprows=4,
                     dtype=[('country', '|U14'),
                            ('pop', int),
                            ('area', float),
                            ('gdp', int)])

selected = eu_data[[0, 8, 9, 10, 11, 13]]
fig, ax = plt.subplots()
width = 0.2
ticks = np.arange(len(selected['country']))
# Unit conversions for nicer scales:
selected['area'] = selected['area'] / 10000      # in ten-thousand hectares
selected['pop'] = selected['pop'] / 1000000    # in millions
ax.barh(ticks - width, selected['pop'], width, align="center")
ax.barh(ticks,         selected['area'], width, align="center")
ax.barh(ticks + width, selected['gdp'],  width, align="center")
ax.set_yticks(ticks)
ax.set_yticklabels(selected['country'])
ax.set_ylabel("States")
```

```python
ax.set_title("Population, Area, GDP")
ax.legend(["population", "area", "GDP"],
          loc="lower right")
```

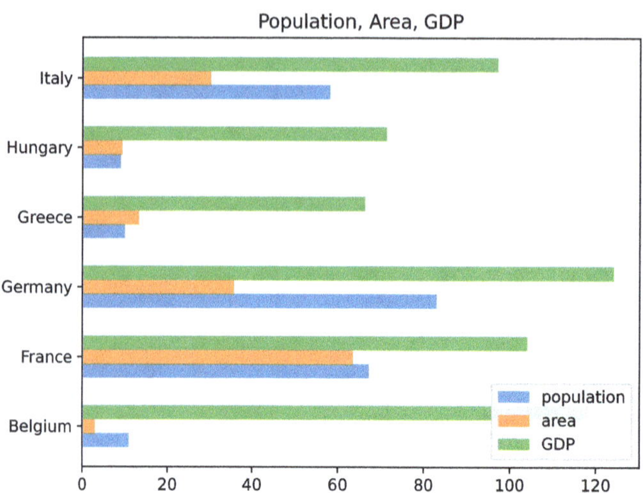

Solution to Exercise 5

```python
import matplotlib.pyplot as plt

# Data: company profit from 2015 to 2025
years = list(range(2015, 2026))
profits = [132456.43, 132789.12, 133102.55, 133560.77, 133800.22,
           134120.00, 134560.66, 134900.88, 135300.99, 135700.11,
           135800.00]

with plt.xkcd():
    fig, ax = plt.subplots(figsize=(10, 5))
    ax.bar(years, profits, color='skyblue', edgecolor='black')
    ax.set_title("Growing Profits")
    ax.set_xlabel("Year")
    ax.set_ylabel("Profit in Euros")
    ax.axhline(y=131000, color='black', linewidth=1)
    ax.set_ylim(132000, 136000)  # intentionally compressed y-axis
    ax.set_xticks(years)
    ax.tick_params(axis='x', rotation=45)
    fig.tight_layout()
```

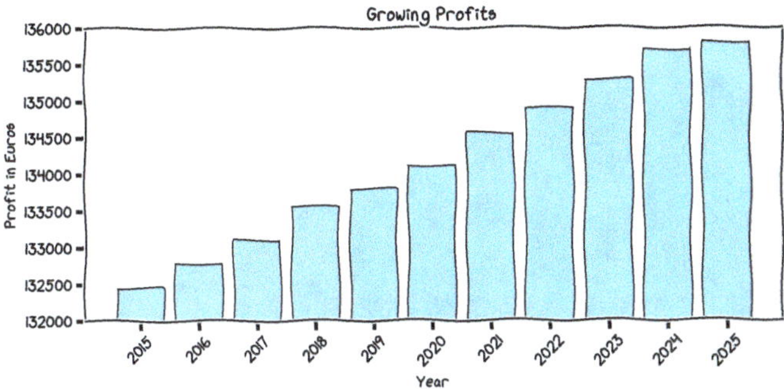

33.12 Solutions to Chapter 19 (Pandas:Series)

Solution to 1. Exercise

```python
import pandas as pd
from numpy.random import choice, randint


first_names = ['Lena', 'Max', 'Finn', 'Hannah',
               'Paul', 'Hendrik', 'Sarah']
last_names  = ['Schulz', 'Müller', 'Schmidt', 'Weber',
               'Fischer', 'Huber', 'Peters']


n = 8
# Generate random grades from 1 to 10:
grades = randint(1, 11, size=n)


# Combine first and last names:
names = [choice(first_names) + ' ' + choice(last_names)
         for _ in range(n)]


grade_series = pd.Series(data=grades, index=names)
print(grade_series)
```

Script output:

```
Hendrik Huber      4
Hendrik Schulz     1
Paul Huber         7
Hendrik Weber      6
Sarah Müller      10
Hendrik Fischer    7
Finn Weber         3
Hendrik Peters     3
dtype: int64
```

Solution to 2. Exercise

```python
import pandas as pd
from numpy.random import choice, randint


first_names = ['Lena', 'Max', 'Finn', 'Hannah',
               'Paul', 'Hendrik', 'Sarah']
last_names  = ['Schulz', 'Müller', 'Schmidt', 'Weber',
               'Fischer', 'Huber', 'Peters']


n = 8
# Generate random grades from 1 to 10:
grades1 = randint(1, 11, size=n)
grades2 = randint(1, 11, size=n)

# Combine first and last names:
names = [choice(first_names) + ' ' + choice(last_names)
         for _ in range(n)]

grade_series1 = pd.Series(data=grades1, index=names)
grade_series2 = pd.Series(data=grades2, index=names)
print("Average grades:\n", (grade_series1 + grade_series2) / 2)
```

The result of the code is:

```
Average grades:
 Sarah Peters      3.0
Sarah Müller       5.0
Hendrik Schulz     8.5
Hannah Huber       2.5
Finn Huber         4.5
Hannah Schmidt     6.0
Sarah Weber        3.5
Lena Müller        5.5
dtype: float64
```

Solution to 3. Exercise

We provide two solutions: the first uses times as simple strings, the second uses
date_time (timestamps).

1. Variant:

```python
import numpy as np
import pandas as pd
```

```python
temperatures = [22.0, 23.1, np.nan, 25.4, 27.0, 28.5, np.nan,
                np.nan, 32.2, 33.0, np.nan, 31.8, 30.0, 28.3,
                26.4, 24.8]

times = ["03:00", "04:00", "05:00", "06:00", "07:00", "08:00",
         "09:00", "10:00", "11:00", "12:00", "13:00", "14:00",
         "15:00", "16:00", "17:00", "18:00"]

s = pd.Series(data=temperatures, index=times)

ff = s.ffill()
bf = s.bfill()
interp = s.interpolate()

print(f"{'Time':<8} | {'Original':<8} | {'ffill':<8} | {'bfill':<8} | {'
    interp':<8}")
print("-" * 50)
for t, o, f, b, i in zip(s.index, s, ff, bf, interp):
    print(f"{t:<8} | {o!s:<8} | {f:<8.1f} | {b:<8.1f} | {i:<8.1f}")
```

The result is:

```
Time     | Original | ffill    | bfill    | interp
--------------------------------------------------
03:00    | 22.0     | 22.0     | 22.0     | 22.0
04:00    | 23.1     | 23.1     | 23.1     | 23.1
05:00    | nan      | 23.1     | 25.4     | 24.2
06:00    | 25.4     | 25.4     | 25.4     | 25.4
07:00    | 27.0     | 27.0     | 27.0     | 27.0
08:00    | 28.5     | 28.5     | 28.5     | 28.5
09:00    | nan      | 28.5     | 32.2     | 29.7
10:00    | nan      | 28.5     | 32.2     | 31.0
11:00    | 32.2     | 32.2     | 32.2     | 32.2
12:00    | 33.0     | 33.0     | 33.0     | 33.0
13:00    | nan      | 33.0     | 31.8     | 32.4
14:00    | 31.8     | 31.8     | 31.8     | 31.8
15:00    | 30.0     | 30.0     | 30.0     | 30.0
16:00    | 28.3     | 28.3     | 28.3     | 28.3
17:00    | 26.4     | 26.4     | 26.4     | 26.4
18:00    | 24.8     | 24.8     | 24.8     | 24.8
```

Here, `interpolate()` performs linear interpolation along the time axis. For temperature series this usually yields more realistic values than plain forward or backward fill. You can also see this in the second variant:

```python
import numpy as np
import pandas as pd

temperatures = [22.0, 23.1, np.nan, 25.4, 27.0, 28.5, np.nan, np.nan,
                32.2, 33.0, np.nan, 31.8, 30.0, 28.3, 26.4, 24.8]

times = pd.date_range("2025-07-01 03:00",
                      periods=len(temperatures),
                      freq="h")

s = pd.Series(data=temperatures, index=times)

ff = s.ffill()
bf = s.bfill()
interp = s.interpolate()

print(f"{'Time':<19} | {'Original':<8} | {'ffill':<8} | {'bfill':<8} | {'
    interp':<8}")
print("-" * 65)
for t, o, f, b, i in zip(s.index, s, ff, bf, interp):
    time = t.strftime("%Y-%m-%d %H:%M")  # or just "%H:%M"
    o_str = f"{o:.1f}" if not pd.isna(o) else "nan"
    print(f"{time:<19} | {o_str:<8} | {f:<8.1f} | {b:<8.1f} | {i:<8.1f}")
```

The result of the code is:

```
Time                | Original | ffill    | bfill    | interp
-----------------------------------------------------------------
2025-07-01 03:00    | 22.0     | 22.0     | 22.0     | 22.0
2025-07-01 04:00    | 23.1     | 23.1     | 23.1     | 23.1
2025-07-01 05:00    | nan      | 23.1     | 25.4     | 24.2
2025-07-01 06:00    | 25.4     | 25.4     | 25.4     | 25.4
2025-07-01 07:00    | 27.0     | 27.0     | 27.0     | 27.0
2025-07-01 08:00    | 28.5     | 28.5     | 28.5     | 28.5
2025-07-01 09:00    | nan      | 28.5     | 32.2     | 29.7
2025-07-01 10:00    | nan      | 28.5     | 32.2     | 31.0
2025-07-01 11:00    | 32.2     | 32.2     | 32.2     | 32.2
2025-07-01 12:00    | 33.0     | 33.0     | 33.0     | 33.0
2025-07-01 13:00    | nan      | 33.0     | 31.8     | 32.4
2025-07-01 14:00    | 31.8     | 31.8     | 31.8     | 31.8
2025-07-01 15:00    | 30.0     | 30.0     | 30.0     | 30.0
2025-07-01 16:00    | 28.3     | 28.3     | 28.3     | 28.3
2025-07-01 17:00    | 26.4     | 26.4     | 26.4     | 26.4
2025-07-01 18:00    | 24.8     | 24.8     | 24.8     | 24.8
```

33.13 Solutions to Chapter 20 (DataFrame)

Solution to 1. Exercise

```python
import pandas as pd

cities = ["Vienna", "Vienna", "Vienna",
          "Hamburg", "Hamburg", "Hamburg",
          "Berlin", "Berlin", "Berlin",
          "Zurich", "Zurich", "Zurich"]

data = ["Austria", 414.60, 1805681,
        "Germany", 755.00, 1760433,
        "Germany", 891.85, 3562166,
        "Switzerland", 87.88, 378884]

index = [cities, ["country", "area", "population",
                  "country", "area", "population",
                  "country", "area", "population",
                  "country", "area", "population"]]

city_data = pd.Series(data, index=index)
print(city_data)
```

The result of the code is:

```
Vienna    country           Austria
          area                414.6
          population        1805681
Hamburg   country           Germany
          area                755.0
          population        1760433
Berlin    country           Germany
          area                891.85
          population        3562166
Zurich    country       Switzerland
          area                87.88
          population         378884
dtype: object
```

Solution to 2. Exercise

```python
city_data = city_data.sort_index()


city_data = city_data.swaplevel()
city_data.sort_index(inplace=True)
print(city_data)
```

This follows from the code:

```
area        Berlin            891.85
            Hamburg            755.0
            Vienna             414.6
            Zurich              87.88
country     Berlin           Germany
            Hamburg          Germany
            Vienna            Austria
            Zurich        Switzerland
population  Berlin           3562166
            Hamburg          1760433
            Vienna           1805681
            Zurich            378884
dtype: object
```

Solution to 3. Exercise

```python
import pandas as pd

people = {
    "Name": ["Henry", "Sarah", "Sofia", "Lulu",
             "Vera", "Toni", "Maria", "Chris"],
    "Height_cm": [179, 165, 172, 154,
                  150, 189, 176, 175],
    "Weight_kg": [65, 58, 58, 45,
                  43, 99, 68, 60],
}


df_people = pd.DataFrame(people)
df_people = df_people.set_index("Name")[["Weight_kg",
                                         "Height_cm"]]


bmi = (df_people["Weight_kg"] /
       (df_people["Height_cm"] / 100) ** 2)
```

```python
bmi_okay = df_people[bmi.between(18.5, 25,
                                 inclusive="both")]
# alternatively:
#bmi_okay = df_people.loc[(18.5 < bmi) & (bmi < 25)]


print(bmi_okay)
```

The result of the code is:

```
       Weight_kg  Height_cm
Name
Henry         65        179
Sarah         58        165
Sofia         58        172
Lulu          45        154
Vera          43        150
Maria         68        176
Chris         60        175
```

Solution to 4. Exercise

```python
print(df_people.loc[df_people.index.str.contains("i")])
```

The result appears as follows:

```
       Weight_kg  Height_cm
Name
Sofia         58        172
Toni          99        189
Maria         68        176
Chris         60        175
```

Solution to 5. Exercise

```python
df_people.insert(loc=len(df_people.columns),
                 column="BMI",
                 value=(df_people.Weight_kg / ((df_people.Height_cm / 100)
                     ** 2)))
print(df_people)
```

The code produces the following result:

```
        Weight_kg  Height_cm        BMI
Name
Henry          65        179  20.286508
Sarah          58        165  21.303949
Sofia          58        172  19.605192
Lulu           45        154  18.974532
Vera           43        150  19.111111
Toni           99        189  27.714790
Maria          68        176  21.952479
Chris          60        175  19.591837
```

Solution to 6. Exercise

```python
print(df_people.sort_values(by="BMI", ascending=False))
```

Executing the code yields:

```
        Weight_kg  Height_cm        BMI
Name
Toni           99        189  27.714790
Maria          68        176  21.952479
Sarah          58        165  21.303949
Henry          65        179  20.286508
Sofia          58        172  19.605192
Chris          60        175  19.591837
Vera           43        150  19.111111
Lulu           45        154  18.974532
```

Solution to 7. Exercise

```python
bmi_okay = (18.5 < df_people['BMI']) & (df_people['BMI'] < 23.5)
name_contains_a = df_people.index.str.contains('a')
print(df_people.loc[bmi_okay & name_contains_a])
```

Here is the result of the code:

```
        Weight_kg  Height_cm        BMI
Name
Sarah          58        165  21.303949
Sofia          58        172  19.605192
Vera           43        150  19.111111
Maria          68        176  21.952479
```

Solution to 8. Exercise

```python
import numpy as np
import pandas as pd


names = ['Jonas', 'Leon', 'Finn', 'Guido',
         'Lara', "Hannah", "Mila", "Lina"]
index = ["January", "February", "March",
         "April", "May", "June",
         "July", "August", "September",
         "October", "November", "December"]
df = pd.DataFrame(np.random.randint(120,
                                    200,
                                    size=(len(index),
                                          len(names))),
                  columns=names,
                  index=index)
print(df)
```

Result:

```
             Jonas   Leon   Finn   ...   Hannah   Mila   Lina
January        188    146    163   ...      128    157    187
February       142    171    184   ...      163    191    176
March          121    132    173   ...      129    185    162
April          191    151    197   ...      149    140    196
May            189    137    190   ...      174    136    179
June           185    183    136   ...      179    189    144
July           199    152    138   ...      170    131    147
August         185    190    148   ...      134    149    199
September      135    145    193   ...      177    149    141
October        142    187    151   ...      151    163    147
November       137    127    170   ...      139    142    154
December       188    147    126   ...      195    187    120

[12 rows x 8 columns]
```

Solution to 9. Exercise

```python
new_df = df.transpose()
print(new_df)
```

The evaluation yields:

```
          January  February  ...  November  December
Jonas         188       142  ...       137       188
Leon          146       171  ...       127       147
Finn          163       184  ...       170       126
Guido         148       120  ...       158       132
Lara          124       145  ...       157       194
Hannah        128       163  ...       139       195
Mila          157       191  ...       142       187
Lina          187       176  ...       154       120

[8 rows x 12 columns]
```

33.14 Solutions to Chapter 21 (Styling)

Solution to Exercise 1

```python
import pandas as pd

df = pd.DataFrame({
    'Zurich':   [15600, -4500, 13400],
    'Frankfurt':[-2400, 18200, -3200],
    'Hamburg':  [10200,  9800,  7500],
    'Munich':   [12000, -1000, -2000]
}, index=['January', 'February', 'March'])

def highlight_values(val):
    """Highlight values:
    Green for profits, red for losses."""
    if val < 0:
        # Losses (red)
        return 'background-color: red; color: white; font-weight: bold'
    else:
        # Profits (green)
        return 'background-color: lightgreen; color: black; font-weight: \
            bold'

# Apply styles
styled_df = (df.style
    .map(highlight_values)
    .set_table_styles([
        {'selector': 'th',
         'props': [('background-color', 'yellow'), ('color', 'black'), ('\
            font-weight', 'bold')]},  # column headers
```

```python
        {'selector': 'th.index',
         'props': [('background-color', 'yellow'), ('color', 'black'), ('
            font-weight', 'bold')]}   # row index
    ])
    .format("{:,.0f}")   # thousands separator for readability
)

styled_df
```

	Zurich	Frankfurt	Hamburg	Munich
January	15,600	-2,400	10,200	12,000
February	-4,500	18,200	9,800	-1,000
March	13,400	-3,200	7,500	-2,000

Solution to Exercise 2

```python
import pandas as pd

df = pd.DataFrame({
    'Berlin': [12500,  8700,  3000, 15500,  9200,  4500],
    'Paris':  [ 9800, 11200, 14000,  5000,  6800,  7100],
    'Rome':   [ 6200,  3500, 10500,  9600,  4200, 15000],
    'Madrid': [11000, 13400,  8500,  7800, 12500,  9000]
}, index=['January', 'February', 'March', 'April', 'May', 'June'])

# Color highlighting based on revenue
def highlight_values(val):
    """Apply color formatting based on revenue."""
    if val >= 10000:
        return 'background-color: lightgreen; color: black; font-weight:
            bold'  # high revenue (green)
    elif 5000 <= val < 10000:
        return 'background-color: yellow; color: black'  # moderate
            revenue (yellow)
    else:
        return 'background-color: red; color: white; font-weight: bold'  #
            low revenue / loss (red)

# Apply styles
styled_df = (df.style
    .map(highlight_values)
    .set_table_styles([
```

```
        {'selector': 'th',
         'props': [('background-color', 'blue'), ('color', 'white'), ('
             font-weight', 'bold')]},
        {'selector': 'th.index',
         'props': [('background-color', 'lightgray'), ('color', 'black'),
             ('font-weight', 'bold')]}
    ])
    .format("{:,.0f}")  # thousands separator
)


styled_df
```

	Berlin	Paris	Rome	Madrid
January	12,500	9,800	6,200	11,000
February	8,700	11,200	3,500	13,400
March	3,000	14,000	10,500	8,500
April	15,500	5,000	9,600	7,800
May	9,200	6,800	4,200	12,500
June	4,500	7,100	15,000	9,000

33.15 Solutions to Chapter 22 (File Processing)

Solution to 1. Exercise

```
pop = pd.read_csv("data1/countries_population.csv",
                  header=None,
                  names=["Country", "Population"],
                  index_col=0,
                  quotechar="'",
                  sep=" ",
                  thousands=",")
print(pop.head(5))
```

The result appears as follows:

```
                Population
Country
China           1355692576
India           1236344631
European Union   511434812
United States    318892103
Indonesia        253609643
```

Solution to 2. Exercise

```python
lands = pd.read_csv('data1/bundeslaender.txt', sep=" ")
print(lands.columns.values)
```

The script returns:

```
['land' 'area' 'male' 'female']
```

```python
# Reorder the columns of our DataFrame:
lands = lands.reindex(columns=['land', 'area', 'female', 'male'])
print(lands[:2])
```

The result follows:

```
               land      area  female  male
0  Baden-Württemberg  35751.65    5465  5271
1             Bayern  70551.57    6366  6103
```

```python
lands.insert(loc=len(lands.columns),
             column='population',
             value=lands['female'] + lands['male'])
print(lands[:3])
```

The processing yields:

```
               land      area  ...  male  population
0  Baden-Württemberg  35751.65  ...  5271       10736
1             Bayern  70551.57  ...  6103       12469
2             Berlin    891.85  ...  1660        3396

[3 rows x 5 columns]
```

```python
lands.insert(loc=len(lands.columns),
             column='density',
             value=(lands['population'] * 1000 / lands['area']).round(0))
print(lands[:4])
print(lands.loc[lands['density'] > 30000])
```

After execution we get:

```
               land      area  ...  population  density
0  Baden-Württemberg  35751.65  ...       10736    300.0
1             Bayern  70551.57  ...       12469    177.0
2             Berlin    891.85  ...        3396   3808.0
3        Brandenburg  29478.61  ...        2560     87.0
```

```
[4 rows x 6 columns]
Empty DataFrame
Columns: [land, area, female, male, population, density]
Index: []


[0 rows x 6 columns]
```

```python
print(lands.loc[(lands.area > 30000) & (lands.population > 10000)])
```

Here is the result of the code:

```
                      land       area  ...  population  density
0      Baden-Württemberg   35751.65  ...       10736    300.0
1                 Bayern   70551.57  ...       12469    177.0
9    Nordrhein-Westfalen   34085.29  ...       18058    530.0

[3 rows x 6 columns]
```

Solution to 3. Exercise

```python
pop = pd.read_csv("data1/person_data.txt",
                  header=None,
                  names=["FirstName", "LastName", "Height",
                         "Weight", "Sex"],
                  index_col=0,
                  quotechar="'",
                  sep=" ",
                  thousands=",")

pop.insert(loc=len(pop.columns),
           column='BMI',
           value=pop["Weight"] * 10000 / (pop["Height"]**2))

print(pop.head(10))
```

The result appears as follows:

```
              LastName  Height  Weight      Sex         BMI
FirstName
Randy           Carter     184    73.0     male   21.561909
Stephanie        Smith     149    52.0   female   23.422368
Cynthia         Watson     174    63.0   female   20.808561
Jessie          Morgan     175    67.0     male   21.877551
```

```
Katherine   Carter     183    81.0   female   24.187046
David         Reed      187    60.0     male   17.158054
Stephen      Jones      192    96.0     male   26.041667
Jerry        Allen      204    91.0     male   21.866590
Billy       Wright      180    66.0     male   20.370370
Earl         Green      184    52.0     male   15.359168
```

Solution to 4. Exercise

We solve the problem using `converters` functions. These are functions specified per column during file import. The `converters` parameter is a dictionary whose keys are column names and whose values are the functions to apply to those columns. Our function `convert2floats` is applied to both the purchase and sale price: it replaces commas with dots, removes spaces, and converts the result to a floating-point number.

```python
import pandas as pd


def convert2floats(x):
    return float(x.replace(" ", "").replace(",", "."))


# Read file and convert prices to floats
df = pd.read_csv("data1/used_car_prices.csv",
                 delimiter=";",
                 converters={"Purchase Price": convert2floats,
                             "Sale Price": convert2floats})


print(df)
df.to_csv('data1/used_car_prices2.csv', index=False)
```

Result:

```
          Brand      Model   Purchase Price   Sale Price
0    Volkswagen       Golf           8200.0      11500.0
1        Toyota      Yaris           7800.0      10900.0
2           BMW   3 Series          15500.0      19800.0
3  Mercedes-Benz   C-Class          17200.0      22500.0
4          Audi         A4          14800.0      19200.0
5          Ford      Focus           6900.0       9800.0
6       Peugeot        308           7600.0      10400.0
7    Alfa Romeo     Giulia          13500.0      18200.0
8       Porsche    Cayenne          38000.0      46500.0
```

The contents of `used_car_prices2.csv` are as follows:

```
Brand,Model,Purchase Price,Sale Price
Volkswagen,Golf,8200.0,11500.0
Toyota,Yaris,7800.0,10900.0
BMW,3 Series,15500.0,19800.0
Mercedes-Benz,C-Class,17200.0,22500.0
Audi,A4,14800.0,19200.0
Ford,Focus,6900.0,9800.0
Peugeot,308,7600.0,10400.0
Alfa Romeo,Giulia,13500.0,18200.0
Porsche,Cayenne,38000.0,46500.0
```

We used the converters to demonstrate their usage. However, in this case, the task can be solved more easily with the built-in parameters `thousands` and `decimal` of `read_csv`. With these options, Pandas automatically interprets spaces as thousands separators and commas as decimal points:

```python
import pandas as pd

# Much simpler: let pandas handle thousands and decimals directly
df = pd.read_csv("data1/used_car_prices.csv",
                 sep=";",
                 thousands=" ",
                 decimal=",")

print(df)
df.to_csv("data1/used_car_prices2.csv", index=False)
```

This follows from the code:

```
            Brand      Model  Purchase Price  Sale Price
0      Volkswagen       Golf          8200.0     11500.0
1          Toyota      Yaris          7800.0     10900.0
2             BMW   3 Series         15500.0     19800.0
3   Mercedes-Benz    C-Class         17200.0     22500.0
4            Audi         A4         14800.0     19200.0
5            Ford      Focus          6900.0      9800.0
6         Peugeot        308          7600.0     10400.0
7      Alfa Romeo     Giulia         13500.0     18200.0
8         Porsche    Cayenne         38000.0     46500.0
```

33.16 Solutions to Chapter 23 (Pandas: groupby)

Solution to 1. Exercise

```python
x = product_prices.groupby("products").mean(numeric_only=True)
print(x)
```

We obtain this output:

```
          customer_price  non_customer_price
products
Crosteron         3100.00             3400.00
Dreaker           2490.50             2575.50
Lotadilo          2020.00             2060.00
Oppilume          2445.89             2545.89
Wazzasoft         1934.50             2055.50
```

Solution to 2. Exercise

```python
grouped = product_prices.groupby("colours")
price_sums = grouped[["customer_price", "non_customer_price"]].sum()
print(price_sums)
```

Output:

```
        customer_price  non_customer_price
colours
blue           8340.89             8842.39
green         10456.39            10841.39
red            2084.50             2190.00
```

Solution to 3. Exercise

```python
import pandas as pd

df = pd.read_csv("data1/project_times.txt", index_col=0)
print(df)
```

The corresponding output can be seen here:

```
           programmer project  time
date
2020-01-01        Hella    XTOR  1.00
2020-01-01        Hella    BIRDY  1.50
2020-01-01       Fatima    NSTAT  0.25
2020-01-01      Mariola    NSTAT  0.50
2020-01-01      Mariola    BIRDY  1.75
...                 ...      ...   ...
2030-01-30      Antonie    XTOR  0.50
2030-01-31        Hella    BIRDY  1.25
2030-01-31        Hella    BIRDY  1.75
2030-01-31      Mariola    BIRDY  1.00
2030-01-31        Hella    BIRDY  1.00

[17492 rows x 3 columns]


times_per_day = df.groupby("date")["time"].sum()
print(times_per_day.head(10))
```

The following result is generated:

```
date
2020-01-01     9.25
2020-01-02     6.00
2020-01-03     2.50
2020-01-06     5.75
2020-01-07    15.00
2020-01-08    13.25
2020-01-09    10.25
2020-01-10    17.00
2020-01-13     4.75
2020-01-14    10.00
Name: time, dtype: float64
```

Solution to 4. Exercise

```
days_projects = df.groupby(['date', 'project'])['time'].sum()
print(days_projects.head(10))
```

The script returns:

```
date         project
2020-01-01   BIRDY      3.25
             NSTAT      1.50
             XTOR       4.50
2020-01-02   BIRDY      3.75
             NSTAT      2.25
2020-01-03   BIRDY      1.00
             NSTAT      0.25
             XTOR       1.25
2020-01-06   BIRDY      2.75
             NSTAT      0.75
Name: time, dtype: float64
```

Solution to 5. Exercise

```python
print(df.groupby(['project'])['time'].sum())
```

The resulting output is:

```
project
BIRDY    9605.75
NSTAT    8707.75
XTOR     6427.50
Name: time, dtype: float64
```

Solution to 6. Exercise

```python
print(df.groupby(['programmer'])['time'].sum())
```

Here is the output:

```
programmer
Antonie     1511.25
Elise         80.00
Fatima       593.00
Hella      10642.00
Mariola    11914.75
Name: time, dtype: float64
```

Solution to 7. Exercise

```
x = df.groupby([df.index, 'project', 'programmer']).sum()


x = x.unstack()
print(x)
```

This follows from the code:

```
                          time
programmer          Antonie Elise Fatima Hella Mariola
date        project
2020-01-01  BIRDY       NaN   NaN    NaN  1.50    1.75
            NSTAT       NaN   NaN   0.25   NaN    1.25
            XTOR        NaN   NaN    NaN  1.00    3.50
2020-01-02  BIRDY       NaN   NaN    NaN  1.75    2.00
            NSTAT       0.5   NaN    NaN   NaN    1.75
...                     ...   ...    ...   ...     ...
2030-01-29  XTOR        NaN   NaN    NaN  1.00    5.50
2030-01-30  BIRDY       NaN   NaN    NaN  0.75    4.75
            NSTAT       NaN   NaN    NaN  3.75     NaN
            XTOR        0.5   NaN    NaN  0.75     NaN
2030-01-31  BIRDY       NaN   NaN    NaN  4.00    1.00

[7037 rows x 5 columns]


x = x.fillna(0)
print(x[:10])
```

The execution leads to this output:

```
                          time
programmer          Antonie Elise Fatima Hella Mariola
date        project
2020-01-01  BIRDY      0.00   0.0   0.00  1.50    1.75
            NSTAT      0.00   0.0   0.25  0.00    1.25
            XTOR       0.00   0.0   0.00  1.00    3.50
2020-01-02  BIRDY      0.00   0.0   0.00  1.75    2.00
            NSTAT      0.50   0.0   0.00  0.00    1.75
2020-01-03  BIRDY      0.00   0.0   1.00  0.00    0.00
            NSTAT      0.25   0.0   0.00  0.00    0.00
            XTOR       0.00   0.0   0.00  0.50    0.75
2020-01-06  BIRDY      0.00   0.0   0.00  2.50    0.25
            NSTAT      0.00   0.0   0.00  0.00    0.75
```

Solution to 8. Exercise

```python
import pandas as pd
import random
random.seed(42)

# The book titles in this dataset were almost objectively and
# almost randomly selected. Any resemblance to real books by the
# author is purely... intentional :-)
book_prices = {"Introduction to Python 3": 24.99,
               "Python Basics | eLearning": 99.00,
               "Numerical Python": 29.99,
               "Functional Programming with Python": 39.99}
books = list(book_prices.keys())
bookstores = ["Paper & Ink", "Book Island", "Bookmark",
              "Book Palace", "Chapter & Co.", "Pagewise", "Wordsmith"]
# Random assignments:
customers = [random.choice(bookstores) for _ in range(14)]
items = [random.choice(books) for _ in range(14)]
unit_prices = [book_prices[item] for item in items]

data = {
    'Customer': customers,
    'Qty': [6, 7, 5, 5, 5, 9, 1, 6, 5, 5, 2, 8, 9, 5],
    'Item': items,
    'Price': unit_prices
}
df = pd.DataFrame(data)
df['Revenue'] = df['Qty'] * df['Price']


customer_revenue = df.groupby('Customer')['Revenue'].sum()


def category_generator(total, medium_threshold, high_threshold):
    """Function to generate a categorization function"""
    def category(revenue):
        if revenue < medium_threshold * total:
            return 'low'
        elif revenue < high_threshold * total:
            return 'medium'
        else:
            return 'high'
    return category


total_revenue = df['Revenue'].sum()
category_func = category_generator(total_revenue, 0.15, 0.25)
categorized = customer_revenue.apply(category_func)
```

```python
result = pd.DataFrame({
    'Total Revenue': customer_revenue,
    'Category': categorized
})


print(result.sort_values('Total Revenue'))
```

This follows from the code:

```
                Total Revenue Category
Customer
Chapter & Co.          224.91      low
Bookmark               495.00      low
Pagewise               884.74   medium
Paper & Ink           1289.88     high
Book Island           1509.99     high
```

33.17 Solutions to Chapter 24 (Pivot Tables)

Solution to 1. Exercise

```python
import pandas as pd

df = pd.read_csv('data1/country_sales.csv',
                 index_col=0)

pivot_df = pd.pivot_table(df,
                          values='Sales',
                          index='Country',
                          columns='Product')


print(pivot_df)
```

Here is the result of the code:

```
Product      Crystal Sound  Heaven's Fire    Stardust      Sundew
Country
Austria         355.250000     294.444444  349.444444  337.666667
Germany         307.250000     308.625000  299.333333  179.333333
Switzerland     263.909091     184.750000  331.600000  297.833333
```

Solution to 2. Exercise

```python
import pandas as pd


data = pd.read_excel('data1/titanic3.xls')
embarked = data.pivot_table('survived', index='sex', columns='embarked')
embarked.columns = ['Cherbourg', 'Queenstown', 'Southampton']
print(embarked)
```

This output is obtained:

```
        Cherbourg  Queenstown  Southampton
sex
female   0.902655    0.616667     0.680412
male     0.305732    0.111111     0.170144
```

The high survival rate of passengers from Cherbourg can partly be explained by their disproportionately high representation in first class compared to the other ports. We can see this when we also take class membership into account:

```python
df = data.pivot_table('survived',
                      index='sex',
                      columns=['embarked', 'pclass'])

print(df.round(2))
```

After execution we get:

```
embarked      C                 Q                 S
pclass        1     2     3     1     2     3     1     2     3
sex
female      0.97  1.00  0.71   1.0   1.0  0.59  0.96  0.87  0.40
male        0.40  0.29  0.21   0.0   0.0  0.12  0.31  0.13  0.14
```

33.18 Solutions to Chapter 25 (Handling NaN)

Solution to Exercise 1

All we need to do is set the keyword parameter thresh to 4, i.e. we require that at least 4 valid values occur in a row. This means, conversely, that now two values may be NaN:

```python
cleansed_df = disturbed_data.dropna(thresh=4, axis=0)
print(cleansed_df[:7])
```

Output:

```
            sensor1  sensor2  sensor3  sensor4  sensor5  sensor6
time
06:00:00      23.3     22.7     23.2     23.3     22.5     22.6
06:30:00      23.6      NaN      NaN     24.3     23.0     23.2
06:45:00      23.8     23.5     24.6     24.2     23.7     23.6
07:00:00      24.0     23.9      NaN     24.6     23.0      NaN
07:15:00      24.2     24.2     23.6     24.3     24.5     23.9
07:30:00      24.4      NaN     24.6     24.6     23.7     24.1
07:45:00      24.5      NaN     24.4     24.5      NaN     23.9
```

Solution to Exercise 2

```python
average_temp_series = cleansed_df.mean(axis=1)
sensors = cleansed_df.columns.values
df = cleansed_df.drop(sensors, axis=1)

df = df.assign(temperature=average_temp_series)
print(df[:6])
```

Output:

```
            temperature
time
06:00:00      22.933333
06:30:00      23.525000
06:45:00      23.900000
07:00:00      23.875000
07:15:00      24.116667
07:30:00      24.280000
```

33.19 Solutions to Chapter 26 (Binning)

Solution to Exercise 1

We use pd.cut() to divide the values into three defined intervals.

```python
import pandas as pd
income = [12, 25, 35, 41, 52, 63, 71, 85]
bins = [0, 30, 60, 90]
income_categories = pd.cut(income, bins=bins)
print(income_categories)
```

The output shows:

```
[(0, 30], (0, 30], (30, 60], (30, 60], (30, 60], (60, 90], (60, 90], (60,
↪ 90]]
Categories (3, interval[int64, right]): [(0, 30] < (30, 60] < (60, 90]]
```

Solution to Exercise 2

```python
import pandas as pd


students = ['Anna', 'Bob', 'Charlie', 'Dave', 'Emma', 'Frank']
grades = [1.4, 2.4, 1.5, 1.4, 3.4, 1.8]


df = pd.DataFrame({'Student': students, 'Grade': grades})
bins = [0, 1.5, 2.5, 5]
labels = ['magna cum laude', 'cum laude', 'rite']
df['Grade Group'] = pd.cut(df['Grade'], bins=bins, labels=labels)
print(df)
```

We obtain this output:

```
   Student  Grade       Grade Group
0     Anna    1.4  magna cum laude
1      Bob    2.4        cum laude
2  Charlie    1.5  magna cum laude
3     Dave    1.4  magna cum laude
4     Emma    3.4             rite
5    Frank    1.8        cum laude
```

33.20 Solutions to Chapter 27 (Multi-level Indexing)

Solution to Exercise 1

```python
growth_rates = {("Germany", 2019): 1.05,
                ("Germany", 2020): -4.56,
                ("Germany", 2021): 2.79,
                ("Switzerland", 2019): 1.24,
                ("Switzerland", 2020): -2.52,
                ("Switzerland", 2021): 3.72,
                ("Austria", 2019): 1.49,
                ("Austria", 2020): -6.74,
                ("Austria", 2021): 4.48}
```

```
growth_rates_series = pd.Series(growth_rates)
print(growth_rates_series)
```

The script returns:

```
Germany       2019     1.05
              2020    -4.56
              2021     2.79
Switzerland   2019     1.24
              2020    -2.52
              2021     3.72
Austria       2019     1.49
              2020    -6.74
              2021     4.48
dtype: float64
```

Solution to Exercise 2

```
growth_rates_series = growth_rates_series.swaplevel()
growth_rates_series.sort_index(inplace=True)
print(growth_rates_series)
```

The evaluation yields:

```
2019  Austria       1.49
      Germany       1.05
      Switzerland   1.24
2020  Austria      -6.74
      Germany      -4.56
      Switzerland  -2.52
2021  Austria       4.48
      Germany       2.79
      Switzerland   3.72
dtype: float64
```

Solution to Exercise 3

Two solutions are possible.

1. Solution with pd.MultiIndex.from_tuples:

```python
import pandas as pd

# We create two arrays for the index levels
cities = ['Vienna', 'Hamburg', 'Berlin', 'Zurich']
categories = ["Country", "Area", "Population"]

# Create an array of tuples for the index
index_tuples = [(city, category) for city in cities for category in
    categories]

# MultiIndex is created from the tuples:
multi_index = pd.MultiIndex.from_tuples(index_tuples, names=['Cities',
    'Category'])

data = ["Austria", 414.60, 1805681,
        "Germany", 755.00, 1760433,
        "Germany", 891.85, 3562166,
        "Switzerland", 87.88, 378884]

city_series = pd.Series(data, index=multi_index)
print(city_series)
```

What we obtain is:

```
Cities    Category
Vienna    Country          Austria
          Area               414.6
          Population       1805681
Hamburg   Country          Germany
          Area               755.0
          Population       1760433
Berlin    Country          Germany
          Area              891.85
          Population       3562166
Zurich    Country      Switzerland
          Area               87.88
          Population        378884
dtype: object
```

2. Solution with `pd.MultiIndex.from_product`:

```python
# cities, categories, data defined as in the previous example

multi_index = pd.MultiIndex.from_product([cities, categories],
                                         names=['Cities', 'Data'])

city_series = pd.Series(data, index=multi_index)
print(city_series)
```

Since the output is identical to variant 1, we have omitted it here to save space.

Solution to Exercise 4

```python
city_series_swapped = city_series.swaplevel()
city_series_swapped.sort_index(inplace=True)
print(city_series_swapped)
```

We obtain this output:

```
Data        Cities
Area        Berlin              891.85
            Hamburg             755.0
            Vienna              414.6
            Zurich              87.88
Country     Berlin             Germany
            Hamburg            Germany
            Vienna             Austria
            Zurich         Switzerland
Population  Berlin             3562166
            Hamburg            1760433
            Vienna             1805681
            Zurich              378884
dtype: object
```

Solution to Exercise 5

```python
city_series_df = city_series.unstack()
print(city_series_df)
```

What we obtain is:

```
Data        Area       Country Population
Cities
Berlin     891.85      Germany    3562166
Hamburg    755.0       Germany    1760433
Vienna     414.6       Austria    1805681
Zurich     87.88   Switzerland     378884
```

Solution to Exercise 6

```python
city_series_df = city_series.unstack(level=0)
print(city_series_df)
```

After execution we get:

```
Cities        Berlin  Hamburg   Vienna       Zurich
Data
Area          891.85    755.0    414.6        87.88
Country      Germany  Germany  Austria  Switzerland
Population   3562166  1760433  1805681       378884
```

Solution to Exercise 7

```python
import pandas as pd
ft = pd.read_csv('data1/colors_tab.csv')
print(f"-------- DataFrame after reading -------\n{ft}")
s = ft.pivot(index=['Color', 'Intensity', 'Place'], columns=[], values='
    Values')
print(f"\n-------- Series object after pivot -------\n{s}")
df = s.unstack()
print(f"\n-------- DataFrame after unstack -------\n{df}")
```

We obtain this output:

```
-------- DataFrame after reading -------
    Color Intensity     Place  Values
0     red     light    inside       4
1     red     light   outside     148
2     red      dark    inside     120
3     red      dark   outside     226
4   green     light    inside       2
```

```
5    green      light   outside      24
6    green      dark     inside      27
7    green      dark    outside     239
8     blue      light    inside     130
9     blue      light   outside      74
10    blue      dark     inside      67
11    blue      dark    outside     224


-------- Series object after pivot -------
Color  Intensity  Place
red    light      inside       4
                  outside    148
       dark       inside     120
                  outside    226
green  light      inside       2
                  outside     24
       dark       inside      27
                  outside    239
blue   light      inside     130
                  outside     74
       dark       inside      67
                  outside    224
dtype: int64


-------- DataFrame after unstack -------
Place             inside   outside
Color Intensity
blue  dark            67       224
      light          130        74
green dark            27       239
      light            2        24
red   dark           120       226
      light            4       148
```

33.21 Solutions to Chapter 28 (Data Visualization with Pandas)

Solution to Exercise 1

```python
import pandas as pd
fname = "data1/exchange_rates_eu_us_tr_ch.csv"
exchange_rates = pd.read_csv(fname, sep="\t", index_col=0)
exchange_rates[['CHF', 'EUR']].plot(figsize=(6,3.5))
```

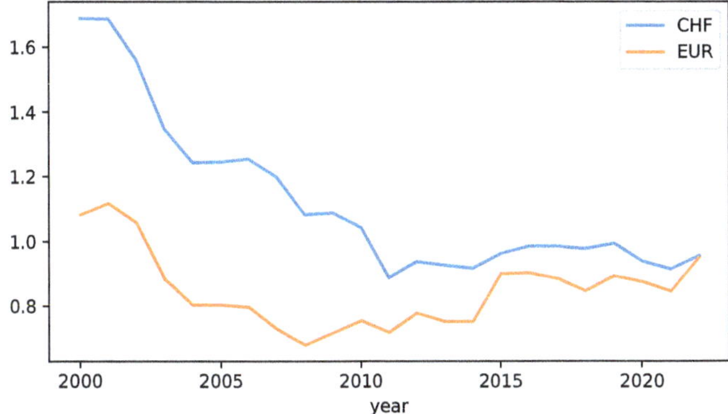

Second part of the task:

```python
exchange_rates[['TRY']].plot(figsize=(6,3.5))
```

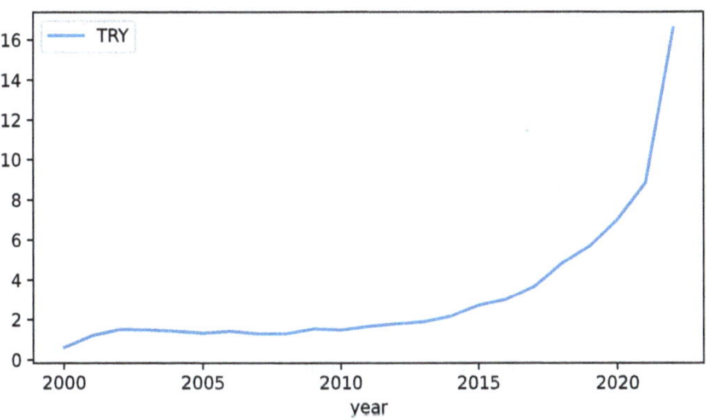

Solution to Exercise 2

```python
import pandas as pd

# Read CSV file into DataFrame
filename = 'data1/drinks_january2025.csv'
df = pd.read_csv(filename,
                 index_col=0)

# Group by name and compute sums
grouped = df.groupby('Name').sum()

# Display DataFrame
print(grouped)
```

```python
# Create grouped bar plot
grouped.plot(kind='bar')
```

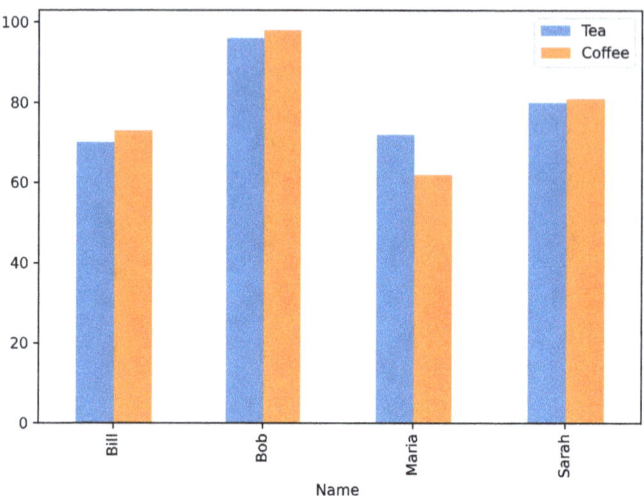

33.22 Solutions to Chapter 30 (Time Series)

Solution to Exercise 1

```python
import pandas as pd
dr = pd.date_range('2023-02-05', '2023-05-17', freq="W-WED")
print(f'There were {len(dr)} Wednesdays in that period!')
```

What we obtain is:

```
There were 15 Wednesdays in that period!
```

Solution to Exercise 2

```python
import pandas as pd

# Generate time series with all days between June 1, 1998 and April 1,
    2023:
date_rng = pd.date_range(start='1998-06-01',
                         end='2023-04-01',
                         freq='D')
```

```python
# Filter Fridays that fall on the 13th:
friday_13ths = date_rng[(date_rng.day == 13) & (date_rng.dayofweek == 4)]


print(f'Between June 1, 1998 and April 1, 2023 there were')
print(f'{len(friday_13ths)} Fridays that fell on the 13th of a month!')
```

This is the result of the code:

```
Between June 1, 1998 and April 1, 2023 there were
42 Fridays that fell on the 13th of a month!
```

33.23 Solutions to Chapter 31 (Image Processing Techniques)

Solution to Exercise 1

```python
import matplotlib.pyplot as plt
import matplotlib.image as mpimg
import numpy as np


path = mpimg.imread('images/weg_und_weide.png')
baltic = mpimg.imread('images/ostsee.png')
chair = mpimg.imread('images/regiestuhl.png')


image = np.where(chair > [0.9, 0.9, 0.9],
                 path,
                 baltic)


plt.imshow(image)
plt.axis("off")
```

Solution to Exercise 2

- Cropping and repainting the bench

```python
import matplotlib.pyplot as plt
img = plt.imread('images/bench.jpg')
img_new = img.copy()
# Paint the bench green
img_new[220:480,420:910] = [100, 180, 100]
plt.imshow(img_new)
```

- Horizontal mirroring of the image

```python
import matplotlib.pyplot as plt
img = plt.imread('images/bench.jpg')
# Horizontally mirror the image:
img = img[::, ::-1]
plt.imshow(img)
```

Index